Cicero in Letters

Cicero in Letters

Epistolary Relations of the Late Republic

PETER WHITE

OXFORD
UNIVERSITY PRESS

OXFORD

UNIVERSITY PRESS

Oxford University Press, Inc., publishes works that further
Oxford University's objective of excellence
in research, scholarship, and education.

Oxford   New York
Auckland   Cape Town   Dar es Salaam   Hong Kong   Karachi
Kuala Lumpur   Madrid   Melbourne   Mexico City   Nairobi
New Delhi   Shanghai   Taipei   Toronto

With offices in
Argentina   Austria   Brazil   Chile   Czech Republic   France   Greece
Guatemala   Hungary   Italy   Japan   Poland   Portugal   Singapore
South Korea   Switzerland   Thailand   Turkey   Ukraine   Vietnam

Published by Oxford University Press, Inc.
198 Madison Avenue, New York, New York 10016
www.oup.com

First issued as an Oxford University Press paperback, 2012.

Oxford is a registered trademark of Oxford University Press.

Library of Congress Cataloging-in-Publication Data
White, Peter, 1941–
Cicero in letters : epistolary relations of the late republic / Peter White.
    p.   cm.
Includes bibliographical references.
ISBN 978-0-19-538851-0 (hardcover); 978-0-19-991434-0 (paperback)
1. Cicero, Marcus Tullius—Correspondence.   2. Cicero,
Marcus Tullius—Contemporaries—Correspondence.
3. Latin letters—History and criticism.   4. Statesmen—
Rome—Correspondence—History and criticism.
5. Letter writing, Latin—History—to 1500.   I. Title.
PA6298.W55 2010
876'.01—dc22   2009031757

Printed in the United States of America
on acid-free paper

D · M · D · R · S · B

Preface

In 1968 my wife, Diana, bestowed on me a handsome dowry of books in classics, the finest of which was Shackleton Bailey's not quite finished edition of Cicero's *Letters to Atticus*. When the two volumes of his *Epistulae ad Familiares* turned up on the shelves of Powell's a few years later, a line was drawn that I felt impelled to follow.

But the aims of Cicero's correspondence for a long time baffled me. He wrote letters differently than I did, and not just better and more often. He practiced different exordial moves, rarely engaging his addressees by way of an anecdote or a description of something, for example. He could take more about their identity for granted, he tended to be more solicitous both of their dignity and his own, and he operated with more abstract notions of what motivates people. He was more leery of revealing himself, though he seemed to give away a great deal unwittingly. What he wrote did not always correspond to what he really thought or, at any rate, not to things he said elsewhere.

At the same time, Cicero's letters bore little resemblance to the letters of his compatriot Pliny, which I had first read in a seminar with Glen Bowersock and enjoyed without especially liking them. Pliny's correspondence was like a smooth train ride over a route punctuated by intermittent vistas and by scheduled stops which the conductor passed back and forth announcing. The Ciceronian letter corpus offered another sort of ride. The route was not picturesque, and it passed over stretches of bad track that occasioned halts and slowdowns. The station signs were difficult to make out, and any announcements from the cab were drowned in static. On the next seat in a second-class coach sat a well-dressed passenger who meant to talk all the way to the last stop and who, despite the urbanity of his conversation, was nervous about something.

Anyone might be pardoned for wondering what was the sense of a journey so taxing.

In order to understand what gave Cicero's published correspondence the look and feel that it has, I decided that I needed points of orientation beyond that particular set of texts. And so, apart from ruminating on my store of Shackleton Baileys, I learned what I could about the people to whom Cicero wrote and the circumstances under which he wrote to them, tracing each one back through Pauly's *Realencyklopädie* and other prosopographical studies into the primary sources. Hoping also to discover a more instructive comparandum for Cicero's correspondence than Pliny's, I browsed in some of the great British and French epistolary collections. If a comparable oeuvre exists there, I failed to discover it. But critics of the letter collections, especially French letter collections, did provide useful models for thinking about the effects that informal letters can have when they are aggregated into a book.

The third resource I found was in the borderland between linguistics and social studies, in subfields marked off by such labels as "symbolic interactionism," "pragmatics," "discourse analysis," and "conversation analysis." It consisted of research into those elements that are implicit in a given situation or in the minds of subjects, and that affect behavior and speech. Cicero's correspondence lends itself to a pragmatics-oriented approach for at least three reasons. The first is that when the letters were published, little or no effort was made to adjust the original communicative framework to the perspective of secondary readers. In the second place, his letters are often intensely situational. A standout example would be *Fam.* 6.15 = 322 SB, which reads in its entirety:

> Cicero to Basilus, greetings.
>   For you I am thrilled, and for myself, glad. I give you my love, and I am looking out for you and yours. I desire your love, and to hear what is up, and what you are up to.

> *Cicero Basilo s.*
>   *Tibi gratulor, mihi gaudeo. te amo, tua tueor. a te amari et quid agas quidque agatur certior fieri volo.*

Secondary readers always need assistance in recovering what was taken for granted by writer and recipient, but nowhere more than here, where the only contextual clues are the name of the addressee, which happens to match the name of one of Caesar's assassins, and the editor's placement of the text within a series of letters to anti-Caesarian diehards. But sometimes opacity of context is offset by a third feature of the correspondence that lends itself to pragmatic analysis. The corpus occasionally preserves two sides of an exchange, so that the inputs of both parties can be compared. Apart from the light it casts on Cicero, the sociolinguistic approach had also the private appeal of reinforcing my long-held suspicion that every social encounter was governed by rules, whether all participants were aware of it or not.

It would have been no hardship to have spent many more hours reading Janet Altman, Erving Goffman, Sacks and Schegloff, the *Journal of Pragmatics*, and the like. But in the wake of Shackleton Bailey's project of recuperation, research on Cicero's correspondence began heating up. Starting in the mid-'80s, Cotton (1985 and 1986) and later Déniaux (1993) treated the letters of recommendation. Hutchinson (1998) studied the literary techniques that Cicero applied to letter writing. Monographs on separate parts of the correspondence continued to appear, and good papers of smaller compass were published by Miriam Griffin (1995 and 1997), Jon Hall (1996 and 1998), Eleanor Leach (1999 and 2006), and Mary Beard (2002) among others. In an increasingly crowded field, it became evident that claims should be staked without dawdling.

The point of this study, then, is to relate the letters of Cicero to the letter-writing habits of a particular Roman milieu. I assume that readers are already acquainted with handbook information about the life of Cicero and the components of his oeuvre. Points on which I wish to elaborate will be taken up as they become relevant to the argument. I assume as well that readers have already encountered some of the letters and that they are interested in them less as historical sources or literary compositions than as a peculiarly mannered form of social intercourse. I will focus on the manners. My primary purpose is to explain what Cicero and his correspondents took for granted about letters and about one another when they corresponded, and to investigate the significance of some of the topics they treated. I hope also to bring out the sense these letters convey that they were written in circumstances in which the principals had something to lose (a sense which, in my view at least, is almost completely missing from Pliny's letters). Although I cover no more than a fraction of the nearly 950 letters that survive, I have tried to keep in view the entirety of the collection. I hope that readers of Cicero's correspondence will find that what I write about those letters I do discuss will carry over to many I do not. Finally, I translate frequently from the letters, partly to anchor the argument and partly because I had an unexpectedly good time trying to channel the voices of Cicero and his correspondents.

The book consists of two parts. Part I concerns features of the letters that are subordinate to their message content, and it moves progressively from an outer ring of social constraints to signals in the physical letter itself. Chapter 1 analyzes effects that follow from the widespread use of secretaries, slow and precarious postal arrangements, the strong Roman preference for face-to-face over written interaction, and the correlation between letter writing and extended absences from Rome. Chapter 2 argues that the impact of Cicero's correspondence as a published whole was largely planned by an editor, even though the collection contains no statement of editorial principles. The editor made a drastic selection from a far larger body of archival material, favoring letters on politics over many other subjects and arranging them in series that highlighted particular episodes in Cicero's life. (Since this chapter concerns forms of outside interference with the letters, it may provide a helpful addendum to Andrew Lintott's recent discussion [2008] of problems with which historians must cope in drawing evidence from Cicero's works.) Chapter 3 explains how an original reader's experience of the letters would have been conditioned by material elements (whether the letter was written on papyrus or on a tablet, whether it was in Cicero's own hand or was dictated to a secretary, whether it carried a seal or not) and by generic conventions (the heading, opening and closing formulas, and dateline). It also studies efforts by the letter writer to project an image of the addressee that complements the purpose of the letter.

Part II turns from context to content and explores three concerns that resonate through Cicero's correspondence: literature, the exchange of advice, and the exercise of leadership. All relate to ways in which members of the Roman elite sought to motivate one another to cooperate when cooperation was difficult. Chapter 4 develops the point that, despite Cicero's deep literary culture, discourse about literature rarely occurs for its own sake in his letters. If he and one of his addressees share a common literary culture, it is put to practical use in interpreting social interactions between them. Chapter 5 argues that the purpose of giving and getting advice in the correspondence is not to exchange practical information or even to reach practical decisions, but to monitor perceptions of one's behavior by others. Chapter 6 concerns an extended series of letters that Cicero wrote to a half-dozen army leaders and provincial governors as he was trying to organize resistance to Mark Antony after the assassination of Caesar. The effort was unsuccessful: Cicero and almost all his correspondents were killed within a year and a half. But the interest of the letters is that they articulate personal and moral obligations which Cicero believed were at least as important to mobilize in a crisis as military resources.

Three essays can hardly do justice to all the ingredients that go into Cicero's letters. As papers by Griffin and by Leonhardt (1995) have shown, philosophy is as important as literature in providing a frame of reference by which Cicero and his correspondents interpret their actions and relationships. Similarly, advising is only one among many speech acts, or letter acts, that could be profitably explored on the basis of material in the corpus. The offering of accounts or explanations would be another. In a number of passages in the letters, a writer undertakes to defend behavior that is problematic from the addressee's point of view, tendering an apology in the "apologia" sense of that word. (On the other hand, so far as I can see, Cicero's letters do not contain a single passage that we would recognize as an apology in the ordinary sense, a matter of some curiosity, given the indispensability of expressions like "sorry," "excuse me," and "I beg your pardon" in our own discourse.) Readers of chapter 6 will notice another omission in my discussion of letters and leadership. I have limited treatment of that topic to a period of military crisis, saying nothing about issues of leadership that arise in letters written apropos of Cicero's experience as governor in Cilicia or his brother's as governor in Asia. Again, though many letters with a focus on Cicero's private life appear to have been excluded from the corpus, enough evidence about his finances remains for them to have been the subject of good studies by Rauh (1986) and Ioannatou (2006). But that subject, too, will not come in for discussion here. My aim is to deal with three concerns of the letters that are representative but not all-inclusive, and I am less interested in them as subjects in their own right than as tokens of the exchange between Cicero and his epistolary partners.

As for the style of exposition, abbreviations for primary texts are given according to the *Oxford Latin Dictionary* or the *Oxford Classical Dictionary*. Letters are cited first according to the numeration of the relevant Oxford classical text. Each citation is then cross-referenced with the number assigned by Shackleton Bailey in his three commented Cambridge editions of the letters (the numbering in his separate translation of Cicero's *Letters to His Friends*, which includes the letters to Quintus and Marcus Brutus as well as the *Ad Familiares* proper, occasionally differs). The resulting cites are cumbersome, but that is largely a fault of the canonical method of citation, which is particularly uncouth in the *Ad M. Brutum*. And no sensible reader of a book on Cicero's letters would want to be without instant access to what Shackleton Bailey has to say about them. In the text but not in the notes, quotations are given in translation, with the Latin immediately appended for anyone who wants a control. Unless otherwise noted, I follow Shackleton Bailey's text, including his use of angle brackets for editorial supplements and square brackets for editorial deletions. Because my argument is topically rather than chronologically organized, I skip around a good deal as I discuss the letters. But I have tried to supply enough context for readers to make sense of each text that I quote, including its date if that is relevant. All year dates not otherwise qualified refer to years B.C. Background information that readers may desire about the number and distribution of letters, books, and correspondents, or about the date of publication, has been collected in appendix 1.

Having introduced my book, I now introduce and thank its nurturers. This project began to take shape in the space afforded by a fellowship from the National Endowment for the Humanities in 1994/95. A course reduction from the Humanities Division of the University of Chicago two years ago enabled me to complete the last remaining spadework for it. Persons as well as institutions have provided much-appreciated help. Audiences at Colgate, Hamilton, and Harvard and at the Universities of Indiana, Michigan, and Missouri gave a kindly but not uncritical hearing to prior versions of several chapters, and smaller pieces of the argument were floated at annual meetings of the American Philological Association. Along the way, John Ramsey and Bruce Redford commented on excerpts, and then Elizabeth Asmis, Andrew Dyck, Elaine Fantham, and Robert Kaster joined the classics editor for Oxford University Press, Stefan Vranka, and other readers whom he consulted in critiquing a nearly final draft. I took counsel from all according to my lights. I am indebted also to Deirdre Brady, Linda Donnelly, and Norma McLemore who shepherded my compuscript into print.

There was never a question in my mind but that this book would be dedicated to the great enabler of work on the letters in our time. But it would not be finished still without unremitting prompts from Robert Kaster to "show me something you've written."

Contents

I

READING THE LETTERS FROM THE OUTSIDE IN

Constraints and Biases in Roman Letter Writing

Of all the literary forms that were current in the Roman period, the familiar letter appears to have altered least in the course of its descent to us. Histories are no longer written on the Roman model, with invented orations and a profound aversion for the documentary. Verse satire, epic, and political oratory, if they are not now extinct, have at least gone into hibernation, and the literary dialogue has sunk to the status of a quaint exercise. Modern novels, love poetry, and tragedies bear little resemblance to their Roman forerunners. The only Roman form to have held its own as successfully as the letter is slapstick comedy, as adaptations of Plautus's plays on Broadway have demonstrated. But personal letters remain the main exception to the general impression of unfamiliarity that Roman literature makes. Reading a letter by Cicero or one of his correspondents, one can still imagine that it communicates in an idiom which our own literary and social competence prepares us to understand.

Take, for example, a note that Cicero wrote to his friend Atticus in the spring of 59 B.C., while he was enjoying a holiday at a home he had on the coast south of Rome:

> Cicero to Atticus, greetings:
>
> I promised you in an earlier letter that I would produce something in the course of this jaunt, but I'm not sticking by that claim very firmly now. I am so caught up in relaxation that I cannot be pried loose. So I luxuriate in books, of which I have a fine supply here at Antium, or I count the waves (the weather is not right for fishing).
>
> I am completely down on the idea of writing. The geographical piece I had in mind to do is a huge project. Eratosthenes, my

intended model, comes in for heavy criticism from Serapion and Hipparchus; can you imagine if Tyrannio chimes in? Besides, the subject matter is hard to put across and tedious. It doesn't lend itself so easily to decorative effects as I imagined.

But the chief thing is that any pretext for slacking off seems good enough to me. I even debate whether I shouldn't get through this whole period by installing myself here at Antium, where I'd rather I had been mayor than consul at Rome. You were smarter than I when you bought the house at Buthrotum, but trust me, the next best thing to your town is this commonwealth of Antium. To think that there is a place so close to Rome where many have never laid eyes on Vatinius! Where no one but I cherishes kindly sentiments for any member of the Board of Twenty! Where no one pesters me and everybody loves me! No question about it: this is the place to be in politics, which is not merely not an option at Rome, but a bore. So I will set to work on private memoirs which I will read just to you, in the style of Theopompus or even a lot more caustic. I don't do anything political nowadays but hate the villains, and even that not with rancor, but with a certain savor.

But to get down to business, I have written to the urban quaestors about the transaction concerning my brother Quintus. See what they say—whether there is any chance of denarii, or whether we are stuck with Pompey's cistophores. Also, you decide what should be done about the wall.

Anything else? Yes: let me know when you think you will be leaving town.

Cicero Attico sal.:

Quod tibi superioribus litteris promiseram, fore ut opus exstaret huius peregrinationis, nihil iam magno opere confirmo. sic enim sum complexus otium ut ab eo divelli non queam. itaque aut libris me delecto, quorum habeo Anti festivam copiam, aut fluctus numero (nam ad lacertas captandas tempestates non sunt idoneae).

A scribendo prorsus abhorret animus. etenim γεωγραφικὰ quae constitueram magnum opus est. ita valde Eratosthenes, quem mihi proposueram, a Serapione et ab Hipparcho reprehenditur. quid censes si Tyrannio accesserit? et hercule sunt res difficiles ad explicandum et ὁμοειδεῖς nec tam possunt ἀνθηρογραφεῖσθαι quam videbantur.

Et, quod caput est, mihi quaevis satis iusta causa cessandi est; qui etiam dubitem an hic Anti considam et hoc tempus omne consumam, ubi quidem ego mallem duumvirum quam Romae fuisse. tu vero sapientior Buthroti domum parasti. sed, mihi crede, proxima est illi municipio haec Antiatium civitas. esse locum tam prope Romam ubi multi sint qui

Vatinium numquam viderint, ubi nemo sit praeter me qui quemquam ex
viginti viris vivum et salvum velit, ubi me interpellet nemo, diligant
omnes! hic, hic nimirum πολιτευτέον. *nam istic non solum non licet sed*
etiam taedet. itaque ἀνέκδοτα *a nobis, quae tibi uni legamus, Theopompio*
genere aut etiam asperiore multo pangentur. neque aliud iam quicquam
πολιτεύομαι *nisi odisse improbos, et id ipsum nullo cum stomacho sed*
potius cum aliqua †scribendi† *voluptate.*

   Sed ut ad rem, scripsi ad quaestores urbanos de Quinti fratris negotio.
vide quid narrent, ecquae spes sit denari an cistophoro Pompeiano
iaceamus. praeterea de muro statue quid faciendum sit.

   Aliud quid? etiam: quando te proficisci istinc putes fac ut sciam

Att. 2.6 = 26 SB.

There are certainly details in this letter that invite explanation. It is helpful
to know, for example, that Caesar was now consul, and that Vatinius was a tribune helping him force through radical legislation; that the Board of Twenty
was in charge of privatizing public lands; that Quintus wanted to collect a sti-
pend he was owed for serving the government in a province overseas; and that
cistophores were a non-Roman currency. Nevertheless, the letter is largely
accessible even without that background. Its language is simple, concrete, and
conversational (worlds apart from the language of one of Cicero's speeches),
and the Greek words that creep in are a sure sign that Cicero is writing casually.[1] The authorial stance is recognizably that of a personal letter rather than of
an official letter, or an open letter, or a tract directed to a merely nominal
addressee. Cicero highlights his relationship with Atticus at the start by recall-
ing a promise made to him and continues stroking him as he compares his
pied-à-terre to Atticus's own, whets Atticus's curiosity about a sensational work
in progress, and consults him on business matters. Phrases expressing
deference are sprinkled throughout: "I promised you," "can you imagine," "you
were smarter than I," "trust me," "just to you," and "you decide."

   But it is Cicero's strategy of self-presentation that is most responsible for
conjuring a sense of familiarity as we read this letter. He eases into it with
remarks about the weather and the scenery and proceeds to talk about what he
has been reading. Only afterward does he shift to a more intimate register and
begin discoursing about his state of mind. Nowadays, too, weather is a topic
that is apt to come in for comment at the start of a personal letter, along with
comments about the health of the letter writer or the addressee or reports of
chance events of no particular significance. Beginnings are hard in most
writing, and the beginning of a letter presents a social challenge on top of the
literary one. The epistolary equivalents of "Nice day" and "How are you?" make
a safer lead-in than any topic that is likely to surface later.[2] Even Cicero's report
about his reading has its analogue in contemporary letters, when correspondents trade reactions to books and movies. All such gambits serve to lay down

stepping-stones that lead from the external to the internal, or from neutral to sensitive matters.

Yet the example I have quoted is anything but typical of the way Cicero and his friends engage each other in the nearly 950 pieces of their correspondence that survive.[3] In fact, Cicero almost never deigns to take note of weather or scenery. On another occasion when the subject intrudes (in another letter written from the seaside), he promptly dismisses it. The letter begins, "Nothing could be sweeter than my isolation here." He notes that he has had to put up with one brief intrusion, but that "otherwise, I tell you, nothing could be more appealing than the house, the beach, the view of the sea—than everything." Then he breaks off: "But that is no matter for a longish letter" (nihil hac solitudine iucundius . . . cetera noli putare amabiliora fieri posse villa, litore, prospectu maris, tum his rebus omnibus. sed neque haec digna longioribus litteris, Att. 12.9.1 = 246 SB). Similarly with the topic of health: although there are Latin letter writers who might be counted among the world's great hypochondriacs—Atticus himself, to judge by Cicero's replies to him, and certainly Fronto—Cicero infrequently says anything about his health. Again although many of his correspondents were well acquainted with Cicero's family, he does not ordinarily indulge in domestic chit-chat unless he is writing to another member of the family, which happens to be the case here. Quintus, mentioned at the end, is both Cicero's brother and Atticus's brother-in-law.[4] And finally, although Cicero does allude to a couple of writing projects in this letter, it is striking how little space is taken up with literary and other cultural pastimes in the letters overall. Cicero had ties to dozens of writers and intellectuals both Greek and Roman, he enjoyed some reputation as a supporter of poets, and he was almost continually engaged in literary production himself. Yet relatively little of this side of his life is reflected in the correspondence, as we will see in chapter 4.

For a more representative piece of Roman epistolary discourse, we may turn to a letter from Cicero's miscellaneous correspondence, the *Letters to Friends,* as they have been known since the Renaissance. It may seem that I am about to contradict what I have just written, since this letter does in fact dwell on both family and literary interests. But it will become apparent that those topics are being exploited for ends different from those in the letter with which I started. The writer this time is not Cicero, but one of his correspondents—a little more than 10 percent of the letters preserved in the Ciceronian corpus were written by persons other than Cicero (as detailed in appendix 1). Trebonius was a fellow senator, traveling from Rome to Asia Minor to take charge of a province he had been sent to govern in the year 44. During a layover in Athens, he encountered Cicero's twenty-year-old son, who was enjoying the philosophical study tour with which the sons of the Roman elite often concluded their education. The encounter resulted in the following letter:

Trebonius to Cicero, greetings and good wishes.

I hope you are well.

I reached Athens on May 22nd and there, as I heartily wished, I found your son engaged in the most commendable pursuits and enjoying a fine reputation for uprightness. It hardly requires any words on my part for you to appreciate how pleased I was. You know how highly I regard you. The affection between us is so genuine and long-standing that every bit of good which comes your way tickles me, let alone something so important as this. Do not imagine, my dear Cicero, that I say this to humor you. There is no one better liked by everyone at Athens, or more devoted to those fine arts which you treasure, than your, or rather *our* young man (since nothing that touches you can be indifferent to me). We are bound to cherish him no matter how he behaves, but I am glad that in all honesty, too, I can congratulate both you and myself because in Marcus we have someone whom it is a pleasure to cherish.

When he mentioned to me in conversation that he had a yen to see Asia, I not only invited but urged him to come during the period when I would be governor. You should have no doubt that I will take up your part toward him with love and affection. I will also make sure that he has Cratippus along with him. You needn't worry that he will be taking time off from the studies to which your pep talks have roused him. I can see that he is primed and well under way, and I will not let up on urging him to make daily progress in his lessons and exercises.

At the moment I write this, I have no idea how you all are doing on the political front. I hear about certain disruptions which naturally I want to be baseless, so that we may at last enjoy our liberty in peace. But that has hardly been my own experience so far.

During the sea passage, however, I did snatch a bit of free time and have put together one of my patented little gifts for you. I have recast in verse a witticism of yours that included a handsome compliment to me (it is written out at the end of the letter). If some of the language in these verses strikes you as a bit *outré*, I take refuge in the scabrousness of the individual against whom my rather blunt assault is directed. You will also excuse the rancorous tone as appropriate to persons and citizens of that ilk. And anyway, why should Lucilius be entitled to express himself more freely than I? Even if he could match me in hating those he assailed, he certainly did not have targets who were more deserving of such outspoken vituperation.

You for your part please put me into your dialogues at the first opportunity, as you promised. And if you should write something about the death of Caesar, I am sure that you will not accord me the least important part in what happened or in your love.

Goodbye, and consider my mother and other kin as commended to your care.
Posted on May 25th at Athens.

Trebonius Ciceroni s.

S. v. b.

Athenas veni a. d. XI Kal. Iun. atque ibi, quod maxime optabam, vidi filium tuum deditum optimis studiis summaque modestiae fama. qua ex re quantam voluptatem ceperim scire potes etiam me tacente. non enim nescis quanti te faciam et quam pro nostro veterrimo verissimoque amore omnibus tuis etiam minimis commodis, non modo tanto bono, gaudeam. noli putare, mi Cicero, me hoc auribus tuis dare. nihil adulescente tuo atque adeo nostro (nihil enim tibi a me potest esse seiunctum) aut amabilius omnibus his qui Athenis sunt est aut studiosius earum artium quas tu maxime amas, hoc est optimarum. itaque tibi, quod vere facere possum, libenter quoque gratulor nec minus etiam nobis, quod eum quem necesse erat diligere qualiscumque esset talem habemus ut libenter quoque diligamus.

Qui cum mihi in sermone iniecisset se velle Asiam visere, non modo invitatus sed etiam rogatus est a me ut id potissimum nobis obtinentibus provinciam faceret. cui nos et caritate et amore tuum officium praestaturos non debes dubitare. illud quoque erit nobis curae ut Cratippus una cum eo sit, ne putes in Asia feriatum illum ab iis studiis in quae tua cohortatione incitatur futurum. nam illum paratum, ut video, et ingressum pleno gradu cohortari non intermittemus, quo in dies longius discendo exercendoque se procedat.

Vos quid ageretis in re publica, cum has litteras dabam, non sciebam. audiebam quaedam turbulenta, quae scilicet cupio esse falsa, ut aliquando otiosa libertate fruamur; quod vel minime mihi adhuc contigit. ego tamen nactus in navigatione nostra pusillum laxamenti concinnavi tibi munusculum ex instituto meo et dictum cum magno nostro honore a te dictum conclusi et tibi infra subscripsi. in quibus versiculis si tibi quibusdam verbis εὐθυρρημονέστερος videbor, turpitudo personae eius in quam liberius invehimur nos vindicabit. ignosces etiam iracundiae nostrae, quae iusta est in eius modi et homines et civis. deinde qui magis hoc Lucilio licuerit adsumere libertatis quam nobis? cum, etiam si odio par fuerit in eos quos laesit, tamen certe non magis dignos habuerit in quos tanta libertate verborum incurreret.

Tu, sicut mihi pollicitus es, adiunges me quam primum ad tuos sermones; namque illud non dubito quin, si quid de interitu Caesaris scribas, non patiaris me minimam partem et rei et amoris tui ferre.

Vale, et matrem meosque tibi commendatos habe.

D. VIII Kal. Iun. Athenis.

Fam. 12.16 = 328 SB

One thing that is immediately striking about this letter is its dialogic intensity. In formal terms, that is signaled from the start in the texture of the first full paragraph, every sentence of which is thickly interlaced with first-person and second-person expressions. But it also comes out in Trebonius's approach to his subject. No one could think that the main point of this letter was to pass on news about Cicero's son that Trebonius had picked up during a casual encounter in Athens. In the first place, the visit was almost certainly not casual. As courtesy required, Trebonius would have called on Cicero before leaving Rome and offered to look up the young Marcus, and Cicero would have encouraged him to do so. In the second place, Trebonius's account of the meeting may not be entirely objective. Cicero's son, the only male of his family to survive the civil wars, gained a reputation in later life as a drunkard and a hothead. Already at this date, his father was anxious about his comportment in Athens (and Trebonius's remark that "no one is better liked by everyone at Athens" might well have caused an unintended twinge). In any case, Cicero did not depend on Trebonius for news about Marcus, which we know was being reported to him more amply through other channels.

In Trebonius's letter, the young Marcus serves less as a topic of news than as a token of the relationship between Trebonius and Cicero. Trebonius brings up the encounter with Marcus by way of assuring Cicero how much pleasure he takes in Cicero's successes, and he insists that he owns as great a stake in Marcus and any congratulations he inspires as Cicero himself. Furthermore, it is not just in rhetorical and figurative terms that Marcus is being made a pawn here. Trebonius volunteers to attach him to his entourage and take him under his wing. And finally, we should notice that this effort to appropriate Cicero's family works in the other direction as well. At the close of the letter, Trebonius commends his relatives in Rome to Cicero's care.

The second topic of the letter is exploited in very much the same way as the first. Although Roman writers often circulated samples of work in progress, the verses that Trebonius sent to Cicero represent a more concerted transaction than that. They had as their theme a witticism by the latter—Cicero prided himself on his reputation as a wit, and many of his quips are not bad—while at the same time they reflected positively on Trebonius, since Cicero's quip carried a compliment to Trebonius. And again, like the discourse about Cicero's son, this part of the letter tacitly aligns the present with a prior moment of the friendship. In sending his poem, Trebonius was renewing an initiative he had taken a year or two earlier, when he had presented Cicero with a whole anthology of Ciceronian witticisms dressed up in Trebonian verse (*Fam.* 15.21 = 207 SB). Cicero had reciprocated by offering Trebonius one of his essays (*Fam.* 15.20 = 208 SB), and now Trebonius nudges him to raise the ante by creating a speaking role for Trebonius in one of Cicero's dialogues.

Trebonius's effort to bolster his ties to Cicero is surely to be interpreted in light of a preoccupation that is barely made explicit in this letter. The date given at the close—May 25th of the year 44—falls nine weeks after the assassination of Julius Caesar on the notorious ides of March. That event, which lies behind Trebonius's allusion to long-awaited liberty, precipitated a renewal of civil war in Rome, the first stirrings of which are here characterized delicately as "disruptions." Both Cicero and Trebonius were deeply embroiled in the consequences, Cicero as a former opponent of Caesar's who had become a grudging collaborator, Trebonius as an early henchman of Caesar who later took a major part in the assassination. Just eight months after writing this letter, Trebonius was to have his head cut off and paraded on a spear by the Caesarian who invaded his province.[5] Coincidentally, the killer was Cicero's former son-in-law Dolabella, who was in turn eliminated a couple of months afterward. A year and a half after Trebonius's letter, Cicero perished in the shakeout that took almost a decade and a half to subside.

Trebonius, then, was writing at an exceptionally precarious juncture when an individual's fortunes were as likely to be affected by family or personal connections as by money, arms, ideology, or luck. In Roman civil wars, ideology counted for much less than connections. Stocking up on friends could not guarantee survival, as the experience of both Trebonius and Cicero illustrates, but it afforded better options than isolation. From the outbreak of the civil war, Cicero worked diligently to cultivate ties on both sides. Diversifying one's network was all the more prudent because people (Trebonius, for example) sometimes switched sides.

Trebonius magnified his allegiance to Cicero because he, too, was nervous about the future. Yet politics at Rome was always a hazardous practice. Open warfare raised the penalties, but the regular penalties were brutal enough: political prosecutions, forced bankruptcy, electoral defeat, double-crosses, organized street violence, and scandal. No one could hope to escape them without laboring constantly to neutralize rivals and to line up friends.

The illustrative value of Trebonius's letter is that it expresses in heightened form anxieties pervading Cicero's correspondence, which is overwhelmingly a political correspondence. Three-quarters of the persons represented in it are members of Rome's governing elite, much of whose epistolary effort was devoted to repairing, protecting, or improving their position vis-à-vis their peers.[6] Letters were not the sole means by which this process was carried on, but they do provide our best look at it, for two reasons. First, with rare exceptions, Romans exchanged letters only when one of the parties was away from Rome, and it was at just such times that one's position became most vulnerable.[7] Apart from that, letters constitute a record that is simply missing in the case of most face-to-face transactions. No other form of elite interaction is as copiously documented.

It is the work these letters had to do in managing peer relations that modern readers are apt to find hardest to fathom. Upper-class society of the late Republic was organized so differently from the way our society is that the etiquette which governed relationships within it inevitably seems arcane sometimes. But what makes the Ciceronian correspondence even more unfamiliar, and perhaps unique, is the affinity we observe in it between manners and power. For as long as the Senate governed, Cicero and his colleagues were collectively responsible for distributing or redistributing the wealth, arms, honors, and other resources that their society generated. Whether their letters overtly addressed such topics or not (and it should be noticed that, except for Publius Clodius, no major politician of the 50s and 40s is unrepresented in the published corpus by a letter either sent or received), their relationships were always grounded in politics. Political stakes were the ultimate sanction behind good manners.

Etiquette, however, is only one area in which the use that Cicero and his friends made of letters diverges from the uses to which we put them. In this chapter, I will outline the material and social circumstances that impinge on Roman epistolary communication, beginning with the most familiar and elementary, and ending with those most closely implicated in the play of competition and accommodation.

Distance and Time

The most elementary difference between ancient and modern letters is a fact of the material order: ordinarily, an ancient letter could not move faster than its human bearer could travel by land or sea.[8] The speed of delivery therefore depended directly on the distance a letter traveled. It could vary from hours for a letter sent from Rome to someone in a Roman suburb, to a few days or a week for a vacationer on the Bay of Naples, to a month or two or three for a general in Britain or an official in Syria.[9]

Private Delivery

The distance problem was compounded by a second problem. In Cicero's time, every letter writer had to arrange for delivery of the letter as well. A dedicated postal system did not yet exist, and a system available to ordinary users would not come into being for more than a millennium and a half. Broadly speaking, Cicero and his correspondents had three options. They could ask one of their own friends or dependents to carry a letter, they could utilize someone connected with the addressee, or they could rely on the good offices of one or a series of third parties who happened to be traveling in the right direction.[10] Under each of these arrangements, the social status of the bearer might vary from high to low, which had a direct effect on performance. Friends had to be allowed leeway in carrying out such errands. Delivery of the letter may have been only incidental to their movements, after all. At the opposite extreme, a letter could be entrusted to a slave or freedman courier (*tabellarius*) whose sole function was to accomplish its delivery. Couriers were expected to proceed directly and quickly to the addressee, and since they made round-trips, they usually carried mail in two directions.[11] Furthermore, unlike a free agent, a slave who had completed a mail run could promptly be turned around and sent on to someone else.[12]

But couriers represented a significant investment for whoever resorted to them. They had to be provided with travel expenses (Pliny *Epist.* 3.17.2 and 7.12.6), and while they were absent their services were unavailable to the household to which they belonged. Although Cicero occasionally attempted to establish a chain of couriers between himself and one of his correspondents, it was always a strain.[13] Great distances made the sustained use of couriers prohibitive. It would take two couriers to keep up a daily correspondence with a person living a day's journey away. But daily letters to someone a month's journey away would have required thirty couriers (half that number if the other party contributed to the delivery arrangement), a manpower requirement that would tax the resources even of very great houses.

Very often, the burden of arranging for a letter to be delivered lay not on the writer but the addressee. Because it was crucial to remain informed about developments in the capital, Romans who went abroad for any length of time made sure to leave trustworthy agents behind (which is the main reason that Cicero and Ovid left their wives in Rome when they were obliged to be away). The city residence of an absent senator or knight became a sort of clearinghouse where outbound mail was collected and incoming mail was distributed. A team of relatives, friends, clients, freedmen, and simple couriers did the legwork. All Cicero had to do to communicate with governors like Decimus Brutus in north Italy or Appius in Cilicia or Cornificius in Africa was to drop off a letter at the man's house in Rome. And as often as not, he did not have to do even that much, because an agent would call to ask if he had anything he wanted to send.[14]

The way that letters were delivered had certain consequences for the way they were written. Private letter carriers were exposed to the same hazards as other travelers, including shipwreck, highway robbery, and, in periods of turmoil, search and seizure.[15] If a message had far to go and was particularly important, Cicero and his friends sometimes dispatched duplicate letters to maximize the chances of delivery.[16]

By far their most frequently expressed concern, however, was not about the safety of the routes but about the trustworthiness of the carriers. Although everyone could find emissaries who would transmit letters without opening or gossiping about them (the phrase *certi homines* [reliable people] is a cliché in this context), one was not always available when needed. If Cicero was writing to Rome from southern Italy, for example, he might have to wait a few days for the arrival of one of the slaves shuttling between him and his town house. A letter could be sent sooner if he gave it to an acquaintance passing through on the way to Rome or to the courier who had just delivered somebody else's letter to him. But in those cases he had to weigh the possibility that the content of the letter might leak out, and adjust accordingly.

An elliptical note to his wife in the year 47 may illustrate. Cicero was preparing to negotiate the divorce of their daughter at a moment when her husband, Dolabella, who had followed Caesar's star during the civil war, was in the ascendant:

> Tullius to his Terentia, greetings.
>
> Apropos of what I wrote you in the last letter about sending formal notice, I have no idea of the man's strength at this point or of the general volatility. If making him angry would be dangerous, hold off. Still, an overture may come from him. You will size up the whole situation and adopt whatever course you find least dismal in dismal circumstances. Goodbye.
>
> July 10th.

> *Tullius s. d. Terentiae suae:*
>
> *Quod scripsi ad te proximis litteris de nuntio remittendo, quae sit istius vis hoc tempore et quae concitatio multitudinis ignoro. si metuendus iratus est, quiesces. tamen ab illo fortasse nascetur. totum iudicabis quale sit, et quod in miserrimis rebus minime miserum putabis id facies. vale.*
>
> *VI Id. Quintilis*
>
> *Fam.* 14.13 = 169 SB

It is easy to interpret the curtness of these lines in light of Cicero's deteriorating relations with Terentia, whom he divorced a few months later. We expect a letter to signal the writer's attitude toward the addressee. But Roman letter writers had to think about who carried their letters as well. Cicero was always as anxious to shield his domestic business from alien scrutiny as he was his political dealings. And so this guarded message about his daughter's divorce, in which politics and domestic business converge, may reflect more on his lines of communication than on Terentia.

Misgivings about the messenger come out explicitly in a letter from the summer of 54, in which Cicero breezes through a succession of mostly innocuous topics in response to a long letter from Atticus. In the middle of the letter (sections 5–6), however, where he takes up some questions from Atticus about politics, the style suddenly becomes more terse:

> Now for your queries about Gaius Cato. You know he was acquitted under the Junian and Licinian Law. I predict he will be acquitted under the Fufian Law, to the relief more of prosecutors even than his own counsel. However, good relations have been restored between him and Milo and myself. Drusus has been charged by Lucretius.

Jury challenges are set for July 3rd. About Procilius the buzz is not good, but you know what the courts are like. Hirrus is reconciled with Domitius....

nunc ad ea ‹quae› quaeris de C. Catone. lege Iunia et Licinia scis absolutum. Fufia ego tibi nuntio absolutum iri, neque patronis suis tam libentibus quam accusatoribus. is tamen et mecum et cum Milone in gratiam rediit. Drusus reus est factus a Lucretio. iudicibus reiciiendis ‹dies› a. d. V Non. Quint. de Procilio rumores non boni; sed iudicia nosti. Hirrus cum Domitio in gratia est....

Att. 4.16 = 89 SB

The motive behind this spare and allusive presentation emerges at the close of the letter: the messenger was not someone Cicero felt he could trust. "Nevertheless, I thought I better give a letter to this whoever-he-is because he looked likely to be seeing you" (huic tamen nescio cui, quod videbatur is te visurus esse, putavi dandas esse litteras, sec. 9).[17] At *Att.* 10.11.1 = 202 SB, Cicero says that fears about a messenger prompted him not to send a letter he had already written.

The hazards of delivery not only prompted defensive strategies in writing letters. They could also serve as excuses for not writing at all. Realities quickly acquire a second-order value as pretexts, and the lack of trusty emissaries and the possibility of interception are two among the many claims that delinquent correspondents put forward to explain their silences. A letter that Cicero wrote to Servilius Isauricus in the aftermath of the civil war provides a good example. In it Cicero cautions Servilius, "I will not often be writing to let you know my views on key political issues because of the danger of such letters. But I will report on the news from time to time" (ego ad te de re publica summa quid sentiam non saepe scribam propter periculum eius modi litterarum; quid agatur autem scribam saepius, *Fam.* 13.68 = 211 SB). There are in fact no letters to Servilius about either news or politics, and Cicero's words here are disingenuous. As Shackleton Bailey observes in his commentary, "Cicero was not in any case likely to open his mind on political matters to a Caesarian like Servilius, but he politely implies the contrary."[18]

One of the logistical limitations of private delivery probably affected letter writing more than fears about security, however. The moment at which a letter was dispatched could be controlled only if the sender charged a personal agent to carry it. Otherwise the schedule depended on someone else: on the courier who brought a message requiring a reply or who called merely to collect a letter, or on a third party who volunteered to deliver one. One consequence was that letters often had to be dashed off on the spur of the moment, whenever a potential bearer turned up. Another was that they were sometimes written even if the writer had nothing in particular to communicate (since it would have been tactless to send back someone's courier empty-handed).[19] Both of these situations are frequently reflected in epistolary discourse, but two illustrations will suffice. Cicero complains to Cassius at one point, "your couriers...would show more consideration if they left me a little time to write, but they keep turning up dressed for the highway and saying that their companions are waiting by the gate" (tabellarii...facerent commodius si mihi aliquid spati ad scribendum darent; sed petasati veniunt, comites ad portam expectare dicunt, *Fam.* 15.17.1 = 214 SB). And he writes to Atticus, "Cincius tells me you are back in Italy and that he is sending his lads to you. I didn't want them to leave without a letter from me—not that I have anything to write, especially as you will be here so soon" (Cincius...dixit enim mihi te esse in Italia seseque ad te pueros mittere. quos sine meis litteris ire nolui, non quo haberem quod tibi, praesertim iam prope praesenti, scriberem, *Att.* 4.4. = 76 SB). The pressure of waiting couriers may be suspected even in cases where they are not mentioned, as in many brief letters of the Atticus corpus.[20] The unpredictability of delivery arrangements probably affected even letters written before a courier's arrival. Postscripts are much more frequent in letters of the Ciceronian corpus than in modern letters, and a likely reason is that during the wait between writing and sending, new material accrued that the writer wanted to add (as at *Att.* 12.1.2 = 248 SB).

Finally, the improvisational character of Roman postal arrangements seems to have had a much broader effect on the rhythms of correspondence. In certain periods, Cicero and Atticus exchanged letters every day.[21] But for reasons already noted, that was possible only when they were living relatively close by. The regularity of their exchanges dropped off markedly as the distance between them increased, and Cicero's correspondence with others, including his brother, was even more sporadic. It is also noteworthy that in the extant corpus there is no one with whom Cicero cultivates a purely epistolary relationship. That is to say, there is no one residing more or less permanently away from Rome with whom he exchanges letters regularly.[22] The lack of a dedicated system for communicating at a distance may not have been the only reason that the Romans did not develop long-term epistolary relationships that maintained a rhythm.[23] But it is probably one reason.

Involvement of the Household

The fact that most letters were delivered by a personal agent of either the sender or the recipient is just one aspect of a broad household involvement in the letter-writing process. Roman society was of course a patronal and slaveholding society, in which the well-to-do depended on staffs of slaves and freedmen to help them organize their lives and on networks of clients to extend their reach. Handling the master's correspondence was one of the specialties that a household was set up to perform, starting with production of the letter itself. Cicero corresponded too widely and too often to have been able to write every letter in his own hand. More often he dictated, with the consequence that on certain topics the presence of a secretary inhibited what he was willing to say (*Att.* 4.17.1 = 91 SB, 13.9.1 = 317 SB). Furthermore, the secretary produced not only the original that was to be sent to the addressee, but usually a file copy, and in some cases copies to be mailed to other persons, as well as a variety of enclosures that might accompany the original such as other letters, literary compositions, and official documents.[24] In our copy machine–dependent age, it is easy to underestimate how easily slave societies could muster resources for services like copying and filing. The fact that letters were freely copied and kept handy for subsequent use complicates their status as private exchanges tied to particular occasions. There was nothing to prevent a person from later passing on a copy of a letter that he had written or that he had received to third parties.[25]

But a more important consequence of domestic involvement is that a Roman letter was not typically self-contained. Whether carried by an agent of the sender or of the addressee, it was often supplemented by an oral message, to which the letters themselves repeatedly draw attention. Cicero tells one friend, for example, "from Marcus Plaetorius you will have excellent information on all matters...touching you personally....You will also have information from him about the overall political situation, the details of which are not easy to put in writing" (de omnibus rebus quae ad te pertinent...optime ex M. Plaetorio cognosces....ex eodem de toto statu rerum communium cognosces; quae quales sint, non facile est scribere, *Fam.* 1.8.1 = 19 SB). He tells another, "if the country itself possessed a voice to tell you how it is doing, you could not easily learn more than from your freedman Phanias....He will give you a full account, which allows for brevity on my part and prudence about things in general" (si ipsa res publica tibi narrare posset quo modo sese haberet, non facilius ex ea cognoscere posses quam ex liberto tuo Phania....ille tibi omnia explanabit; id enim mihi et ad brevitatem est aptius et ad reliquas res providentius, *Fam* 3.1.1 = 64 SB). And he informs yet another, "I gave [a letter] to Caninius, but since he is a knowledgeable person and very close to you, I also had a conversation with him which I assume he has reported to you" (Caninio dedi; sed cum eo ut cum homine docto et amantissimo tui locutus ea sum quae pertulisse illum ad te existimo, *Fam.* 9.2.1 = 177 SB). Contrariwise, a letter that arrived *without* its live counterpart could cause annoyance, as Cicero says of a message from his fellow consular Servius: "When I read your letter, I realized that Philotimus had shown poor judgment. Though he had been briefed by you on all points, as you say in the letter, he did not come to me in person, but had your letter sent on" ([litteris] lectis cognovi non satis prudenter fecisse Philotimum, qui, cum abs te mandata haberet, ut scribis, de omnibus rebus, ipse ad me non venisset, litteras tuas misisset, *Fam.* 4.2.1 = 151 SB). Combining a written with an oral message gave Romans some of the same advantages we can obtain by following up a letter with a telephone call.[26]

There is one last curiosity about letters in the Ciceronian corpus that household involvement helps to explain. Remarkably few of them contain narratives of political or other public events. Except in letters to his brother and to Atticus, Cicero rarely gives accounts of senatorial debates or public trials—not even of trials in which he took a starring role. He never describes (though he sometimes mentions) triumphs or electoral upsets. No letter reports on the killing of Clodius or of Caesar, though Cicero was in town when those events took place. The reason is not that such news would have seemed unimportant to his correspondents, but rather the opposite. Senators abroad could not afford to remain ignorant of events that altered the equilibrium of power and status back home. But as noted above, they depended on their own people—the *sui*—to relay that information, not on peers.[27]

Cicero himself can be seen pumping his inner circle for news whenever he is away from Rome. From his place of exile in 58, for example, he appealed to his brother, "I beg you to write back to me about everything" (te oro ut ad me de omnibus rebus rescribas, *QFr.* 1.4.5 = 4 SB). A decade later, when he was stranded for months in Brundisium after the first round of civil war, he instructed his wife, "I want you to set up regular couriers so that I get some letter(s) from you every day" (velim tabellarios instituatis certos, ut cottidie aliquas a vobis litteras accipiam, *Fam.* 14.18.2 = 144 SB). But his appetite for political news was most intense during the year when he was abroad as governor, and events back home were leading toward war between Caesar and the Senate. In the summer of 51, he wrote to Atticus, "I am signally concerned about being out of touch with everything back there for so long. And so, as I wrote to you before, make sure I hear about things, especially politics" (mirifice sollicitus sum quod iam diu mihi ignota sunt ista omnia. qua re, ut ad te ante scripsi, cum cetera tum res publica cura ut mihi nota sit, *Att.* 5.15.3 = 108 SB). At the same time, he counted also on his protégé Caelius, who as a senator and magistrate was privy to facts that Atticus did not always have and who loved to chatter. Caelius is told, "Please write me in fullest detail about the overall political situation—I will take as most reliable whatever I learn from you" (tu velim ad me de omni rei publicae statu quam diligentissime perscribas; ea enim certissima putabo quae ex te cognoro, *Fam.* 2.11.2 = 90 SB).[28]

The general reliance on confidential informants had a corollary that is made evident in letters to persons outside one's inner circle. It becomes a commonplace of Cicero's letters to say that the addressee will have no need of being told the latest news: "I know that you are sent careful reports of what is and has been going on" (acta quae sint quaeque agantur scio perscribi ad te diligenter, *MBrut.* 1[2.1].3 = 1 SB). "I believe you have been informed about what is and has been going on here through written and oral communications from a number of sources" (hic quae agantur quaeque acta sint [ea] te et litteris multorum et nuntiis cognosse arbitror, *Fam.* 1.5b.1 = 16 SB). "There's no news to pass on to you, and even if there were any, I know you are apprised of it by your own people" (novi quod ad te scriberem nihil erat et tamen, si quid esset, sciebam te a tuis certiorem fieri solere, *Fam.* 6.4.1 = 244 SB). Rarely was Cicero in a position to assume that he possessed news which the addressee would not have already heard.

Letters versus Face-to-Face Exchanges

From what Cicero's letters generally do not do, I return to what they do do. Letters substituted for face-to-face contact when Roman peers were unable to interact directly. To appreciate the way letters function, we must appreciate the primary role of the live encounters they replaced. Much of a Roman's day was arranged so as to foster personal contact, from the morning open house to the daily promenade around the Forum and to the evening dinner party. When a senator went on holiday to one of his villas in the south, he expected peers and clients to call on him there if they happened to be in the vicinity. Such rituals were extremely important in moderating the adverse effects of aristocratic competition. Various episodes could be cited in which a social call not paid leads a Roman grandee to take offense.[29] But a particularly striking one comes from a letter of Cicero written about a month before the outbreak of the civil war between Caesar and Pompey:

> I saw Pompey on December 10th, when we spent perhaps two hours together.... On the political front, he spoke as though beyond any doubt we were facing war. Nothing offered a prospect of reconciliation. He said he had recently concluded that Caesar was plainly at odds with him (though he knew it already): Hirtius came from Caesar, with whom he is very tight, but paid no call on *him*. He came the evening of the 6th and then in the dead of night headed back to Caesar, even though Balbus was planning to come to Scipio's place for a general discussion before dawn on the 7th. That seemed to Pompey a tell-tale sign of alienation.

> *Pompeium vidi iiii Id. Dec.; fuimus una horas duas fortasse.... de re publica autem ita mecum locutus est quasi non dubium bellum haberemus: nihil ad spem concordiae; plane illum a se alienatum cum ante intellegeret, tum vero proxime iudicasse; venisse Hirtium a Caesare, qui esset illi familiarissimus, ad se non accessisse et, cum ille a. d. viii Id. Dec. vesperi venisset, Balbus de tota re constituisset a. d. vii ad Scipionem ante lucem venire, multa de nocte eum profectum esse ad Caesarem. hoc illi τεκμηριῶδες videbatur esse alienationis.*

Att. 7.4.2 = 127 SB

Pompey was not necessarily mistaken in the inference that Cicero says he drew. In addition to avoiding Pompey, Hirtius evidently ducked out of a morning meeting that was to discuss the possibility of reconciliation. What seems extraordinary, however, is that Pompey would fix on the neglect of a courtesy in first place as proof that a civil war was imminent.

An important function of letters was to serve as prophylactics against such estrangement—as stopgaps for the face-to-face encounters in which members of the elite were temporarily unable to engage. The connection between letters and direct engagements is at issue in a letter of the year 45, in which Cicero toys with the alternatives and hints at a hierarchy in which they can be arranged:

> You ask me to look out for that exceptional lady, your wife Pompeia. On reading your letter, I promptly had a talk with our friend Sura. I told him to tell her from me that she should notify me of anything she needed, and that I would do all she wished with the greatest of enthusiasm and care. And so I will, and I will call on her as well, should that be necessary. For your part, please write to her and say she should consider no charge so great that I would find it burdensome or so small I would find it demeaning. Any exertions on your behalf will seem not bothersome but even creditable.

> *quod mihi feminam primariam, Pompeiam, uxorem tuam, commendas, cum Sura nostro statim tuis litteris lectis locutus sum ut ei meis verbis diceret ut, quicquid opus esset, mihi denuntiaret; me omnia quae ea vellet summo studio curaque facturum. itaque faciam eamque, si opus esse videbitur, ipse conveniam. tu tamen ei velim scribas ut nullam rem neque tam magnam neque tam parvam putet quae mihi aut difficilis aut parum me digna videatur. omnia quae in tuis rebus agam et non laboriosa mihi et honesta videbuntur.*

> *Fam.* 5.11.2 = 257 SB

Onc would not go wrong in suspccting bad faith bchind this fog of words about how contact is to be made with Pompeia. Nothing could have been easier, after all, since she and Cicero were both in Rome at the time. And so it becomes relevant to know that the addressee of the letter is Vatinius, the erstwhile antagonist whom Cicero had detested for a decade and a half (and disparaged in the letter with which this chapter began), but with whom he had been forced to reconcile. Now etiquette requires him to communicate with Vatinius's wife, and he proceeds in the most roundabout way imaginable. He first taps someone from Vatinius's circle in Rome, not his own, to serve as go-between (Sura is mentioned nowhere else in Cicero's letters). He does not write to Pompeia but sends an oral message instructing her to get in touch with *him*. Rather than write to her himself, Cicero suggests that Vatinius should write to her from overseas. And he makes it as plain as he can that he expects a personal call on Pompeia to be unnecessary. By combining a series of backhanded gestures with polite expressions, Cicero flaunts his repugnance for contact while he submits to the necessity of it.

If Cicero's behavior toward Vatinius's wife represents a calculated reversal of courtesy, by the same token it preserves the code of normal priorities. A personal visit takes precedence over a letter, as a letter takes precedence over an oral message. (Whether the messenger is a slave or a known friend and confidant or someone in between contributes to the semiotic as well.) That letters are second-best is made explicit elsewhere. In one of the earliest letters to Atticus, Cicero reports that he has visited an estranged friend of Atticus and done his best to repair the grievance between them. But he has made no headway: "Something is eating at him that is too deep inside, something that neither your letters nor my diplomacy can remove as easily as you in person, and not just by words but by your good old face" (habet quiddam profecto quod magis in animo eius insederit, quod neque epistulae tuae neque nostra legatio tam potest facile delere quam tu praesens, non modo oratione sed tuo vultu illo familiari).[30] It is surely the premium put on face-to-face interaction that explains why so few of the letters in the Ciceronian corpus were exchanged between persons in Rome. If efficiency were the first consideration, it would often have been simpler for two persons living in different parts of the city to communicate by letter than to visit each other. Under normal rules of social intercourse, however, that would have conveyed aloofness.

The preference for live contact is often acknowledged even in circumstances in which letters are the only interaction possible. And perhaps a hint of it comes out also in an often-described ritual whereby a letter is shown around or read aloud to those in the company of the person who has received it. At Att 13.46.2 = 338 SB, for example, Cicero describes a visit to Caesar's agent Balbus on which he was greeted with the news that Balbus had just received a letter from Caesar. Cicero continues, "I read the letter. Lots about my piece on Cato. Caesar said that his own eloquence had been improved by several readings of it, whereas a reading of Brutus's *Cato* encouraged him to congratulate himself on his style" (legi epistulam. multa de meo Catone, quo saepissime legendo se dicit copiosiorem factum, Bruti Catone lecto se sibi visum disertum). Balbus could certainly have conveyed Caesar's compliment without handing the letter to Cicero, or he could have sent a copy for Cicero to read in private, as he did on other occasions. But by being read in the context of a tête-à-tête between mutual friends of Caesar, the letter acquired a value beyond its content, as a momentary presentification of the bantering, back-slapping Caesar himself. Cicero deployed a letter to similar effect in a situation he describes at Att. 15.1.2 = 377 SB. After Caesar's death, Atticus had sought Cicero's aid in winning ratification of an oral agreement that he had obtained from Caesar. Cicero reports that he could not arrange a meeting with Mark Antony but did raise the issue with another power in post-Caesarian Rome, the consul-designate: "But it chanced I had Hirtius with me at Puteoli when I read your letter. I read it to him and followed up. He said first of all that he counted himself in your corner no less than I was. Then he declared that he was at my complete disposal, not only as regards this matter but his consulate overall" (sed casu, cum legerem tuas litteras, Hirtius erat apud me in Puteolano. ei legi et egi. primum, quod ad te attinet, nihil mihi concedebat, deinde ad summam arbitrum me statuebat non modo huius rei sed totius consulatus sui). The reading of the letter to Hirtius lent greater weight to Atticus's request than a simple statement of it would have had; hence Hirtius responds by first asserting his own credentials as Atticus's friend. In situations in which letters are read in company, the point is not simply to communicate information. The reading is an effort to capture the presence of the letter writer and to inject it into the social dynamic of the occasion.[31]

Uses of Letters

If letters could be seen as a substitute for live conversation, it was presumably because they discharged some of the same functions that conversation did. Fortunately we do not have to depend entirely on intuition to orient us here. Long before the age of Cicero, the personal letter had developed an array of conventions which reflected a broad social consensus about its aims and methods and which passed with surprisingly little alteration from Greek into Roman letters. That letter writers were conscious of hewing to a generic model is evident not only from the standardization of the salutation, opening, close, and dateline (formalities which will be discussed in more detail in chapter 3), but also from conventional utterances scattered through the body of letters.[32] Several of these elements (the opening, the close, and many politeness formulas) mimic the progress and etiquette of face-to-face encounters.[33]

Epistolary format would not have acquired the degree of uniformity it has in the absence of prescriptions about it. Although no extant pattern book or manual on letter writing can confidently be dated as early as Cicero's time, it is likely that rhetorical writers had already articulated the rudiments of a theory of the letter by then because Cicero and his correspondents sometimes seem to appeal to one.[34] The opening of a letter to Curio is a good example:

> You are well aware that, among the several types of letter which exist, the most basic one and the cornerstone of the genre is that we inform persons who are absent about anything which it serves their interest or ours for them to know. Yet for letters of this sort you do not look to me, since you have members of your household to report and write about your own affairs, and in mine there is nothing new. Two other types of which I am very fond are the friendly, joshing letter and the stern and serious kind respectively. I cannot say which of these it would be less suitable for me to write. Should I joke with you in

letters? I swear I do not believe that anyone who could laugh in these times is a patriot. Should I write more seriously? On what subject could a serious letter be written by a Cicero to a Curio except on politics? Yet in this department my situation is such that I don't dare write what I think and don't want to write what I do not think.

epistularum genera multa esse non ignoras, sed unum illud certissimum, cuius causa inventa res ipsa est, ut certiores faceremus absentis si quid esset quod eos scire aut nostra aut ipsorum interesset. huius generis litteras a me profecto non exspectas. tuarum enim rerum domesticos habes et scriptores et nuntios, in meis autem rebus nihil est sane novi. reliqua sunt epistularum genera duo, quae me magno opere delectant, unum familiare et iocosum, alterum severum et grave. utro me minus deceat uti non intellego. iocerne tecum per litteras? civem mehercule non puto esse, qui temporibus his ridere possit. an gravius aliquid scribam? quid est quod possit graviter a Cicerone scribi ad Curionem nisi de republica? atqui in hoc genere haec mea causa est est, ut ‹neque ea quae sentio audeam› neque ea quae non sentio velim scribere.

Fam. 2.4.1 = 48 SB

That such typologies are felt as commonplaces is consistent with the fact that they often occur at the beginning of letters, where (as here) a writer is laboring to establish common ground with the addressee.

One of the claims most often made about the familiar letter, in Cicero and throughout antiquity, was that it not only substituted for live conversation but somehow approximated it.[35] What was meant in part was that it drew more on the style and gambits of talk than did most kinds of classical writing. But it was also implied that the letter served some of the same objectives as conversation.[36] That is most obvious in the case of the second letter type to which Cicero refers. While joshing (*iocari*) would probably not rank among the primary functions assigned to letters in any modern classification, wit or, more precisely, competitive banter was central to the Roman aristocratic ideal of *urbanitas*.[37] Its role in letters mirrors its importance in conversation.[38] Similarly with another type mentioned: letters about politics are a continuation of the incessant talk about politics in which Cicero and his peers engaged when they met. And certain of the functions that Cicero associates with letters elsewhere, such as conveying consolation (*Fam.* 6.10.4 = 222 SB), congratulations (*Fam.* 15.14.3 = 106 SB), and *mandata* or calls on friends for help of various kinds (*Att.* 5.5.1 = 98 SB), are also grounded in the routines of face-to-face interaction. A call for help that Cicero put out during the year he governed Cilicia affords a particularly clear illustration of the carry-over from oral to epistolary communication. After conducting successful military operations in his province, he wanted the Senate to vote a public thanksgiving in his honor, and to that end he says he wrote to all but one of his approximately six hundred fellow senators.[39] This is the sort of intensive lobbying which he would have carried out in person if he had been in Rome, and which friends on the spot did take up on his behalf.[40]

The classificatory scheme with which Cicero and his friends operated— political, newsy, and bantering letters, letters of condolence and congratulation, recommendation letters and *mandata*—has the virtues of reflecting their perceptions rather than ours and of accounting for many letters that they wrote. It also bears on the present argument, in that it helps draw attention to the strong overlap between the subjects of letters and of conversation. But another sign that this classification is more conventional than descriptive is that it corresponds to practice only roughly. As Cicero has many occasions to remark, his fellow senators could generally obtain news through channels that preempted the need for him to report it. And although he often makes jokes in letters, letters devoted to joking are rarer than his treatment of them as a type would suggest. Fewer than two dozen in the corpus fit that description, and most of those are reserved for just two among his correspondents.[41] There are also certain types of letters in the corpus that the conventional classification does not accommodate at all—the many letters which open with the writer's avowal that "I have nothing particular to write about," for example, and a large category which could be labeled "letters of advice" (to be discussed in chapter 5).

At this point, however, rather than add categories in order to improve the scheme, let us step back for a more synoptic look at what the letters do. Often a writer does confront some limited practical objective: to canvass a vote, to introduce a protégé, to negotiate a purchase or sale, or to discharge an obligation of congratulation or condolence, for example. But it can be deceptive to approach the letters of the Ciceronian corpus simply in terms of their immediate goals. For one thing, they often pursue more than one at a time. But more important is that practical objectives are usually subordinate to, or at least accompanied by, a larger purpose.

Letters containing *mandata* are a case in point. The literal meaning of the word ("things assigned," "commissions," "charges") might suggest that it was most at home in relationships of top-down authority and that the emphasis was all on the task to be discharged. In fact, however, Cicero and his peers regularly make a fuss of giving and getting *mandata* from one other. Not only that, but the mandatee often goes out of the way to volunteer his services, as, for example, "please be assured that there is not the slightest matter of interest to you which is not dearer to me than all my own concerns" (tu velim tibi ita persuadeas, nullam rem esse minimam quae ad te pertineat quae mihi non carior sit quam meae res omnes, *Fam.* 1.8.6 = 19 SB); "please pass along…instructions about all matters which you want me to handle or supervise" (omnibus…de rebus quas agi, quas curari a me voles mandata des velim, *Fam.* 3.1.2 = 64 SB), "for the time being, I think it is enough to let you know that, without needing to be asked, I will do whatever I see will advance your wishes, advantage, or status" (satis esse hoc tempore arbitratus sum hoc ad te scribere, me, si quid ipse intellegerem aut ad voluntatem aut ad commodum aut ad amplitudinem tuam pertinere, mea sponte id esse facturum, *Fam.* 5.8.5 = 25 SB). The solicitation of *mandata* forms part of the ritual of leave-taking when a friend goes abroad.[42] In such contexts, the imperative overtone of the word does not signal a status differential between the parties but serves a politeness strategy which is familiar also in English ("your wish is my command"). The open-ended nature of these offers is significant as well. Often enough a particular piece of business *is* at issue, and getting it accomplished is not unimportant. But the rhetoric associated with *mandata* in the letters also aims at inserting particulars into the texture of an ongoing relationship.

The same habit colors another practically oriented letter type. The arguments made in letters of recommendation turn as much on the relationship between letter writer and addressee as on the deserts of the recommendee. They are too numerous and varied to do more than paraphrase some of the most typical: "so-and-so enjoys the same sorts of things that you and I do"; "you will be doing as much for me as for so-and-so"; "demonstrate to so-and-so that my word carries weight with you"; "I am appealing to you in the name of our friendship"; "your many past kindnesses encourage me to ask…"[43] While it might appear that such overtures merely exploit a relationship to elicit a favor, a relationship is not something distinct from its fruits. In Cicero's society, personal ties were created and sustained by that stream of favors and other attentions which are collectively termed *officia*. Even a note of condolence can be made to foreground the relationship between writer and recipient:

> Marcus Cicero bids greeting to Gaius Curio:
>   In your distinguished father, I have lost a powerful witness to my love for you. By virtue of his own accomplishments and of your being his son, he would have surpassed the fortune of all others, had it only been granted him to see you before he passed from this life.
>   Still, I hope that the friendship between you and me needs no witnesses. May the gods prosper your legacy from your father! You can count on me to cherish and rejoice in you as much your father did.

> *M. Cicero s. d. C. Curioni:*
>   *gravi teste privatus sum amoris summi erga te mei patre tuo, clarissimo viro; qui cum suis laudibus tum vero te filio superasset omnium fortunam si ei contigisset ut te ante videret quam a vita discederet.*
>   *sed spero nostram amicitiam non egere testibus. tibi patrimonium dei fortunent! me certe habebis cui et carus aeque sis et iucundus ac fuisti patri.*

Fam. 2.2 = 46 SB

Every *officium* thus contributes something above and beyond its immediate purpose, and the letters rarely fail to draw attention to that dimension of particular transactions.

An instructive parallel for the effect that letters are meant to exert can be found in another transaction to which the letter corpus is our best witness. One instance of it is found in the Trebonius letter quoted at the beginning of the chapter, in which Trebonius turns an encounter with Cicero's son into an occasion for reaffirming his connection with Cicero. The display of lavish interest in another's son is the main exception to the generally low frequency of discourse about family in the letters. Outside the confines of the Atticus series, about a dozen other examples can be cited.[44] Attention to a son can substitute for attention to the parent when the latter is absent, since the son is a natural surrogate, or in Cicero's parlance, a "mirror of mind and body" (imago animi et corporis, *Fam.* 6.6.13 = 234 SB) of the father. Moreover, as the Trebonius letter illustrates, talk about a son foregrounds exactly those themes of affection, values, and social position that are most central to the discourse by which correspondents construct their relationship with each other.

The symbolic value so apparent in the use of this topic is operative also in many others. The letters appeal to a variety of persons and practices as concrete tokens of the friendship between correspondents. In the dominant metaphor, such tokens are characterized as *vincula* or "bonds" between them, and they include mutual friends (*Fam.* 13.17.1 = 283 SB), tenure of the same office (*Fam.* 3.4.2 = 67 SB), shared investments in oratory (*Fam.* 13.29.1 = 282 SB), philosophy (*Fam.* 15.4.16 = 110 SB), and literature (*Fam.* 3.10.9 = 73 SB, 13.29.1 = 282 SB), and *officia* of all sorts (*Fam.* 1.9.18 = 20 SB and 6.10.2 = 223 SB).[45]

The word *vinculum* helpfully anchors the abstract idea of mutuality or friendly intercourse in that it offers one way of imagining a connection between two persons. But it is a remarkable keying of that idea. According to the *OLD*, the first meaning of *vinculum* is "bond," "chain," "fetter," or "shackle," and the suggestion of duress is not irrelevant to other senses. It is revealing that, whereas the *vinculum/devincire* metaphor occurs often in letters and speeches, it is completely absent from Cicero's discussion of friendship in his dialogue on that theme.[46] On the ideal plane on which the argument there moves, friendship is consistently represented as a union of soul mates.[47] The letters, by contrast, are a window onto the rockier experience of friendship that senatorial Romans actually had. In that milieu, friends were always liable to slip loose because they were at the same time competitors.[48] Friendship could be maintained only by strenuous efforts, and the *vinculum* metaphor betrays an obsession with establishing secure attachments.

Concern about the security of one's position also underlies a closing motif of the letters, which can take two forms. One is illustrated (again) by Trebonius's letter, in the final words of which he commends his mother and the rest of his household to Cicero's care. Women do not ordinarily have much of a role to play in public life, and so this commendation is perfunctory. But like sons, the women of a household can stand as surrogates for the head of it, and to commend them is another way of commending oneself.[49]

In the more frequent variation of the motif, the letter writer actually does commend himself, for example: "I beg you to show your customary generosity in defending me while I am abroad" (peto a te ut tuam consuetudinem et liberalitatem in me absente defendendo mihi praestes, *Fam.* 5.9.1 = 255 SB); "goodbye, and cherish me as I cherish you, and protect my dignity so far as I deserve" (fac valeas meque mutuo diligas dignitatemque meam, si mereor, tuearis, *Fam.* 10.17.3 = 398 SB); "please cherish and defend me while I am abroad, as you always do" (tu velim, ut consuesti, nos absentis diligas et defendas, *Fam.* 15.3.2 = 103 SB). Like the image of constraint in the *vinculum* metaphor, the language of defense and protection in these passages is no idle figure. Political figures did run into dangers in which they needed strong allies. The careers of Cicero and Caesar provide well-known examples, and the correspondence of Cicero provides others. After his friend Lentulus Spinther left Rome to govern a distant province, Lentulus's colleagues in the Senate moved not only to foreclose a potentially lucrative side commission, but to strip him of his command altogether. Cicero's efforts to thwart those maneuvers are the subject of most of his letters to Lentulus in book 1. His correspondence with Appius in book 3 discloses an episode in which he was able to help when he himself was far from Rome. Appius, who had preceded Cicero as governor of Cilicia, returned to the capital only to be assailed with two separate prosecutions for provincial misconduct. Cicero made sure that information favorable to the defendant was forthcoming from the province (*Fam.* 3.10.1 = 73 SB, 3.11.3 = 74 SB).

But the dangers against which upper-class Romans looked for defenders were not confined to occasional high-stakes contests such as these. A man's position vis-à-vis his peers could also be harmed by the gossip that bubbled in public and private conversations every day. Gossip did not subside but merely became more difficult to counteract when someone went away, and so it was prudent to leave watchdogs behind. While Cicero was away in his province, his wife, who had remained in Rome, negotiated the engagement of their daughter to Dolabella. Though Cicero was personally satisfied with this match, at least initially, it could not have taken place at a more awkward moment. Dolabella was the very person responsible for prosecuting Appius, whom Cicero wanted to be seen as helping at that point. After being warned in a letter that Dolabella would aggravate matters by crowing about his new tie (*Fam.* 8.6.1–2 = 88 SB), Cicero wrote to Appius deploring his son-in-law's actions and declaring that he himself had played no part in arranging the marriage (*Fam.* 3.10.5 = 73 SB, 3.12.2–3 = 75 SB). When, some years later, another friend wrote warning that comments from a hostile source were threatening to impair Cicero's good relations with Caesar, Cicero replied that he was already taking care to ingratiate himself with several friends of Caesar's.[50] There are also letters in which Cicero takes up the defense of someone else who has been the victim of malicious talk, as in this letter to Brutus:

Cicero to Brutus, greetings.

The tribune-elect Lucius Clodius is very close to me, or to speak more forcefully, cherishes me dearly, and from that standpoint I am sure you realize that I cherish him in turn. You know what I am like. There is nothing I consider less civilized than failure to rise to the level of those who challenge us in affection.

Clodius has evidently formed the suspicion—to his deep distress—that your regard for him has cooled as the result of something reported to you by, or with the connivance of, his enemies. I am not prone to issue rash affirmations about others, my dear Brutus, as I think you know. It is too risky, given that people have hidden hearts and many layers. But I have seen into the mind of Clodius and read and approved it. There are several pointers, which, however, do not have to be put down in writing: I want you to take this rather as my affidavit than a letter. Clodius was advanced by the favor of Antony (no small part of which favor was in fact owed to you), and so it was natural to align himself with Antony's interests, consonant with the interests of us as well. But he sees that things have reached a point—he is no fool, as you know—where the interests of the two sides cannot coexist. He therefore takes our side, and toward you he holds and voices the most friendly sentiments.

So if anyone has written or spoken differently about him to you, I beg you most earnestly to believe me instead. I am in a better position to judge than your nameless informant, and I love you more. Accept that Clodius is devoted to you and that he is the kind of citizen a sober person of excellent fortune ought to be.

Cicero Bruto salutem

L.Clodius, tribunus pl. designatus, valde me diligit vel, ut ἐμφατικώτερον *dicam, valde me amat. quod cum mihi ita persuasum sit, non dubito (bene enim me nosti) quin illum quoque iudices a me amari. nihil enim mihi minus hominis videtur quam non respondere in amore iis a quibus provocere.*

Is mihi visus est suspicari, nec sine magno quidem dolore, aliquid a suis vel per suos potius iniquos ad te esse delatum quo tuus animus a se esset alienior. non soleo, mi Brute, quod tibi notum esse arbitror, temere adfirmare de altero (est enim periculosum propter occultas hominum voluntates multiplicisque naturas): Clodi animum perspectum habeo, cognitum, iudicatum. multa eius indicia, sed ad scribendum non necessaria; volo enim testimonium hoc tibi videri potius quam epistulam.

auctus Antoni beneficio est (eius ipsius benefici magna pars a te est).
itaque eum salvis nobis vellet salvum. in eum autem locum rem adductam
intellegit (est enim, ut scis, minime stultus) ut utrique salvi esse non
possint. itaque nos mavult. de te vero amicissime et loquitur et sentit.

Qua re si quis secus ad te de eo scripsit aut si coram locutus est, peto a
te etiam atque etiam mihi ut potius credas, qui et facilius iudicare possum
quam ille nescio quis et te plus diligo. Clodium tibi amicissimum existima
civemque talem qualis et prudentissimus et fortuna optima esse debet.

M Brut. 6(1.1) = 13 SB[51]

Gossip was hardly the gravest danger that Cicero and his class encountered, but it did inflict wounds, and it was a weapon in constant use.[52]

In this section, I have been arguing that, apart from the practical short-term objectives which letters served, they also aimed to bolster the long-term relationship between writer and recipient. In the Ciceronian correspondence, this function is often highlighted by rhetorical strategies that frame the letter topic in terms of the relationship and by images of security and defense. And while letter writers often appeal to others to defend them and sometimes write in defense of others, the defensive work of letters consisted mainly of self-defense. The surest defense in the long term was to minimize the chances of estrangement from one's peers by maximizing communication with them.

During absences, that was possible only by letter. Writing to Cassius at a moment when both he and Cassius happened to be abroad, Cicero regrets that they have been unable to meet, but he argues that they can still accomplish by letter most of the things they would have accomplished—more pleasurably, to be sure—in person. Of the several goals he has in mind in the present letter, he says, "last on my list is the confirmation of our friendship, about which few words are required" (extremum illud est de iis quae proposueram, confirmatio nostrae amicitiae; de qua pluribus verbis nihil opus est). And after a quick glance back over the experiences which made them friends, he concludes: "So I would say that a good deal of my present honor and enjoyment has been the result of talent and effort from your side. I ask you earnestly to confirm it with a ready will and to send me a letter right away, and then on a regular basis once you get back to Rome" (itaque in vestro ingenio et industria mihi plurimum et suavitatis et dignitatis constitutum puto. id tu ut tuo studio confirmes et vehementer rogo, litterasque ad me et continuo mittas et, cum Romam veneris, quam saepissime, *Fam.* 15.14.6 = 106 SB). Nowhere does Cicero make more explicit that the ultimate point of engaging in correspondence was to keep a relationship active while two people were separated. And again his choice of language is telling. In Latin the word for "confirmation" (*confirmatio/ confirmare*), which he uses three times in this letter, still retains a concrete sense of strengthening and fortifying that has faded from the English word.[53] That is to say, it belongs to the same realm of ideas as *vinculum* and *defendere*.

It is true that most of the time, the kind of defense which letters could afford amounted to little more than an exchange of words between the correspondents. The value of mere talk should not be discounted, however. Talk verifies that some kind of transaction has engaged two people. Roman Jakobson argued that among the multiple functions which operate in all verbal communication, one is exclusively procedural and that in some messages it is the dominant function. "There are messages primarily serving to establish, to prolong, or to discontinue communication, to check whether the channel works...to attract the attention of the interlocutor or confirm his continued attention.... This...phatic function may be displayed by a profuse exchange of ritualized formulas, by entire dialogues with the mere purport of prolonging communication."[54]

Jakobson's "phatic function" seems, if anything, more pronounced in letters than in live encounters. When two friends come face to face, chatter is so hard to avoid that it can easily pass unremarked. But a letter consisting of chatter stands out because the letter writer appears to have taken the trouble to establish a contact only to let it go to waste. So far from being inconsequential, however, the quality of pure communicativeness is treated in modern discourse theory as being close to the heart of a letter.[55] In the Ciceronian corpus, moreover, a letter does not typically present itself as an isolated act of communication. Letters, especially letters written after a lapse of contact, tend to open with an effusion of friendship language expressing that a previous tie is still in force. The writing of a letter represents the renewal of a personal alliance, and it is by upholding the alliance that epistolary talk functions as a form of defense.

Cicero and his friends were not familiar with Jakobson's helpful analysis of communicative functions. But they did perceive that the *officium litterarum* or "work of letters" (*Fam.* 6.6.1 = 234 SB) figured significantly in the exchange of performances by which their relationships were formed and maintained. In the present chapter, I have outlined some of the constraints on letter writing in Cicero's time, and I have argued that his correspondence evinces a preoccupation with security beyond the more immediate purposes that letters served. In the second part of this study, I will consider the content and purpose of some of his letters in more detail. But before continuing in that direction, it will be necessary to take account of a complication in our reading of them. It is doubtful that we have Cicero's letters exactly as he left them.

The Editing of the Collection

What sort of literary artifact do we confront when we read the letters of Cicero in a standard edition of his works? Certainly they have much in common with other Latin texts we read. A given letter, whether by Cicero or one of his correspondents, is a composition that a writer shaped and released and that subsequently fell prey to the distortions of transcribers, booksellers, and annotators and to lesions in the manuscripts which transmitted it. Readers of classical texts expect to take account of such vagaries. But Cicero's letters differ from most other Latin texts and from all his other extant works in two respects. Cicero probably did not arrange for the mass of his correspondence to be published, and, when it was published anyway, whoever took responsibility acquired a significant role in shaping what we read.[1]

From Private to Published

The first of these points cannot be proved. In fact, it has not been found unthinkable that Cicero did arrange for his correspondence to be published. The latest letters that can be dated were written in midsummer of 43, when Cicero's public role had completely unraveled.[2] By that time, his erstwhile protégé Octavian had taken full charge of his own career and begun negotiations with rival army leaders that would lead to the proscription and death of Cicero in December. Virtually nothing is known about Cicero's activities during the last four or five months of his life. But if he discerned what was coming, he might have dropped out of sight to put his affairs in order and to gather letters and papers he wished to have published after his death. Papers reserved for posthumous publication are a recurrent phenomenon of Roman literary life.[3]

Yet the only positive indication that Cicero thought of publishing his letters points to a project of very different scale. A year and a half before his death, he wrote to Atticus that "there is no collection of my letters. But Tiro has something on the order of seventy, and of course some must be obtained from you. I should look through them and correct them—then and only then will they be published."[4] It seems obvious that Cicero must be referring here to letters culled for eventual publication rather than to all the letters he had on file. No one could believe that out of the thousands he had written, his secretary retained copies of only seventy.

But which letters Cicero considered publishing and whether the project was ever brought to term we do not know. The conventional view is that the seventy letters constitute the core of the eighty-one letters now gathered in book 13 of the *Letters to Friends*.[5] If so, Cicero could be and sometimes is credited with editorial responsibility for at least this book of the published correspondence. However, all that links Tiro's store of letters with the recommendations is an approximate coincidence between the numbers seventy and eighty-one. That coincidence would acquire significance only if one can assume as well that Cicero's word "collection" (συναγωγή) implies a physical unit of text, and that the seventy-plus letters would necessarily emerge as a single book.

Furthermore, the circumstances of Cicero's remark need to be taken into account. Atticus had informed him that a mutual friend of theirs, the litterateur Cornelius Nepos, would soon be writing to Cicero. Nepos was eager to see something Cicero had written, Atticus said, and was not interested in the philosophical works but was interested in some of the letters. Nepos's esteem for Cicero's letters is confirmed by his own testimony elsewhere. In a biography of Atticus written a few years later, he extolled the historical value of the letters Atticus received from Cicero, in which "all has been set down touching the ambitions of leading men, the shortcomings of generals, and transformations of the political order" (omnia de studiis principum, vitiis ducum, mutationibus rei publicae perscripta sunt, Nep. *Att*. 16.4). But if this is the sort of content Nepos valued, he would hardly have been angling for a look at letters of recommendation when he wrote to Cicero.

Although the exchange with Atticus does not reveal which seventy letters Cicero had in mind, it does establish two points of interest. The first is that when, seventeen months before his death, Cicero contemplated an edition of his letters, he envisioned a relatively small project, not one that would cover his entire correspondence. The other is that by that date he had apparently not readied *any* letters for release: "I should look through them and correct them—then and only then will they be published."[6]

Cicero spent most of the next five months after writing those words away from his house in Rome, and when he returned in December, he was caught up in a struggle against Mark Antony that engrossed him until the middle of 43. The scarcity of opportunity for literary work during this time is the most compelling reason to doubt that he could have expanded and carried through the plan for an edition of the letters before he died.[7] Merely to sort through them all would have been a large task. The surviving correspondence takes up thirty-six books, references to letter collections which have perished suggest that they filled at least as many more (see appendix 1), and these seventy-odd books had to be compiled from the still larger body of letters Cicero wrote and received. But from his own words we know that more than sorting would have been involved: he took it for granted that letters selected for publication would have to be revised.

How soon after his death the letters came into circulation has been the most contentious question in the scholarly literature surrounding them.[8] But we do have evidence that they were not issued right away—at least, not the largest and most important corpus. Nepos indicates that the letters to Atticus which he so admired were still unpublished when he saw them, and it is not apparent from his words that publication of them, or of any other part of the correspondence, was then imminent.[9] The slowness of the letters to appear after Cicero's death affords further reason to doubt that he left them ready for release before he died.

Finally, the correspondence as it has come down to us contains editorial slips unlikely to have been committed had Cicero been the editor. Book 7 of the *Letters to Friends* provides a notable example. Throughout this corpus, letters to the same person are often grouped together. Five letters of book 7 are addressed to someone named "Gallus": numbers 23, 24, and 25 to "M. Fabius Gallus," according to the salutation line, and numbers 26 and 27 simply to "Gallus."[10] The first four are to a wealthy friend who, like Cicero, lived in Rome under the Caesarian regime of the mid-40s. The fifth is to Cicero's ex-quaestor Titus Fadius, living somewhere in exile since the late 50s. It seems evident that the editor of the collection has mistakenly combined letters to persons with similar names whom Cicero himself would have had no trouble distinguishing.[11] The two Brutuses appear to have been confused in book 11. Letter 16, in the middle of a series addressed to Decimus Brutus, entreats support for a protégé of Cicero in an upcoming election. The following letter, also to Brutus, is differently phrased but asks support for the same candidate in the same election. It was probably directed to Marcus Brutus rather than to Decimus.[12]

To return to the caveat expressed at the outset, it cannot be taken as certain that Cicero did not arrange for his collected correspondence to be published. But a better argument can be made for that view than for the opposite. The premise of the following pages will be that it was someone else who edited and published the letters.

No evidence has survived to tell us who that person was, whether more than one person was involved, or when, how, and why the project was carried out. The published correspondence is devoid of any kind of editorial statement, and independent sources have nothing to say about the circumstances under which

Cicero's letters were made public. Scholars have tried to cross the evidential chasm by laying down a variety of hypotheses in which Cicero's secretary Tiro, his friends Atticus and Nepos, and sometimes other persons play more or less important parts.[13] Elements of these theories seem entirely believable. Tiro is likely to have had a hand in publishing the letters since he had charge of them during Cicero's lifetime and survived him by thirty years. There is also the coincidence that one whole book of the collection preserves letters written to Tiro.[14] Atticus, too, is a plausible agent. He was the recipient of the largest single set of letters, and it can be argued (not proved) that he saved and shared them after Cicero's death. But questions of who, when, and why will not drive the present argument. I believe that speculation in this direction has been pushed as far as it profitably can be without firmer anchor points. The market for it collapsed when Carcopino floated a hypothesis (1947) so gaudy and inventive that it was seen to burst of its own excess.[15] But even before Carcopino, theories about the formation of the collection were guided by assumptions about editorial motive that could only be judged by standards of good storytelling.

Instead, I want to take the collected correspondence more or less as it stands and to proceed on the assumption that it displays its purpose on its face. I believe that we were intended to read the letters which have been included and not to read letters which have not been. This proposition may sound vacuous to the point of simple-mindedness, and it may lead to results which are no more certain or less circular than other inquiries have yielded. But at least it will bring some fresh considerations into play.

To avoid the cumbersome neutrality of referring always to an "editor or editors," I will anticipate one conclusion from the start and speak of "the editor" throughout. I hope it will become apparent that the editorial procedures I will describe are broadly similar in different parts of the corpus and that the publication project therefore follows a uniform approach. But I would not question that more than one executor may have been at work.

Finally, readers who find that the terms in which the following argument is conducted make for a more rebarbative exposition than they care to accompany are invited to skip ahead to the closing section, where conclusions are summarized without argumentation.

Missing Letters

The first and most important step is to clarify that the epistolary corpus as we have it represents a selection.[16] What I mean at a minimum is that when the editor gathered letters to various individuals for publication, he declined to publish other letters to them that there is no reason to think were unavailable. Missing letters can be discerned in almost every sequence within the published correspondence, from the relatively short blocks of the *Letters to Friends* to the sixteen books of the *Letters to Atticus*. So far as I am aware, no one has attempted to collect testimonia concerning Cicero's unpublished letters.[17] But for a few letter series, the situation can be quickly set out in tabular form.

Cicero's correspondence with his son-in-law, the Caesarian partisan Publius Cornelius Dolabella, is gathered in the middle of book 9 of the *Letters to Friends*. It consists of six letters. One dates from a few months before the battle of Pharsalia and was written by Dolabella in Caesar's camp to Cicero in Pompey's. The remaining five, all by Cicero, were written later, over a period of a year and a half in 45 and 44. One additional letter to Dolabella exists but does not formally belong to the series; Cicero incorporated a copy of it into one of his letters to Atticus.

Although one letter from Dolabella is extant, and references exist to approximately a dozen others that are missing, for purposes of argument it will be best to limit scrutiny to Cicero's side of this exchange. In table 2.1, I list his extant letters to Dolabella together with references to those that are missing. For the year and a half that the table spans, we know of six letters that are extant and six that are not. But notice that for the editor of the *Letters to Friends*, the perspective was slightly different: only five letters were incorporated into the collection, and seven others were not (since item 12, the enclosure to Atticus, is not found within the Dolabella series of book 9).

What conclusions can be drawn from this evidence of choice I will consider in due course, but first let us look at some other letter sequences that present gaps. Book 10 of the *Letters to Friends* contains the letters that Cicero exchanged with Munatius Plancus during the years 44 and 43, when Plancus was the army commander in northern Gaul. In this series, both men are well represented, with almost as many letters to Plancus's credit as to Cicero's. I list

TABLE 2.1. Cicero's letters to Dolabella, 45–44 B.C.

Letter	Date
1. *Fam.* 9.10 = 217 SB	early 45
2. *Fam.* 9.11 = 250 SB	April or May 45
3. *Fam.* 9.13 = 311 SB	early 45
4. ▶ *Att.* 13.50.1 = 348 SB	August 45
5. ▶ *Att.* 15.3.1 = 380 SB; implied also at *Att.* 13.21.2 = 351 SB	by August 45
6. *Fam.* 9.12 = 263 SB	November or December 45
7. *Fam.* 9.14 = 326 SB, repeated as *Att.* 14.17A = 371A SB	May 3, 44
8. ▶ *Att.* 14.19.4 = 372 SB, 14.18.1 = 373 SB, 14.21.1 = 375 SB	May 8, 44
9. ▶ *Att.* 15.4a = 382 SB, 15.12.1 = 390 SB	before May 25, 44
10. ▶ *Att.* 15.8.1 = 385 SB	before May 31, 44
11. ▶ *Att.* 15.18.1 = 395 SB	June 15, 44
12. *Att.* 15.14 = 402 SB	June 26, 44

Extant letters are indicated by the usual book and number notation. Missing letters are indicated by an arrow ▶ pointing to a passage in an extant letter that refers to a letter not extant. Multiple references after an arrow indicate that a missing letter is mentioned more than once.

them in table 2.2, again melding the extant letters with indications of missing letters.[18] Admittedly, the data are less clear-cut than in the Dolabella series. Although items 1, 3, 19, and 32 point unmistakably to a prior communication that is being answered, there is no explicit mention of letters, and so one cannot rule out the possibility that in these cases a messenger brought merely an oral communication instead of a letter. Item 17 is also ambiguous, since it may point either to a missing letter or to an extant letter that has been abridged for publication (a problem to which I will return). To sum up in a way that allows for the uncertainties, we can say that in the Plancus series, four to nine letters are missing, as against twenty-four that are extant.

TABLE 2.2. The Cicero-Plancus Correspondence, 44–43 B.C.

	Letter	Sender	Date
1.	▶ *Fam.* 10.1.4 = 340 SB	Plancus	Latter half of 44
2.	*Fam.* 10.1 = 340 SB	Cicero	Latter half of 44
3.	▶ *Fam.* 10.2 = 341 SB	Plancus	Latter half of 44
4.	*Fam.* 10.2 = 341 SB	Cicero	Latter half of 44
5.	*Fam.* 10.3 = 355 SB	Cicero	September or October 44?
6.	*Fam.* 10.4 = 358 SB	Plancus	December 44
7.	*Fam.* 10.5 = 359 SB	Cicero	December 44 or January 43
8.	*Fam.* 10.6 = 370 SB	Cicero	March 20, 43
9.	*Fam.* 10.7 = 372 SB	Plancus	late March 43
10.	▶ *Fam.* 10.10.1 = 375 SB, *Fam.* 10.12.1 = 377 SB	Plancus	March 43
11.	*Fam.* 10.10 = 375 SB	Cicero	March 30, 43
12.	*Fam.* 10.12 = 377 SB	Cicero	April 11, 43
13.	▶ *Fam.* 10.11.1 = 382 SB	Cicero	after April 11, 43
14.	*Fam.* 10.9 = 379 SB	Plancus	ca. April 26, 43
15.	*Fam.* 10.11 = 382 SB	Plancus	late April 43
16.	*Fam.* 10.14 = 384 SB	Cicero	May 5, 43
17.	▶ *Fam.* 10.15.1 = 390 SB	Plancus	May 43
18.	*Fam.* 10.13 = 389 SB	Cicero	May 43
19.	▶ *Fam.* 10.21a = 392 SB	Cicero	May 43
20.	*Fam.* 10.15 = 390 SB	Plancus	ca. May 11, 43
21.	*Fam.* 10.21 = 391 SB	Plancus	ca. May 13, 43
22.	*Fam.* 10.21a = 392 SB	Plancus	May 43
23.	*Fam.* 10.19 = 393 SB	Cicero	May 43
24.	*Fam.* 10.18 = 395 SB	Plancus	ca. May 18, 43
25.	*Fam.* 10.17 = 398 SB	Plancus	ca. May 20, 43
26.	*Fam.* 10.16 = 404 SB	Cicero	late May 43 ?
27.	*Fam.* 10.20 = 407 SB	Cicero	May 29, 43
28.	*Fam.* 10.23 = 414 SB	Plancus	June 6, 43
29.	▶ *Fam.* 11.15.1 = 422 SB	Plancus	June 43
30.	▶ *Fam.* 10.22.1 = 423 SB	Plancus	June 43
31.	*Fam.* 10.22 = 423 SB	Cicero	late June 43
32.	▶ *Fam.* 10.24 = 428 SB	Cicero	July 43
33.	*Fam.* 10.24 = 428 SB	Plancus	July 28, 43

Extant letters are indicated by the usual book and number notation. Missing letters are indicated by an arrow ▶ pointing to a passage in an extant letter that refers to a letter not extant.

The published collection features many more letters dating from the 40s than from the 50s and before, and this disparity has been taken to indicate that files of Cicero's correspondence were not systematically preserved until relatively late in his career. In broad terms, this assumption may be true even if the inference is circular. But apropos of the letters just surveyed, let me point out that the amount of material published does not necessarily mirror the condition of Cicero's archives. The exchanges with Dolabella and Plancus date from years in which his files should have been most complete, and yet as published, both sequences have significant gaps. The paradox also holds in the other direction: few gaps reveal themselves in some earlier sequences, such as the letters to Appius in book 3. There seems to be no correlation between the completeness of a series and its date. That should make us cautious about invoking archival unevenness to account for what was published and not published.[19] If lacunae in later portions of the correspondence cannot be blamed on ill-kept files, that may not be the explanation for earlier exclusions either.

I turn now to a longer series. Cicero's letters to his brother Quintus have survived as a three-book collection numbering (in modern editions) twenty-seven letters. None of the letters from Quintus's side of this exchange was published except for one short note concerning Tiro, which was included in the last book of the *Letters to Friends*.[20] In table 2.3, I list the twenty-seven extant letters to Quintus together with references to some twenty letters that do not survive. It is possible that some of the references listed as items 4 through 8 concern different passages in a single letter rather than separate letters, but overall table 2.3 presents a decidedly conservative picture of what is missing. Items 2 and 6 imply more letters than just one or two. At the end of the year 59, Cicero promised his brother frequent news of politics (*QFr.* 1.2.16 = 2 SB), but no such letters survive. We have only three letters from the early months of 54, when he was promising Quintus to write every day.[21] The collection includes no letters dating from the second year of Cicero's exile, though during this period Cicero received at least two letters from Quintus that he is likely to have answered.[22] But the most striking lacuna in the Quintus series is that it terminates abruptly at the end of the year 54, even though Quintus remained with Caesar in Gaul for two full years after that.

At this point it will be less useful to extend the inventory to other parts of the corpus than to consider the data from which it has been constructed. It will be apparent from the tables that missing letters come to light in different ways. The most common clue is that a letter within a series alludes to a letter which was written previously but which cannot be identified with any extant letter of the series. Sometimes evidence comes from a parallel text outside the series, as when Cicero happens to mention in a letter to Atticus that he has written to Quintus or Dolabella. In those series in which we have letters from both sides, it is often possible to discern that party A is replying to something B has written, and if the reply does not pick up anything extant in B's letters, it can be

TABLE 2.3. Cicero's Letters to Quintus, 68–44 B.C.

	Letter	Date
1.	▶ *Att.* 1.5.2 = 1 SB	before November 68
2. + ?	▶ *QFr.* 1.1.1, 31, 40 = 1 SB	60
3.	*QFr.* 1.1 = 1 SB	late 60 or early 59
4.	▶ *Att.* 2.16.4 = 36 SB	before May 59
5.	▶ *QFr.* 1.2.2 = 2 SB	59
6. + ?	▶ *QFr.* 1.2.7–9 = 2 SB	59
7.	▶ *QFr.* 1.2.11 = 2 SB	late 59
8.	▶ *QFr.* 1.2.12–13 = 2 SB	late 59
9.	*QFr.* 1.2 = 2 SB	late 59
10.	▶ *QFr.* 1.4.4 = 4 SB	April 58 ?
11.	▶ *QFr.* 1.3.4 = 3 SB	May or June 58
12.	*QFr.* 1.3 = 3 SB	June 13, 58
13.	*QFr.* 1.4 = 4 SB	ca. August 5, 58
14.	▶ *Fam.* 14.3.4 = 9 SB	ca. November 30, 58
15.	▶ *QFr.* 2.1.1 = 5 SB	ca. December 15, 57
16.	*QFr.* 2.1 = 5 SB	ca. December 15, 57
17.	*QFr.* 2.2 = 6 SB	January 17, 56
18.	▶ *QFr.* 2.3.1 = 7 SB	before February 12, 56
19.	*QFr.* 2.3 = 7 SB	February 15, 56
20.	*QFr.* 2.4 = 8 SB	March 56
21.	*QFr.* 2.5(4.3–7) = 9 SB	March 56
22.	▶ *QFr.* 2.6(5).1 = 10 SB	before April 9, 56
23.	*QFr.* 2.6(5) = 10 SB	April 9, 56
24.	*QFr.* 2.7(6) = 11 SB	ca. May 15, 56
25.	*QFr.* 2.9(8) = 12 SB	ca. February 11, 55
26.	*QFr.* 2.8(7) = 13 SB	55?
27.	*QFr.* 2.10(9) = 14 SB	early February 54
28.	*QFr.* 2.11(10) = 15 SB	ca. February 13, 54
29.	*QFr.* 2.12(11) = 16 SB	February 14, 54
30.	*QFr.* 2.13(12) = 17 SB	May 54
31.	*QFr.* 2.14(13) = 18 SB	early June 54
32.	*QFr.* 2.15(14) = 19 SB	late July 54
33.	*QFr.* 2.16(15) = 20 SB	late August 54
34.	*QFr.* 3.1 = 21 SB	September 54
35.	*QFr.* 3.2 = 22 SB	October 11, 54
36.	*QFr.* 3.3 = 23 SB	October 21, 54
37.	*QFr.* 3.4 = 24 SB	October 24, 54
38.	▶ *QFr.* 3.5.6 = 25 SB	November 54
39.	*QFr.* 3.5(5–7) = 25 SB	November 54
40.	*QFr.* 3.6(8) = 26 SB	late November 54
41.	*QFr.* 3.7(9) = 27 SB	December 54
42.	▶ *Fam.* 16.16.1 = 44 SB	May 53
43.	▶ *Att.* 11.16.4 = 227 SB	before June 47
44.	▶ *Att.* 13.41.1 = 344 SB	mid-August 45
45.	▶ *Att.* 13.47a.2 = 352 SB	August 45
46.	▶ *Att.* 13.21.2 = 351 SB	August 25, 45
47.	▶ *Fam.* 16.27.1 = 352 SB	December 44

Extant letters are indicated by the usual book and number notation. Missing letters are indicated by an arrow ▶ pointing to a passage in an extant letter that refers to a letter not extant.

deduced that a letter from B must be missing. Beyond these relatively certain indications are others that are merely suggestive, such as a correspondent's promise to write or the social expectation that a letter received entails a reply.

Two things must be understood about the character of this evidence. First, we have little hope of discerning letters that are missing unless we have a good run of extant letters to start with. Second, our criteria of detection are always hit-or-miss. Letter writers do not always or even usually refer back to previous letters they have written, for example, and not every return letter goes over ground covered in the letter that it follows. Thus it would be naive to suppose that we can balance missing letters against extant ones and conclude that such-and-such percent are missing. Whereas the number of extant letters is a fixed quantity, a tally of missing letters can never be regarded as more than a minimum.

Traces of missing letters in the published correspondence seem too numerous and too widely distributed to be explained by postal failure, deficient archives, or other impersonal causes. Whoever published Cicero's letters must first have sorted through them, selecting and discarding in light of guidelines nowhere made explicit. But once we accept that editorial choice was being exercised, we can begin to perceive types of letters that were passed over. More often than not, when Cicero and his correspondents refer to letters that have not survived, they provide some indication of content. Thus it becomes clear that one of the missing letters to Dolabella (item 8 in table 2.1) concerned personal finances. Cicero was trying to recover the dowry that Dolabella had an obligation to return to him when he and Tullia divorced. In the correspondence between Cicero and Caelius Rufus, the extant letters have a mostly political cast, but a letter of Caelius concerning money that he wanted Cicero to help him collect in Cilicia is not included in the series.[23] In a letter missing from Cicero's exchange with Paetus, Cicero wrote of his efforts to purchase real estate in Paetus's neighborhood (*Fam.* 9.15.5 = 196 SB). Similar choices come to light even in the Atticus corpus, which is often taken to comprise everything available at the time of publication. Although in the extant letters to Atticus we frequently find comment about finances interspersed with other topics, at least three letters concerning money matters were not included, perhaps because they were too narrowly focused on that topic.[24]

Another category that was deemphasized if not excluded consists of letters regarding senatorial business. This claim will seem surprising both because it is counterintuitive—anyone would expect to find scores of such letters preserved—and because several of Cicero's letters (especially those to Atticus, Quintus, and Lentulus Spinther) and many of Caelius Rufus's letters to Cicero do in fact report on proceedings in the Senate. Nevertheless, there are cases in which letters in this vein have just as plainly been excluded. In the collection as published, Cicero's correspondence with loyalist army leaders during the struggle against Antony is focused on the volatile military situation. The exclusion of several letters about debates in the Senate has made the focus sharper. In one of the missing letters of the Plancus series (item 13 in table 2.2), for example, Cicero gave an account of measures honoring Plancus that he managed to push through in spite of opposition.[25] Senate business was also the theme of a missing letter by Plancus (item 30 in table 2.2) in which he urged Cicero to promote legislation making land available for his troops. After the liberation of Mutina from Antony's siege, Cicero moved honors for Decimus Brutus as well, and duly reported the news to him. But the letter was not included in the published exchange with Decimus in book II of the *Letters to Friends*.[26] Missing from the Cornificius series in book 12 is a letter in which Cicero discussed the implications of a Senate decree for Cornificius's position as governor in Africa.[27] Yet it should not be thought that a bias against senatorial reportage came into play only when there was an abundance of more dramatic letters to choose from. During the quiescent period of Caesar's domination, Cicero worked to bring about the restoration of several exiles, Marcus Claudius Marcellus among others. When Caesar surprised a meeting of the Senate by abruptly granting permission for Marcellus's return, Cicero sent Marcellus a letter describing the session (*Fam.* 4.11.1 = 232 SB). But it was not one of the letters selected to make up the Marcellus series in book 4 of the *Letters to Friends*.

Letters about domestic concerns were also apt to be dropped from consideration for the collection, notwithstanding that more than half of the existing books consist of letters to Cicero's wife, brother, freedman, and closest friend (whose sister was married to Cicero's brother). Deselection is most apparent in the correspondence with Quintus, which as published includes none of the aggrieved, scolding, and quarrelsome communications that we know he received from Cicero (items 1, 5, 8, 43, 44, and 45 in table 2.3). Letters discussing possible husbands to whom Tullia might be consigned for her third marriage have disappeared from both the Terentia series and the Caelius series.[28] Asinius Pollio sent Cicero an account of offensive behavior by the latter's nephew which was not included with other letters from Pollio (*Att.* 12.38.2 = 278 SB). And although one book of the *Letters to Friends* contains letters that Cicero wrote to his freedman Tiro, letters that Cicero wrote *about* Tiro are not in the Curius series or the Quintus series.[29]

A last category of missing letters to which I want to draw attention may seem scarcely worthy of remark. As Cicero and his peers moved back and forth between the capital and their villas and their destinations abroad, they often arranged to visit one another if their paths converged. Travel did not halt the routine of courtesy calls that characterized their life in Rome. When they correspond, they give notice of their itineraries and negotiate points at which to rendezvous. Existing letters often contain material of this sort, but it is also a feature common to several of the letters left out.[30] That an editor might have suppressed messages concerned with arranging the details of visits would not be surprising; they were practically devoid of long-term interest. But signs of editorial cutting in this area prompt questions about other letter types which are underrepresented in the published books. Cicero must have had occasion to compose many more thank-you letters, condolences, and congratulations than the few that have been preserved.

Uncertainties in the argument I have just sketched are not to be dissembled. Material akin to that in missing letters can readily be found in published letters, which suggests that the editorial principles I have been trying to identify were not absolute. I have supposed that missing letters about personal finances, for example, were left out because they were entirely or mainly concerned with finances. But that need not have been the case. An indication that a missing letter had something to say about finances is no guarantee that it did so exclusively. The subject may have come up along with others, as it does in many an extant letter. Moreover, the categories into which I have sorted omitted material may not always be the most relevant. Alternative explanations can be imagined for the exclusion of some letters I have mentioned, and in fact some letters may have been discarded for a combination of reasons. Finally, it is not after all impossible that in some cases a letter is missing because it was lost in transit or destroyed or mislaid upon receipt rather than because it was suppressed.

What remains reasonably certain is that for whatever reasons, a substantial number of letters were discarded at the editorial stage. The evidence for missing letters would repay further study. As patterns of exclusion become clearer and more fully documented, they should help to fix more exactly the character of material selected for publication. In the meantime, the fact of deselection can stand as the first and most salient indication that whoever published Cicero's correspondence was also concerned to give it shape and measure.

Internal Deletions

About deletions of a bolder sort, the record is inscrutable. We cannot tell whether the editor freely deleted passages within letters that were published. Internal cuts do not ordinarily leave behind clues like those cross-references which point to whole letters that are missing and which allow us to infer an editorial policy. Skillful editing should leave no trace, and when a letter jumps casually from topic to topic, as many in the Ciceronian corpus do, excisions hardly require much skill. Where a lacuna can be detected even so, it would be foolish to start from the assumption that it is deliberate. The published letters contain many serious lacunae, but the most plausible explanation in almost every case is that they have resulted from faulty transmission.

There are four places, however, in which it is difficult to resist the conclusion that text has been deliberately abridged. One occurs in a letter that Cicero wrote to Appius Claudius Pulcher (*Fam.* 3.10 = 73 SB), the man he succeeded as governor of Cilicia. At this point in their exchange, each was accusing the other of actions that slighted and undermined him. Cicero insists that he has acted only from the most generous motives, which he enunciates at length. At the very end of the letter, he turns to steps he has taken to ensure that no discreditable evidence reaches Rome during Appius's trial for official misconduct. The transition is as follows: "But so much for all that; perhaps I have even gone on at greater length than was necessary. Now let me inform you what initiatives and arrangements have been forthcoming on my side." The next sentence in the manuscripts reads, "And these things we have done and will continue to do, more in furtherance of your dignity than in aid of your trial" (sed haec hactenus; pluribus enim etiam fortasse verbis quam necesse fuit scripta sunt. nunc ea quae a me profecta quaeque instituta sunt cognosce * * * atque haec agimus et agemus magis pro dignitate quam pro periculo tuo, *Fam.* 3.10.11 = 73 SB). A passage recounting helpful interventions in Cilicia has evidently disappeared.

The second passage occurs in a letter to Atticus and concerns the younger Quintus, nephew of both Cicero and Atticus, who was then pursuing a scandalous flirtation with the Caesarian cause. Cicero passes on the latest he has gleaned from a conversation with friends: "Then the subject changed to Quintus. There were plenty of shocking things that don't bear repeating, but one thing particularly, which I could not bring myself to put in writing, much less dictate to Tiro, if it were not known all over the army." The next sentence is the closure formula, "But so much for that." (ventum est tamen ad Quintum. multa ἄφατα, ἀδιήγητα, sed unum eius modi quod, nisi exercitus sciret, non modo Tironi dictare sed ne ipse quidem auderem scribere * * * sed haec hactenus, *Att.* 13.9.1 = 317 SB). The natural implication both of the contrafactual statement and of the close is that Cicero did relate some anecdote about Quintus that has been suppressed.[31]

The other two cases involve identical anomalies in the opening of a letter from Plancus to Cicero and the opening of another from Cicero to Marcus Brutus. In its transmitted form, Plancus's letter begins, "After writing this letter, I thought it a matter of public importance to let you know what happened subsequently" (his litteris scriptis quae postea accidissent, scire te ad rem publicam putavi pertinere, *Fam.* 10.15.1 = 390 SB). Plancus goes on to report a new development in the struggle to eliminate Mark Antony after the battle of Mutina. Cicero's letter to Brutus begins, "When my letter was already written and sealed, a letter from you was handed to me that was full of news" (scripta et obsignata iam epistula litterae mihi redditae sunt a te plenae rerum novarum, *MBrut.* 7[1.2].1 = 14 SB), which Cicero proceeds to summarize. Neither letter makes sense as it stands because neither contains a ground of reference for the already-written letter. However, formulas like *his litteris scriptis* and *obsignata iam epistula* occur repeatedly in the collected correspondence at points where a letter writer makes a fresh start on a missive already begun—usually, as in these two cases, because he has just received a piece of new information.[32]

Their appearance at the start of a letter can best be explained as the result of an editorial decision to excise the early portion of the respective texts and to retain only the more newsworthy part.

These are the clearest indications that an editor has deleted material within letters. But they should be considered together with less intrusive operations on the margins which nonetheless suggest a willingness to cut. In a letter devoted to flattering pleasantries, Trebonius reports that he has taken a note-worthy sally of Cicero's and recast it as a satirical utterance in verse. "I have written it out below," he says (infra subscripsi, *Fam.* 12.16.3 = 328 SB). But Trebonius's verses did not survive the transfer of his letter into the published correspondence.

Cicero, who never resists a wisecrack at the expense of his lawyer friend Trebatius Testa, writes in one letter, "since the sureties you people draft are not so foolproof, I send you one in my own hand—in Greek" (quoniam vestrae cautiones infirmae sunt, Graeculam tibi misi cautionem chirographi mei, *Fam.* 7.18.1 = 37 SB). Trebatius had been telling Cicero how eager he was to make money from his stint with Caesar in Gaul, and so it is likely that this *cautio* contained cautionary advice.[33] Cicero sometimes switched to Greek when he had something confidential to say. But whatever it was, the editor did not include it with the rest of the letter.

Few as these examples are, they nevertheless justify a qualm of uncertainty. We are not free to adopt on a priori grounds the position that any particular text in the collection was surely published intact. For what it is worth, let me add that my inclination is to believe that in general, the editor *did* refrain from deleting material. But the way is certainly open to anyone to argue a case that deletions were more systematic.

Numerous traces of excluded letters plus a smaller number of internal excisions prove that Cicero's published correspondence is an editorial construction rather than a transcription. And with these reminders of an editor's presence, we can see that some of the most salient formal characteristics of the collection must be ascribed to an editor as well. I have in mind the treatment of enclosures and of letters of recommendation, the grouping of letters into discrete series, and the inclusion of letters written by some of Cicero's correspondents. In each of these efforts at arrangement, the editor can be seen struggling with problems of presentation that were the consequence of preserving certain kinds of letters while discarding others.

Enclosures

At various points in the Ciceronian corpus, a letter addressed to one person incorporates or precedes a letter addressed to a second party which the sender has passed along for perusal by the first. Although Latin lacks a comparable word, we have no difficulty recognizing in these texts what we call "enclosures" or "attachments" in modern letters.[34] A total of thirty-nine enclosed letters or parts of letters were published together with their carrier texts.[35] But internal evidence points to as many enclosures that were not published as were.[36] And so we must again try to infer an editorial policy from its results.

Enclosures are more abundantly provided in the Ciceronian corpus than in any other published collection. Neither Pliny's nor Fronto's correspondence, for example, offers anything comparable to the number in Cicero's.[37] But one criterion of selection was evidently based on genre. Although many kinds of documents were sent as enclosures, those taken into the corpus consist almost invariably of other letters.[38] The sole exception is found in a letter of Caelius (*Fam.* 8.8 = 84 SB), into the middle of which Caelius has copied a series of senatorial resolutions. The position of the documents within the body of his letter presumably helped to protect them from editorial deletion.

If we suppose that letters integrated into the text of their cover letters may have been preserved for the same reason, there remain about thirty true attachments whose presence in the corpus invites an explanation. In the majority of cases, the reason they were published cannot have been that they were needed to make the primary text intelligible. For example, in the early days of the civil war, Cicero sent Atticus two successive letters that were each accompanied by four attachments. The first four are copies of letters Pompey had written to him and of his replies to Pompey (*Att.* 8.11A–D = 161A–D SB), which Cicero says he has sent along so that Atticus can observe Pompey's "disorganization" (*neglegentia*) in contrast with his own sharp eye for consequence. The attachments are interesting in their own right and do illustrate his point. But the letter to Atticus is perfectly comprehensible without them, both because in it Cicero sums up the lesson to be gleaned from the enclosures and because his views about Pompey's disorganization are amply developed in letters to Atticus that precede and follow this one. The same holds true for the following set of attachments, which consist of letters Pompey had written to the consuls and to the proconsul Domitius Ahenobarbus when Domitius let himself be trapped by Caesar at Corfinium (*Att.* 8.12A–D = 162A–D SB). Cicero tells Atticus that the enclosures will show that Pompey is foisting all the blame onto Domitius, which they do. But the letter to Atticus hardly needs them to be understood, any more than numerous letters in the corpus that have been stripped of their enclosures.

The eight letters have in common that either the writer or the addressee or both had politically important roles, as did Caesar, his agents Balbus and Oppius, Mark Antony, Dolabella, and the officials who figure in other extant attachments. That these letters featured prominent people undoubtedly contributed to their being published alongside letters of Cicero (even in cases where they were written neither to nor by Cicero). Letters were selected partly according to the status of the correspondent, as we shall see, and in the subset of enclosed letters the status of the correspondents is higher than in the collection overall. But status does not quite explain why the letters were preserved in the form of attachments. Many could just as well have been published as primary texts in those parts of the corpus comprising Cicero's exchanges with Caesar, Pompey, Dolabella, and others.[39] Moreover, the status of the correspondents does not obviously distinguish enclosures that were published from those that were not. Most of the latter involved prominent personages as well, including again Caesar and Pompey.

The focus of the respective letters differs, however. Whereas enclosures that were suppressed covered a range of public and private topics, published enclosures consist of two types only. A handful are letters of recommendation (a category that will be considered in the next section), but the majority are letters about dramatic public events and Cicero's part in them. A summary is the simplest way to illustrate. The enclosures accompanying letters written early in the civil war have to do with Cicero's bid to broker a peace agreement between Caesar and Pompey, his military charge on the coast, the fall of Corfinium to Caesar, Pompey's evacuation of Italy, and Caesar's efforts to dissuade Cicero from following him.[40] Enclosures from the period following Caesar's assassination concern Cicero's relations with the consuls Mark Antony and Dolabella, and later the contest between Caesarians and Republicans for control of the east. The subject matter, together with the tenuous claim of some of these texts to be the correspondence of Cicero, suggests that enclosures were likely to be published when they cast vivid sidelights on events discussed in the primary letters, whether or not they directly implicated Cicero.

Five letters from the *Letters to Friends* that I have not yet mentioned point in the same direction.[41] Like several from the Atticus corpus, they are neither to nor by Cicero, and although they are not accompanied in our edition by cover letters, commentators are almost certainly correct in supposing that that is how they came into Cicero's hands. They all have plausible sources in persons with whom Cicero is known to have been in contact, and they have a dramatic interest equal to that of the enclosures just described, as a summary will again illustrate. One is a letter from Decimus Brutus to Marcus Brutus and Cassius. Written just a few days after Caesar's death, it describes Antony's early moves to neutralize the assassins who remained in Rome. Two were written by Brutus and Cassius to Mark Antony several weeks later and concern preparations by both sides for an eventual war. A letter from Decimus Brutus and Plancus to the Senate in the following year announces that they have combined their armies and are prepared to act on behalf of the Senate, while another dispatch from Lepidus to the Senate announces the more fateful merger of his army with Mark Antony's. Every one of these letters illustrates a fresh turn in the power struggle that was a consequence of Caesar's removal.

But their presence in the corpus does more than confirm that dramatic interest was one criterion guiding the selection of material. If they have been correctly identified as enclosures detached from cover letters, they also suggest that letters serving merely to transmit other letters may have been another category liable to editorial rejection.[42] Perhaps more significant, they show that the editor was prepared to tolerate anomalies for the sake of retaining good material. In the absence of their cover letters, the five letters in question lack even a tenuous claim to be included in the correspondence of Cicero.

Letters of Recommendation

More than 10 percent of the published letters urge the recipient to act on behalf of some third party, which makes letters of recommendation one of the most conspicuously favored types within the corpus.[43] Book 13 of the *Letters to Friends* contains an almost solid block of eighty.[44] An additional thirty-three recommendations are scattered through other books of that collection, as well as through the letters to Marcus Brutus, to Atticus, and to Quintus.[45] Yet in a society that allowed so much influence to the advocacy of friends, even this large number can be no more than a fraction of the total that Cicero wrote.[46] Some clear patterns are discernible in the selection presented to us. In the first place, while the published correspondence includes about a hundred letters written by persons other than Cicero, very few of them are recommendations *to* Cicero. The extant recommendations occur almost exclusively in Cicero's letters.[47] It is also curious that of the extant recommendations, two at most are for a member of his own family. Part of a letter commending Quintus to Caesar survives as an embedded enclosure.[48] There is also a letter in which Cicero asks Brutus to permit the young Marcus, then serving under Brutus, to travel to Rome to stand for an election, which perhaps does not quite qualify as a letter of recommendation (*M Brut.* 13[1.5].3 = 9 SB). But there are no other letters on behalf of Cicero's brother or son, or on behalf of his nephew or sons-in-law or freedmen or other agents, though these are kinds of letters that any Roman magnate would have had many an occasion to write. What the extant letters most obviously have in common, however, is the high status of those whose intervention Cicero solicits. At least thirty-eight of the forty-five addressees are fellow senators, most of whom are approached when acting in some official capacity.[49]

It seems fair to conclude that, as published, the letters of recommendation are intended to project an image of Cicero as a man with effective ties in all parts of Roman society. The individuals for whom he exerts himself range from young nobles to freedmen and from politicians and businessmen in the capital to municipal and provincial notables.[50] Most are persons of some standing in their society. But on average, the persons who receive the letters are of much higher status. And what is worth pondering here is not so much that Cicero has recourse to important people as that he can be assumed to have some sort of claim over almost every one of them. As Déniaux has emphasized, a Roman letter of recommendation presupposes and trades on a personal relationship between writer and recipient to a much greater extent than is typical in modern recommendations.[51] The published letters thus present Cicero as a man who can help because he always knows someone at the top of whatever hierarchy is relevant—the consul, the praetor, the general, the governor, the finance officer, or the mayor.

But these letters posed editorial challenges that other kinds did not. The examples we have show that formal commendations tended to follow a conventional pattern. Cicero often alludes to the difficulty of saying something fresh as he is writing them,[52] and the underlying sameness will only be rendered more apparent if such letters are later juxtaposed in a collection. At the same time, the editor confronted a problem that was practically the reverse of the first. As our corpus again illustrates, many recommendations did not take the form of self-contained letters but were casually appended to letters about something else. They would look incongruous if they were placed alongside fuller and more formal recommendations. But if they were not grouped with other recommendations, that element of the letter would not come into focus. Furthermore, a letter of recommendation, unlike other letters, always testifies to at least two relationships, one with the protégé and one with the addressee.[53] An editor therefore had to decide in which context to present it. Formal considerations might argue that it be published with other letters to the same addressee. Yet a recommendation would normally have much more to say about Cicero's relationship with the protégé than with the recipient of the letter.

Perhaps no perfectly consistent resolution of these dilemmas was to be had, and certainly the outcome does not have a tidy aspect. More than two-thirds of the letters of recommendation are collected in one book of the *Letters to Friends,* the remainder are scattered all over, and as noted earlier, three letters appear twice, once in the collected set and again somewhere else. But first impressions notwithstanding, there is a rough logic to the distribution. Several of the recommendations that were not gathered into book 13 of the *Letters to Friends* are of a kind that could not have stood on their own because the endorsement is no more than an epistolary tangent—in some cases only a sentence.[54] In one recommendation, the formal purpose is completely overborne by Cicero's need to brandish his authority vis-à-vis the addressee. This is *Fam.* 5.5 = 5 SB, commending Atticus to Gaius Antonius, Cicero's recent colleague in the consulship. But the letter is so filled with vituperation against Antonius that it hardly resembles a recommendation, and hence it stands with an assortment of letters illustrating Cicero's touchy relations with fellow consulars. But the consideration that most often accounts for placement of a recommendation outside book 13 is clearly the decision to keep it with other letters to a given addressee. So, for example, Cicero's recommendation of Aulus

Trebonius to Lentulus Spinther (*Fam.* 1.3 = 56 SB) appears in a book of letters to Spinther, a recommendation of Milo to Curio (*Fam.* 2.6 = 50 SB) appears with other letters to Curio, and two recommendations for Appius Claudius and Aelius Lamia to Decimus Brutus (*Fam.* 11.22 = 427 SB, and *Fam.* 11.16 = 434 SB) appear with other letters to Brutus.

The broad split in our corpus between recommendations kept with letters to the same addressee and recommendations massed with other recommendations in book 13 of the *Letters to Friends* can serve as a first clue to the order the editor tried to impose. It is relevant to notice also that the latter arrangement was more intrusive than the former. The editor had first to look through a given dossier (whether concerning the addressee of a recommendation or the commendee) and to pick out the letters he wished to publish. He then separated the recommendations from everything else and reassembled them in a thematic mini-corpus. This meant not only putting them into a different context than he had found them.[55] In grouping letters by type rather than recipient, the editor also diverged from the dominant principle by which the rest of the edition was organized.

A further peculiarity of the selection in book 13 is that more than three-quarters of the letter recipients represented in it (twenty-five of the thirty) get no other letters from Cicero except the recommendations in the book. This pattern can be related both to the focus of this particular book on letters of recommendation and to the general tendency of the epistolary corpus to keep letters to the same person together. The circumstances suggest that book 13 was created not so much to be the showcase for Cicero's letters of recommendation as to be a repository for recommendations that did not have a suitable niche elsewhere in the corpus. That is why so many of the recipients turn up only here. These were exchanges from which recommendations were all that the editor culled for publication, and book 13 served as the default location for recommendations that could not be merged with letters to the addressee in other books.[56]

That book 13 was conceived as complementary to the rest of the corpus can be seen even in the few cases in which correspondents represented in it do appear in other books. Though correspondents overlap, the letters rarely do. There are only three duplicates among more than one hundred letters.[57] Otherwise, when the same person receives recommendations in the anthology and in another book, the letters are distinct and purposely divided. There is one recommendation to Plancus in the series of the *Letters to Friends* devoted to him (*Fam.* 10.1.4 = 340 SB). Book 13 contains another (*Fam.* 13.29 = 282 SB), written three years before the other letters begin and at a time when Plancus occupied a different position of influence. The extant book of correspondence with Marcus Brutus, covering spring and summer of the year 43, includes three recommendations from that period (*MBrut.* 14[1.6].2–4 = 12 SB, 15[1.7] = 19 SB, and 19[1.11] = 16 SB). Book 13 of the *Letters to Friends* contains a separate run of five recommendations written two years earlier, when Brutus's resources for bestowing favors were likewise different (*Fam.* 13.10–14 = 277–81 SB). In both cases, it was probably the disparate context that deterred the editor from combining earlier with later letters.[58]

In two other cases, however, the editor has separated recommendations from letters to the same person which are contemporary. Book 13 of the *Letters to Friends* contains five letters of recommendation written to Minucius Thermus when he was governor of Asia (*Fam.* 13.53–57 = 130–33 SB). Another letter to him in the same capacity, though not a recommendation, stands in book 2 (*Fam.* 2.18 = 115 SB). A larger set of letters to Servius Sulpicius Rufus is similarly divided. Book 13 contains thirteen recommendations written to him when he was governor of Greece (*Fam.* 13.17–28a = 283–95 SB), and book 4 contains a partly contemporary exchange of six letters, none of which is a recommendation (*Fam.* 4.1–6 = 150, 151, 202, 203, 248, and 249 SB).

Here again, the editor's rough-and-ready rule of keeping recommendations with other letters to the same person was at odds with counter-considerations. In the case of Thermus, not only would the single letter in book 2 have made a weak nucleus around which to group 5 recommendations, but that letter is itself an element in another series. The second half of book 2 consists of letters that Cicero wrote when he too held a governorship, and it ends with three that focus on departure arrangements. This is the context in which the letter to Thermus fits. The Senate having failed to send out proper successors for either Cicero or Thermus, Cicero advises his colleague to turn over his province to the incoming quaestor, as he himself attempts to do in the very next letter.

It would have been equally awkward to have combined the Servius letters. In the first place, the letters of recommendation would have overwhelmed the six letters in book 4. Servius receives more recommendations than anyone else in the entire corpus, and in no sequence outside book 13 do such letters predominate. The letters of recommendation would also have blurred the focus of the rest. The letters in book 4 have a strongly political cast. They are written from one consular and Pompeian sympathizer to another as both men come to terms with Pompey's abandonment of Italy and later with Caesar's dictatorship. The recommendations would have communicated a suggestion of normal process at odds with the pessimism of their political correspondence.

I have been arguing that book 13 of the *Letters to Friends* is structurally related to the rest of the published corpus and that even where material or correspondents seem to overlap, decisions taken at one point are generally complementary to decisions at another. Book 13 provides one of our best opportunities to study the way the editor worked because it is so obvious that the plan of it is his creation. There can be no temptation to think that this book reproduces the organization of any of Cicero's files. It is because a new order had to be imposed that problems of consistency were especially likely to arise in book 13.

One involves letter 77 (= 212 SB), written to Sulpicius Rufus when he was governing Dalmatia. Although it commends Cicero's friend Bolanus, it is not a full-blown letter of recommendation like the others in book 13. Cicero was replying to a letter from Sulpicius about something else, and two-thirds of his letter has nothing to do with Bolanus. This is just the sort of recommendation that normally turns up outside book 13 in groups of letters to particular persons. But the editor selected nothing from the correspondence with Sulpicius except the one recommendation, and so if it was to be published at all, the only place to put it was book 13.

A pair of recommendations inconsistently placed exposes another ambivalence in the editor's strategy. In these two cases his decision was complicated by the fact that he decided to publish not only the recommendation but also a letter about it from Cicero to the recommendee. That meant that the recommendation could be presented as an enclosure, which was the course adopted in book 6 of the *Letters to Friends*. In a letter to Caecina, Cicero writes that he is attaching a copy of a recommendation for him to Furfanus, the governor of Sicily (*Fam.* 6.8 = 235 SB). The recommendation duly appears immediately following (*Fam.* 6.9 = 236 SB). But a parallel case in book 7 was handled differently. Here Cicero tells Curius that he has attached a letter of recommendation for him to Acilius, the governor of Greece (*Fam.* 7.30 = 265 SB). But that letter was published among the recommendations of book 13 (*Fam.* 13.50 = 266 SB).[59]

By far the most glaring anomaly in book 13 is letter 68 = 211 SB, written to Servilius Isauricus when he was governor of Asia. Although it appears among a half-dozen recommendations to Isauricus of the same period, it does not commend anyone even in passing. It is the only non-recommendation among the eighty-one letters of book 13. Like the letters to Servius in book 4, it is a reflection on politics written by one consular for the eyes of another. Since political letters figure prominently throughout the epistolary corpus, it is unlikely that this one crept in through inadvertence. A more plausible explanation would be that it was the only interesting item the editor found apart from the recommendations[60] and that he did not scruple to disrupt the thematic coherence of the book for the sake of keeping it.

From all these compromises in the treatment of letters of recommendation, it would seem that the material mattered more to the editor than how he presented it. I do not mean that placement was of no concern. Recommendations do not turn up at random in the corpus where they make no sense. But a given letter can usually make sense in more than one location (say, with other letters to the addressee, with letters to the recommendee, or with other recommendations), and the editor juggled the possibilities. His decisions tend to be complementary rather than strictly consistent.

A major decision was the reservation of a separate book to accommodate letters of recommendation not integrated elsewhere, and it has a pendant which now requires notice. The last letter in the Atticus corpus is a short note reporting that Cicero has written on Atticus's behalf to Plotius Plancus and is sending along a copy of the letter.[61] Atticus had asked for Cicero's help in protecting his clients in a town of Epirus from land expropriations which Plancus was in charge of carrying out. Their cause is a motif that runs through the last three books of the corpus, prompting Cicero to object at one point that his friend was writing "too much about Buthrotum" (*Att.* 15.2.1 = 379 SB). What is peculiar about the enclosure mentioned is that, as published, it comprises not only the letter to Plancus promised in the cover message, but two subsequent appeals to him and three letters to colleagues of his whom Cicero asks to intercede (*Att.* 16.16A–F = 407A–F SB). As commentators have noted, only the first letter of recommendation properly belongs with the note to Atticus. The editor has piggy-backed the other five on the first, showing again both his partiality toward letters of recommendation and his readiness to compromise with format to accommodate them.[62]

Here as elsewhere, compromises were a consequence of combining texts which were differently arranged in the letter files that were their source. In considering letters of recommendation, I have paid particular attention to book 13 of the *Letters to Friends* because that is the editor's most ambitious attempt to construct a letter series. But signs of editorial improvisation can be glimpsed everywhere that letters have been put into coherent sequences. To other cases I now turn.

Letters in Series

In formal terms, what is most noticeable about Cicero's epistolary corpus is that it consists of a multiplicity of separate letter series.[63] The major components of the corpus are of course defined by correspondent. We have the *Letters to Atticus*, the *Letters to Brother Quintus*, and a remnant of the *Letters to Marcus Brutus*. That principle of organization persists even in the collection *Letters to Friends*, in which separate books are reserved for the correspondence with Lentulus Spinther, with Appius Pulcher, with Cicero's wife Terentia, and with his secretary Tiro. A still larger number of series occupy only parts of books. Thus, for example, Cicero's letters to Curio and to Caelius—two doomed young adventurers—are collected back to back in book 2; those to Trebatius are collected in the middle of book 7; and those to Cornificius at the end of book 12.

To arrange all letters to a given person in a sequence might seem a simple enough scheme, but more editorial thought went into the execution of it than might at first appear. The *Letters to Quintus*—the only multibook series to survive apart from the *Letters to Atticus*—do not represent a complete publication of all Cicero's letters to his brother, as we have seen. Not only are many letters missing, but one effect of the missing letters is to divide the Quintus series into thematic clusters. It begins with two long letters about Quintus's governorship in Asia which were written late in his administration (60–59) and continues with two more about Cicero's exile a year later. It then picks up again with seven letters reporting on a period of about six months after Cicero's restoration, when he was reclaiming his role in the courts and the Senate. Then after a year and a half represented by only two letters, the series picks up again with fourteen letters written in the year 54. All but two of these belong to Quintus's first months of service with Caesar in Gaul, and they concern in equal measure public business in Rome and the Ciceros' relationship with Caesar. Except for two letters in the middle that do not seem to fit the pattern, the selection has a markedly political orientation, focusing by turns on Cicero's reactions to his brother's gubernatorial performance, his own experience of exile, his reinsertion into public life, and his rapprochement with Caesar. What the correspondence as published clearly does *not* attempt to do is to track the rhythm of the epistolary relationship. There are only two letters to show from the three years that Quintus spent in Asia and two from the year and a half that Cicero passed in exile. There are fourteen letters dating from the first year of Quintus's sojourn in Gaul, then none at all from the next two years.

The Lentulus series in book 1 of the *Letters to Friends* presents a similar aspect. Publius Lentulus Spinther was one of Cicero's staunchest friends among the aristocracy, and, as consul in 57, he took the lead in organizing Cicero's recall from exile. At the end of that year, he left Rome to govern Cilicia, where he remained for the next three years. The published letters all belong to this period, even though Cicero and Lentulus demonstrably wrote each other before and after that.[64] Furthermore, the published series by no means comprises all the letters that Cicero sent Lentulus in Cilicia.[65] Of the eleven items selected, two are undatable and concern persons recommended to the governor. Of the nine letters remaining, seven date from the first months of his term and are dominated by a single issue. In combination with his provincial charge, Lentulus had been authorized by the Senate to restore the king of Egypt, who had been overthrown by his subjects. As soon as Lentulus was out of Rome, however, maneuvers began to reassign the free-spending king to someone else's advantage. Most of the published correspondence with Lentulus consists of letters written in this period, in which Cicero reported on the progressive breakdown of the Egyptian mandate. Only two letters were included from the two and a half years that follow.

In the same way that a run of letters written early in Lentulus's governorship is used to focus that series, a run of letters written late in the term of another governor anchors the series contained in book 3 of the *Letters to Friends*. Appius Pulcher was Lentulus's successor in Cilicia, as it happened, but he became one of Cicero's correspondents as the result of a political shift in Rome. Down to the year 54, the feud between Cicero and Clodius, Appius's brother, had kept them at odds. But Appius became the target of a reconciliation no less ostentatious than the feud after he was elected consul and Pompey compelled Cicero to make up with him. Cicero advertised their newfound amity during Appius's consulship. When Appius went out to his province, Cicero promised to champion his interests at home, and he escorted Appius's entourage as far as the Bay of Naples. Two and a half years later, as Appius's term was winding down, Cicero discovered to his dismay that he would be taking over from him as governor of Cilicia.

What is striking about the published correspondence with Appius is that it includes almost nothing written to him before the end of his term (the one exception, *Fam.* 3.1 = 64 SB, is in part a letter of recommendation). Yet it can hardly be imagined that Cicero neglected to write earlier, given his effort to ingratiate Appius. One episode that must have called for some sort of communication, however oblique, was the murder of Clodius by Cicero's protégé Milo one year into Appius's term; Cicero then defended Milo at the subsequent trial. A positive occurrence that required notice was a gesture of homage by Appius to Cicero. When Cicero was elected augur in 53 or 52, Appius, now a priestly colleague, dedicated and sent to him the first book of a treatise on augury. Although the dedication is mentioned later on, there is no letter acknowledging Cicero's receipt of it.[66] Finally, in letters written toward the end of Appius's governorship, Cicero more than once recalls earlier exertions on Appius's behalf—in securing the vote of a *supplicatio* for Appius's military exploits, for example.[67] Yet there are no letters reporting on these efforts at the time they occurred, of the sort we have for Lentulus. With the one exception mentioned, the thirteen extant letters are confined to the last four months of Appius's term, when Cicero was trying to negotiate the transition, and to the ensuing twelve months of Cicero's term, when he kept having to defend his interference with Appius's policies in Cilicia.

The great majority of letter series in the collected correspondence evince a comparable pattern. What gives them their coherence is not simply that they have a single addressee, but that they are dominated by one or more sequences of topically related letters selected from a more diffuse exchange. A kind of nodal organization sometimes makes itself felt even in the *Letters to Atticus.*[68] Book 3 consists of twenty-seven letters that Cicero wrote during exile, all concerned with recriminations over the personal betrayals that he thought contributed to his plight and with exhortations about resolving it. That the uniformity of tone may be partly a result of editorial selection is suggested by the distribution of the letters. Twenty-five of them date from March through December of the first year of exile, with only two short letters included from the seven months that it continued into the year 57. To take another example, the letters that Cicero wrote after Caesar's invasion of Italy in 49 have an obsessive focus that every reader quickly notices. They repeatedly solicit Atticus's advice in helping Cicero decide whether he should remain in Italy, join Pompey, or pursue some other alternative. But the focus of this sequence may have been sharpened by the elimination of those letters that the editor chose to discard.[69] Another node is formed by the twenty-two letters Cicero wrote from Brundisium when he was stalled there for eleven months after Caesar's defeat of Pompey's army at Pharsalia. What lends thematic coherence to this set is Cicero's constant mulling of scenarios under which he might be able to return to Rome. But here again there are unexplained gaps in the correspondence and evidence of missing letters.[70]

In none of these cases, obviously, were motifs invented that were not present in the letters themselves. But it is likely that editorial intervention has privileged certain motifs at the expense of others. And still bolder initiatives in series construction are noticeable at other points. Book 4 of the *Letters to Friends* contains a sequence of five letters exchanged between Cicero and Marcus Marcellus in the year 46 (*Fam.* 4.7–11 = 229–33 SB). After Caesar's victory in the civil war, Marcellus had declined to sue for permission to return to Italy. Cicero wrote several times urging him to reconcile and come home, and when Caesar finally granted permission without insisting that Marcellus beg for it, Marcellus wrote Cicero that he would soon return. The sequence closes with a sixth letter written neither by Cicero nor Marcellus, but by the then-governor of Greece (*Fam.* 4.12 = 253 SB). It reports that Marcellus was murdered outside Athens by a disgruntled member of his entourage during the course of his journey home. This series has clearly been shaped by the same taste for the dramatic that led to publication of some of the enclosures considered earlier.[71]

Less dramatic but no less contrived is the placement of a letter in the Tiro series that fills book 16 of the *Letters to Friends*. Most of the book consists of letters to Tiro from Cicero, interspersed with a handful from his brother and his son (no letters of Tiro himself are included). But midway through the book stands one (*Fam.* 16.16 = 44 SB) not addressed to Tiro. It is a letter from Quintus to Marcus—the only such letter extant in the published corpus—rejoicing in the news of Tiro's elevation to freedman status. Here, too, a letter series has been supplemented with strictly extraneous material for the sake of a pertinent story element.

Both these cases illustrate again that although grouping letters by recipient was the default arrangement, it was not the only guideline the editor followed. More ambitious schemes can often be discerned in those books that combine letters to a number of different correspondents. Book 15 of the *Letters to Friends* consists of twenty-one letters to eight addressees, no one of whom accounts for more than six items. The first fourteen foreground Cicero's role as proconsul in Cilicia. There are two official reports to the Senate; an exchange of four letters with Cato about Cicero's desire to be voted a *supplicatio* and triumph; seven letters to consuls, consuls designate, or their kin seeking to enlist their goodwill; and finally a letter asking support from Cassius Longinus, who was then about to return to Rome after governing the adjacent province of Syria.

What makes this aggregate into a series is not a particular addressee but a particular focus. All the letters belong to the year of Cicero's proconsulate, all reflect concerns about his position at home, and all are addressed to senators whose support he counted on. In the last seven letters of the book, the focus shifts, however. The letter to Cassius served as a sort of hinge to which to attach five more letters to or from him, plus two to Trebonius, all written roughly four years later, in the doldrums between Caesar's early victories and his assassination. For the most part, these letters skirt political topics and self-consciously parade the writers' philosophical and literary culture (an unusual emphasis in the correspondence overall). But it is perhaps not coincidental that both Cassius and Trebonius were shortly thereafter to achieve notoriety as tyrannicides.[72]

Book 5 features an even more disparate makeup than book 15. It contains twenty-two letters to twelve addressees, no one of whom is represented by more than four items. It covers a broader time span as well, running from letters of the late 60s to letters of the mid-40s. But in this case, too, the editor has relied on rough categories to organize material. With one exception, the first twelve letters are to senior senators and proconsuls with whom Cicero had (or had had) strained relations (Metellus Celer, Metellus Nepos, Gaius Antonius, Pompey, Crassus, and Vatinius).[73] The letters mostly illustrate these strains. The five remaining correspondents appear to have nothing in common with the first group. Not all are senators, and none is a consular, for example. But they form a distinct group within the book by virtue of the fact that they all either write or receive letters of consolation.

Book 6 contains twenty-three letters to eleven different addressees. Five persons with whom the book leads off and the two with whom it closes are former partisans of Pompey whom Caesar has barred from Rome, and all the letters relating to them (seventeen of the twenty-three) are about their plight. All but one of the six correspondents represented in book 7 are non-senators, making that the only composite book reserved to non-senators in the published collection.[74] The four correspondents of book 4, by contrast, are not only senators but longtime friends who, like Cicero, have been marginalized under Caesar's rule (this is the book containing the letters to Marcellus and Servius mentioned above).

I do not mean to exaggerate the sophistication of the ordering schemes at work. As was true in the treatment of recommendation letters, alternate principles are inconsistently applied, and often one scheme is dropped in favor of another when it has been only partly carried through. In book 5, for example, which combines a group of letters written during Cicero's proconsulate with another group written four or five years later, the editor could easily have filled the entire book with letters from Cicero's proconsulate.[75] Book 6 could have been entirely rather than just mainly devoted to Pompeian exiles if the letters to Marcellus and Figulus in book 4 had been added to it. Letters to one of

Cicero's closest equestrian friends, Papirius Paetus, have been combined not with letters to other non-senators in book 7, but with letters to Varro and Dolabella in book 9. Chronology is carelessly regarded at many points. In general, the editor tried to keep together letters that date to approximately the same period, both in prosopographically defined series and in other kinds of series. Yet often letters that belong to a given period do not stand in the proper order within the period. The editor has not always arranged in correct sequence even letters that are explicitly dated.[76] No principle of order is absolute, including the principle of grouping letters by recipient, as we have already had several occasions to notice.

Nevertheless, the present order of the letters is anything but mindless, in the sense either that it is random or that it can have resulted from a process of mechanical transcription. In all parts of the corpus themes emerge too clearly not to suspect that they have been editorially enhanced. And there is almost no point at which the placement of individual letters cannot be seen to make sense in at least local terms.

The construction of letter series was the most creative editorial input into the publication of Cicero's correspondence.[77] Conceivably one purpose of it was to compensate for the absence of all orienting comment on the editor's part. More than anything else, it is the fact that nearly every letter is integrated into a larger set that discloses background and makes letters intelligible. But anyone who hopes to mine the correspondence for evidence about Cicero and his milieu has to keep a further consequence in mind. The construction of series was at least potentially a filter. As the editor ransacked letter files for publishable material, he had to have had the ultimate plan of the collection in mind. Material not pertinent to his rough-and-ready categories was perhaps liable to be discarded.

Letters from Correspondents

The novelty that most distinguishes Cicero's published correspondence from other collections is that it incorporates many letters written *to* Cicero along with the letters written by him—by my count, eighty-nine letters from thirty-two different persons, or almost 10 percent of the total.[78] One-sixth of these letters take the form of enclosures, which have been discussed above. But most occur as formally separate items in the *Letters to Marcus Brutus* and in several of the books constituting the *Letters to Friends*.

If it is surprising that such letters should be included at all, the next noteworthy thing about them is how selective the editor was in choosing them. Since we have already considered the selection criteria for enclosures above, let us here disregard those items and consider only letters to Cicero that were published as independent pieces of correspondence. Of twenty-four letter writers

involved, fifteen are responsible for only one letter apiece, and two are responsible for two apiece. These writers, at least, are too slightly represented for us to
imagine that the intended effect was to balance the epistolary portrait of Cicero
with portraits of selected correspondents. A more plausible hypothesis might
be that letters from correspondents were sometimes included to contextualize
or complement a companion text by Cicero. So, for example, the famous letter
from Matius (*Fam.* 11.28 = 349 SB) responds to a letter just before it in which
Cicero criticizes Matius's devotion to Caesar. Vice versa, a letter from Metellus
Celer (*Fam.* 5.1 = 1 SB) contains a criticism to which Cicero then responds. Yet
isolated letter pairs of this sort are rare in the corpus, and where they occur it is
questionable whether the comprehension of one really depends on the presence
of the other.[79] In a few cases, moreover, the possibility that the editor included
letters from correspondents because they complemented letters of Cicero can
be ruled out. Four of the letter writers are represented by their side of the
exchange only; the editor did not opt to publish any of the letters they received
from Cicero.[80]

   While these unpaired letters obviously cannot have been selected for the
sake of their relevance to letters by Cicero, they did qualify for inclusion under
another criterion of which the editor was fond. All date from the year 43, they
concern episodes in the struggle by Cicero and the Senate against Antony and
his allies, and they were written by authoritative participants. Cassius's and
Lentulus's letters (*Fam.* 12.13 = 419 SB, and *Fam.* 12.14 = 405 SB) report on
operations they conducted against Dolabella in the east. Galba's letter (*Fam.*
10.30 = 378 SB), often anthologized, is an eyewitness account of the battle of
Forum Gallorum by a commander in it. Pollio's three letters (*Fam.* 10.31 = 368
SB, 10.32 = 415 SB, and 10.33 = 409 SB) were written in his capacity as army
commander in Spain and show him temporizing about whether to throw his
weight to Antony or to the Senate. Like several of the enclosures that were
selected for publication, they have the attraction of casting vivid sidelights on
dramatic contemporary events.

   That this quality motivated their inclusion is confirmed by the context in
which they appear. Galba's and Pollio's letters in book 10 are appended to an
exchange with Munatius Plancus, then governor of Gaul, about checking
Antony's movement from northern Italy into Gaul. Cassius's and Lentulus's
letters in book 12 follow a long series to Cassius Longinus which, like their
own letters, focuses on the organization of the Republican cause in the east.
Books 10 and 12 share an affinity with book 11 (comprising letters to Decimus
Brutus, the Republican general in north Italy) and with the surviving book of
Letters to Marcus Brutus in that they are more sharply focused on military
affairs than any other portion of the extant correspondence.[81] It is probably no
coincidence that close to half (forty-one) of all the letters Cicero receives from
others and most of the letter writers credited with multiple letters are concentrated in these four books.

But although a predilection for dramatic reportage seems more marked here than elsewhere, that alone cannot explain the editor's inclusion of so many letters by Cicero's correspondents. Not all letters of Cassius, Plancus, and the two Brutuses have the intensity of bulletins from the front. But collectively they do offer an unusually sustained view of Cicero's performance in a public role. Cicero's leadership against Antony was the second star turn of his career, and by contrast with the struggle against Catiline, it left an abundant record in his correspondence because the other players were situated far from Rome. Many of their letters have an undeniable documentary interest, and some must have been included mainly for that reason. But what made them relevant to the publishing project overall was that in praising, questioning, or criticizing Cicero's conduct of policy, they seemed to put him at the center of momentous events. I will return to these letters in chapter 6.

That letters by others were apt to be included if they highlighted Cicero is particularly noticeable in those cases where a series features multiple letters by Cicero but only one from his correspondent. The exchange with the exiled senator Marcellus has been mentioned in the preceding section. The one letter of Marcellus in it begins, "You can be sure that your authority has always carried the greatest weight with me both in general and especially in this episode" (plurimum valuisse apud me tuam semper auctoritatem cum in omni re tum in hoc maxime negotio potes existimare, *Fam.* 4.11 = 232 SB), and it credits Cicero with major responsibility for his return. The exchange with Servius Sulpicius in the same book also includes one contribution by the epistolary partner. It is a letter consoling Cicero on the death of his daughter and urging him "not to forget that you are Cicero" (noli te oblivisci Ciceronem esse, *Fam.* 4.5 = 248 SB). The only letter by Lucceius to be published (*Fam.* 5.14 = 251 SB) was likewise written after Tullia's death and exhorts Cicero to resume his accustomed public role. The one letter by Dolabella included in that series (*Fam.* 9.9 = 157 SB) is an effort to cajole Cicero out of Pompey's camp and into Caesar's. The Cato series in book 15 includes one letter from Cato's side (*Fam.* 15.5 = 111 SB) praising Cicero's varied accomplishments but declining to support his bid for a Cilician triumph. Most of the Caecina series consists of letters from Cicero urging Caecina to bear up under the stress of exile. But it also includes one from Caecina in which he describes a tribute he has paid to Cicero in a recent literary composition, praises Cicero's "superlative and towering intelligence" (summum atque excellens ingenium, *Fam.* 6.7.4 = 237 SB) and begs him to exert his intimate influence with Caesar on Caecina's behalf.

But whether their letters report on great events or merely contribute to a multidimensional image of Cicero, what almost all the writers represented in the collection have in common is that they are important persons. Of the twenty-four correspondents, twenty-one are senators, and most play prominent roles. The simplest message communicated by the editor's selection is that Rome's great and powerful took pains to stay in touch with Cicero.

Selection and Social Status

The point just made about letters from correspondents was also true of enclo-sures and letters of recommendation: the editor has selected material that privileges the topmost stratum of Roman society. And what is true of these subsets is true of the collection as a whole—both of the extant books and of books which are now lost. Élisabeth Déniaux's table of correspondents in the extant books lists ninety-seven named persons, of whom seventy-four are senators.[82] Thirty-six books or more that are lost once contained a correspondence with Pompey, Brutus, Caesar, Octavian, Pansa, Hirtius, Axius, Licinius Calvus, Marcus junior, and Cornelius Nepos, of whom all but the last two are senators.[83]

This concentration on Cicero's relations with fellow members of the gov-erning class may seem unremarkable, since it undoubtedly suits the tastes of most readers ancient and modern. But let us nevertheless take a moment to inventory some of the available correspondents whom the editor passed over. The published collection preserves almost none of Cicero's letters to magnates in the towns of Italy or in the provinces. It contains no letters to persons in his hometown of Arpinum, for example, or to regional clients he accumulated as quaestor in Sicily and afterward, and almost none to some three dozen people whom he identifies as *hospites*.[84] And while the editor made a point of including letters of recommendation, he retained little of the background communica-tion with the persons on whose behalf the recommendations were written. The collection also contains none of Cicero's exchanges with Greek intellec-tuals whom he cultivated, such as the philosophers Aristus, Diodotus, Cratippus, and Posidonius and the *grammatici* Nicias and Tyrannio.[85] The only member of his domestic staff represented in the edition is Tiro, though Cicero often wrote to Philotimus and the tutor Dionysius as well, and nothing sur-vives of an active correspondence with the businessmen Vestorius and Vettienus. Finally, the editor did not see fit to publish an extensive political exchange that Cicero had with Balbus. During the 50s and 40s, when Balbus was acting as Caesar's intermediary, Cicero was in more frequent contact with him than with Caesar himself. But as a knight and a Spaniard, Balbus lacked status, and the few letters from this exchange to be published appeared only as enclosures.[86]

There are certainly components of the collection that cannot be explained in terms of their prestige value (the letters to Tiro and to fringe characters such as Curius of Patrae and Marius, for example). But the overwhelming majority of the letters focus attention on Cicero's relations with the high elite. What the editor evidently set out to construct was an epistolary portrait of a great *princeps civitatis* who over a long period dominated discourse in his milieu even if he was unable to control events.

A Scenario of the Editor at Work

Thus far in this chapter I have attempted to develop a slow, inductive argument about the way the editor worked. I end with a short retrospect that I hope will leave a more focused impression of his activity.

Whoever took the decision to publish Cicero's letters faced procedural problems that were daunting and of a sort not previously addressed in Roman literary history. Over the course of his lifetime Cicero churned out an immense correspondence, much of which he took care to have copied and filed. The sheer abundance of material must have made publishing all of it unthinkable from the first. It may also have discouraged any temptation on the editor's part to seek out additional material in the hands of Cicero's correspondents.

If a surfeit of material was the first problem, the next was deciding what to select. Letters may be written with some ideal of epistolary form in mind, but beyond that they do not regularly subdivide into tidy categories. The elaborate distinctions of letter-writing manuals are scholastic refinements of a later age. In Cicero's practice, even recommendations, congratulations, and thanks are apt to be ingredients of an epistolary mix. Since the letters themselves offered few cues about sorting, the editor had to devise criteria of his own. No one who has had experience of putting together a survey or anthology of texts will be surprised that the process was sometimes arbitrary and inconsistent.

The editor cared most about the social identity of Cicero's correspondents. He organized the letters primarily by correspondent rather than, say, by date or topic, yet in no case—not even in that of Atticus or Quintus—did he try to publish all the letters a correspondent received. A letter series usually resolves into one or more vignettes representing an exchange over a particular matter during a limited stretch of time. This structure enhances the comprehensibility of the letters for readers and also tends to accentuate the social dynamic between the epistolary partners. Cicero receives the major exposure since it is predominantly his side of the exchange that is featured. But even where no letters from his correspondents are included, a letter series almost always conveys a good sense of who and where they were and what they were doing and how important it made them. The editor's consciousness of their relative status is evident also in sequences where he groups them by type, as leading senators or knights or exiles.

Three-quarters of the correspondents represented are senators, a ratio that is largely a consequence of the editor's partiality for letters about politics, government, and public life. These matters are prominent even in letters to several knights (Atticus, Caecina, and Matius, for example). At the same time, however, the selection of elite correspondents serves to enhance Cicero's image. He is shown to be important by the importance of people who corresponded with him. But it is not impossible that the editor allotted space to certain correspondents simply because he was pressured to. During his lifetime, Cicero was often entreated to write appearances by friends into his dialogues. The publisher of the letters may have had to cope with publicity seekers as well, just as Pliny did when he began publishing his letters.[87]

Some idea of the subject matter that the editor favored can be gained by comparing extant letters with letters that are missing. The most obvious bias is, as just noted, toward political content, dramatic political content above all, for which the editor was willing to stretch the parameters of his project. He included some letters he discovered in the files that were not only not written by Cicero, but not written to him either. He was also fond of letters in which a writer spread himself in the "O tempora, o mores!" vein, and less interested in detail about parliamentary discussions or public trials. The editor discarded many letters covering Cicero's life out of the public spotlight: letters about family relations, business affairs, literary and other cultural pursuits, and purely social interactions. He was also leery of including isolated letters that could not be integrated into a context of some sort.

We have no reason to suspect that the editor ventured to revise letters when he published them, as Cicero himself was planning to do. But on a few occasions (it is impossible to estimate how many) he did excerpt them, and he was not always scrupulous about retaining the exact form of headings and closings where the letter text melted into formulas.[88] He organized the material he had selected into intelligible sequences, usually by putting together all letters to or from a particular person and then clustering those letters by time period. But he did not always bother to put them into exact chronological order even when they were dated. In the briefer letter series of the *Letters to Friends*, he enlarged his schemes of arrangement, taking into consideration also the status and location of correspondents and their themes.

We cannot afford to forget that between us and Cicero's letters stands someone who did a great deal to determine how we read them.

3 〰

Frames of the Letter

That the Romans often compared the letter to a live exchange, as noted in chapter 1, reveals much about the value they placed on face-to-face interaction but little about their epistolary practice. The differences between an exchange of letters and a conversation are more consequential than the resemblances.[1] In the first place, a correspondence is a delayed exchange between parties who occupy separate and often distant positions in space and in time. Each therefore communicates in a social void, beginning and concluding without interruption, challenge, or reaction from the other side. In the second place, a letter is an exclusively written form of communication. Even a dictated letter is produced more slowly and usually more circumspectly than talk. Letter writers, moreover, are unable to exploit the bodily signals—intonation, facial expression, gesture, and other modes of body language—that help to convey meaning in conversation. For that matter, they draw on a more limited range of speech than speakers do. A scrupulous transcript of any conversation will contain more discourse particles, expletives, nonword sounds, and breaks than a letter will. That a letter is itself the transcript of a discourse is a further consequence of writing. Every letter writer by that act creates and entrusts to someone else a material record of a sort that is rarely obtained for conversations, even in our era when sound recordings are technically possible. A third way in which an exchange of letters differs from a conversation is that participation is typically more restricted. In a strict sense, of course, only one party to a correspondence is active at any moment, as already noted. But even if the time delay is disregarded, most correspondence consists of two-party communication only. Finally, letters tend to be more goal-oriented than conversations. A conversation can come about by accident and proceed in directions that the participants did not anticipate, particularly when several persons are involved. Correspondents, on the other hand, must take some trouble to establish communication, and once they have done so, they know where they are going.

The Significance of Externals

As socially competent actors, the Romans can be taken to have understood these differences between correspondence and conversation as well as we do, and their letters afford plenty of evidence that they exploited peculiarities of the medium. An epistolary equivalent of body language, for example, could be based on the materials of which letters were made.[2] Two physical formats were regularly available. Messages could be inscribed with a dry stylus on small, hand-held, wax-coated wooden tablets consisting of two or more leaves. Such letters could be written almost anywhere, since a tablet required no ink and always offered a hard, flat surface on which to write. Apart from whatever the text made explicit, therefore, the format alone hinted at a letter's circumstances: that the sender was writing from an unusual location, that the message was urgent or written in haste, that its content would be limited, or (since tablets were often associated with financial transactions) that it would concern a matter of business.[3]

In addition to the comparative informality of the medium, however, tablets had the disadvantage of being cumbersome to transport and to store. The majority of Cicero's correspondence was written in the second format, with a reed pen and ink on papyrus, as he describes at *QFr.* 2.15(14).1 = 19 SB.[4] The letter text formed a progression of short, parallel columns written perpendicular to the long side of a prefabricated sheet, which could be cut or joined to another sheet as the length of the message required. In physical appearance, a letter on papyrus thus bore some resemblance to a book roll, not least in being rolled up in cylindrical form when it was done, rather than being folded like a modern letter.[5]

As with a tablet, a letter on papyrus could convey signals before the first word of it was read. A long letter was instantly recognizable by the diameter of the roll. A message that was literally as fat as a book might be received with misgiving or with pleasure depending on the circumstances, but in either case it advertised itself as falling outside the bounds of conventional correspondence.[6] It was also noticeable whether a letter had been written on the proper material. Papyrus was a specialty product not readily available outside an urban market.[7] Hence persons who wanted to maintain an active correspondence sometimes presented the epistolary partner with letter paper (just as they had to arrange for delivery).[8] Irregular stationery provoked comment. When Cicero's friend Trebatius was with Caesar in Gaul, he once wrote back on a used piece of papyrus which he had cleaned off. Cicero interpreted that to be another symptom of the deprivation in distant barbary which Trebatius was making into a refrain of his letters home.[9]

But the letter sign on which Roman readers remarked most often was the handwriting. Given that most correspondence between members of the elite was dictated to secretaries, the recipient of a letter would normally have had little expectation of reading something written in the sender's own hand. The very fact of its rarity, however, made a correspondent's handwriting available as a sign. Since it involved more exertion than dictation, it could serve first of all as a token of special care and esteem.[10] Cicero says that under ordinary circumstances he made a practice of writing in his own hand to his friend Atticus and to his brother Quintus.[11] In such cases, it was his occasional recourse to a secretary that then invited interpretation—as, for example, that he was overwhelmed with work, or suffering from eye trouble, or not in a convenient spot in which to write.[12] Though the meaning could vary, Cicero takes it for granted that the script of letters is a sign on which the recipients will base inferences and judgments.[13]

A writer's autograph can yield clues about the person that a dictated letter does not divulge, and some comments in the Ciceronian corpus show readers poring over such clues. Cicero concluded from the shaky penmanship of one of Tiro's letters that his secretary was ill, and in a letter of his own to Atticus he paraded his frugality by writing in a close, tight script; Cicero's brother inferred from one carelessly written letter he received that Cicero must be distracted or out of sorts.[14] But comment on a letter's script or on the possible sign value of erasures, blots, or marginal and interlinear insertions is rare. Graphic indicators can be revelatory only in cases in which correspondents do their writing themselves, as no more than a handful in the Ciceronian corpus do. Perhaps, indeed, the preference for dictating letters reflects not simply the number there were to be written, but also a conscious effort to depersonalize the writing. In communicating with peers and rivals, there would have been every incentive to eliminate a channel of unintended signals.

Even in exchanges with peers and rivals, however, Cicero and his correspondents did on occasion pen their own letters or parts of them. Some of these autographic interventions seem to coincide with passages of sensitive content. During the lead-up to the civil war, for example, Caelius reported in his own hand on a sudden realignment affecting Caesar; soon after the outbreak, Pompey concluded a military briefing with a personal charge to Cicero; and later, another army commander wrote about the possibility of changing sides.[15] But it is difficult to say whether the change of script was intended to signal an aura of confidentiality or to add a stamp of personal authority to what was written.[16] At times, the switch may have communicated neither the one thing nor the other, but resulted from the vagaries of Roman postal arrangements. Once a letter was written, it had to await the availability of a bearer before it could be dispatched. If the next possibility to turn up was a courier from the very person to whom one had written, or another courier who had just brought pertinent news, the pending letter would often be updated. In that case it could be as quick to add a note personally as to call on a secretary.[17]

Although in this way a letter might conclude with a passage in the writer's own hand, no Ciceronian parallel can be verified for those passages in the Pauline epistles in which St. Paul purposely writes a line or two in his own hand to personalize them.[18] And of course, the Romans did not sign letters as we are accustomed to do. Sender and recipient were identified together in the heading at the beginning of a message; the good-bye formula at the end did not include a signature.[19]

Finally, the fact that Roman correspondents were conditioned to accept letters that lacked all trace of the sender's handwriting enabled the production of letters to which the ostensible sender might have contributed nothing at all. When distress sapped Cicero's spirit, as during his exile, during his later internment at Brundisium, and after the death of his daughter, he often deputized Atticus to write for him to anyone who Atticus thought needed to receive a letter.[20] We are in no position to determine whether any of the extant letters were in fact drafted by Atticus or someone else. But for various reasons, the likelihood seems slight. Letters from the depressive phases of Cicero's life are few to begin with. Letters ghostwritten by Atticus surely had less chance of being copied and preserved in Cicero's files than those Cicero generated himself. And it seems reasonable to suppose that the collection editor would have eliminated manifestly supposititious items, given the apparent purpose behind the publication project.

But the possible use of epistolary deputies in any case presented a somewhat different problem for original readers of the letters than it does for us. Others besides Cicero sometimes allowed letters to be written in their name by agents.[21] Such letters could not be dismissed as simply counterfeit. The circumstances of delivery would have left no doubt that they emanated from someone closely associated with the ostensible sender and therefore in some sense authorized. What was questionable was the exact degree of authority behind them, and that could encourage a skeptical reading if the reader objected to the content. After Pompey's defeat, when Cicero was hoping that Caesar would pardon him and allow him to return to Rome, he received instead a letter indicating that he would first have to sue for pardon in person. As it turned out, Cicero did finally go to Caesar and make his peace several months later. But when he initially received the distasteful message, he preferred to doubt that it originated with Caesar.[22] Later in the civil war, Brutus addressed a letter to the Senate expressing a conciliatory stance toward Mark Antony's brother, whom he had captured. Cicero, who objected to any quarter with Antony, threw up a cloud of doubts about the letter: the bearer was disreputable, the letter carried neither seal nor date, and none of Brutus's friends in Rome (Cicero, for one) had received the usual epistolary backup. Small wonder, then, that one of

Cicero's senatorial colleagues "wanted to infer that the letter was bogus, and, if you care to know, he won assent" (hoc cogere volebat, falsas litteras esse, et, si quaeris, probabat, *MBrut.* 5[2.5].4 = 5 SB).

As the preceding example suggests, it was the external seal rather than the sender's handwriting or signature that typically signaled authenticity, whether the letter had been written on a tablet or on papyrus. The seal actually served a double purpose, at the same time identifying the sender and keeping the message enclosed during transit. Before being dispatched, the tablet or scroll was wrapped with string or a strand of papyrus, and that was held in place by a dollop of wax or clay with the imprint of the sender's signet ring. At our end of the textual tradition, there is naturally no way to know if the original of a particular letter carried a seal or not. But seals are mentioned so often and so casually in Cicero's correspondence that they appear to have been regular in both formal and informal letters. With their personalized emblem of the writer, they count as the last of the material elements that could signify before a word of the letter was read.

Nevertheless, the case of Brutus's dispatch shows that some letters were not sealed. Because Cicero preferred to impeach this letter, he ignored the possibility that Brutus might have had a reason for leaving it unsealed. One likely motive was that Brutus wanted his confidants in Rome to vet the letter before it was delivered to the Senate.[23] But usually the reason for dispensing with a seal would have been more ominous. Cicero often worried that the content of his letters might compromise him if they fell into the wrong hands, and he considered sending truly sensitive letters incognito.[24] It was more difficult to tag the sender with a letter if it carried no seal.[25] And that safeguard for the sender would in turn convey a signal to the recipient. A letter that arrived without the sender's seal could be expected to concern itself with political or military affairs.

Formal Conventions of the Letter

The features of Latin letters discussed up to this point were obvious at the very first glance: the choice of tablet or papyrus, the handwriting, the seal. Yet unsophisticated as they were, each lent itself to interpretation on the part of the reader and therefore to manipulation on the part of the writer. The features to be considered next required at least a partial reading of the text. A piece of writing was revealed to be a letter (as opposed, say, to a literary text or a legal document) by conventional elements at beginning and end which are roughly analogous to those of modern letters.[26] Roman letters opened with a heading that comprised the names of letter writer and addressee and usually an abbreviated greeting formula. In the Ciceronian corpus, spare headings are the most frequent, for example, "Cicero bids greetings to Trebatius" (Cicero s. d. Trebatio,

Fam. 7.6 = 27 SB), "Cicero to Plancus, greetings" (Cicero Planco s., *Fam.* 10.2 = 341 SB), "Cicero to Varro" (Cicero Varroni, *Fam.* 9.3 = 176 SB). Letters often closed with a short valedictory formula, such as "farewell" (vale, *Fam.* 3.1.3 = 64 SB) or "take care to be well" (cura ut valeas, *Att.* 2.2.3 = 22 SB), sometimes followed by a date. These stereotypical elements, all of which were imported from Greek letter-writing practice, could be customized in ways that implicitly commented on the relationship between writer and addressee.

The most important locus of variation was the letter heading.[27] Since the names of sender and addressee stood in the third person, by contrast with the "I-you" discourse in the body of the letter,[28] and since the heading was self-contained and syntactically independent of the rest, the opening bore something of the character of a label. At the same time, the modulation of names in the heading lent itself to the articulation of social nuances. Most men in the upper ranks of society (and the majority of Cicero's correspondents) had names consisting of praenomen, nomen gentilicium or family name, and one or more cognomina. Since as a rule the full complement of names was not needed for identification purposes, name elements could be deployed separately or in different permutations to convey other things.[29] In the heading of letters to his wife and daughter and to his freedman Tiro, but to no one else, Cicero usually named himself simply "Tullius." The family name thus signaled a letter about family business. Letters to his brother, on the other hand, were inscribed "Marcus to his brother Quintus," since both men shared an identical family name and cognomen.[30] Otherwise, however, the bald use of one's praenomen was too casual for letter headings. Cicero does not repeat it in letters to anyone else, and apart from his brother, the only addressees he so identifies are three noblemen who affected name styles based on rare praenomina.[31]

At the other extreme from the informal letter heading was the ultraformal. When Cicero inscribes all three parts of his name, he is invariably ruffling his feathers, whether in writing aggrievedly to Pompey about Pompey's disrespect of Cicero's services as consul (*Fam.* 5.7 = 3 SB) or to another noble who had slighted him (*Fam.* 5.2 = 2 SB), or when as governor he informs the Senate of matters affecting his province (*Fam.* 15.1–2 = 104–105 SB) or welcomes the young nobleman who is to succeed him (*Fam.* 2.19 = 116 SB), or when he assumes the mien of elder statesman in writing to a colleague en route to his own province (*Fam.* 13.68 = 211 SB). If Cicero arrogates the three names to himself, he usually accords them to his addressees too, and sometimes also if they happen to be holding office when he writes to them.[32]

It is even more common for titles of office to be advertised in formal headings than full names, as for example, "Marcus Cicero bids greeting to Consul Quintus Metellus" (M. Cicero s. d. Q. Metello cos., *Fam.* 5.4 = 10 SB), "Commander Marcus Cicero bids greeting to Marcus Cato" (M. Cicero imp. s. d. M. Catoni, *Fam.* 15.4 = 110 SB), and "Commander Marcus Cicero bids greeting to Proquaestor Caius Cassius" (M. Cicero imp. s. d. C. Cassio pro q.,

Fam. 15.14 = 106 SB). Finally, a formal element that is rarely deployed except in combination with one of the other two is the use of a patronymic, as in this example: "Marcus Cicero bids greeting to Proconsul Quintus Ancharius, son of Quintus" (M. Cicero s. d. Q. Anchario Q. f. pro cos., *Fam.* 13.40 = 59 SB).

In general, heading styles fall between the extremes of formality and informality. Letter writers sought to blend intimacy and hauteur in a dosage suitable to each correspondent, and the variables in the heading afforded them a way to do it.[33] Admittedly, we are not always in a position to interpret the effects. Not everybody possessed a cognomen, for example, and to further muddle the picture, not everyone who had a cognomen cared to use one. Some name styles reflect only the quirks of individuals and not broad trends. Nevertheless, certain trends are evident. In none of the examples quoted so far does the name style consist of nomen plus cognomen (as in "Tullius Cicero"), and that holds true throughout the corpus.[34] The default style in headings consists of the praenomen in combination with either cognomen or nomen ("Marcus Cicero" or "Marcus Tullius"). It is against that base that variations can be interpreted.

We have Cicero's word for it that the shortening of the name by omission of the praenomen was regarded as a sign of familiarity (*Fam.* 7.32.1 = 113 SB). That corresponds with his practice in a series of seventeen letters to his junior friend Trebatius Testa, fourteen of which are headed simply "Cicero to Trebatius." The intimacy quotient rose still higher if the letter writer attached the possessive adjective *suus* to the name of the addressee, as in the heading "Cicero to his very own Capito, greetings" (Cicero Capitoni suo sal., *Att.* 16.16 C = 407C SB). Except for this wheedling letter to Capito, however, Cicero applied the possessive only to members of his family and household.[35] But other correspondents bestowed it more promiscuously, and it was no doubt to Cicero's deep chagrin that he found himself claimed as "his very own Cicero" by the egregious Vatinius.[36]

An effect of intimacy could also be obtained by the omission of titles in correspondence between officeholders (Cic. Dom. 22; compare *Phil.* 13.22), which is likewise reflected in Cicero's practice. When his protégé Plancus was governing Transalpine Gaul, they exchanged twenty-four letters, and in only one was Plancus's title inscribed by either man. Titles figure in only three of the twelve letters that Cicero wrote to Appius throughout a period in which one or the other of them and sometimes both were holding public office.

In other headings, however, it is the insistence on a title that is meant to catch attention. During the year when Cicero was governor of Cilicia, he kept in touch with his young friend Caelius Rufus in Rome. In all nine extant letters, he inscribed his title, and when in the course of the year Caelius won election to an aedileship in Rome, Cicero began to inscribe Caelius's title, too. This formality is striking not only because Caelius was one of Cicero's more intimate acquaintances and because in letters of the same period to others Cicero often omitted his title, but also because it was completely at odds with Caelius's practice. According to the manuscripts, every one of his seventeen letters to Cicero carried the casual heading "Caelius to Cicero, greetings."[37] Whether Cicero was twitting Caelius with his junior status or trying to model correct epistolary deportment for his insouciant friend, these headings seem to communicate on a plane apart from the letters proper.

Another letter from Cilicia in which Cicero flaunts his title is addressed "Commander Cicero to Paetus" (Cicero imp. Paeto, *Fam.* 9.25 = 114 SB). The heading style here is uniquely dissonant. Everywhere else that Cicero asserts a title (as in the contemporary letters to Caelius), he also inscribes his praenomen. But this heading combines the formal use of a title with the familiar address form "Cicero to Paetus" that occurs in all other letters to Paetus. The anomaly is surely deliberate. As a rule, Paetus, a mere equestrian, receives bantering letters about books, cuisine, and social life rather than about serious matters. But in one of his own letters, apropos of Cicero's campaigns on the frontier, he had evidently strayed onto the topic of strategy, which elicited this response from Cicero:

> Your letter turned me into a general extraordinaire. Really, I had no idea you were so up on military science—it's obvious that you have been poring over the books of Pyrrhus and Cineas. Well, I intend to follow your instructions, and to keep a few boats on the coast for good measure. They say that no better fighting arm can be devised against Parthian cavalry. But why do I jest?

> *summum me ducem litterae tuae reddiderunt. plane nesciebam te tam peritum esse rei militaris; Pyrrhi te libros et Cineae video lectitasse. itaque obtemperare cogito praeceptis tuis; hoc amplius, navicularum habere aliquid in ora maritima. contra equitem Parthum negant ullam armaturam meliorem inveniri posse. sed quid ludimus?*

Cicero's letter is a put-down which he previews in the heading. The inconcinnity of the style hints at the grotesqueness of Paetus's presumption, and the title of office demarcates the commander from the preposterous amateur.[38]

A title of office that is any way peculiar also draws attention to itself. One of the rare letters to Appius Pulcher featuring a title is headed "Cicero bids greeting to—as I hope—Censor Appius Pulcher" (Cicero Appio Pulchro, ut spero, censori s. d., *Fam.* 3.11 = 74 SB). The style is eccentric in that a first-person interjection disrupts the third-person formula. Moreover, Appius's office was not yet official: Cicero had not actually heard whether he had won his election. But the oddness of the formulation merely cloaks an assurance that Appius was a shoo-in for the censorship (as indeed he was). Once again, a heading cues the tone of a whole letter. Up to this point, Cicero and Appius had been engaged in a series of testy exchanges. But in this letter, written a month before Cicero was to leave his province and head back to the capital, he changes tack and plies Appius with compliments.[39] The letter ends as it began, with an augury of his censorship.

Another anomaly occurs in the heading "Marcus Cicero bids greeting to Jurisconsult Lucius Valerius" (M. Cicero s. d. L. Valerio iurisconsulto, *Fam.* 1.10 = 21 SB). The addressee in this case was another of Cicero's protégés, and his title was a spoof, like the whole of the short letter that follows. "Jurisconsult" was not the name of a proper office but of a function, like "orator" or "clerk." And Cicero no sooner bestows the title than he debunks it by commenting, "I don't see why not to make you a present of this, the more so in the present age when nerve can pass for expertise" (cur enim tibi hoc non gratificer nescio, praesertim cum his temporibus audacia pro sapientia liceat uti). This letter heading served to let a social inferior know his place, as Cicero's joking letters often do.[40]

The majority of Cicero's correspondents were senators, however, who normally did one another the courtesy of pretending that they were peers. The juxtaposition of names in the letter heading presented a perfect facade for the display of solidarity. A heading in which both parties were named in the same onomastic style and were accorded matching titles of office made a graphic declaration of equality. That Cicero and his correspondents generally sought to strike this note is suggested by the fact that their letter headings fall into reciprocal patterns more often than not. Especially noteworthy are cases in which correspondents who happen to hold the same office do not name it, but rather style each other as "colleague" (collega).[41] On the other hand, when it was important to register distinctions, unbalanced address styles could be employed to communicate deference, dignity, or distance.

The letter headings in the Ciceronian corpus are the least carefully transmitted element of the text and, for modern readers, probably the least closely scrutinized. But their significance for the original readers is proven not only by Cicero's care in composing them, but also by the frequency with which he comments on them when interpreting other people's letters or his own.[42] Simply by reading the heading, the recipient of a letter could infer where he or she stood in the hierarchy of the writer's esteem, and sometimes what the letter would be about.

None of the remaining epistolary formulas was as essential or as subtly calculated as the address line. The formula "bids greeting" (dicit salutem) was usually abbreviated and often left implicit.[43] On rare occasions, mostly but not exclusively in letters to family, Cicero would add the word "exuberant" or "heartiest" (plurimam, also abbreviated) to the word for "greeting," but even that was formulaic.[44] The greeting formula was basically the same for everyone.

It could, however, be supplemented by a preset expression that was not regularly employed: "If you are well, it is good; for my part, I am well" (si vales, bene est; ego quidem valeo).[45] This formula, which like the formal greeting was more often abbreviated than not, functioned as a bridge to the body of the letter. The shift from indirect to direct address established the appropriate conversational tone, and the topic of health eased the writer into the letter by means of the most conventional of all polite gambits. Seneca and Pliny, writing a century after Cicero, regarded this opening as the habit of an earlier generation, and in fact it was already current in Latin as far back as the time of Plautus in the third century B.C.[46]

But it was not a particularly organic cliché. It did not help to articulate a letter, like the address line or valedictory phrase. Insofar as it introduced, however stiltedly, a topic of discourse, it preempted other openings that might have been more lively or effective. Cicero sometimes likes to plunge into a letter with an exclamation or a question, for example, which would have followed incongruously on the heels of "s. v. b. e. v." Furthermore, as the epistolary equivalent of a conversational icebreaker, the formula best suited situations in which correspondents were feeling their way. It was less in place when a lively exchange was already in progress. Hence it never occurs in Cicero's letters to Atticus or to his brother, and rarely in other letter series. One last disadvantage is that it was so perfunctory as to be useless on those occasions when the health of a correspondent was actually a matter of concern.

It should come as no surprise, then, that this opening shows signs of being obsolescent in the epistolography of Cicero and his friends. It is found only thirty-four times, or in less than 4 percent of all letters in the collection. But although its propositional content was virtually nil, it did have the singular quality of being an utterance that would be encountered only within a letter. Occurring at the outset, what it therefore communicated was the intention to write a proper letter. It crops up most often in letters that have an official tinge, for example, when Pompey and Pollio write in their capacity as army leaders to Cicero (*Att.* 8.11C = 161C SB, *Fam.* 10.33 = 409 SB), or when Cicero and Lepidus write to the Senate (*Fam.* 15.1 = 104 SB, 10.35 = 408 SB). Here the phrase can easily be read as a token of formality.

At other times, however, it is employed by persons who have no official role and who are not trying to distance themselves from an addressee. Lucceius, for example, was a longtime acquaintance whom Cicero had once asked to write the story of his consulate. In a letter after the death of Cicero's daughter, he presumed on their relationship to urge that Cicero shake himself out of a protracted funk (*Fam.* 5.14 = 251 SB). In this context, Lucceius's use of a standard opening connoted that he was taking pains to produce a serious communication on a sensitive matter. During the civil war, Cicero's son-in-law Dolabella had recourse to it in a letter exhorting Cicero to detach himself from Pompey (*Fam.* 9.9 = 157 SB). In the second half of the opening he worked in mention of Cicero's daughter and wife: "If you are well, I'm glad; I am well, and our Tullia quite well. Terentia hasn't been so good..." (s. v. g. v. et Tullia nostra recte v. Terentia minus belle habuit...). The purpose of this preamble, as the letter shortly makes explicit, was to reassure Cicero that Dolabella was writing in a spirit of dutiful affection (*pie*) and not as Caesar's partisan. In this case, the conventional opening suggested the transparency and good faith of the letter writer.

Other instances of it can be similarly elucidated in terms of context, but the hardest cases to interpret are presented by a series of letters from Cicero to his wife. Not only is the appearance of the formula surprising in a letter series, but most of the letters to Terentia in which it occurs date from a year or two before Cicero divorced her. That circumstance, taken together with the formality of the preamble and the lack of warmth in the messages, led Adams to infer that Cicero "was clearly delivering a rebuff" when he began letters to Terentia in this way.[47] But that somewhat misstates the effect. Though conventional, the opening does not inherently convey distance, as the letters of Lucceius and Dolabella illustrate. In Cicero's letters to his wife, in fact, it is often combined with the heading "to his very own Terentia," a gesture of intimacy Cicero would not have allowed himself if he were delivering an overt rebuff. Here as elsewhere, the formula is best seen as a warrant of epistolary propriety. Although much of its communicative value had leached away by Cicero's time, it always carried the sanction of formal correctness. Why a letter writer would want to underscore the correctness of a message naturally varied with the nature of the message: an authoritative communiqué from a general, straight talk from an old friend, affectionate regard from a son-in-law.

And in letters to Terentia? Perhaps it was a tic. Two-thirds of the seventeen letters in which Cicero uses the formula are addressed to her, and the less he found to say to her, the more often he resorted to it. From his perspective, the *suus* formula and the conventional opening—and these are not the only marks of politeness the letters contain—no doubt signified civility.[48] But any mannerism, conscious or not, tempts interpretation from the other side. The problem with Cicero's letters from his wife's vantage point might have been that they communicated little more than civility. The epistolary proprieties would have sounded not so much brusque as hollow.

The two remaining conventions of a Roman letter were employed at the close, though neither had as firm a footing as the corresponding elements of modern letters. Overall, about 20 percent of the letters in the Ciceronian corpus wind up with an expression generally translated as "good-bye" or "farewell."[49] The key word literally means "be well" (*vale*) and is identical to the key word in the opening formula (although at the end of a letter it never seems to be abbreviated). The polite solicitude about a correspondent's health that provided a pathway into the letter thus served for an exit as well.

Despite its relatively low frequency in the corpus, the valedictory formula was clearly felt to be appropriate no matter what degree of status or intimacy the recipient of a letter enjoyed. Cicero uses it in letters to his brother, his wife, his freedman, his confidant Atticus, grandees like Caesar and Varro, and lesser friends like Paetus. Nor does it appear to be meaningful whether a letter writer opts to employ or omit the formula. Whereas the end of a modern letter is traditionally marked by a sign-off phrase such as "sincerely," "love," or "best regards," closure in the letters of Cicero and his friends was less cut-and-dried. It was signaled more often by closural themes than formulas. The writer may look forward to the pleasure of a letter in response or of a visit soon to be shared; ask to be remembered to someone in the addressee's household, pass along greetings from someone in the writer's own household, or commend a friend; beg to be allowed to perform services beyond any that could reasonably be expected; or call upon the addressee to reaffirm the affection that they both cherish for each other. The business of cementing ties that was discussed in chapter 1 accounts for many of the themes sounded at the end of letters. The close was also where a letter writer was most likely to say something substantive about the addressee's health if circumstances required it. The "farewell" ending was therefore only one among several possible modes of closure and no more privileged than any other.

That having been said, the fact remains that the use of it shows some sharp variations from one addressee to another. The overall frequency of 20 percent gives little sense of the degree of fluctuation. The formula occurs in less than 10 percent of Cicero's letters to Atticus, for example. But what is truly striking is that seventeen of those instances, or a good 40 percent, are concentrated in a single book of letters (book 11), most of which date from a period after the battle of Pharsalia when Cicero was detained at Brundisium. In other words, Cicero used the formula in only about 5 percent of his letters to Atticus, except for one stressful period in which he used it about 60 percent of the time. It is difficult to explain this transient preference as anything but a tic of which Cicero himself may have been unaware.[50]

Cicero also favored the valedictory formula in letters to his brother, where it occurs about a third of the time. Yet that frequency pales beside its use in letters to Terentia, all twenty-four of which have some form of it. And lest one be tempted to interpret repetition of this formula, too, as a sign of chilliness, it occurs in letters written long before the marriage was under strain, and in every one of Cicero's twenty-one letters to his freedman Tiro. Use of the formula is more strangely skewed in these two series than anywhere else in the corpus.

Terentia and Tiro are both projected as valetudinarians in Cicero's discourse with them, and so, to the extent that the "farewell" formula echoes a real concern about health, it had perhaps a stronger motivation in letters to them than to most others. But that alone would not explain such a sharp spike in its frequency. Terentia and Tiro were not *always* ailing, after all, and both managed to live exceptionally long lives.

Another peculiarity that may be relevant is that Cicero fiddles with the formula in these two series more often than he does anywhere else. Not that the fiddling is complicated. Usually it amounts only to some form of repetition. For example, in the letters to Terentia, he closes with "Farewell...farewell" (valete...valete, *Fam.* 14.2.4 = 7 SB); "Take care to be well. Farewell" (cura ut valeas. vale, *Fam.* 14.8 = 164 SB); "Take care for your well-being. Farewell" (valetudinem cures. vale, *Fam.* 14.9 = 161 SB). And in the letters to Tiro, he writes, "I want you well first for your sake, then for mine...farewell" (te valere tua causa primum volo, tum mea...vale, *Fam.* 16.3.2 = 122 SB); "Farewell...farewell, farewell and thrive...farewell" (vale...vale, vale et salve...vale, *Fam.* 16.4.4 = 123 SB); "Again and again, take care to be well...again and again, farewell" (tu etiam atque etiam cura ut valeas...etiam atque etiam vale, *Fam.* 16.11.3 = 143 SB). But artless though it is, this doubling is found in fully half the letters in each series, while being almost unexampled in letters to anyone else.

An ending like "Take care for your well-being. Farewell" cannot fail to make anyone who encounters it acutely aware that in Latin letters, the word *vale* teeters between sentiment and empty expression. I suggest that in the letters to Terentia and Tiro, Cicero himself was particularly conscious of this problem and trying to compensate. Yet his freedman and his wife were not correspondents who he believed required the same degree of investment that others required. As noted earlier, his letters to them are not written in the rhythmic prose he employs with the great majority of his correspondents.[51] Furthermore, their status as members of his household precluded many of the themes of closure that he employed with others. To his mind, the relationships with Terentia and Tiro did not need cementing. To personalize the ending of letters to them, he was therefore content to do the equivalent of underlining a stock phrase ("Farewell—literally"). The high frequency and awkward repetitions of the formula can be explained partly by the dearth of things to talk about apart from health, and partly by Cicero's unwillingness to make an extra effort.

The last stereotypical element of a Roman letter was the dateline, in the format "(Letter) sent (literally, "given," *data*—the origin of our word "date") on such-and-such a day."[52] The word for "letter" was always omitted, and often the word for "sent" as well. On the other hand, letter writers sometimes made a point of recording, by degrees of scrupulosity, the place of dispatch, the hour, and (very rarely in the Ciceronian corpus) the year.

Like all other elements except the heading, the dateline was optional. Only about 15 percent of letters in the corpus are dated in this way. For that reason, and perhaps also because the dateline occurred at the end rather than the beginning of Roman letters, it did not acquire the reference function it has today, when the date is the ordinary means by which to identify a particular letter. When Romans wished to identify an item of correspondence, they were as likely to cite the place of origin, the bearer, or the content as the date.

One reason that letters in the Ciceronian corpus do not feature a dateline more frequently is that the writers often found occasion to specify the date in connection with some topic covered earlier in the letter, for example, "But the Senate will be in session today, that is, October 1st" (sed senatus hodie erat futurus, id est Kal. Oct., *Att.* 4.17.4 = 91 SB). If that was the case, there was no need to repeat the information at the end. In many cases, too, it sufficed that the content of a letter indicated an approximate time of writing. More often still, a writer would have seen no reason to communicate a date. The moment of writing rarely seems an important detail until an epistolary present has become the past. There were even circumstances which could make it advisable to suppress the date. The fact that none of the eighty letters of recommendation in book 13 of the *Letters to Friends* is dated probably reflects a wish on the part of both recommender and recommendee to keep the endorsement open-ended.[53]

Because the dateline was generically standard and yet not required, patterns of use differed from one writer to another. Cicero observes that Atticus habitually dated his letters (*Att.* 3.23.1 = 68 SB), and Suetonius reports that the emperor Augustus made a point of recording the hour as well as the day of dispatch on his (*Aug.* 50). In Cicero's own letters, the dateline occurs a little less often on average than in the collection as a whole. But as in the case of the valedictory formula, an average does not disclose how much his practice fluctuated. Half of the letters to Tiro and 80 percent of those to Terentia include a dateline, showing once again that Cicero was more scrupulous about epistolary format with them than with anyone else. But whatever motives may lie behind his use of other conventions, he had a strong practical reason for dating letters to them. In both series, the use of a dateline coincided with periods in which Cicero was abroad. A knowledge of the date of dispatch enabled the recipient of a letter to calculate how much time it would take to write back, and also where to write, if the place of dispatch was added, as it is in many of these letters.[54] Cicero counted on being able to maintain contact with his wife because she was a principal conduit through whom letters from persons in Rome reached him, and with Tiro because he was Cicero's most trusted secretary.

In letters that Cicero addressed to others, too, and in letters that he received from others, a dateline signified that the writer was in transit in the vast majority of cases. In letters from Plancus, the two Brutuses, and other generals in the field,[55] it is so common as to seem virtually a military affectation. But the use most evocative of symbolic meaning occurs in the letters that Cicero wrote to Atticus while he was detained in southern Italy after Pharsalia. He was away from home, and at least technically he retained the rank of army commander, and so the use of a dateline would not have seemed out of place. But the point of it could not have been to keep Atticus current with his whereabouts. Since Cicero was stuck at Brundisium for nearly a year, there was no doubt about where he was to be found. Yet he dated 60 percent of the letters that he sent to Atticus from there. If under ordinary circumstances a dateline implies that the writer is on the move, in this case it seems to express more a sense of alienation and uprootedness.[56]

Engagement of the Addressee

Even if a letter came stripped of all the generic trappings just discussed, however, no reader could mistake it for any other sort of text. What constitutes a
letter is ultimately the "I-you" polarity that frames it. Underlying every other
statement that it makes is the message "I am communicating (something) to
you." The following chapters will examine some characteristic forms that the
"something" takes in Cicero's correspondence. Here I want to focus on the
personal frame of the letter, and more particularly on the "you." Writers project
some sort of self-image in all forms of writing, but in letters, it is the construction
of the addressee that is most distinctive and most important to the interaction.

One indication that letters have a meaning beyond anything they say is that a
lack of things to say presents no obstacle to writing them. The refrain "I have nothing
to write about" is common in Cicero's letters, as in this short note to Atticus:

> Though I have nothing to write to you about, I write anyway because
> it lets me imagine I am chatting with you. We have Nicias and
> Valerius staying here. We are looking forward [literally, "were looking
> forward"] to a letter from you this morning. Maybe there will be a
> second one this afternoon, if your Epirus correspondence doesn't get
> in the way—on which I am not the one to intrude. I am sending
> [literally, "sent"] you letters for Marcianus and Montanus. Please
> include them in the same packet, if you haven't already sent it off.

> *Ego, etsi nihil habeo quod ad te scribam, scribo tamen quia tecum loqui*
> *videor. hic nobiscum sunt Nicias et Valerius. hodie tuas litteras*
> *exspectabamus matutinas. erunt fortasse alterae postmeridianae, nisi te*
> *Epiroticae litterae impediunt, quas ego non interpello. misi ad te epistulas*
> *ad Marcianum et ad Montanum. eas in eundem fasciculum velim addas,*
> *nisi forte iam dedisti.*[57]

The slightness of this message is obvious. Not even the information about the
visit from Nicias and Valerius is new, since Cicero had mentioned that to
Atticus a couple of days earlier (*Att.* 12.51.1 = 293 SB). The letters that he asks
Atticus to forward are likewise a nod in the direction of something mentioned
earlier. Marcianus and Montanus were hometown relations on tour with
Cicero's son in Greece. Cicero had asked Atticus to intervene over a money difficulty that arose during their trip (*Att.* 12.52.1 = 294 SB). But neither that nor
any other topical concern motivates this note, which communicates a desire for
contact for its own sake. Cicero imagines a conversation and savors the prospect
of a letter without seeming to care what either is about.

The near-absence of substantive content has the effect of throwing the
"I-you" frame of the note into high relief. A third of its fifty-seven words are

first- or second-person verbs or pronouns: eleven in the first person, seven in the second. But whereas expressions in the first person outnumber those in the second, the rhetoric of the text is concentrated mainly on developing an image of the latter. The opening sentence twice balances a "you" in the predicate against a subject "I." But with his very first words ("though I have nothing to write"), Cicero deprecates his letter as an empty offering, whose only value is that, on his side at least, it conjures an illusion of Atticus's presence. What he has to offer presents a sorry contrast with the copious letters of Atticus to which he, or he and his guests, look forward.

Cicero plays to Atticus's self-esteem in other ways as well. Instead of saying plainly that he wants Atticus to write again in the afternoon, he makes a tentative forecast that leaves unstated both his desire to get a letter and Atticus's need to write one: "Perhaps there will be a second letter." And he quickly takes two steps back even from that veiled request, raising on Atticus's behalf the objection that Atticus may have more pressing business to attend to, and disavowing any wish to distract him from it. The closing request is similarly circumspect. When Cicero asks Atticus to forward letters to Marcianus and Montanus, he is careful to use a Latin equivalent of "please," and he suggests that it is a matter of no great importance if the letters have to wait until Atticus's next posting to Greece.

One last detail requires comment. Two verbs in Cicero's letter that would most naturally stand in the present tense if the letter had been composed in English are in fact past tenses, as noted in the translation above. *Exspectabamus* ("we were looking forward") and *misi* ("I sent") are so-called "epistolary tenses," which represent a shift out of the time frame of the letter writer and into that of the addressee.[58] Cicero *is* looking forward to letters from Atticus at the moment when he writes his own letter, as he *is* sending two enclosures with it. But rather than present the actions from his own perspective, he adopts the perspective of Atticus, for whom those actions will have receded into the past by the time he reads the letter.

The use of epistolary tenses is not systematic in Latin letters. On the contrary, as other verbs in this very letter indicate, writers ordinarily keep to their own time frame. Since tense shifting is a hallmark of the genre yet never required, it is available for purposes other than expressing time, and often it serves to signal deference to the viewpoint of one's interlocutor. Cicero shifts tense just at the point when he tells Atticus that he is waiting for a letter from him.[59] By stepping out of his own time and into that of Atticus, he tempers his request, tacitly inviting Atticus to put his own perspective ahead of Cicero's. (The second tense shift also occurs in connection with a request.)

The courtesies and hedges woven into this note are readily identifiable as politeness strategies, about which a large literature has now accumulated in the field of sociolinguistics.[60] It would be impractical here to try to catalog all relevant devices used in the Ciceronian corpus: there are far too many of them. The

outline of politeness strategies provided by Brown and Levinson (1987) is extensive enough to serve as a guide to much of Cicero's practice. And to the extent
that linguistic politeness can be reduced to a set of fixed expressions, some of
the formulas most common in Latin have been compiled by Cugusi.[61] But
readers of the letters are apt to find that they do not need much outside
assistance to appreciate this aspect of Cicero's correspondence. We intuit how
we are being treated by others in letters, phone calls, or conversations more
quickly than we process anything else they say. It is not difficult to redirect this
social expertise when we read or hear something in which the reference of a
"you" has changed from ourselves to someone else.

Yet in one important respect, the courtesy displayed in letters between
Cicero and his friends probably does not correspond with our own experience
of it. As Hall (1996, 19) has noted, "Cicero and his contemporaries seem to
employ polite expressions of goodwill with one another far more extravagantly
and expansively than do most modern Anglo-Saxon societies." Furthermore,
there is reason to suspect that elite Romans cultivated a higher standard of
politeness in their letters than they did in face-to-face encounters, although
without recordings of the latter, the point can never be proved. But at least it is
true that Cicero showed more respect to his friend Servius Sulpicius in personal
letters than in one of his speeches.[62] The same applies to Servilius Isauricus,
and even to Cicero's enemy Mark Antony.[63] In one case we can catch a glimpse
of the difference in tone between letters and a face-to-face discussion of the
same subject. Early in the year 49, Cicero and Caesar exchanged a series of
polite letters about whether Cicero would consent to serve in the Senate under
Caesar's regime. But when they finally met to discuss the matter, they had a
conversation that Cicero describes as blunt on both sides.[64]

If Roman letters tend to be more polite than live exchanges, it is probably
not just because writers can manage words more easily than talkers can. In
Cicero's milieu, letters typically span periods of separation when relationships
have become more precarious than ever, and therefore require extra care. The
politeness of letters is an effort to mount a sort of idealized reality until normal
social processes can be resumed.

But it is a more pervasive phenomenon than the model of politeness dominant in current theory seems to account for. Brown and Levinson view politeness as behavior that is transactional and largely compensatory. It consists of
mechanisms to offset particular actions ("face-threatening acts") by one person
that are likely to infringe another person's self-esteem or to encroach on another's autonomy. There is no question that this model accounts for many interactions documented in the correspondence of Cicero. The letters contain an
abundance of advice, criticism, and requests sweetened in all the ways that
Brown and Levinson describe. What the model does not explain is the amount
of apparently gratuitous politeness that the letters present when no face-
threatening acts are involved.[65] The following letter (*Fam.* 7.20 = 333 SB) to

Cicero's longtime friend Trebatius is a good example. It was written in the summer of 44, as Cicero was about to resume a voyage down the west coast of Italy after a short layover in Trebatius's hometown:

Cicero to Trebatius, greetings:

I feel the more fond of Velia because I feel how fond it is of you. But why should I say "you" (who is *not* fond of you?): I swear that people miss even your man Rufio as much as if he were somebody like you or me. Not that I blame you for transferring him up to your construction site. Even if Velia is no vile match for the Lupercal, still, I prefer your spot there [in Rome] to all that you have here.

But: if you pay me your customary heed, you will hang on to your family estates down here—the people of Velia are somewhat nervous—and not renounce the noble River Hales nor quit the Papirian manse. True, the place has its lotus, which is known to entrap even chance visitors—though you could improve the sight-lines if you chopped it down. But in these times especially, it seems opportune to retain as a refuge, first of all a town of people who cherish you, and second the home and lands you have, and in a remote, salubrious, and lovely location besides. And I believe there is something in it for me too, my dear Trebatius.

But you will stay well, and keep an eye on my affairs, and expect me back before the dead of winter, gods willing.

I got from Sextus Fadius, Nicon's student, a book titled *Nicon on Gourmandise*. What an amiable physician, and how responsive I am to such a regimen! But our friend Bassus kept me in the dark about this book—though not you, evidently.

The wind is picking up. Take care of yourself.

July 20th, from Velia.

Cicero Trebatio s.

Amabilior mihi Velia fuit quod te ab ea sensi amari. sed quid ego dicam "te," quem quis non amat? Rufio medius fidius tuus ita desiderabatur ut si esset unus e nobis. sed te ego non reprehendo qui illum ad aedificationem tuam traduxeris. quamquam enim Velia non est vilior quam Lupercal, tamen istuc malo quam haec omnia.

Tu, si me audies quem soles, has paternas possessiones tenebis (nescio quid enim Velienses verebantur), neque Haletem, nobilem amnem, relinques nec Papirianam domum deseres. quamquam illa quidem habet lotum, a quo etiam advenae teneri solent; quem tamen si excideris, multum prospexeris. sed in primis opportunum videtur, his praesertim temporibus, habere perfugium, primum eorum urbem quibus carus sis, deinde tuam domum tuosque agros, eaque remoto, salubri, amoeno loco; idque etiam mea interesse, mi Trebati, arbitror.

sed valebis meaque negotia videbis meque dis iuvantibus ante brumam exspectabis.

    ego a Sex. Fadio, Niconis discipulo, librum abstuli Νίκωνος περὶ πολυφαγίας. *o medicum suavem meque docilem ad hanc disciplinam! sed Bassus noster me de hoc libro celavit; te quidem non videtur.*

    ventus increbrescit. cura, ut valeas.

    XIII. Kal. Sext. Velia.

What prompted this letter is not made explicit. Cicero gives no indication that he is responding to a letter received from Trebatius, and he does not write to pass along personal or public news. The one request he makes (that Trebatius look after Cicero's affairs in Rome) can only be a reminder of arrangements made before his departure, since he says nothing specific on the subject. He does give Trebatius advice about the latter's property in southern Italy, but on careful examination, the offer of advice looks contrived. The possibility that Trebatius might sell is presented only as a local rumor, not something that Cicero has heard from Trebatius himself. The subtext of the passage concerns Cicero rather than Trebatius, in any case.

The letter would have a plausible motivation if we supposed that Cicero was writing to acknowledge Trebatius's hospitality in absentia after a stop at his place in Velia.[66] But the manner so overwhelms the matter of this message that it seems more important to try to understand that than to pinpoint the occasion of writing. Like the note to Atticus, this letter is geared mainly toward courtship of the addressee. The "I-you" frame is if anything more salient here than there, and polite strategies are again in evidence. Cicero softens the request that Trebatius look after his affairs by imagining the desired action as a future reality, as in the letter to Atticus, and he subordinates his request to the injunction that Trebatius first look after himself. Epistolary tenses likewise crop up.[67]

Yet Cicero wields politeness more relentlessly here than in the letter to Atticus. He treats Trebatius to the rhythmic prose that he regularly employs in formal writing, including letters to persons outside his domestic circle.[68] And the expression of politeness goes beyond locutions such as "not that I blame you," "if you pay me heed," and "my dear Trebatius." Every topic on which Cicero touches is chosen to promote good feeling. He compliments Trebatius on his estate in Velia and on the house he is building in Rome. He credits him with enough literary culture to catch an allusion to the *Odyssey* that some classical scholars have missed.[69] He expatiates on the affection with which Trebatius is regarded by his Velian compatriots. He enthuses over the science-based gourmandise to which he was treated while a guest at Trebatius's house. Even Cicero's jokes about the lotus and the food have a softer tone than his jokes in earlier letters. Ten years before, when he sent the young Trebatius to Gaul to seek his fortune with Caesar, his banter often had a mocking edge, but now the tone is respectful. There is nothing injurious in this letter that polite strategies would be needed to offset, yet it is awash in politeness from start to finish.

The manner is the message of this text, and it bears witness to a reversal of fortune. Trebatius had long since outgrown his role as Cicero's protégé. In Gaul he was taken into Caesar's inner circle, and after Caesar was killed he continued to maneuver adroitly as Caesar's partisans split into feuding groups. Eventually he aligned himself with Octavian, who had launched his challenge to Mark Antony's hegemony a couple of months before this letter was written.[70] Cicero, by contrast, was stymied at this point. In his view, the ides of March had eliminated one tyrant only to make way for the more brutal tyranny of Antony. Isolated and intimidated, he was sailing from Rome to Greece, where he planned to sit out the year of Antony's consulate.[71]

None of this background is given explicit comment in the letter. But it lurks in the reference to "these times." And when Cicero writes about enjoying the love of one's compatriots and having a congenial place of refuge, he is drawing an implicit contrast between Trebatius's situation and his own, as he virtually admits ("I believe there is something in it for me too").[72] The politeness lavished on Trebatius carries a message that he is in a position to be helpful, and that his help may be needed now that Cicero is short of other allies.[73]

To illustrate how the personal frame contributes to the effect of a letter, I have chosen two letters that consist of almost nothing except their frame. With little message content to distract attention, they show particularly well how Cicero strives to engage the goodwill of his addressees. Not many letters communicate the ardent politeness of the letter to Trebatius, but all engage the addressee in some way.[74] Even a letter that did not make the least gesture toward its addressee after the heading would count as a mode of engagement, because it would be interpreted as a snub. To vary the frame metaphor, letters are stereophonic. Alongside the message channel runs a stream of signals ranging from polite turns of phrase to tokens of care in writing to outright compliments and declarations of affection (or their opposites). That is the channel to which any reader is instantly attuned, and it presents another set of elements that invite interpretation along with the content of the letter itself.

Controlling the Frame

One last point to be made about the epistolary frame can be seen as a corollary of its focus on the addressee. The letters of Cicero tend to underrepresent engagements he has with persons apart from the addressee. But what is meant by this claim, and why it is worth bearing in mind, is best understood by thinking again about the kind of society in which Roman letter writers were based.

At most times in his life, Cicero received a constant and broad stream of information, rumor, and opinion. As a senior member of the Senate, he was among the first to hear of official news. But he was also privy to a great deal of unofficial information. Much of it came to him live, through conversations in which he engaged during his morning open house, his perambulation of the Forum, and dinner parties at night. The daily round of visits and consultations continued even when he left the capital to sojourn in one of his houses on the coast. He also received an enormous number of letters. It can always be assumed, therefore, that input from many sources contributed to what he thought, said, and did.

Some of his letters lift the curtain on this background. This is especially true when he discusses money matters in his correspondence with Atticus, who often functioned as his business agent. In a brief message about an estate to which Cicero had been named part-heir, for example, he lets Atticus know that he has already discussed arrangements for disposing of the property with one of his joint heirs, with an agent for another, and with a businessman he often consulted about his investments (Att. 13.37a = 340 SB). Atticus needed such information if he was to represent Cicero effectively, and especially if, as in this case, he was expected to follow up on negotiations that Cicero had already begun.

Cicero is also more forthcoming with Atticus than with anyone else except his brother about contacts he has had on the subject of politics. In a letter written when he had hopes of being granted a triumph for his operations in Cilicia, he tells Atticus about encouraging letters he has received from friends in the Senate, and also about letters he has written to both prospective supporters and opponents (Att. 7.1.7–8 = 124 SB). Again, as in letters about his financial business, he is especially likely to refer to his other contacts when something has arisen that he wants Atticus to pursue with them.

Finally, Cicero makes a point of letting many of his correspondents know about communications he has had with Pompey. In this case, however, his purpose is usually to parade his connectedness rather than to convey specific information. After Caesar becomes dominant in Roman politics, Cicero begins to flaunt connections with him in the same way. The conflict between his desire to be seen hobnobbing with the powerful and his reluctance to share information is perfectly captured in a letter in which he tells Caelius, "over several days I was involved in conversations with Pompey that focused exclusively on politics. They neither can nor should be put down in writing. But know this much: Pompey is an outstanding patriot, and ready in heart and thought for every step that must be taken on the political front" (cum Pompeio compluris dies nullis in aliis nisi de re publica sermonibus versatus sum. quae nec possunt scribi nec scribenda sunt; tantum habeto, civem egregium esse Pompeium et ad omnia quae providenda sunt in re publica et animo et consilio paratum, Fam. 2.8.2 = 80 SB).[75]

Cicero's chariness with sources is all the more apparent if his letters are read alongside those he receives from Caelius. Caelius gossips uninhibitedly about capital scandals and scheming behind the scenes. In *Fam.* 8.10 = 87 SB, for example, he tells Cicero about private interests that have caused the consuls to stall Senate action on Parthia, and about plans that his senatorial colleagues Curio and Furnius intend to put into effect when they take office as tribunes at the end of the year. In *Fam.* 8.11 = 91 SB, he reports at length how with Furnius and Lentulus he has lobbied the consuls as well as Curio and Hirrus to support a decree honoring Cicero. At *Fam.* 8.12 = 98 SB, he describes the personal politicking on which he has embarked as a result of a feud with Appius Pulcher.

Cicero's letters to Caelius, on the other hand, rarely volunteer information about contacts with others, and what little he does say is guarded. Apart from the mention of his conversation with Pompey, he refers to letters or meetings involving only three other people. On one occasion, he tells Caelius about an apologetic note he has written to Appius about the marriage of Tullia to an enemy of Appius (*Fam.* 2.15.2 = 96 SB). He shares this information because it was Caelius who had warned him about Appius's annoyance in the first place. On another occasion, at the end of a letter, he tells Caelius that he has encountered a mutual friend of theirs (*Fam.* 2.8.3 = 80 SB). To advert to ties shared with an addressee is a regular closing strategy of Roman letters. Finally, in response to a letter from Caelius chiding him for siding with Pompey at the start of the civil war, Cicero recalls a visit he received from an outspoken Pompeian partisan (*Fam.* 2.16.3 = 154 SB). He uses it to argue his aversion from either side. In each case, a contact is disclosed only if something in the context calls for it.

The comparative insulation of one source from another may be observed at another point as well. Most of Cicero's correspondence with Caelius dates from a period of about sixteen months in which he also happened to be corresponding regularly with Appius Pulcher and with Atticus. Over that time, the three of them receive a total of forty-seven letters.[76] Yet only once does Cicero allude to his correspondence with Caelius in letters to Appius (*Fam.* 3.10.5 = 73 SB) or vice versa (*Fam.* 2.15.2 = 96 SB), and to neither does he mention his exchanges with Atticus. Only twice does he mention to Atticus anything he has heard from Appius or Caelius (*Att.* 6.1.2 and 21 = 115 SB), and in both cases, it concerned information from Appius and Caelius about themselves. Contrast *Att.* 6.9.5 = 123 SB, where Cicero queries Atticus about a political rumor he has heard, without specifying that Caelius was his source (*Fam.* 8.14.4 = 97 SB).

The pattern of the Caelius correspondence is repeated in many other parts of the collection. Cicero wrote both to his brother and to Trebatius when they were serving with Caesar in Gaul, and often via the same couriers—thirteen letters to Trebatius and eleven to Quintus.[77] But he never tells Quintus anything about his correspondence with Trebatius. And in letters to Trebatius, he alludes only twice to letters received from Quintus: once by way of complaining that he has received no letters from Trebatius, and once to report that he has thanked Quintus for a favor done to Trebatius.[78]

Even when Cicero is writing to a fellow senator about a political matter, he tends to present it in abstraction from the part played by others, as though it involved chiefly himself and his correspondent. In the early months of the civil war, when a colleague consulted him about the advisability of leaving Italy to join Pompey, Cicero replied without reference to discussions we know he was having with others on this very question (*Fam.* 4.2 = 151 SB). Although most of Cicero's letters to Curio are remarkably bare of political details, in one he asks Curio to support a protégé of his who was campaigning for the consulate (*Fam.* 2.6 = 50 SB). His appeal is framed entirely in terms of his relationship with the candidate and with Curio, and it identifies no one else involved in the campaign.

But the most instructive case is the correspondence that Cicero conducted with Lentulus Spinther when Lentulus's enemies in the Senate were trying to circumscribe his governorship and then strip him of it. The whole point of Cicero's letters is to demonstrate zeal on Lentulus's behalf, and he duly mentions visits he has paid to Pompey, resolutions he has cosponsored with other Senate leaders, and consultations he has kept up with Lentulus's friends and family. He reports at length on the formalities of Senate debate as it affected Lentulus's interests. And yet he gives away so little about who—apart from Cicero—was actually doing what that Lentulus eventually had to ask him about it.[79] Moreover, Cicero says almost nothing about the networking in which he engaged to improve his own political position at the same time that he was working on behalf of Lentulus. Not until his last letter to Lentulus does he relate how during this period he came to ally himself with Crassus, Pompey, and especially Caesar. And the only reason he finally does so is that Lentulus had already learned from others of Cicero's volte-face and had demanded an explanation.[80]

Under certain circumstances, Cicero is prepared to let recipients of his letters know about exchanges he has had with others in his network. But the circumstances are limited, as the examples considered indicate. Cicero does not readily *volunteer* this kind of information. No doubt one reason is that the dyadic frame of a letter always encourages a writer to magnify the addressee and to downplay other attachments. But there were also practical advantages in screening one's contacts from an addressee. The more successfully one could isolate the issues discussed in letters from persons, the easier it became to set any discussion on the plane of principle, which was Cicero's favorite way of dealing with every issue. Concealing the input of others also made it easier to offer an assessment of the issues as the fruit of one's own political insight. Finally and perhaps most important, it kept correspondents from knowing who had one's ear and how one was aligned at any given time. But, of course, all those advantages of the letter frame disappeared as soon as letters were juxtaposed in a published collection, which introduced a new frame that Cicero did not anticipate.

The elements considered in this chapter have brought us from the situation of writing into the letter itself, and yet as generic features, they obviously do not take us far. Although they were subject to the writer's control in the sense that they presented themselves as choices, the options were limited. Every letter had to be handwritten by somebody and inscribed on some kind of writing material; every letter began and ended somehow, and posited some image of the person to whom it was addressed. A reader was rarely in a position to know what a letter would be about until such universals had given way to particulars. In the second half of this book, I will focus on three themes that involve us with epistolary content.

II

EPISTOLARY PREOCCUPATIONS

The Letters and Literature

For explanatory power, the idea of the literary would seem to have sunk in our day to about the level of phlogiston. A generation of critics has questioned whether it is a property that can be predicated of texts rather than of the social conditioning or mental processes of those who read them, or whether indeed it means anything at all.[1] I borrow the word "literature" for the chapter title nevertheless, not from any wish to rehabilitate it, but because its expansivity makes it a handy umbrella category.[2] This chapter will discuss letters that may be called "literary" in various senses having mostly to do with their affinities to books, in that they are written to or by the writers of books, they are about books or invoke them, or they themselves acquire or aspire to book form. The direction of argument will be clearer if I declare at the outset that my goal is not to assess whether "literary" is a more appropriate label for one than for another of these attributes, or whether it is the ideal label for any. Rather, it is to bring to bear an admittedly loose set of criteria that can still be exploited to improve our appreciation of one side of Cicero's correspondence. And second, my focus here as throughout this book is on the letters, not on Cicero per se. I am concerned with what the letters do, not with the performance of their writers on any wider stage. Because we know that Cicero was intensely engaged with literature as both reader and creator, we may expect that the letters will reveal him to us in that light. But in fact, they afford only a partial and obstructed view of his literary interests. The following pages will illustrate that point and try to explain it. But before examining the part that literary activities play in his correspondence, it will be necessary to discuss a more basic idea of what makes a letter a literary letter.

Literary versus Ordinary Letters

The most elusive sense of the expression "a literary letter" has been the one most often discussed. It refers to qualities of a letter that are associated more with its form than its message content, and it goes back to a distinction that Adolf Deissmann laid down more than a century ago.[3] Only a personal letter written with no thought of anyone beyond the party to whom it is addressed is a true letter, he held. A letter aimed at an audience beyond the ostensible addressee is a secondary and artificial phenomenon, which should be designated as a "literary letter" or an "epistle" (the term *Epistel* being chosen precisely for its exotic ring in German). The question for us is what this distinction can contribute to an understanding of Cicero's letters.

Deissmann's treatment of letters was aprioristic and idealizing in the extreme. A given letter fell into either the one category or the other, with nothing in between. Or rather, the possibility of a hybrid—a letter genuinely meant for the addressee but written with some thought for others who might read it, too—was relegated to the status of being simply a bad letter. Deissmann did not claim that his distinction between "letter" and "epistle" was based on the way the corresponding words were actually applied in Latin.[4] He was careful to stipulate that the difference between them could not be determined from formal qualities alone, nor from the mere fact that a letter text later happened to be gathered into a book and published. Everything depended on whether the letter writer intended to communicate only with the person or persons addressed, or with an audience beyond.

The concept of authorial intention was cast into disgrace a couple of generations after Deissmann, and it would be a hardy critic today who would claim to know, or even care, what an author (if there was an author) was thinking. Yet the distinction between a literary letter and an ordinary letter persists in criticism.[5] It is freely invoked even by those who would reject out of hand the meaning it had for Deissmann. If the term "literary letter" is to retain any value in the discussion of Cicero's letters, however, it must refer to something about them that can be reified outside the mind of the writer. Four such criteria can be tested against the Ciceronian corpus.

1. *Publication.* Since most letters that are written are *not* published, publication can serve as a prima facie marker of the special status that makes a letter "literary." As a matter of literary history, publication certainly does confer status, not just by making letters available to general readers, but in thereby bringing them into the company of other texts that readers read. The act of publication made Cicero's correspondence literary by making it a literary exemplar, to be assimilated in due course by Pliny and Petrarch and others. The merit of this test is that it is relatively simple and not absurd.

But like many a simple test, that of publication has its shortcomings. One consequence is that if the act of publication sufficed to make Cicero's letters literary, it should have had the same effect on, say, the letters of Vatinius, which were published alongside Cicero's and which actually outnumber Cicero's to him. That Vatinius was thereby transformed into a literary exemplar is a more difficult idea to swallow, especially in light of Velleius Paterculus's assertion that the foulness of Vatinius's intellect was a fit match for the deformity of his body (2.69.4). But more to the point, the publication of letters may occur under circumstances so remote from a writer's knowledge or control that it is irrelevant to the writing of them. What we want to know is how the possibility of publication impinged on Cicero as he was composing letters. We have no way of knowing whether he did in fact publish any of them (though for the reasons given in chapter 2, I doubt that he did), and in the prevailing critical climate it would be taboo to ask whether he wrote with the intention of publishing. But it seems allowable to take one step back from that question, and to consider what prospects a person in Cicero's position could have had that his letters *might* be published.

What seems obvious is that letters were the least likely part of a Roman writer's output to end up in general circulation (which probably holds true for most authors of today as well). Cicero himself paid lip service both in public and in private to the idea that letters are expected to remain confidential.[6] At the same time, however, he was well aware that writings which their authors made no move to disseminate did sometimes find their way into the hands of the public. That had happened with an essay by the orator Antonius in the generation before him (*De Orat.* 1.94) and with a speech of his own (*Att.* 3.12.2 = 57 SB). He says that it happened even with an exchange of letters between himself and Licinius Calvus on the subject of oratory.[7] Cicero was also aware of precedents for the publication of whole letter collections, most notably the letters of Aristotle, who was newly in vogue in the Rome of his day.[8] He believed that the Platonic collection was authentic as well, and he quoted from it and from Epicurus's letters.[9] In his own language, he may have been familiar with a collection of letters by Cato the Elder.[10] But so far as we know, there was no precedent, in terms of either scale or type, for the edition of a correspondence like his own. On balance, then, Cicero could well have thought it conceivable that letters of his might be published, with or without his cooperation. But the publication of letters was still unusual enough in his day that he probably did not hold that possibility constantly in view as he wrote—surely less so than a British aristocrat of the eighteenth century, when epistolary collections had become a fashion.

Moreover, even if the possibility of publication sometimes occurred to Cicero, there is no reason to think that it altered the way he wrote letters. In a letter to Trebonius about the published exchange with Calvus, he says, "I wrote that letter [or "those letters"] to Calvus no more thinking that it [or "they"] would get out than this letter you are reading now. We have one way of writing what we think will be read only by people to whom it is sent, another way of writing what we think will be read by many" (ego illas Calvo litteras misi non plus quam has quas nunc legis existimans exituras; aliter enim scribimus quod eos solos quibus mittimus, aliter quod multos lecturos putamus, *Fam.* 15.21.4 = 207 SB). Apart from insisting that he did not write his letters to Calvus or Trebonius for public consumption, he implies that he never wrote letters that way. That implication is supported by another passage which might at first glance seem to point the other way. Discussed already in chapter 2, it is the passage in which, near the end of his life, Cicero mentions a group of about 70 letters set aside for possible publication, and adds, "I should look through them and correct them—then and only then will they be published" (eas ego oportet perspiciam, corrigam; tum denique edentur, *Att.* 16.5.5 = 410 SB). It is unlikely that he is here worrying about spelling errors or grammatical mistakes in his old letters. "Correct" means "fix." He must be referring to some aspect of the letters that was not on his mind when he wrote them, but that would be problematic if they became public. He may have wanted to clear away cobwebs of *deixis,* for example, or to extinguish possibly offensive sidelights cast on contemporaries.

In the end, the touchstone of publication seems a poor guide to identifying what might be literary about Cicero's letters. While there can be little doubt that he conceived the possibility of publication, he implies that it made no difference in the actual writing of the letters. In the only case in which he mentions letters he thought about publishing, he gives no hint of which ones they were, and so we have no idea what qualities made a letter potentially publishable in his eyes. Even those letters, he implies, he would not have published as they were, but only after they were fixed in some way he does not specify.

2. *Accessibility to second readers.* If Cicero gave little thought to a general public that might one day read his letters in books, there were other categories of ulterior reader that did preoccupy him. He habitually worried that his letters might fall into the hands of outsiders, and at the opposite extreme he sometimes wanted his letters to be seen by third parties. Both concerns could have consequences for the way he wrote.

Cicero's obsession with the confidentiality of letters was illustrated in chapter 1. Risks arose not only from carelessness or worse on the part of the bearer (who was often not under the letter writer's control) or from interception of a letter en route. Once a letter had been safely delivered, the recipient might pass it along to others, as is shown by the abundance of enclosures mentioned or extant in our corpus, and by occasional entreaties from letter writers that their missives be destroyed as soon as they have been received.[11] The fear that a letter may become known to strangers often leaves more or less tangible traces in the text in the form of guarded expressions. Cicero may curtail or obfuscate comment about sensitive political or family business, avoid referring to people by name, switch from Latin into Greek, or make a point of taking over the writing of a letter from the secretary.[12]

At times, however, he actually arranged for his letters to be seen by people in addition to the addressee. No one was privy to more of his correspondence than Atticus, to whom he showed letters he had written to Caesar, Pompey, Varro, Marcus Brutus, Cassius, Dolabella, Antony, Plotius Plancus, and Octavian.[13] Some of his letters to Caesar, at least, he also showed around more widely, and that was probably true of letters to others, too.[14] Letters of recommendation in particular must often have been shared with the persons on whose behalf they had been written.[15]

Cicero's reasons for bringing in extraneous readers varied. In the case of letters on politics, he sometimes wanted to test the reaction of an independent party before he approached the addressee. If, on the other hand, he sent a copy of a letter after the fact, he was apt to be concerned about defending his position. He copied Atticus on letters to Brutus and to Varro in part because Atticus had been encouraging Cicero's relations with them. When he copied the beneficiaries of his letters of recommendation, he was letting them know that a favor had been posted to their account. He wanted Atticus to see his letter soliciting a write-up of the Catilinarian affair from the historian Lucceius because, he said, the letter was "very nice" (valde bella, Att. 4.6.4 = 83 SB), but also because Atticus and Lucceius were longtime friends, and he wanted Atticus to back up the request.

Since Roman letters lacked the equivalent of a "cc:" formula, an addressee usually had no way of knowing whether anyone else had been copied, nor do we, except through chance remarks independent of the letter. The circumstances under which the writer might want to circulate a letter to others were too various to leave a consistent imprint on the text, unlike worries about confidentiality. But whether it would be shown to persons other than the addressee was one of the calculations that necessarily weighed in the writing, and, once in a while, effects are unmistakable. While Cicero was serving abroad as a provincial governor in 50, he learned that back in Rome a new possibility had materialized for marrying off his daughter. But the informant, his friend Caelius (Fam. 8.6 = 88 SB), explained that there was a problem. The new suitor was just about to prosecute Appius Pulcher, Cicero's predecessor as governor, with whom Cicero had been at odds but now wished to have good relations. Caelius's letter elicited the following reply:

> Marcus Cicero Commander bids greeting to Marcus Caelius Curule Aedile:
>
> Infrequent as the letters that come from you have been (perhaps the failure is on the delivery end), they are sweet. Take the one I have just received: what a sagacious letter, and how full of courtesy and advice! Though I had already made up my mind to act as you advise,

nevertheless our purposes are bolstered when we see that wise and
true advisers think the same.

I have a profound affection for Appius, as I have often said to
you, and I felt that it began to be reciprocated the moment we laid
aside our quarrel. As consul he treated me with respect, he has been
a dear friend, and a fan of my own favorite pursuits. On my side, you
can testify that my attentions to him do not fall short.

M. Cicero Imp. s. d. M. Caelio Aedili Curuli:

*Raras tuas quidem (fortasse enim non perferuntur) sed suavis accipio
litteras; vel quas proxime acceperam, quam prudentis, quam multi et offici
et consili! etsi omnia sic constitueram mihi agenda ut tu admonebas,
tamen confirmantur nostra consilia cum sentimus prudentibus fideliterque
suadentibus idem videri.*

*Ego Appium, ut saepe tecum locutus sum, valde diligo meque ab eo
diligi statim coeptum esse ut simultatem deposuimus sensi. nam et
honorificus in me consul fuit et suavis amicus et studiosus studiorum
etiam meorum. mea vero officia ei non defuisse tu es testis.*

Fam. 2.13.1–2 = 93 SB

Cicero continues in this vein for several lines, itemizing proofs of his devotion
to Appius, then says, "I have written at length because your letter contained a
whiff of doubt about my good will toward him. I suppose you have heard some
rumor. Trust me, anything you have heard is false" (haec eo pluribus scripsi
quod <non> nihil significabant tuae litterae subdubitare qua essem erga illum
voluntate. credo te audisse aliquid. falsum est, mihi crede, si quid audisti).
True, he acknowledges, he and Appius did bring different philosophies of
government to the task of administration (in fact, he considered Appius cor-
rupt, as contemporary letters to Atticus make clear), but those were mere differences of opinion. He avers that he would not dream of saying or doing
anything to Appius's discredit, and he declares his solidarity with him during
the upcoming trial.

Given that Caelius is told of things he is already supposed to know and has
imputed to him sentiments he did not express, the primary function of this
letter cannot be to answer his. The burden of it is to communicate Cicero's
esteem for Appius. Whether Caelius was supposed to pass the letter on, or
whether Cicero himself ensured that Appius received a copy, the second reader
of this letter was at least as important to its conception as the first.[16]

Unlike the expectation of publication, the fear or desire that letters would
become known to individuals beyond the addressee frequently intruded on
Cicero's letter writing. Deissmann's strictures about letters composed for the
benefit of anyone but the addressee seem particularly untrue to the realities of
Roman society. But although an awareness of second readers undoubtedly

influenced the way some letters were written, it is not obvious that it has anything to do with the literariness of those letters. Neither Cicero's gymnastics in the letter to Caelius nor his evasive maneuvers in others seem to put them beyond the bounds of what was ordinary for him.

3. *Topic.* One way in which a private letter acquires the potential to engage a wide readership is through avoidance of details that are known, pertinent, or interesting to the addressee alone. In the terms popularized by Umberto Eco, such a letter is able to draw on the general encyclopedia of interpretative competencies available to all readers rather than on an idiolectal encyclopedia peculiar to one.[17] The "I-you" frame that defines the epistolary genre is minimized, while the topic treated is magnified. One strategy of maximization, in turn, is to limit the content of the letter to a single topic.

Although letters containing scant personal material are well suited for publication, they do not necessarily presuppose it. Letter writers may strike a general note because they lack a more personal basis on which to engage the addressee or because they do not care to engage on that basis for some reason. Nevertheless, one of the clearest overall differences between the letters of Pliny, who was able to review them for publication, and the letters of Cicero, who was not, is that the letters of Pliny's corpus are largely monothematic, while those of Cicero's are not. Maximization of topic has the effect of turning letters into set pieces, which is what makes Pliny's letters so much easier for us to anthologize than Cicero's.

However, a few letters of Cicero's do exhibit the qualities of being depersonalized, theme-driven, and monothematic. The best example is the longest letter of the corpus, written to his brother around the turn of the year 60 B.C., when Quintus's term as governor of Asia was extended for a third year (*QFr.* 1.1 = 1 SB). At a few points Cicero does touch on matters specific to Quintus: his unhappiness over the extension of his term, his bad temper, and some of his gubernatorial acts during the previous two years. But on the whole, the letter is pitched in very general terms. In orderly fashion and with illustrations from Xenophon and Plato, Cicero discourses on the standards to which a governor's staff should be held, on the appropriate treatment for different grades of provincial resident, and on the virtues to be practiced and vices to be avoided by the governor himself. The tone and the length, together with the fact that Cicero's advice was dispensed two years after Quintus took up his post, led Shackleton Bailey (1980, 147) to infer that this letter was "a tract...doubtless intended for wider circulation."

The letter to Lucceius (*Fam.* 5.12 = 22 SB) that was mentioned a couple of pages earlier is another example. At four and a half pages, it is much longer than average, carefully structured, and replete with references to Greek history and Greek historians. From beginning to end, it presses the argument that Lucceius should compose a monograph on Cicero's handling of the Catilinarian conspiracy. Another long and largely monothematic letter, written to a friend who rarely visited Rome, reports on the theatrical shows with which Pompey inaugurated his grand new theater in the year 55 (*Fam.* 7.1 = 24 SB). "This letter," opined Shackleton Bailey in his commentary, "is in the nature of a literary exercise...reminiscent of Pliny the Younger."

As it happens, all three letters have been taken to be models for Pliny. In a recent study of Pliny's letters, Marchesi finds "entire letters modeled on recognizably Ciceronian antecedents," and the letters just discussed are the exemplars to which she points.[18] The point that wants emphasizing here, however, is that we find scarcely a dozen pieces in this vein by Cicero.[19] They are as unrepresentative of his corpus as they are typical of Pliny's. Even if it were known for certain that he circulated these few letters to a reading public, therefore, their rarity would only underscore the otherness of most of his correspondence.[20]

4. *Language and manner.* The considerations that critics have usually had in mind when they characterize a letter as "literary" are based on language. They mean that, vis-à-vis a more ordinary missive, its language has been heightened by the manipulation of cadence, diction, phrasing, allusivity, and rhetorical artifice. Like depersonalization of the topic (and unlike evidence regarding ulterior readers), this criterion is basically internal to a letter. To be sure, it does not allow for hard-and-fast distinctions between literary and unliterary, since the effects involved will be a matter of degree. Almost any letter is apt to present some feature that can be labeled as "literary" according to this definition.[21] But heightened language makes a handy criterion precisely insofar as it does lend itself to quantification. If one cannot distinguish between literary and unliterary absolutely, one can at least distinguish between more and less literary.

A further advantage is that the criterion of heightened language parallels a standard which Roman letter writers often invoked. In their parlance, the opposite of an ordinary letter is "the carefully written letter" *(litterae accurate scriptae)*.[22] The opening lines of a letter that Cicero claims to have written carefully (at *Att.* 5.11.6 = 104 SB) will serve as an example. Cicero wrote it after a stopover in Athens on his way out to govern his province in the year 51. The addressee is Gaius Memmius, most famous as the dedicatee of Lucretius's *On the Nature of Things* and the butt of abuse by Catullus, but who by this date had been relegated to the sidelines. After a conviction for electoral bribery (his conviction being the "wrong" to which the letter alludes), he was living out his days as an exile in Greece. At the behest of Atticus and his Epicurean friends, Cicero had agreed to approach Memmius about selling a property he owned in Athens that had been the site of Epicurus's house. But on learning that Memmius was temporarily out of town, he wrote to him instead:

> Marcus Cicero bids greeting to Gaius Memmius:
>   I could not tell whether seeing you at Athens would have brought me a sensation rather of distress or of cheer. The wrong that has

been done you fills me with sadness, and yet the wisdom with which you bear it fills me with joy. Still, I would rather have seen you, for my distress is hardly the lighter because I did not see you, whereas the pleasure I could have had would certainly have been greater if I did. And so I will not hesitate to try to see you as soon as there is a good opportunity to. In the meantime, I want to broach with you now something that can be broached by letter, and I believe actually accomplished. For a start, I will ask you not to go against your inclination on my account. If, however, there is something that you find makes a great deal of difference to me but none to you, please do it—provided that you first take the view that you are happy to do it.

M. Cicero s. d. C. Memmio:

    Etsi non satis mihi constiterat cum aliquane animi mei molestia an potius libenter te Athenis visurus essem, quod iniuria quam accepisti dolore me adficeret, sapientia tua qua fers iniuriam laetitia, tamen vidisse te mallem; nam quod est molestiae non sane multo levius est cum te non video, quod esse potuit voluptatis certe, si vidissem te, plus fuisset. itaque non dubitabo dare operam ut te videam, cum id satis commode facere potero. interea quod per litteras et agi tecum et, ut arbitror, confici potest, agam nunc, ac te illud primum rogabo, ne quid invitus mea causa facias, sed id quod mea intelleges multum, tua nullam in partem interesse ita mihi des si tibi ut id libenter facias ante persuaseris.

Fam. 13.1.1–2 = 63 SB

The letter continues for another couple of pages, but the proem establishes the tone. Its bravura is no doubt the reason that this piece was chosen by the collection editor to be first in the book of recommendation letters. The interlacing of "you" and "I" constructs a virtual dialogue in place of the conversation that did not occur, and Cicero rings changes on about a dozen antitheses disposed in carefully balanced phrases within a periodic framework that my translation does not capture. The language is as contrived as the conceit that in writing to an Epicurean fellow traveler about Epicurus's house, Cicero would lead off with a little disquisition on pleasure and pain.[23]

    For all its artifice, the letter to Memmius illustrates only a few of the linguistic effects that can go into a "carefully written letter." Other letters explicitly identified as such could enlarge the repertory.[24] But there should be no need to elaborate: such letters contain the elements of heightened language that we could predict they would contain.

    The criterion of language therefore does provide us with an empirical means of distinguishing between more ordinary and less ordinary letter writing, whether we want to label the second category as "careful," "heightened," or "literary." But there are two obstacles in the way of drawing from it any broader inferences about the correspondence of Cicero. One is that, as already noted, the distinction is not precise. In reference to letters, "ordinary" may in fact be a pole that is never quite reached, like the temperature of absolute zero. That it is a dubious standard, especially for a practiced writer like Cicero, is suggested by the simple fact that the greater part of his correspondence, apart from the Atticus letters, is written in rhythmic prose. "The difference from other letter-writers," as Hutchinson (1998: 12) observes, "does mean that Cicero's letters would have seemed highly distinctive, and distinctively polished." Within the confines of the Ciceronian corpus, we may be dealing with the paradox that the marked category is not the special, but the ordinary.

The second problem is that while heightened language is easy enough to discern, it is not a self-explanatory phenomenon. With its emphasis on careful-ness, the Latin "accurate scriptae" focuses the issue better than distinctions like "ornate" and "ordinary," because it directs attention to the situation rather than the quality of writing. A letter writer will have reasons for writing more care-fully at some times than at other times, but not always the same reasons. Pliny may have produced carefully written letters because he was already thinking about publication when he wrote them (*Epist.* 1.1.1). But when Cicero says that he wrote carefully to the doctor who had taken the ailing Tiro under his care (*Fam.* 16.4.1 = 123 SB), publication would have been the last thought on his mind. Then, he wanted the doctor to understand that Tiro's recovery was important to him, and to provide the highest standard of treatment despite the patient's freedman status.

It is significant that many of the letters described as "carefully written" in the Ciceronian corpus happen to be recommendation letters. The letters to Tiro's doctor and to Memmius both fall into this category.[25] Because recom-mendations always call on an addressee to do something, the problem of moti-vation is particularly acute in them. The care that they require is focused in the first instance upon the person they must engage rather than on the language in which they are dressed. Even in Cicero's letter to Memmius, cajolery is upper-most. Cicero condoles with Memmius over the miscarriage of justice that brought about his exile, compliments him on his *sapientia* (using a word that suggests both learning and intelligence), recalls explicitly and implicitly his ties with the school of Epicurus, alludes to his many friends (among whom Cicero insinuates himself), and makes Memmius's convenience the paramount interest to be protected. Eloquence is no more than a contributing element of Cicero's epistolary strategy here.

What is meant by the term "a literary letter" varies widely from one per-son's understanding to another's, but the meaning can always be reduced to something more tangible. In this section I have considered alternative defini-tions based on facts regarding circulation, readership, topic, and language, each of which can and should have a bearing on how we interpret a letter. Yet they are not interchangeable. A letter circulated to readers beyond the addressee is not necessarily a letter that treats a general topic, nor is a letter about a general topic necessarily a letter written in elegant prose (although, of course, a letter *may* be all three at once). To the extent that the blanket category of "literary letter" obscures what we really mean, it only encourages us to talk past one another. Even if we renounce it in favor of more empirical descriptors based on readership, topic, or language, however, we still do not arrive at terms that explain a letter, since a letter writer can manipulate any of these elements for divergent ends. To fix on them as criteria of literariness simply distracts us from reading carefully.

Contemporary Literature in the Letter Corpus

A more content-related sense in which a letter might be considered "literary" is that it is written by one literary figure to another. A crude but handy measure is available to determine who in the letter corpus might be categorized as writer friends of Cicero. Of the approximately 110 correspondents attested for the published corpus, thirty-eight also gain mention in the Schanz-Hosius history of Latin literature because they are attested as having written something (the something being of broader scope than just a letter to Cicero).[26] As it happens, they include all contemporary prose writers of whose work any substantial part survives: Caesar, his continuator Hirtius, Cornelius Nepos, Varro, and Cicero's brother Quintus, too, if we are prepared to count the *Campaign Memo* as an authentic work of his. About twenty more belong to a shadowy crowd of pamphleteers, memoirists, historians, jurists, and learned specialists in other departments known to have written in this period, but whose writings have perished. A half dozen or so contributed only some of their speeches to Latin literature.

Cicero also counts among his correspondents several persons known to have written verse: Asinius Pollio, Atticus, Cassius Parmensis, Cornificius, Licinius Calvus, Memmius, and Trebonius. Some of the prose writers just mentioned also composed verse: Caesar, Varro, and Quintus. At this point, however, the category of "literary friends" begins to ring hollow. None of the big names in Latin poetry for this period and few even of the minor ones figure among Cicero's correspondents: not Lucretius, Catullus, or Aemilius Macer, or the new wave represented by Cornelius Gallus, Cinna, Vergil, and Varius Rufus, or the veterans Furius Bibaculus and Varro of Atax, or the stage writers Laberius and Publilius Syrus.

Let me suggest first that this absence should strike us as somewhat peculiar. Although the corpus contains no letters to or from Lucretius or Catullus, both surely enjoyed some sort of relationship with Cicero. St. Jerome reports that Cicero "emended" Lucretius's books, and Cicero himself implies that he had read his poems.[27] As for Catullus, we have from him a lavish compliment to Cicero in poem 49. Whether written with tongue in cheek or not, it required Cicero to reciprocate in some form, and since the tribute to Cicero takes the form of a thank-you poem, it should imply a prior transaction as well as a sequel. Cicero was acquainted with the mimographer Laberius, too.[28] Further-more, it was taken for granted by Pliny and his friends that Cicero once "fostered the talents of poets with wonderful kindness" (M. Tullium mira benignitate poetarum ingenia fovisse, Pliny *Epist.* 3.15.1). As Elaine Fantham has suggested to me, this belief, like that about the emendation of Lucretius's poem, very likely goes back to testimony from Cicero himself in one of his lost works. But whatever the source, there is nothing improbable about the information. In literary dialogues, Cicero often assumes that Roman leaders of preceding gen-erations cultivated relations with poets of their day, and the assumption must in part be a projection onto the past of his own experience.[29] And given that verse writing at Rome always had a significant social dimension, Cicero's youthful verse experiments should also imply personal contact with the literary avant-garde on whose techniques he sometimes drew.[30]

One thing that is peculiar about the extant correspondence, then, is that Cicero's relationships with contemporary Latin poets seem largely unrepre-sented in it. Nor does the subject of poetry loom large in letters exchanged with poets to whom he did write, except for those to Quintus and Atticus. Both the Cicero brothers wrote verse, and the letters show that they sometimes discussed it as well. But Pollio's letters to Cicero allude neither to the New Poetry that Pollio himself had written and that Vergil later praised, nor to anything that Cicero was turning out. The point of his single reference to literary activity is to deride his scapegrace quaestor Balbus, one of whose crowning extravagances was to have staged an autobiographical drama in his provincial seat (*Fam.* 10.32.3 = 415 SB). In sixteen letters to Cornificius in book 12 of the *Letters to Friends*, Cicero does not allude to Cornificius's earlier career as a poet, and the focus of the now lost letters he exchanged with Licinius Calvus was not Calvus's poetry, but a dispute over current trends in oratory (*Fam.* 15.21.4 = 207 SB). As we saw in chapter 1, the only poetry that comes up in his correspondence with Trebonius is verse in celebration of Cicero.[31] The subject does not come up at all in the letters Cicero wrote to Memmius and Varro, or in the letter he received from Cassius Parmensis.[32]

If we broaden our scope from poetry to literature more generally, the pic-ture is not much different. The only correspondents whom Cicero could be said to project as literary personalities in his letters to them are Ampius Balbus, Appius Pulcher, Atticus, Caecina, Lucceius, Quintus, and Varro. Although some three dozen of Cicero's correspondents might plausibly be identified as literary friends, therefore, that figure does not convert into a corresponding body of literarily oriented letters within the collection. The subject of literature is generally downplayed even in correspondence with other writers.

Having applied one rough test of literariness to the corpus, let me now apply another that is more broadly based. Rather than surveying those correspondents who are known as writers, this survey focuses on literary works that are mentioned in the letters. So far as possible, however, it is restricted to works produced within Cicero's lifetime, since the question it is meant to address is still the question with which I have been concerned since the beginning of this section: What sort of engagement do the letters manifest with contemporary literary life? Moreover, the survey covers only works that take the form of written texts (not speeches, therefore, unless it is clear that they could be read in addition to being heard)[33] and works that can be presumed to have had some circulation to a reading public (not ordinary private letters, therefore).

Details are set out in appendix 2. The broad results are that in the extant letters, about 110 works are mentioned, and reference is made to them about 250 times. Although references have been culled from the entire letter corpus, they represent Cicero's outlook almost exclusively. Only a dozen of the references occur in letters written by his correspondents.

Despite the number and range of works cited—which include both poetry and prose and Greek books as well as Latin—they mirror poorly the output that we know from this period. Important names in history, oratory, philology, and poetry are missing, and the oeuvre of some authors who are mentioned is oddly stunted in this presentation of it. The letters advert to only a fraction of the writings that Atticus, Caesar, and Varro produced.

Furthermore, Cicero has little to say about most of what he does mention: the great majority of his citations consist of no more than a bare reference to a text. With two exceptions, he never quotes from the contemporary literature to which he alludes, and both the exceptions are self-quotations.[34] This restraint contrasts markedly with his attitude toward earlier Latin and Greek literature, from which he quotes profusely.[35] The spareness of his references is well illustrated by the handful of *testimonia* to contemporary poetry in his letters (omitting verse by Cicero and his brother, who are the poets most abundantly cited). In one, he thanks Trebonius for the complimentary verses mentioned above (*Fam.* 15.21 = 207 SB), and in another he refers to epigrams by Atticus likewise praising Cicero (*Att.* 1.16.15 = 16 SB). He mentions epic poetry by Archias in honor of Roman grandees that inspired in Cicero a hankering for something similar (*Att.* 1.16.15 = 16 SB). He approves of Atticus's liking for a picture book with epigrams by Varro (*Att.* 16.11.3 = 420 SB), and he praises a lampoon by Calvus against a person whom Cicero, too, found offensive (*Fam.* 7.24.1 = 260 SB). He pays tribute once to the Neoteric poets by concocting a neat line in imitation of their style (*Att.* 7.2.1 = 125 SB). He characterizes the mimes of Laberius and Publilius as tedious (*Fam.* 12.18.2 = 205 SB) and judges that the author of a Greek geographical poem which he consulted is "clumsy as a poet yet ignorant of the material, but not a waste of time" (poeta ineptus, et tamen scit nihil; sed est non inutilis, *Att.* 2.20.6 = 40 SB). And he delivers the pronouncement familiar to every student of Latin literature, that "Lucretius's poems...have many flares of genius and yet much art as well" (Lucreti poemata ut scribis ita sunt, multis luminibus ingeni, multae tamen artis, *QFr.* 2.10[9].2 = 14 SB).[36] The surprising thing is how infrequently such remarks occur in the letters.

Apart from the meagerness of Cicero's reflections on contemporary literature, what is most salient about the works noticed in the letters is that more than 40 percent of them consist of writings by Cicero himself, and that more than 60 percent of his references are to that plus-40 percent. To be sure, most references even to his own work involve little comment. (Some exceptions will be considered later.) Typically, he says no more than that he is busy with such-and-such a project or that he is sending such-and-such a finished book to friends.

The conclusions to be drawn from this patchwork of citations are, I think, as follows. The literature most on Cicero's mind in the letters was the literature he happened to be producing himself. Though he was aware of other books, he tended to bring them up only when they impinged on some concern of his own. And whether he referred to works written by himself or by his contemporaries, rarely did the mention of something broaden into a discussion of it. In the extant corpus, at any rate, Cicero does not use the letter form as a platform from which to launch essays in criticism, as Horace would later do.[37] By contrast with politics, literature is not a topic of discourse that he is inclined to develop for its own sake.

Admittedly, the evidence on which I base these conclusions affords only a partial view of Cicero's literary interests. Not only have I narrowed the question of literary culture to contemporary literature, but I have not cited all the contemporary literature that Cicero knew. His dialogues refer to many such works that are not mentioned in his letters. The meagerness of his literary comments in the letters likewise gives an impression that needs to be corrected from the dialogues. That he was capable of writing serious, sustained, and informed criticism is shown by the *Brutus,* the *Orator,* and the *De Oratore.*

Moreover, as noted earlier, it is likely that the letters underrepresent the extent of Cicero's involvement with other litterateurs. Most letters in the corpus were written by someone in Rome to someone away from Rome, or vice versa. But literary activity in this period, insofar as it consisted in the production, circulation, and reception of texts, took place almost entirely within the confines of the capital. Letters written abroad cannot be expected to carry more than an occasional echo of the literary interactions that went on at home. It is no accident that literary references predominate in the letters to Atticus, many of which were written in the near vicinity of Rome. The personality of an addressee also influences the literary content of a letter, since Cicero tries to tailor his discourse to the sensibility of each recipient. And finally, as I have argued in chapter 2, we cannot rule out the possibility that the epistolary corpus owes its present complexion as much to the anonymous redactor as to Cicero.

The more literary portions of Cicero's extensive correspondence may have been discarded because no place was found for them in the editor's grand mosaic depicting Cicero the public man.

The published letters, therefore, are far from being a full expression of Cicero's persona as a writer and literary savant. Yet they do constitute fair evidence for the use he makes of literature as an epistolary topic, which is my concern here. And the relative slightness of this theme for Cicero is best appreciated by comparison with Pliny's letters. Although more than two and a half times as many letters by Cicero as by Pliny survive, the respective collections disclose considerably less about Cicero's involvement in the Roman literary milieu than about Pliny's. The Ciceronian corpus includes no counterparts to the portraits Pliny composes of fellow writers like his uncle the elder Pliny, Silius Italicus, and Martial, for example, or to the many accounts Pliny provides of recitations.[38] In his survey of Pliny's corpus, the commentator Sherwin-White counted forty-three "literary" letters, which he defined as being concerned with the composition, criticism, and publication of speeches and verse by Pliny and his friends.[39] It would be difficult to point to as many as half a dozen letters in the Ciceronian corpus with a comparable focus.

A nice instance of the contrast in orientation comes in a letter that Cicero wrote to Atticus in the year 45, after Caesar's final victory over Pompeian forces in Spain. For some weeks Cicero had been fretting over the prospect of having to meet with Caesar when he returned to Italy, and a meeting finally took place when Caesar paid a call on him at his villa on the Bay of Naples. Later, Cicero reported to Atticus that their encounter went better than expected. He describes Caesar's entourage and his routines while on the road, and he makes much of the hospitality he lavished on Caesar. But their conversation he skips over with the remark that it involved "a lot of literary talk, nothing serious" (σπουδαῖον οὐδὲν in sermone, φιλόλογα multa, *Att.* 13.52.2 = 353 SB). Pliny would have battened on such a conversation.

The disparity between Pliny and Cicero in this regard certainly owes something to historical developments. The profusion of literary opinions and anecdotes poured out in Pliny's letters is partly a consequence of his having less to do with politics than Cicero. As the establishment of the principate diminished the role that senators could play in that arena, their zest for literary pursuits grew. Granted, Cicero successfully balanced a literary career with politics. But even so, he was more hobbled than Pliny was by the aristocratic code that relegated literary endeavor to recreation or *otium* and rendered it suspect as a theme of serious discourse. The restraint on literary content in Cicero's letters can thus be taken as one sign that in his eyes, his correspondence was no pastime but serious business. Nicholas Horsfall has suggested that Cicero's personality also contributed to the bias. He argues that as Cicero aged, his early interest in and sympathy for what contemporary poets were attempting simply evaporated.[40] That is the viewpoint reflected in the extant correspondence, which dates almost entirely from the last twenty years of Cicero's life.

But for present purposes, the circumstances of the letter writers require less attention than the letters themselves. The instructive value of the comparison with Pliny is that it highlights an epistolary topic that might have played a very different part in Cicero's correspondence than it does.[41] We still need to consider exactly what part it does play.

The Uses of Literature

At the least it can be said that the culture of books is taken for granted as a feature of the epistolary background. References to more than a hundred contemporary works mentioned in the letters are collected in appendix 2, and the tally would be much higher if one were to include references to earlier writers. Books and writers figure in the consciousness of Cicero and his correspondents even when specific titles are not mentioned. Literary interests are among the merits singled out in letters of recommendation, as when Cicero praises "an excellent man and a close friend, endowed with that zeal for literature and learning in which I take the highest delight" (virum optimum mihique familiarissimum, iis studiis litterarum doctrinaeque praeditum, quibus ego maxime delector, *Fam.* 13.30.1 = 301 SB).[42]

Books also provide the argument for one of the earliest letters that Cicero wrote after he had given up the Pompeian cause and had been allowed by Caesar to return to Rome in 47. Realizing that his political influence was extinct, he was looking to retool as a man of letters, and so he reached out to Varro. Cicero always tried to align himself with the most potent forces in his field of action, and if cultural pursuits were now to be his primary endeavor, the master was undoubtedly Varro, to whom he writes as follows:

> You should know that since my return to the city I have been
> reconciled with those old friends our books. It was not that I had
> broken relations because I was angry with them, but rather because
> I was ashamed. I felt that I had not properly heeded their counsel
> when I consigned myself to faithless companions and great upheaval.
> But they grant me pardon, and recall me to our old intimacy, and
> declare that you were wiser than I in standing by it.

> *scito ... me, postea quam in urbem venerim, redisse cum veteribus amicis,*
> *id est cum libris nostris, in gratiam. etsi non idcirco eorum usum*
> *dimiseram quod iis suscenserem sed quod eorum me subpudebat; videbar*
> *enim mihi, cum me in res turbulentissimas infidelissimis sociis*
> *demisissem, praeceptis illorum non satis paruisse. ignoscunt mihi,*

revocant in consuetudinem pristinam teque, quod in ea permanseris,
sapientiorem quam me dicunt fuisse.

Fam. 9.1.2 = 175 SB

Cicero's pitch to Varro is ingenious in several respects, most notably perhaps in ascribing his pardon and restoration not to Caesar but to "books" (and in leaving unspoken the thought that Varro himself had been an earlier beneficiary of Caesar's grace). But it has in common with the clichés of recommendation letters that it treats learning as a token of mutual understanding among members of the elite. This function of literature in Cicero's correspondence has recently been stressed in independent contributions by Sander Goldberg and Cynthia Damon.[43] That literary knowledge would become a medium of elite exchange in Roman society occurred the more readily because education was largely restricted to the elite and was more uniform than it is nowadays.

Still, Cicero is more attuned to his correspondents as individuals than as members of a class. Although almost all would have received the usual literary and rhetorical education, he does not presume that all cherished literary interests. In letters to only about a third of them does he touch even lightly on literature, mentioning particular books, for example, or quoting verse or talking of culture (*studia, doctrina, litterae*) in the abstract.[44] One manifestation of reserve in this regard can be seen in his deployment of quotations from Greek poetry. More than a hundred are found in his letters to Atticus (where they are twice as frequent as quotes in Latin).[45] The long stays in Greece that had earned Atticus his name had made him as conversant with Greek as with Roman culture. Not quite a dozen citations of Greek verse occur in Cicero's letters to his brother, who as a young man had accompanied Cicero on his study tour of Greece and Asia in the early 70s. A dozen more quotations are sprinkled through letters to just five other persons.[46] This distribution suggests that Cicero's quotations are neither decorative nor random elements but are carefully calculated, and I would argue that that is true of most of his other evocations of literature. Cicero considered not only the background and interests of the person to whom he was writing but also the particular effects he wanted to achieve when he brought the subject up.

Cicero's views of literary culture as a practical resource are more abundantly illustrated in the letters to Atticus than anywhere else in the correspondence, but they surface in letters to others, too. One use of literature with a long tradition at Rome was that it provided material for gift exchanges. Cicero and his peers use letters to present copies of their writings to one another, just as poets make a point of presenting their verse to friends.[47]

However, it is more common for letters to take a literary turn when the letter writer is seeking to back up some argument he is making. When Cicero's brother was obliged to accept an extension of his assignment as governor of

Asia, Cicero argued that the situation gave him an opportunity to put his study of Plato into practice. He writes:

> Plato, that nonpareil of genius and learning, held that states would flourish only if wise and educated men undertook to govern them, or if those who governed them committed all their effort to learning and philosophy. It was this combination of power and wisdom, he thought, that could be the saving of governments.... Your province is lucky that the man who now holds supreme power in it is someone who from boyhood has put enormous time and passion into gaining knowledge and gaining virtue and breadth of spirit. Make sure, then, that this year which has been added to your burden may seem to have been extended for the good of Asia.

> *ille quidem princeps ingeni et doctrinae Plato tum denique fore beatas res publicas putavit, si aut docti ac sapientes homines eas regere coepissent aut ii qui regerent omne suum studium in doctrina et sapientia conlocassent; hanc coniunctionem videlicet potestatis et sapientiae saluti censuit civitatibus esse posse.... nunc quidem profecto isti provinciae contigit, ut is in ea summam potestatem haberet cui in doctrina, cui in virtute atque humanitate percipienda plurimum a pueritia studi fuisset et temporis. qua re cura ut hic annus qui ad laborem tuum accessit idem ad salutem Asiae prorogatus esse videatur.*
>
> QFr. 1.1.29–30 = 1 SB

When another friend was governing the province of Achaea, and Cicero had a boon to ask on behalf of the people of Sparta, he adopted a similar line: "Please be assured that in my view, considering the troubled times, *all* the communities of Achaea are fortunate to have you in charge of them, and I think that you are and will remain an instinctive friend of Sparta because you are more familiar than anyone not only with all of Roman history but also the history of Greece" (sic velim existimes, me omnis Achaiae civitates arbitrari pro horum temporum perturbatione felicis quod iis tu praesis, eundemque me ita iudicare, te, quod unus optime nosses non nostra solum sed etiam Graeciae monumenta omnia, tua sponte amicum Lacedaemoniis et esse et fore, *Fam.* 13.28a.2 = 295 SB).

Literary backup could also be marshaled when a letter writer ventured beyond exhortation into criticism. A few pages earlier, I quoted a letter that Cicero wrote to ingratiate himself with Appius Pulcher, the blue-blood who preceded him as governor of Cilicia. But the handoff of power had initially gone awry when Cicero, on arriving in his province, learned that Appius was lingering there to extort a few last sesterces and when Appius complained that Cicero snubbed him by dodging a courtesy encounter between them. Cicero defended himself against Appius's accusation by trying to shift the onus of bad manners and bad breeding from himself onto Appius. He has been told, he writes, of Appius's petulant comment on the unfortunate snafu, a comment that in Cicero's rendering of it goes, "Well, well: an Appius took the trouble to greet [his predecessor] Lentulus. A Lentulus greeted Ampius. And a *Cicero* has declined to greet an Appius!" With that huffy remark as his springboard, Cicero takes the offensive:

> I ask you! Can you utter this kind of silliness, when in my view you are a person of surpassing good sense, wide learning too, and vast experience, to say nothing of sophistication, which the Stoics very correctly hold to be a virtue? Do you think that any degree of "Appius-ness" or "Lentulus-ness" counts more with me than the appurtenance of virtue? Even before I had attained those honors which all consider most grand, I never stood in awe of your names (rather, it was the men who left them to you that I thought great). And after I gained and carried out top offices in such a way that I felt no need of further honor and glory, I hoped that I had achieved parity with you people (though never superiority, of course).... If you think otherwise, it would not be amiss for you to study a bit more closely what Athenodorus the son of Sandon has to say on the subject, so that you may understand what constitutes nobility.

> *"quidni? Appius Lentulo, Lentulus Ampio processit obviam, Cicero Appio noluit." quaeso, etiamne tu has ineptias, homo mea sententia summa prudentia, multa etiam doctrina, plurimo rerum usu, addo urbanitatem, quae est virtus ut Stoici rectissime putant? ullam Appietatem aut Lentulitatem valere apud me plus quam ornamenta virtutis existimas? cum ea consecutus nondum eram quae sunt hominum opinionibus amplissima, tamen ista vestra nomina numquam sum admiratus; viros eos qui ea vobis reliquissent magnos arbitrabar. postea vero quam ita et cepi et gessi maxima imperia ut mihi nihil neque ad honorem neque ad gloriam acquirendum putarem, superiorem quidem numquam, sed parem vobis me speravi esse factum.... tu si aliter existimas, nihil errabis si paulo diligentius, ut quid sit εὐγένεια intellegas, Athenodorus, Sandonis filius, quid de his rebus dicat attenderis.*

> *Fam.* 3.7.5 = 71 SB

The effect of Cicero's two invocations of Stoic learning here is to suggest that Appius is perhaps not yet quite up to distinguishing between proper and improper behavior, though he makes a show of leaving that conclusion to Appius's own more considered reflection. As often when he has something critical to say, Cicero puts it off onto a surrogate.

Appius was no doubt as competent a reader as we are, however, and as the cross-fire of aggrieved messages continued, Cicero found himself having to undo the ill will generated by the letter just quoted. But this time, rather than needling Appius further, he tries to dispel bad feeling by making a joke. The joke invites

Appius to scrutinize the offending letter not in his capacity as a social actor—which of course is the only relevant capacity—but rather as a literary critic and a particularly fine one: "I don't understand which letter of mine you are calling 'somewhat testy.' I sent you two in which I defended my own behavior in detail and criticized you slightly over something that you were too hasty to believe. Remonstration in that vein seemed amicable enough to me. But if you object, I will refrain from it in future. However, if the letter was 'inelegant,' as you say, you can be sure that it did not originate with me. Just as Aristarchus repudiates Homeric authorship of any verse with which he finds fault—if I may be allowed a joke—so you should not consider as mine anything which is not elegant" (stomachosiores meas litteras quas dicas esse non intellego. bis ad te scripsi me purgans diligenter, te leviter accusans in eo quod de me cito credidisses. quod genus querelae mihi quidem videbatur esse amici; sin tibi displicet, non utar eo posthac. sed si, ut scribis, eae litterae non fuerunt disertae, scito meas non fuisse. ut enim Aristarchus Homeri versum negat quem non probat, sic tu (libet enim mihi iocari), quod disertum non erit, ne putaris meum, *Fam.* 3.11.5 = 74 SB).

The literary allusions adduced thus far conform to a pattern of use that is commonplace in the Roman milieu. Literature, like history, is regarded as a repository of lessons and models that can be invoked to persuade others to act in desired ways. But one thing that is interesting about the correspondence of Cicero is the frequency with which his literary *exempla* are self-directed. From the store of books inside his head, he often picks out parts to play. In the stream of quotations from the *Iliad* running through the letters to Atticus, his favorite is Hector's apprehensive reference to public opinion, "I fear the Trojans and the long-robed Trojan women" (αἰδέομαι Τρῶας καὶ Τρῳάδας ἑλκεσιπέπλους).[48] As Cicero wrangled with the barons of the Senate, he evidently imagined himself as one of the princes in Homer's story. He channels Agamemnon at *Fam.* 3.7.6 = 71 SB and Nestor at *Fam.* 9.14.2 = 326 SB.[49] Shifting to the repertoire of tragedy, he assumes the voice of Cassandra at *Att.* 8.11.3 = 161 SB and of Amphiaraus at *Fam.* 6.6.6 = 234 SB. He changes script once again apropos of telling Atticus that he has had a talking-to with their wayward nephew, Quintus. The letter opens with a purported dialogue between the youth and his worldly wise uncle which is composed partly in Greek, in the manner of Menander (*Att.* 13.42.1 = 354 SB). Apart from providing Cicero with a sympathetic role in which to present himself, the recourse to Menander encourages Atticus to hope that the troubles with Quintus are destined to have a happy ending.

Cicero does not cast himself only in positive roles, however. After his return from exile in 57, he antagonized members of the aristocracy by aligning himself with Caesar and by defending one of Caesar's henchmen (the ubiquitous Vatinius again) in the courts. When Lentulus Spinther, who had orchestrated Cicero's recall from exile, took him to task, Cicero quoted back a passage of Terence's *Eunuch* (439–45) in which a parasite urges a lover to retaliate against the girl who has rebuffed him by kindling jealousy of another girl. Cicero wrote that he was only following the parasite's advice. Since the aristocrats had been cozying up to his enemy Clodius, he was getting back at them by taking sides with the odious Caesarian.[50] Cicero borrows again from comedy in letters written after the fall of the Republic a decade later. Perhaps because he felt slightly embarrassed to be now hobnobbing and dining with Caesar's triumphant partisans, he pictures himself as a Plautine parasite lapping up rich sauces.[51]

The ease with which Cicero slips into such impersonations suggests that the literature he knew exercised a continuing power of suggestion over him. But that is less remarkable than his evident conviction that texts exert their most powerful effects on the very persons who have created them. This view emerges at one point in the letter to his brother about provincial administration, when he is explaining how important it is to monitor the ethics of subalterns. He extols the integrity of one of Quintus's senior aides, "all the more because he is a historian," who "can pick from his own chronicles many individuals whom he would have scope and inclination to imitate" ([speaking of Tubero] ego arbitror, praesertim cum scribat historiam, multos ex suis annalibus posse deligere quos velit et possit imitari, *QFr.* 1.1.10 = 1 SB). Years later, when a Pompeian partisan was languishing in exile, Cicero urged him to take comfort in the knowledge that he had acted out of conviction and that convictions always carry costs. Then he continues, "Moreover, since you devote your energy to preserving the deeds of brave men for posterity, you should have a care to do nothing whereby you would render yourself the least bit unlike those you praise" (deinde, cum studium tuum consumas in virorum fortium factis memoriae prodendis, considerare debes nihil tibi esse committendum quam ob rem eorum quos laudas te non simillimum praebeas, *Fam.* 6.12.5 = 226 SB).

Cicero's own prolific output naturally made him liable to have such arguments turned upon him by others.[52] But even without their prompting, he seems to have been particularly susceptible to the moral imperatives that emanated from his books. When Caesar and Pompey formed their first coalition in 59 and sought Cicero's help in getting legislation passed, Cicero was tempted to cooperate. He wrote to Atticus that it would certainly ease his problems with Clodius. Yet, he continues, he cannot get out of his head a passage from an epic that he had composed to celebrate his own consulate four years earlier. It is an exhortation put into the mouth of a Muse who descends to counsel him at the close of the third book: "'Steer still that course which you set with courage and spirit in early youth and have set now as consul too, and so enlarge your fame and the plaudits of good men.'" After quoting the verses, he draws the moral: "Since Calliope herself dictated this course to me in that book containing so many things in an optimate vein, I think I must not swerve from the belief"—and here he tops himself with a quote from Homer (*Il.* 12.243)—"The one best augury is to struggle in defense of the fatherland" ("interea cursus, quos prima a parte iuventae / quosque adeo consul virtute animoque petisti, / hos retine atque auge famam laudesque bonorum." haec mihi cum in eo libro in quo multa sunt scripta ἀριστοκρατικῶς Calliope ipsa praescripserit, non opinor esse dubitandum quin semper nobis videatur "εἷς οἰωνὸς ἄριστος ἀμύνασθαι περὶ πάτρης," *Att.* 2.3.4 = 23 SB).

Ten years later, when the civil war finally erupts, Cicero writes of his struggle not to despair: "I worry that...I may even bring disgrace upon my own endeavors in literature. And so I pass the whole time pondering the essence of that great man whom I studiously depicted...in my books. Do you remember the goal by which I wanted the overseer of the state to test things? Scipio speaks as follows, I believe, in book 5." There follows another snatch of self-quotation, this time from the *On the Commonwealth* (vereor ne...etiam dedecori sim studiis ac litteris nostris. consumo igitur omne tempus considerans quanti vis sit illius viri quem nostris <libris> satis diligenter...expressimus. tenesne igitur moderatorem illum rei publicae quo referre velimus omnia? nam sic quinto, ut opinor, in libro loquitur Scipio, *Att.* 8.11.1 = 161 SB).

But the most arresting case of self-indoctrination concerns a text that was created for that purpose. During a months-long depression brought on by the death of his daughter in early 45, Cicero took little comfort from the efforts of friends to rally him. He writes to Atticus: "You act true to form in wanting me to pull out of my present distress. But you can bear witness that I have not been totally passive: there is no book by anyone on the subject of reducing grief that I did not read at your house. But the sorrow wins out over every solace. I have even done something I daresay no one has done before, which is to compose a consolation of myself. I'll send you the book if they are done copying it. I guarantee you, no other consolation is its like" (quod me ab hoc maerore recreari vis, facis ut omnia; sed me mihi non defuisse tu testis es. nihil enim de maerore minuendo scriptum ab ullo est quod ego non domi tuae legerim. sed omnem consolationem vincit dolor. quin etiam feci, quod profecto ante me nemo, ut ipse me per litteras consolarer. quem librum ad te mittam, si descripserint librarii. adfirmo tibi nullam consolationem esse talem, *Att.* 12.14.3 = 251 SB). Cicero's consolation of himself is no longer extant, and so we are in no position to assess his claim of its superiority. But its quality is of less significance than the impulse to write it in the first place. His remarks about it, together with those on the two works mentioned earlier, suggest that for him, literary activity had as practical an orientation as diet or exercise or household finance would have had.

On the evidence of the letters, moreover, practical concerns governed not only the larger purposes for which he wrote but details of how he wrote. His approach can be illustrated by comparing two passages in his letters in which he discusses his literary aims. In the summer of 54, Cicero responded to a comment by Atticus about his dialogue *On the Orator*, written the previous year. Atticus had said that he was sorry that the speaking role Cicero created for the old jurist Mucius Scaevola terminated at the close of book 1, when Scaevola goes home for a siesta. Cicero wrote back that he had in mind Plato's treatment of the elderly Cephalus in the *Republic*, who likewise withdraws early from a dialogue. "No doubt Plato thought it would be unseemly if he continued to keep a person of that age on hand through so long a conversation. I thought I should be even more careful about this in the case of Scaevola, old as he was and in poor health, you remember, and of such rank that it seemed not quite appropriate for him to be lingering for days at Crassus's Tusculan retreat. Besides, the topic of book 1 was akin to Scaevola's interests, whereas the other books bring in specialist material, as you are aware. I didn't want the old fellow around for that—you know how he made light of things" (credo Platonem vix putasse satis consonum fore si hominem id aetatis in tam longo sermone diutius retinuisset. multo ego magis hoc mihi cavendum putavi in Scaevola, qui et aetate et valetudine erat ea qua esse meministi et iis honoribus ut vix satis decorum videretur eum pluris dies esse in Crassi Tusculano. et erat primi libri sermo non alienus a Scaevolae studiis; reliqui libri τεχνολογίαν habent, ut scis. huic ioculatorem senem illum, ut noras, interesse sane nolui, *Att.* 4.16.3 = 89 SB). This paragraph is the longest passage in the letters in which Cicero comments from an artistic perspective on something he has written. He speaks of his desire to emulate Plato, and his efforts to make a dramatic character true both to real life and to the fictional requirements of the dialogue in which he engages. But nothing in this vein exists elsewhere in the letters, and it is not irrelevant that Cicero is here taking a backward look at his treatise *On the Orator*. The appeal to Plato serves partly to validate a work of his own that has entered the public domain and is now out of his hands.

Furthermore, mention of *On the Orator* was incidental to discussion of another work on which Cicero was currently engaged. Atticus had raised the subject by way of leading up to a suggestion that Cicero should create a speaking role for his friend Varro in a new dialogue he was composing, *On the Commonwealth*. Cicero answered that that dialogue was set too far in the past for Varro to have a plausible role in it. When he then went on to describe aesthetic considerations behind *On the Orator*, it was a graceful way of turning aside Atticus's request.

A letter written a few months later, however, shows that more practical concerns in fact weighed heavily as Cicero was writing *On the Commonwealth*. In *QFr.* 3.5[5–7] = 25 SB, he tells Quintus that some criticism he received of an early draft has prompted him to rethink the project. The characters whom he had planned to cast as speakers in the dialogue were great civic leaders of the previous century. But when he organized a reading from it, a friend who was present said that his choice of speakers was ill advised, telling him that "talk about those subjects would have much greater authority if I myself spoke about the state, especially since…I was a former consul, and one who had been involved in crucial affairs of state" (multo maiore auctoritate illis de rebus dici posse si ipse loquerer de re publica, praesertim cum essem…consularis et is qui in maximis versatus in re publica rebus essem, *QFr.* 3.5[5–7].1 = 25 SB). The friend added that the dialogue lost credibility by being retrojected so far into the past, and he suggested that Aristotle provided a good precedent for an author to write about politics in his own voice.

At some point after writing this letter, Cicero evidently changed his mind again and returned to the original plan for the dialogue. But at the time, he told his brother that the critic left him convinced he should rewrite: "He made an impression on me, the more so because I was not going to be able to deal with great disturbances in our body politic because they occurred after the lifetime of the speakers in the dialogue. Of course, it was precisely my original intent not to offend anyone by running afoul of contemporary events. Well, I will steer clear of that, but now you and I are going to be the actual speakers" (commovit me, et eo magis quod maximos motus nostrae civitatis attingere non poteram, quod erant inferiores quam illorum aetas qui loquebantur. ego autem id ipsum tum eram secutus, ne in nostra tempora incurrens offenderem quempiam. nunc et id vitabo et loquar ipse tecum, *QFr.* 3.5[5–7].2 = 25 SB).[53]

Like the earlier passage about the treatise on oratory, this is one of the rare glimpses that the letters allow us of Cicero the author at work. *On the Commonwealth* is a brilliant piece of artistry even in the tattered state in which it has come down to us. Yet here, apart from a passing reference to dramatic structure in section 1 of the letter, neither Cicero nor his critic appraises the work in light of aesthetic considerations. They do not talk about the challenge of emulating Plato in Latin, for example, or delineation of character through dialogue, or finding a style appropriate both to conversation and to exposition. They are concerned above all with social and practical ramifications of the project: the experience, status, and authority of the writer, plausibility, and the risk of offending contemporaries. Those concerns are not irrelevant to the writing of his book, but they are of a very different order than the criteria of "art" and "genius" which Cicero famously invoked apropos of Lucretius.[54]

The Romans were not the first to debate whether utility or pleasure took precedence as the goal of literature. But they exacerbated the controversy, and later critics were able to collect from them more ammunition for the cause of utility than of pleasure. It is hardly surprising that Cicero would have inclined toward that view, which partly explains why his letters do not contain more in the way of aesthetics or criticism, and why he could have said that if his life were twice as long, he would still not have time for lyric poetry (Sen. *Ep.* 49.5). Over and above that bias, the epistolary medium itself encouraged a utilitarian approach to literature, at least in Cicero's case. With each of his addressees, he usually had concrete, practical aims in view. Letter writing was not an occasion for detached reflection on literature or very much else.

To say that Cicero took a utilitarian view of letters and of literature is not to denigrate this facet of his correspondence as dull, however. He is as ingenious in letters and with literary topics as with anything else he writes. One last illustration may serve to close the argument. It comes from a letter written to Varro in mid-46, the latest of seven letters to him over a period of about six months.[55] The sequence opens with Cicero's letter about being recalled to the life of books which was quoted earlier, and which sets the tone for everything to follow. As Cicero and Varro corresponded, they were awaiting the outcome of the civil war in North Africa and then waiting for Caesar to return to Rome. Amid a constant static of rumor concerning the dictator's movements, Cicero rehearses his own conduct during the civil war, defends his return to what was now the seat of Caesar's government, deplores the present state of political life, and extols the pursuit of learning. For a reader of the letter corpus, that is roughly the scope of the exchange with Varro.

Vis-à-vis Varro, however, what is interesting is that every one of these letters but the last is about arranging or failing to arrange a visit between the correspondents. Throughout most of their exchange, Cicero and Varro were no further apart than Rome and Tusculum, which would have made it easy enough for them to meet. But Varro was planning an extended retreat on the Bay of Naples, and that prompted a discussion about whether, when, and where Cicero would join him. Travel plans formed an easy bridge to the subject of literature, because the sojourn in the south was to be a working vacation. But in the latest letter of the sequence, written when Varro was not yet under way himself, it emerges that Cicero has decided to back out of the trip. After another flurry of speculation about Caesar's movements and lamentation over the rush to civil war, the letter winds up as follows:

> I have always viewed you as a great figure in any case, but also
> because you are practically alone in having safe haven amid the
> current storms. You partake of the finest fruits of learning, given
> that you ponder and engage with things the pursuit and enjoyment
> of which should be ranked above all the doings and delights of
> those [warmongers]. For my part, I think that your days at
> Tusculum make the perfect life, and I would gladly yield up any
> sum to anyone in return for the freedom to live as you do, with
> violence eliminated. I do imitate you as well as I can, and am very
> happy to retire into my studies. Now that the country either does
> not care to make use of us or cannot, who could deny us permission
> to return to that life which many learned men have thought
> deserves preference over politics? Wrong though they may be, they
> are numerous. With our country's blessing, why should we not
> plunge into pursuits which great men have held merit exemption
> from public responsibilities? But...I am telling you things that you
> know better than I who tell them to you.

cum enim te semper magnum hominem duxi, tum quod his tempestatibus
es prope solus in portu, fructusque doctrinae percipis eos qui maximi sunt,
ut ea consideres eaque tractes quorum et usus et delectatio est omnibus
istorum et actis et voluptatibus anteponenda. equidem hos tuos
Tusculanensis dies instar esse vitae puto libenterque omnibus omnis opes
concesserim ut mihi liceat vi nulla interpellante isto modo vivere. quod nos
quoque imitamur, ut possumus, et in nostris studiis libentissime
conquiescimus. quis enim hoc non dederit nobis, ut, cum opera nostra
patria sive non possit uti sive nolit, ad eam vitam revertamur quam multi
docti homines, fortasse non recte sed tamen multi, etiam rei publicae
praeponendam putaverunt? quae igitur studia magnorum hominum
sententia vacationem habent quandam publici muneris, iis concedente re
publica cur non abutamur? sed...ego tibi ea narro quae tu melius scis
quam ipse qui narro.

Fam. 9.6.4–5 = 181 SB

From a social perspective, this paean to the literary life can be seen to accomplish four purposes simultaneously. At the most obvious level, it gives Cicero an opportunity to compliment Varro as a distinguished scholar. It also stakes out ground on which Cicero can claim fellowship with Varro, because by their writing they are both engaged in the propagation of important knowledge among their countrymen.[56] Assertions of solidarity are frequent in the letters, but there was an added motive for it in this case, because we know that Cicero found Varro's personality intimidating.[57] Another purpose Cicero has in praising literary endeavor is that it allows him to reinterpret the negative experience of Varro and himself in positive terms. Both men had followed the losing side in the civil war, and that put an end to one kind of effectiveness. Cicero rehabilitates their experience by directing attention away from the failed hopes at its source toward opportunities that are its consequence. Finally, the passage I have quoted conveys a tacit apology. This is the letter in which it finally becomes clear that Cicero does not mean to accompany Varro to southern Italy. But rather than say that directly, Cicero disengages by contrasting Varro's single-minded and incomparable pursuit of learning with his own more modest ambition to follow as best he can. The variety of messages communicated in this one text suggests that the literary tone in Cicero's letters does not rise and fall simply with the erudition of the addressee. It also corresponds to the number and complexity of the social objectives that he is pursuing through the medium of literary discourse.

To sum up, literature enters into the letters when it helps in managing social relations. It offered models and warrants for behavior in the present and material for the exchange of compliments, which helped to induce cooperation in members of the Roman elite. Beyond that, a poetic quotation or the mention of a book could have more tactical applications within a letter.

It might serve to tone down an overly self-assertive statement, to intensify a claim being urged upon the addressee or to mute a criticism, or to point out common ground when obvious discord made conversation awkward. Literature was useful because in relation to certain correspondents, at least, it was one of the ties that people believed connected them, and so obligated them to one another. Cicero could exploit literary culture as a kind of code in the letters not only because it was the product of a common schooling, but also because it continued to be regarded in some sense as a form of practical discourse.

5 𝄢

Giving and Getting Advice by Letter

Consultation—the asking, giving, and taking of advice—ranks along with discussions of politics, the imparting of *mandata,* and the commendation of friends and dependents as a major staple of the epistolary exchange between Cicero and his peers.[1] As with those other concerns, its importance in letters is an extension of its importance in life. Often a passage of consultation in the letters will wind up with the words, "but more on this when we meet" (sed haec coram), which is a good reminder that it was a regular element of the discourse carried on during receptions, dinners, and other face-to-face encounters among the elite.[2] Consultation was also institutionalized in the form of those advisory panels which we discern at the elbow of magistrates, governors, generals, and even of a Roman *paterfamilias* who sits in judgment upon wayward members of his family. "The Romans had an immemorial tradition that men in positions of responsibility should not take decisions alone."[3] There is no way to determine whether they actually consulted one another more often than Greeks did, but they certainly seem to talk about it more often.

With rare exceptions, we have no direct account of how Romans interacted when they conferred face-to-face.[4] But if it is true that effective advice giving has to satisfy the same basic conditions whether the advice is dispensed in person or at a distance, the social and rhetorical strategies evident in letters of advice presumably resemble strategies that Romans practiced when both parties were present. The letters of Cicero should thus provide the fullest information we have about an emblematic form of interaction among members of the Roman elite.

Given the frequency of consultation in the letters, it is odd that Cicero never treats it as forming one of the letter types that he regards as standard.[5] But it seems even more odd that the Romans were so persistent about giving and seeking advice in the first place. The reception of advice cannot help but open the possibility of a breach in personal dignity, of which Roman grandees were notoriously protective. To borrow again from the analysis of politeness by Brown and Levinson (see chap. 3), advice can be characterized as a face-threatening act. It is threatening for the advice giver, who steps onto slippery ground by delivering a message that will entail some cost for the recipient, who gambles a presumption of personal sagacity upon a practical test, and who risks being rebuffed by the recipient of advice. It is still more threatening to the latter, since it always carries an implication that the recipient's unaided understanding is somehow inadequate, and since once it has been delivered, it imposes a choice between the equally disagreeable alternatives of submitting to or rejecting another's direction.[6]

To the risks which accompany advice giving under the best of circumstances, consultation by letter adds at least two extra hazards. An epistolary adviser cannot receive the instant feedback that enables face-to-face advisers to adjust tone and repair missteps. Written advice can therefore go more badly wrong than spoken advice. And secondly, the privacy that protects both parties in a face-to-face encounter is potentially at risk in a letter. Letters sometimes become public, exposing indiscretions that neither party would care to have on record.

That the Romans persisted in trading advice despite these risks to mutual self-esteem should prompt us to wonder what benefits they thought outweighed the costs.[7] And so I begin this consideration of advice in the correspondence of Cicero and his friends by drawing attention to language that signals the sensitivity of the transaction. In the light of that background, I then try to clarify some of the social issues in play and to arrive at conclusions about the function of advice giving in Roman upper-class society.

The Sensitivity of Advice

Face-saving phraseology is most immediately detectable in the utterances of advice givers, and perhaps the most remarkable tactic on this side is to disavow that one is offering advice at all. After Cicero's brother had been sent abroad to govern the province of Asia at the close of the 60s, Cicero drafted a nineteen-page letter advising him on the proper conduct of provincial administration. Near the end of the letter, he declares, "I have written the things written above not in order to instruct you—nor, indeed, does your sagacity stand in need of anyone's direction—but the rehearsal of your fine character as I write has been a source of delight to me" (ea quidem quae supra scripta sunt non ut te instituerem scripsi (neque enim prudentia tua cuiusquam praecepta desiderat), sed me in scribendo commemoratio tuae virtutis delectavit, QFr. 1.1.36 = 1 SB).[8] A letter to the consular Marcus Marcellus begins, "I do not venture to advise a man endowed with such outstanding sagacity as yourself" (neque monere te audeo, praestanti prudentia virum, *Fam.* 4.8.1 = 229 SB), and Cicero tells another consular, his friend Servius Sulpicius, "I am not advising you, of course. I am sure that you are doing the same [as I], which even if it does not help, at least distracts the mind from care" (non equidem te moneo, sed mihi ita persuasi, te quoque in isdem versari rebus, quae etiam si minus prodessent, animum tamen a sollicitudine abducerent, *Fam.* 4.3.4 = 202 SB).

The burden that advice imposes can also be lightened by distributing it. That is the effect sought by using a first-person plural verb instead of the second-person singular. When a friend (Servius again) who had accepted a governorship from Caesar wished to resign and return to Rome, Cicero attempted to dissuade him. He writes—here and below I underscore the relevant pronoun uses—"I still take the line that we should do nothing but what Caesar seems to prefer" (adhuc in hac sum sententia, nihil ut faciamus nisi quod maxime Caesar velle videtur, *Fam.* 4.4.5 = 203 SB). Caelius Rufus resorts to the same tactic when he counsels Cicero about military kudos to be won during Cicero's term as governor of Cilicia. Caelius proposes that Cicero should look to provoke a small war, but the words he chooses suggest that he and Cicero will be fighting it together: "If we could only manage things so that a war developed of just the scale to suit your military strength, and so that we could achieve what was needed for the glory of a triumph while we avoid the really serious and dangerous conflict [with Parthia]—nothing could be so desirable" (nam si hoc modo rem moderari possemus, ut pro viribus copiarum tuarum belli quoque exsisteret magnitudo et quantum gloriae triumphoque opus esset adsequeremur, periculosam et gravem illam dimicationem evitaremus, nihil tam esset optandum, *Fam.* 8.5.1 = 83 SB). With this as with other discourse strategies I point out, speakers of English also have some acquaintance, perhaps as far back as the time we were first advised, "Let's clean up our plate now."

Another palliative is to represent the advice one offers as wisdom of which the recipient must already be well aware. An often quoted passage from another of Caelius's letters takes this form. Shortly before the civil war, Caelius urged Cicero to align himself with Caesar in case the stalemate in the Senate should lead to war. But he credited Cicero with having worked out the logic of that choice for himself: "I am sure it does not escape you that in a domestic conflict, people ought to take the more honorable side so long as an issue is contested as between citizens and without weapons, but the stronger side once it comes down to war and opposing camps. Then they ought to take the position that the better course is the safer course" (illud te non arbitror fugere, quin homines in dissensione domestica debeant, quam diu civiliter sine armis certetur, honestiorem sequi partem; ubi ad bellum et castra ventum sit, firmiorem, et id melius statuere quod tutius sit, *Fam.* 8.14.3 = 97 SB).[9]

The alternative to playing up the sagacity of one's interlocutor, as Caelius does, is to play down one's own. This is the strategy for which Caesar's agents

Balbus and Oppius opt in writing to Cicero when the question of his allegiance in the war is still unresolved: "Even in the case of grand personages, not to mention lowly persons like ourselves, most people are accustomed to judge advice by the outcome rather than by its intention. But trusting in your generosity of spirit, we will impart our most honest advice on the point on which you wrote to us. Should it not prove sagacious, at least it will proceed from the most loyal sentiments and a very good heart" (nedum hominum humilium, ut nos sumus, sed etiam amplissimorum virorum consilia ex eventu, non ex voluntate a plerisque probari solent. tamen freti tua humanitate quod verissimum nobis videbitur de eo quod ad nos scripsisti tibi consilium dabimus. quod si non fuerit prudens, at certe ab optima fide et optimo animo proficiscetur, *Att.* 9.7A.1 = 174A SB). Boisterous self-abnegation is a hallmark of Balbus's letters, even on this occasion on which Cicero had initiated the request for advice. But it has the drawback that it can call in question the worth of what an adviser has to say. Hence the point on which Balbus puts most stress in this passage is that he and Oppius have Cicero's best interests at heart.[10]

Another way in which an advice giver may seek to counteract an impression of bossiness is to use phrases that emphasize the other party's complete freedom to decide. Early in the civil war, when senatorial moderates were trying to decide whether or not to remain in occupied Italy, Servius proposed a visit to sound Cicero out. Cicero suspected that he and Servius had already come to opposite conclusions and that the visit would therefore be a waste of time. And so he responded, "I suggest—with your concurrence—that you forgo the nuisance of this visit if your mind is already made up in such a way that your course and mine are not as one" (tu, si videbitur, ita censeo facias ut, si habes iam statutum quid tibi agendum putes, in quo non sit coniunctum consilium tuum cum meo, supersedeas hoc labore itineris, *Fam.* 4.2.4 = 151 SB).[11] This sentence actually incorporates a second politeness strategy alongside the first. Apart from reserving judgment to Servius, Cicero frames the suggestion that they not meet as though the point of it were to spare him trouble: "I suggest that you forgo the nuisance of this visit."[12]

Cicero in turn is made the target of elaborately hands-off advice from his friend Caelius Rufus in an exchange that was briefly considered in chapter 4. At a certain point when Caelius was hoping to ingratiate himself with the aristocrat Appius Pulcher, he tried to maneuver Cicero into supporting Appius during an upcoming trial. But knowing that Cicero's prior dealings with Appius had been more stressful than pleasant, he could not afford to press too hard. And so he broached the suggestion that Cicero should help Appius out with the diffident overture, "I know that you have no antipathy toward him. How you want to oblige him is up to you" (scio tibi eum non esse odio; quam velis eum obligare in tua manu est, *Fam.* 8.6.1 = 88 SB). Caelius then presented his advice obliquely, in the form of hypotheticals laying out various courses and consequences for Cicero to ponder: "Now, if you had not previously been on the outs with him, you would have had more leeway in this whole business. But as things are, if you stand on claims of right, as in strict objectivity you are entitled to do, there will be the risk that your recent reconciliation with him may not look altogether sincere and aboveboard. Besides, it will be safe for you to tilt in this direction as much as you like, since no one will say that you swerved from duty as the result of friendship or any other tie" (cum quo <si> simultas tibi non fuisset, liberius tibi de tota re esset; nunc, si ad illam summam veritatem legitimum ius exegeris, cavendum tibi erit ne parum simpliciter et candide posuisse inimicitias videaris. in hanc partem porro tutum tibi erit si quid volueris gratificari; nemo enim necessitudine et amicitia te deterritum ab officio dicet).

So far I have described some redressive moves by which advisers attempt to soothe the self-esteem of those they counsel. Let me turn now to a characteristic reaction on the part of persons who have been subjected to advice. To the letter of Caelius just quoted, a reply by Cicero is extant which begins, "What a sagacious letter I have received from you... and how full of courtesy and advice! Though I had already made up my mind to act as you advise, nevertheless, our purposes are bolstered when we see that wise and loyal advisers think the same" (accipio litteras... quam prudentis, quam multi et offici et consili! etsi omnia sic constitueram mihi agenda ut tu admonebas, tamen confirmantur nostra consilia cum sentimus prudentibus fideliterque suadentibus idem videri, *Fam.* 2.13.1 = 93 SB). Guarded as Caelius had been in proffering advice, Cicero was so touchy about receiving it that he could not forbear to intimate that Caelius's advice was scarcely needed. (He had all the more reason to insist on his own perspicacity here because, as argued in chapter 4, he was writing this letter as much for the eyes of Appius as of Caelius.) Cicero reacts similarly to advice from Atticus in a letter that begins, "I am delighted that you are advising me to do something which I had already done of my own accord on the day before" (gaudeo id te mihi suadere quod ego mea sponte pridie feceram, *Att.* 15.27.1 = 406 SB). And lest we suppose that we have to do here only with the hair trigger vanity of Cicero, we can observe the same reaction in a letter of Julius Caesar. After Caesar's successful blitzkrieg early in 49, Balbus and Oppius suggested that he consider renewing negotiations with Pompey. Caesar answered, "Gladly will I follow your advice, and all the more gladly because I had decided of my own accord to show the utmost clemency and to take steps to win over Pompey" (consilio vestro utar libenter et hoc libentius quod mea sponte facere constitueram ut quam lenissimum me praeberem et Pompeium darem operam ut reconciliarem, *Att.* 9.7C.1 = 174C SB).[13] Or advice givers may anticipate this response at the outset, saying that they are sure that an advisee is already doing what should be done.[14]

Three things should be understood about the sampler of formulaic language offered above. One is that the conventions illustrated by it are by no means reserved exclusively for advice giving. Some are also employed when Latin speakers make requests or issue directives, for example, which are ordinarily classified as speech acts of a sort different from the giving of advice. For one thing, they do not necessarily presuppose that the speaker has the interests of the addressee foremost in mind. But as Cicero says in a letter fragment quoted by Quintilian, "the objective of an adviser is the utility of the person one advises" (suasoris enim finis est utilitas eius cui quisque suadet, Quint. *Inst.* 3.8.42).

Nor have I tried to compile the whole formulary of face-saving devices to be found in Latin letters of advice. Such a survey would be much longer and would perhaps only divert attention from the pragmatic finesse of the parties involved. Although efforts to make advice palatable are necessarily expressed in words, competent advisers rely more on their feel for a situation and their knowledge of the person addressed than on a stockpile of formulas. What they say can be extremely varied.

Finally, politeness strategies are not lavished uniformly on everyone. It will be no surprise that situation and status have an important bearing on the tone of the advice that a Roman receives. In the examples quoted above, all the persons being advised are senators, and all but one of them is a consular. But when Cicero is dealing with a dependent, a junior colleague, or an exile, the advice he dispenses can be relatively unvarnished.[15]

These few excerpts from the letters hardly do justice to the amount of mitigation that is mixed into the dispensing of advice, but they should serve to give an overview of the devices to which Romans resorted.

Friendship

If we now ask why a form of social behavior that required such elaborate redress was so freely indulged, a part of the answer has to be that advice giving was perceived to be a social obligation. It was always an acknowledged obligation within the sphere of friendship. In some of the passages quoted above, offers of advice are expressly grounded in the affection and concern that one party owes the other. Cicero goes so far as to make advice a corollary of what he calls the "first law of friendship" (prima lex amicitiae) in his dialogue on that theme. "Let us dare to offer counsel frankly," he writes. "In friendship the authority of friends who urge well should have the greatest scope, and should be deployed in advising not just unabashedly but even sharply, if circumstances require" (consilium vero dare audeamus libere; plurimum in amicitia amicorum bene suadentium valeat auctoritas; eaque et adhibeatur ad monendum, non modo aperte sed etiam acriter, si res postulabit, *Amic.* 44).[16]

Since a nexus between friendship and advice giving is taken for granted in modern society too, it might seem hardly worthy of remark.[17] But the frequency of advice in Cicero's letters is a direct consequence of the fact that almost every letter in the collection is a communication between two persons who can claim to be friends. For Cicero and his contemporaries in the upper echelons of Roman society, *amicitia* was a diffuse connection. It functioned as a kind of circumambient ether that permeated and enabled all social relations. In letters to at least three quarters of his nearly one hundred correspondents, Cicero expressly refers to ties of friendship, and I doubt that there is a single correspondent from whom he would have intentionally withheld the appellation of "friend."[18] Even he and Mark Antony profess their friendship in letters they address to each other.[19] Although our present corpus of Cicero's *Letters to Friends* did not acquire that title from Cicero or indeed from any ancient source, the title accurately reflects the ethos of amity behind the letters.

Authority

Advice, then, is common in the correspondence because advice was one of the primary goods that friends were expected to exchange. But there was also a second dimension in which it was perceived to be a social obligation. For anyone who claimed a leadership position in Roman society, the giving of advice was inseparable from the exercise of personal *auctoritas*. To be called the *auctor* of some course of action is, in fact, one way in which an advisory role is indicated in Latin.[20] Not only are Cicero's correspondents in some degree his friends, but a large proportion of them—again, about 75 percent—are fellow senators who share a corporate responsibility for counseling the officers of the state. In this milieu, we can expect the principal players to be preoccupied with advice giving as a probative token of leadership.

For Cicero, the aspect of leadership that most particularly summoned advisory propensities into play was the power of foresight. He alludes on more than one occasion to Thucydides' exaltation of Themistocles as the "best predictor of things to come, up to the furthest boundary of the future."[21] He incorporated this touchstone into his own model of the statesman, declaring in the *Pro Murena*, for example, that "it is the part of a good consul not only to see what is happening, but also to *foresee* what is *going to* happen" (est boni consulis non solum videre quid agatur verum etiam providere quid futurum sit, *Mur.* 4). Naturally, he was thinking in the first instance of himself, and in the letters he can often be observed plying his powers of divination.[22]

Cicero's record as a prophet is imperfect. Some predictions that he makes are belied by events, and some events that he later claims to have foreseen are at least not foretold in any of the extant correspondence.[23] But whatever the results, his conviction that good leaders possessed the gift of foresight partly explains his need to dispense advice. It also explains why he was touchy about accepting advice, if that could be taken to imply that his own intuition had left him in the lurch. Cicero's concern with foresight may also reflect a deeper moral concern to which I will return at the end of this chapter. Here it will be enough to observe that foresight was not just part of a skill set required of leaders: from a Roman perspective, it overlapped with a principle of conduct indispensable for anyone at all. The Latin word *providentia* is the original form of *prudentia*, which by Cicero's day had already acquired its rank as the first of the four cardinal virtues.[24] Foresight was a matter of surpassing importance if it was considered an aspect of virtue. "Just as ... *prudentia* ... was a virtue and an index of character, failures of *prudentia* were vicious. ... The Romans took such failures to be blots upon their honor and as comments on their worth as persons."[25]

Status Granting

Cicero's indifferent performance as a political seer, however, points us to another issue. Insofar as the role of adviser is an attribute of some other social position—as a friend, or as a leader—consultation is apt to acquire a pro forma quality. Or to put it another way, the frequency with which Romans consulted one another may have had less to do with the quality of advice they expected than with their relationships to the advice givers. One setting in which consultation often took place was the traditional open house which the leaders of society conducted during morning hours. But since good etiquette required lower-ranking friends to present themselves on such occasions whether they craved advice or not, whatever counseling occurred was incidental to the social nature of their call.

One episode of consultation for appearance's sake is recorded in unusual detail. After Caesar invaded Italy early in 49, he was eager to induce Cicero to stay and collaborate with him. In a brief but gracious message he wrote, "As I am confident that I will shortly get to Rome, I particularly request of you that I may see you there, in order that I may draw on your advice, influence, prestige, and aid in all respects" (in primis a te peto, quoniam confido me celeriter ad urbem venturum, ut te ibi videam, ut tuo consilio, gratia, dignitate, ope omnium rerum uti possim, *Att.* 9.6A = 172A SB).[26] By a fortunate and unusual chance, both Cicero's candid reaction to this note and the studied answer he later made to Caesar have been preserved.[27] To Atticus, he first commented, "Caesar writes ... that he wants to draw on my 'advice'—okay, fine: that's a commonplace" (Caesar scribit ... se velle uti 'consilio' meo—age, esto; hoc commune est, *Att.* 9.9.3 = 176 SB). Having dismissed Caesar's reference to *consilium* as cant, he then tried to guess the practical coordinates of the terms "influence, prestige, and aid." To Caesar he responded, "When I read your letter ... I was not so much astonished that you wanted to draw on my 'advice and prestige,' but I did ask myself what you were suggesting in regard to 'influence and aid'" (ut legi tuas litteras ... te velle uti 'consilio et dignitate mea' minus sum admiratus; de 'gratia' et de 'ope' quid significares mecum ipse quaerebam, *Att.* 9.11A.1 = 178A SB). In the remainder of the letter he describes the terms on which he would be prepared to cooperate with Caesar, but he carefully avoids the appearance of dispensing advice on policy.

It is obvious from this exchange that Cicero thought Caesar was merely being polite when he solicited advice. No doubt correctly, he assumed that Caesar's policies would be formed without input from him. Yet Caesar, for his part, did need the endorsement of a compliant Senate to enact policy. Procedurally, it was not pointless for him to make a show of conferring with one of the Senate's senior consulars and its most articulate spokesman.

Cicero expressed less wariness about a consultant role tendered to him a few years later. After Caesar's assassination in the spring of 44, he saw no hope of co-opting the surviving consul Mark Antony, but he cultivated with fresh zeal the two Caesarians slated to succeed Antony at the start of the next year. With Aulus Hirtius, in particular, he embarked upon a program of dinner parties, master classes in oratory, and political reindoctrination. He soon reported to Atticus that Hirtius was willing to cancel a resettlement plan in a region where Atticus held property, and that he was promising even more: "He made me the arbiter not only of this matter, but of his whole consulate" (arbitrum me statuebat non modo huius rei sed totius consulatus sui, *Att.* 15.1.2 = 377 SB). Shackleton Bailey terms this utterance of Hirtius "remarkable" and cautions that "such expressions were obviously not to be taken too literally." To us, as perhaps to Cicero, it sounds as though Hirtius is holding out the prospect of an intimate collaboration. But if pressed, all his words *have* to mean is that as consul, he would call on Cicero to express his views in senatorial debates first—which is the role a senior consular would play in any case. Hirtius might just as easily have borrowed Caesar's language and said that he intended to draw on Cicero's "advice, influence, prestige, and aid in all respects." And Cicero would have had no reason to cavil, because he was guilty of offering the same sort of bland assurances himself. A few years before the civil war, at a time when he had begun creeping into alignment with Caesar, he was called to account by the anti-Caesarian consular Lentulus. Cicero responded by promising that in the future he would make Lentulus "the moderator of all my policies" (tu eris omnium moderator consiliorum meorum, *Fam.* 1.9.22 = 20 SB).[28]

If solicitations of advice sometimes seem to proceed more from an appreciation of another's position than of his wisdom, the same is true of some claims to have benefited from advice in times past. In a letter written to his friend Lucceius many years after the Catiline affair, Cicero harks back to those deeds "which I accomplished at your instance above all" (quas te in primis auctore gessimus, *Fam.* 5.13.4 = 201 SB). It is something of a surprise to hear Cicero credit the defining performance of his career to alien inspiration, and there is nothing else in his writings or in any other source that connects Lucceius with the events of 63. In an account Cicero published of his consulate, he did speak of taking counsel before the arrest of the conspirators, but the advisers he identified there were his brother and another friend, not Lucceius.[29]

On another occasion, when Cicero was in command of armed forces in Cilicia, he wrote to his predecessor, Appius Pulcher, that he had deferred a request for Senate recognition of a victory in the field, and he recalls that he did so because he was "swayed by your lead and counsel" (adductus auctoritate et consilio tuo, *Fam.* 3.9.4 = 72 SB). None of the letters that Cicero wrote to Appius around the time when Appius could have offered this advice makes any mention of it.[30] Perhaps more tellingly, it does not come up in letters to Atticus that Cicero was writing concurrently and that detail his eagerness to secure a decree of thanksgiving if not a triumph for his exploits.

To cite one last case, Cicero tells the Caesarian agent Matius that after giving up the Pompeian cause and returning to Rome, he had taken Matius's advice (*consilium*) about how to act toward Caesar on all important matters (*Fam.* 11.27.5 = 348 SB). At best, this statement must be reckoned an exaggeration, since the rest of Cicero's correspondence from this period gives no hint of such a role for Matius and suggests rather that Atticus was the paramount influence on Cicero's conduct.[31]

All these examples naturally raise the possibility that other consultations on show in Cicero's correspondence, perhaps even a good many of them, may be formalities. Now, to be sure, formalities are not necessarily meaningless formalities. If the consultations in which the Roman elite engaged should turn out to be pro forma exchanges, they might still be socially constructive acts and be so in a way that would call in question the assumption that advice giving is always a face-threatening act. If taking counsel is done for appearance's sake, then at least some of the tension I have claimed that the Romans felt between giving advice and respecting face claims would be defused. Though it may be rude to thrust advice upon another, to seek and receive advice in virtue of the social position which the other occupies is the very opposite of a face-threatening act. It is a compliment.

That there is a strong element of status granting in many consultations attested by the letters seems undeniable. But it can hardly be the universal explanation. It cannot account for those situations in which advice was offered when it was not invited, for example. The next chapter will examine two of Cicero's unsolicited letters of advice, one to Decimus Brutus and one to Munatius Plancus. But even if it is true that every consultation served to reaffirm status hierarchies, that would not be a very interesting explanation for the phenomenon. An interpretation that makes requests for advice just another kind of coin in which respect was paid, like gifts or book dedications or personal calls, displaces attention from the substance of the transaction to manners. And it does not do justice to the range of effects that advice giving creates in personal relationships.

Networking

At several points in the published correspondence, Cicero can be observed seeking advice simultaneously and independently from several sources. When he was dwelling in exile in 58 and 57, he constantly discussed schemes for his recall with Atticus in the series of letters that now make up book 3 of that corpus. During the same period, however, he was also corresponding with and gathering information and advice from fellow senators, including his brother Quintus; his then son-in-law, Piso; Pompey; the consul-elect Lentulus; the incoming tribunes Sestius and Fadius; and others.[32] These were surely not pro forma consultations initiated to flatter his correspondents. Cicero's self-absorption is here fervent and undisguised, and with Atticus at least he courts offense by often complaining, scolding, and criticizing. Furthermore, Cicero desperately desires to utilize the information that reaches him. The difficulty is that because he communicates with each of his confidants separately for the most part, the advice he receives is inconsistent. That sets him churning to no purpose, trying to test one recommendation against another. He finds fault with a tactical decision that Atticus had made, for example, because it is at odds with a course being advocated by his friends among the tribunes-elect (*Att.* 3.24 = 69 SB). This compartmentalizing of advisers and their advice is part of a pattern in the letters that was described in chapter 3. With most correspondents, Cicero seems not to want his lines of communication to cross or merge. Letters to one person give away relatively little about the contacts he maintains with others.

But in any case, let it be noted that Cicero canvassed for advice even when he had less at stake than in the crisis of his exile. When he left Rome to begin his tour of provincial administration in Cilicia, he had not yet managed to find a suitable new husband for his daughter, Tullia. He therefore asked Atticus to continue to explore possibilities while he was away, and at several points consulted with him about the progress of the search.[33] Separately, he had also asked Caelius Rufus to keep an eye out for him as he was leaving town.[34] While abroad, he negotiated directly with one suitor whose candidacy he seems to have discussed with neither Caelius nor Atticus.[35] And ultimately he endorsed a match that he says he had authorized his wife and daughter to conclude independently of these consultations.[36]

A comparatively minor question on which he sought advice arose in the aftermath of Caesar's assassination, when Antony had taken control of the Senate. Cicero withdrew from political activity but then agonized about whether he should also absent himself from Rome and, if so, how far afield he should travel and for how long. Though he looked to Atticus for guidance in this as in all matters, he let him know that he was regularly polling the opinions of others too.[37]

What is interesting about these episodes is that, faced with three problems of disparate urgency, Cicero took trouble to consult about each. Yet it is uncertain in these and other cases whether the advice he received governed what he did in the end. Not that the possibility can be ruled out. Cicero does ascribe some of his past actions to good advice he received, as we have seen, and we will see that he ascribes other actions to bad advice. But the fact that they are retrospective makes such claims somewhat suspect: in each situation, Cicero had an incentive to revise the past. I know of no example of decision making in which the letters show him in the act of embracing a course recommended by someone else for the reasons it was recommended. The paucity of practical results suggests that consultation may have been valued for something other than, or beyond, solutions to problems. Anyone who has engaged in or observed the activity that we now call "networking" will recognize in it a resemblance to what Cicero was doing. Ancient and modern objectives differ, perhaps, but in both societies the process is as important as the ostensible goal.

Positioning

A peripheral benefit of the consultation process was that it established positions from which the consulting parties could maneuver at later points. The adviser acquired a warrant to criticize if events unfolded in such a way as to support a reprimand for disregarding advice. So, for example, on the ides of March when Brutus and Cassius took refuge on the Capitol after killing Caesar, Cicero urged them to summon the Senate and consolidate their political position before Caesar's partisans could react. They did not, and when, a couple of months later, they had been driven from Rome and were on the verge of decamping from Italy, Cicero reminded them of their lost opportunity.[38] The habit of consultation also provided the advisee with a warrant for criticism in the event that he followed advice which turned out badly. Cicero worked this end of the process as well. Under Clodius's onslaught in 58, he decided (probably correctly) that he did not have adequate resources to fight back and that he would do better to take refuge abroad. But later he decided that he had given up too easily, and he blamed his decision to withdraw on advice from false friends.[39]

Criticism is an act that requires even more elaborate face work than advising, and Cicero's correspondence contains a wealth of evidence for the study of it. The affinities between criticism and advice in the letters would repay investigation: criticism can be viewed as a kind of advice after the event, and it was sometimes provoked by the miscarriage of advice. Rather than pursue that tangent here, however, let me note only that opportunities for the kind of retrospective criticism just described were further increased if one had consulted a multiplicity of advisers, as Cicero often did. The wider the range of opinion sampled, the more likely it became that there would be scapegoats to bear the blame for any miscalculation one had made. Cicero eventually felt that it was a mistake for him to have joined Pompey in 49, and in a backward-glancing letter to Atticus two years later he blamed that decision on pressure from his family: "When I saw the complexion of the war—that complete fecklessness and impotence were pitted against perfect readiness—I had made up my mind what to do, and opted for a course which may not have been valiant, but which was more permissible for me than for anyone else. [But] I yielded to my family, or rather obeyed them" (ego enim cum genus belli viderem, imparata et infirma omnia contra paratissimos, statueram quid facerem ceperamque consilium non tam forte quam mihi praeter ceteros concedendum. cessi meis vel potius parui, Att. 11.9.1–2 = 220 SB; compare 9.6.4 = 172 SB). Yet in letters written before he sailed for Greece, the conversations with his wife and brother and children are ranged alongside many other conversations he was having. At one point in those discussions, in fact, he reproached Atticus because Atticus had advised him *not* to join Pompey. "The one thing that torments me," he writes, "is that I have not followed Pompey…like a soldier in the ranks" (me una haec res torquet quod non…Pompeium tamquam unus manipularis secutus sim, Att. 9.10.2 = 177 SB). Then after ventilating his regrets, he declares, "Now, at least, I shall try to take wing from this place, even if the effort entails a risk. Maybe I should have acted sooner. But the things I mentioned, and above all, your authority slowed me down" (nunc si vel periculose experiundum erit, experiar certe ut hinc avolem. ante oportuit fortasse; sed ea quae scripsi me tardarunt et auctoritas maxime tua, sec. 3). With that, he arrives at one of the most remarkable junctures in the epistolary corpus. Announcing that he has just paused to take out a file of letters from Atticus for the previous two months, he quotes back to him fourteen comments to the effect that Cicero should not be in any hurry to join Pompey. (This little chrestomathy preserves almost the only words of Atticus to have survived from antiquity.)

The habit of consulting many persons also provided a second sort of cover: in practice, it reduced the necessity of heeding any of them. Since it was hardly possible in most cases to reconcile conflicting advice, to solicit a range of opinions therefore provided a safeguard against the offense of later ignoring advice.

Finally, in this milieu, even the absence of advice had its uses. Cicero was as willing in retrospect to blame others for not advising him at all as for advising him badly. He recalls that when he let Clodius intimidate him into fleeing Italy, Atticus "contributed only tears" to his distress (tu tantum lacrimas praebuisti dolori meo, Att. 3.15.4 = 60 SB). "You devoted none of your wisdom to my preservation, because you had decided either that I possessed counsel enough within or that you owed me nothing more than to be on hand…and so I cast myself and mine into the hands of my enemies as you looked on and said nothing" (nihil impertisti tuae prudentiae ad salutem meam, quod aut in me ipso satis esse consili decreras aut te nihil plus mihi debere quam ut praesto esses…me, meos tradidi inimicis inspectante et tacente te, sec. 7).[40] This way of thinking was not peculiar to Cicero. At the outset of the civil war, Caelius Rufus wrote that he had chosen Caesar's side with serious misgivings. In part, he felt that his better judgment had been swept away by antipathies or loyalties toward some of the principals, but Cicero, too, was to blame, he said. "You besides, when I visited you the night I was setting out for Ariminum…you neglected the office of a friend and you did not give me counsel" (tu porro, cum ad te proficiscens Ariminum noctu venissem…amici officium neglexisti neque mi consuluisti, *Fam.* 8.17.1 = 156 SB). Preposterous as these accusations may sound coming from responsible adults, they are instructive. For Caelius and for Cicero, advice giving was such an integral part of their intercourse that the default of it could be represented as a violation of social norms.

The Content of Advice

The material surveyed thus far illustrates that advice giving was seen as an obligation associated with the social positions which members of the elite occupied as friends and as leaders, and that on a transactional plane it opened the way for subsequent moves by the consulting parties. But more was involved in the process than social maneuvering, and it is time finally to say something about the actual content of advice.

The first thing to recognize is that little of the advice exchanged in Cicero's correspondence bears on problems of how to accomplish things. So far as we can tell from the extant material, Cicero rarely if ever sought counsel about his forensic practice—which cases to take or how to present them.[41] He evidently needed no guidance about the discharge of senatorial functions, such as articulating policy, framing legislation, lobbying, and voting. When Clodius was brought to trial in 61 B.C. for a sacrilegious intrusion into a Roman women's rite, Cicero gave testimony that demolished Clodius's alibi and so precipitated the feud that led to his own exile. There is no sign that he consulted anyone about that fateful step.[42] Letters to Atticus and others after the assassination of Caesar in 44 give no hint of deliberation preceding Cicero's decision to take the offensive against Antony toward the end of that year. During his brief stint as a governor in 51/50, he did not seek advice about the conduct of military operations or (by contrast, say, with Pliny a century and a half later) about the routines of provincial administration.[43] (It is true that some of his letters to Atticus in this period concerned financial interests that friends of Atticus were trying to press in Cilicia. But Cicero was in no doubt about the policy he wanted to pursue. He wrote to try to persuade Atticus to accept his point of view.) So far as the letters would suggest, Cicero plunged into most activities of his career without consulting anybody.

What, then, were the questions about which he chose to seek advice? Rather than embark upon a catalogue here, let me describe the single most common scenario for consultation. When Pompey and his army evacuated Italy early in the civil war, it took Cicero weeks to follow suit. In the interval he produced a book and a half worth of letters asking Atticus whether he thought he should return to Rome or cast his lot with Pompey or pick a neutral destination, and who else was leaving town or staying on. At many junctures in his life, this quandary recurred in some form. On the eve of his exile in 58, as noted above, Cicero had asked friends whether he should flee from Rome or stay and fight Clodius (this was the occasion on which he complained that Atticus had failed him). After Pompey's defeat, Cicero spent a year at Brundisium checking with Atticus and others about the feasibility of returning home to the capital. And after that, Antony's ascendancy precipitated a new round of indecision about whether to vacate Rome again. Long stretches of the letters to Atticus can be summed up as Cicero dithering about where to go.

But Atticus was not being consulted for his travel experience, and Cicero was rarely seeking facts he needed to plot his itinerary. We have only to read through any sequence of these letters to see that he wanted forecasts about his public image. The underlying question, which sometimes becomes explicit, is, "How will you and others regard me if I take such-and-such a step?"[44] The spirit of these consultations is captured in an exchange which Cicero had with Caesar's agent Oppius at the start of the civil war, and which Cicero recalls in a letter to Oppius written a few years later: "I have always judged that you possess the utmost sagacity in framing advice and the utmost trustworthiness in dispensing it, and I had particular experience of that at the beginning of the civil war, when I consulted you by letter about whether I should go to Pompey or remain in Italy. You advised that I should consult my dignity" (semper iudicavi in te et in capiendo consilio prudentiam summam esse et in dando fidem, maximeque sum expertus cum initio civilis belli per litteras te consuluissem quid mihi faciendum esse censeres, eundumne ad Pompeium an manendum in Italia. suasisti ut consulerem dignitati meae, *Fam.* 11.29.1 = 335 SB). What a non-Roman might easily mistake for a practical question, Oppius interpreted as a question about Cicero's status. More surprising still, Cicero thought, or at least claimed, that the recommendation to consult his dignity was an answer to the question. He continues, "With that, I understood what you thought, and I marveled at your conscientiousness and trustworthiness in giving advice, because, although you thought that your great good friend had a different preference, you placed a higher value on my sense of duty than on Caesar's will" (ex quo quid sentires intellexi et sum admiratus fidem tuam et in consilio dando religionem, quod, cum aliud malle amicissimum tuum putares, antiquius tibi officium meum quam illius voluntas fuit).

It would be disingenuous to pretend that in almost 950 letters concerned with politics, money, literary activities, and family relations, neither Cicero nor his correspondents ever imparted a bit of practical advice.[45] But no distortion is involved in claiming that the consultations were not usually focused on practical "how-to" problems and that, when they seem to be, closer scrutiny often suggests otherwise. Take a consultation about family arrangements. When Caesar began his sweep toward Rome in 49, Cicero wondered whether he should allow his wife and daughter to remain there. But safety, convenience, or sentimental considerations weighed less with him than did matters of image, as this query to Atticus makes clear: "I ask you to look at whether it really does us credit for them to be at Rome, when other women of their stature have departed" (quaeso videas ut satis honestum nobis sit eas Romae esse cum ceterae illa dignitate discesserint, *Att.* 7.14.3 = 138 SB). Or take a literary decision that was examined in chapter 4. In a letter to his brother (*QFr.* 3.5[5–7].1 = 25 SB), Cicero wrote that he had decided to recast his dialogue *On the Republic* so as to make himself and Quintus the interlocutors. The decision was based not on literary grounds but on considerations of status. "I was advised," Cicero explains, "that a discourse on those themes could have much greater weight if I spoke in my own voice about the commonwealth, since...I was a consular and one who had taken a hand in dramatic political events" (admonitus sum ab illo multo maiore auctoritate illis de rebus dici posse si ipse loquerer de re publica, praesertim cum essem...consularis et is qui in maximis versatus in re publica rebus essem, *QFr.* 3.5.1 = 25 SB). Finally, a question about money. As Cicero was returning to Rome for his climactic fight against Mark Antony in late 44, he consulted frequently with Atticus about money problems that were hampering his ability to clear his debts. The latest letter of the Atticus series raises the subject one more time: "I'm anxious about my personal finances. But do I say finances? On the contrary, I mean rather my reputation" (me res familiaris movet. rem dico? immo vero existimatio, *Att.* 16.15.5 = 426 SB).

The Latin terms that come up in these anecdotes and in the exchange with Oppius mentioned earlier—*existimatio, auctoritas, dignitas, honestum, officium*— indicate that the problems under consideration were being construed by both parties as problems of moral action. A moral dimension is even more pronounced in other consultations. The following chapter will discuss the correspondence that Cicero carried on with governors and army leaders during the years 44 and 43, when he was trying to rally them against Antony. Although the military situation was in constant flux, Cicero's letters for that period rarely advert to details of what was happening or to issues of strategy. They are overwhelmingly taken up with abstractions like *dignitas, gloria, auctoritas,* and *fama.*

The quickness with which advisers ascended from the plane of the concrete to the abstract sometimes left the recipients of advice bewildered. As noted previously, the chief preoccupation of Cicero's letters to Atticus in early 49 was whether he should join Pompey after Caesar had driven Pompey out of Italy. Atticus had responded with a stream of advice that is partially extant in the chrestomathy of *Att.* 9.10.4–10 = 177 SB. But after several weeks, Cicero had to ask him exactly what he was recommending: "You say you're glad I have remained, and you write that you are standing by your recommendation. Yet in an earlier letter it seemed there was no doubt in your mind that I should go, if Pompey took ship with a sizable crowd and if the consuls made the crossing. Don't you recall this? Did I not quite understand you? Or did you change your mind?" (gaudere ais te mansisse me et scribis in sententia te manere. mihi autem superioribus litteris videbare non dubitare quin cederem, ita si et Gnaeus bene comitatus conscendisset et consules transissent. utrum hoc tu parum commeministi, an ego non satis intellexi, an mutasti sententiam? *Att.* 9.2 = 168 SB). A week earlier, he had begged Atticus, "Though you have given hints of what you think about all this, please put it down for me more precisely" (haec qualia tibi esse videantur, etsi significata sunt a te, tamen accuratius mihi perscribas velim, *Att.* 8.12.4 = 162 SB). A week later, he expressed confusion about a letter that he said Atticus had written "in rather general terms" (γενικώτερον). "I thought you were intimating in effect that I should leave Italy" (ego mihi a te quaedam significari putassem ut Italia cederem, *Att.* 9.10.6 = 177 SB). But then came a follow-up letter in which Atticus denied he had intimated anything of the kind.

The Roman penchant for sententious abstraction was certainly not the only factor that can be seen working at cross-purposes to effective consultation in the letters. The personality of Cicero, who gives an impression of hearing only as much advice as he wanted to hear, also played a part. And at least equally important was the societal reality that advice was required from members of the upper class whether or not they had any to impart. The pressure to purvey insights which one either did not possess or for which one did not care to take responsibility could turn advising into an exercise in fence-sitting. Atticus's own words show that the gist of his counsel in 49 was "wait and see," which was his message at other points in the correspondence, too.[46] Cicero on occasion temporized in much the same way. In 56, his benefactor Lentulus Spinther was hoping that, as governor of Cilicia and Cyprus, he would be charged with restoring the spendthrift king of Egypt to the throne from which he had recently been toppled. Lentulus's rivals in the Senate, however, had concocted a religious impediment to the use of troops in that connection which Cicero, for all his efforts, was unable to overcome. The best he could do was to report that he and Pompey had thought of a technicality that might allow Lentulus to skirt the problem. Not that they went so far as actually to promote that course, however:

> [Pompey] and I endorse this idea with the caveat that we recognize that people will judge your plan [notice that the plan has suddenly become Lentulus's plan, not Cicero and Pompey's] according to its outcome—that if it turns out as we wish and hope, everyone will declare that you acted wisely and bravely, but if there is some slip-up, the same people will say that you acted with reckless cupidity. It is

not so easy for us to judge what you can accomplish as for you, who sit practically in sight of Egypt. Our view is that if you are sure that you can gain the mastery of that kingdom, you should not delay, but if you are in any doubt, you should not try.

> *sed haec sententia sic et illi et nobis probabatur ut ex eventu homines de tuo consilio existimaturos videremus; si cecidisset ut volumus et optamus, omnis te et sapienter et fortiter, si aliquid esset offensum, eosdem illos et cupide et temere fecisse dicturos. qua re quid adsequi possis non tam facile est nobis quam tibi, cuius prope in conspectu Aegyptus est, iudicare. nos quidem hoc sentimus, si exploratum tibi sit posse te illius regni potiri, non esse cunctandum; si dubium sit, non esse conandum.*

Fam. 1.7.5 = 18 SB

There was good reason for Cicero not to be too forward with advice on this occasion. When a neighboring governor less cautious than Lentulus later went ahead and restored the Egyptian king, he was prosecuted for treason.[47] If Lentulus had been the one to end up on trial, Cicero would not have wanted to be on record as having encouraged him, and yet he could not dodge the responsibility of providing guidance to a friend. Equivocal advice was the inevitable compromise.[48]

Presumably the advice traded between Romans was colored by the subjective factors that also impinge on advice giving today: the large- or closed-mindedness of the consulting parties, their wisdom or naiveté, tact or clumsiness, and altruism or conceit. The correspondence of Cicero amply attests the contributions of personality to the process. But to return the focus again to the content of advice, the letters also show that in Cicero's milieu, advising consisted above all in relating questions of practical action to generally accepted moral values. It was easier for an adviser to expatiate on values, however, than to analyze exactly how they were implicated in a given situation. When Cicero wanted advice about joining Pompey in 49, he found that Atticus responded with "intimations" and "generalities." What he missed were the argumentative steps that would guide him from the practical alternatives he faced to the moral abstractions by which others would judge his conduct.

This orientation toward moral values is, of course, one of the features that mark the style of advice giving practiced in the letters as distinctively Roman. The correspondence of Cicero illustrates just how constant the stream of judgments was. The nature of the advice conveyed in turn accounts for another feature that distinguishes Roman from modern practice—or at least from modern, urban, American practice. In our society, advice has become institutionalized to a great extent. It has been turned over to professionals who can claim expertise in such fields as physical and mental health, school and career problems, personal finances, marriage and child rearing, and even lonely hearts counseling.[49] The differentiation of professions in Roman society, on the other hand, was much less developed. Yet even if there had been a greater number of niches for expert knowledge at Rome, advice giving would probably not have been assigned a place among them. Since the advice that members of the upper class wanted consisted largely of moral or social assessment, it was hardly a scarce good. Everybody possessed a fund of it, at least everybody whose opinion in society counted for anything, and everyone whose opinion counted was ipso facto authorized to promulgate opinions. And not only were there many people on hand waiting to advise, but advice seekers had incentives to consult many of them. They were usually polling opinion rather than seeking information, and the habit of implicating others in their deliberations had tactical advantages apart from any guidance they received.

For these reasons it seems inevitable that the exchange of advice should have been frequent in Cicero's letters. But to say that is perhaps to say no more than that advice was plentiful because there was plenty of it on tap. A slightly more dynamic hypothesis might propose that advice circulated freely because it was a commodity that could be easily exchanged, and because society requires a steady process of exchange if it is to remain cohesive. To that extent, advice would be on a par with other staples of epistolary trade mentioned at the beginning of this chapter: news, *mandata*, favors, and recommendations.

But there was something distinctive about this particular commodity that caused it to be particularly prominent in letters. I have tried to show that Roman consultations turned in large part on the defining of social position. The letters of the Ciceronian corpus often coincided with moments when the social position of either the letter writer or the recipient was vulnerable. At a minimum, one party was away from Rome and therefore unable to participate in the day-to-day transactions by which public standing was normally maintained. Sometimes a correspondent's position was more seriously compromised than that as a result of exile, threats from enemies at home, or relegation to the political sidelines. In these moments Cicero and his correspondents might have been particularly anxious to assure each other that, despite appearances, the moral standards that had always defined position and right conduct were still in force.

6 𝕊

Letter Writing and Leadership

Chapters 4 and 5 discussed two of the epistolary topics that Cicero and his peers employed variously to cajole, compliment, or criticize one another or to aggrandize themselves. Advice giving and literary talk serve on the whole to smooth the give-and-take of social life. They are among the routines that enabled members of the elite to interact positively while always competing with one another. This chapter concerns letters that Cicero wrote at a rare moment in his life when he was able to take charge in the public sphere and was trying to bring about a realignment of political forces. More was at stake here than smooth relations: the cause for which Cicero sought to enlist or consolidate support entailed serious costs for everyone who rallied to it. My purpose is to examine how Cicero's private letters contributed to his efforts in support of a broad public objective.

The Post-Caesarian Correspondence

The published correspondence gives lavish coverage to letters written in the years 44 and 43, following the assassination of Julius Caesar. Letters of this period fill the last three books of the Atticus series, which breaks off enigmatically in the middle of it, in November 44. The one book of correspondence with Marcus Brutus that survives contains letters from the spring and summer of 43—evidently the last letters of that series. Books 10, 11, and 12 of the *Letters to Friends* contain exchanges with other governors and army leaders of the period (Plancus, Decimus Brutus, Cassius, Cornificius, Trebonius, Lepidus, and Pollio) and with lesser players in the same events. Moreover, these books of the *Letters to Friends* have been arranged so as to set their thematic and chronological coherence in relief. Although the default principle for organizing the collection was clearly to gather all material relating to a given correspondent in one place, the principle was modified here. Exchanges with Cassius and with Trebonius that took place prior to Caesar's death have been relegated to a different part of the collection (book 15). Editorial principles have been stretched in other ways as well. Not only do books 10 through 12 contain the most copious selection of material from Cicero's epistolary partners—including some correspondents, including Pollio, to whom Cicero's own letters do not appear in the collection—but they also include official dispatches to the Senate and other letters not addressed to Cicero at all.

Ancient readers of the letters had an even richer trove of post-Caesarian material available to them than we do. Judging by the distribution of letters in the one surviving book, at least one if not two more books of the Brutus series must have been devoted to letters of the years 44 and 43. Citation formulas in Nonius Marcellus indicate that there were twelve books of correspondence with the Caesarian leaders Hirtius and Pansa, much of which demonstrably dates from this time. Finally, all of the letters in three similarly attested books to Octavian, or "the younger Caesar," as the collection termed him, must have been written after the death of the elder Caesar. It would be a conservative estimate that in addition to the seven books of letters from this period that survive, the published correspondence once comprised as many more that do not.[1]

Since many other features of the corpus appear to be the result of design rather than chance, the inclusion of so many letters from these two years—amounting to more than 20 percent of the number extant—presumably reflects an editorial preference as well. It is easy to imagine why a compiler would be tempted to mine this material. The letters cover a span of about sixteen months in which Cicero found an opportunity to take center stage as he rallied the Senate to assert its authority against Caesar's creature Mark Antony. Even though the effort ultimately miscarried, with fatal consequences for Cicero, it was one of the two great sustained performances of his career. Cicero himself compared the struggle against Antony to his struggle against Catiline twenty years earlier when he was consul (*Phil.* 4.15, 12.24). And unlike his record as consul, his activity in 44 and 43 was exceptionally well documented in the letters. Much of the action in the Catilinarian affair took place in Rome, which limited the possibilities that Cicero's maneuvers vis-à-vis allies and antagonists would be reflected in his correspondence—the extant corpus contains no letters at all from the year 63, in fact. The struggle against Antony, on the other hand, unfolded largely outside Rome and led Cicero into an extended correspondence with army leaders around the Mediterranean.

Cicero's Role in the Senatorial War of 44–43

The editor of the collection was doubtless as aware as we are that the letters of 44 and 43 offered a unique view of Cicero. They are the only letters of his career in which he figures not just as a witness to important events but as a leader attempting to direct them. That the letters were selected to highlight his public role is suggested by the fact that the selection comes to an end with the end of the performance. By midsummer of 43, Cicero had run out of resources to throw into the struggle against Antony, and that is the point at which the published collection terminates. It includes no letters written during the last four months of Cicero's life, though it is most unlikely that he wrote none during that time.

Cicero's correspondence is not, of course, the only source for the history of this period. We have also 14 *Philippic Orations* from him and detailed narratives from Appian and Cassius Dio, to instance only the fullest among an unusually diverse array of sources. The background of the present chapter is less the history of the period per se, however, than Cicero's perception of it, which necessarily differs from our perception of it. Cicero was reacting and contributing to events before they had been emplotted into the historical narrative that we know, and with a less informed idea than we have of the direction in which events were moving. But in that respect, weak as his position may now look to us, he operated on roughly the same footing as Antony, Octavian, Lepidus, Plancus, Brutus, Cassius, and the rest. Each of them was working the levers available to him without foreknowledge of the results.[2]

The lever available to Cicero was not money or an army or a clientele, but the Senate. As he himself observed, "The Senate was my instrument" (ὄργανον enim erat meum senatus, *Fam.* 11.14.1 = 413 SB), and in the early stages of the contest he probably had a firmer grasp of his instrument than others did of money or armies. The Senate had come into play again at Caesar's death because no single individual was then in a position to appropriate the overwhelming power that Caesar had been able to amass. Even Antony's most high-handed actions in the months after the assassination rested on his use of conventional consular authority, and that was set to expire at the end of the year 44. Other pretenders to power had weaker credentials than Antony. And so it was at least conceivable that with Caesar gone, government might revert again to the Senate, as had happened after Sulla's regime. In the absence of an unquestioned strongman, all members of the political class needed the authority of the Senate to underwrite the arrangements, opportunities, and honors on which their careers depended. As long as it appeared that the Senate had the capacity to make good on its guarantees, it would have a political role.

But the post-Caesarian Senate was fractious, and Cicero's command of it was tenuous. At the time, the Senate comprised—and these were not mutually exclusive blocs—survivors of the Pompeian coalition during the civil war, former partisans and allies of Caesar now jostling one another, and those participants in the assassination who had not yet left Rome, together with their sympathizers.[3] Consensus among them did not form easily, so that Antony was able to represent decisions taken against him as mere manifestations of factional wrangling.[4]

As for Cicero, although he was a senior senator, he held no magistracy or command that enabled him to direct affairs. He had no authority to convene the Senate, and he was not even the head consular whom the presiding magistrate invited to frame debate by speaking first. His seniority ensured that he could always make his views heard, yet he could impose them only by persuading others to share them. He could deliver an address to the People only when a magistrate invited him to do so.

Yet despite these handicaps, Cicero did succeed in becoming leader of the Senate for several months beginning in December of 44. That he had taken charge was certainly his own understanding of his position at the time. Although he kept clear of words that might have had an official ring, he spoke of having taken the tiller of the Republic and of holding primacy (*principatus*), and of being the chief (*dux*) and mentor (*auctor*) of the Senate.[5] More to the point, friends and enemies agreed. Both Brutus and Antony acknowledged that, on the home front at least, Cicero was the person in charge.[6]

In the last of the *Philippics*, delivered at a juncture when Cicero mistakenly believed that the struggle against Antony was all but won, he looked back on the part he had played in it:

> Everyone remembers how on December 20th I took the lead in calling back our liberty, and how from January 1st until the present hour [on April 21st] I have stood watch over the nation: night and day, my home and my ears have been open to the injunctions and the admonitions of all, and people everywhere have been rallied to the defense of the country by my letters, my messages, and my exhortations.

> *omnes...memoria tenent me ante diem XIII Kalendas Ianuarias*
> *principem revocandae libertatis fuisse, me ex Kalendis Ianuariis ad hanc*
> *horam invigilasse rei publicae, meam domum measque auris dies noctesque*
> *omnium praeceptis monitisque patuisse, meis litteris, meis nuntiis, meis*
> *cohortationibus omnes qui ubique essent ad patriae praesidium excitatos.*
>
> Phil. 14.20

As he indicates, his activities were manifold. He frequently availed himself of opportunities to address the Senate and the People (only a few of which are documented by the *Philippics*), and, apart from making speeches, he engaged in consultations and negotiations behind the scenes. He battled colleagues vigorously to maintain control over the Senate's war policy. But this chapter does not purport to offer a comprehensive account of Cicero's campaign against Antony; that story can be read in the penultimate chapter of almost any biography of Cicero. The one area of his activity on which I want to focus attention here is the letter writing to which the passage above alludes. That is the focus consistent with the orientation of this book, the letters in question are numerous and understudied, and the goals to which Cicero aspired in writing them give them a distinctive place within the correspondence. But it would certainly be misleading if the following discussion were to leave an impression that his leadership could be reduced to what he accomplished or failed to accomplish through his letters alone. For Romans of Cicero's class, letter writing was not an optimal mode of interaction under the best of circumstances, as we have seen, and the problems were only aggravated during wartime, when lines of communication became more precarious and events outran the pace of correspondence.

Indeed, it may seem surprising that Cicero's letters should have played any part at all in the war effort because, as noted, Cicero was not authorized to direct the actions of others. None of his letters to Plancus, Marcus and Decimus Brutus, and the others constituted an official communication, nor did their letters to him.[7] Official letters from the Senate, often conveying notification of Senate decrees, emanated from consuls or from magistrates acting in their stead. From the other side, the official correspondence of governors and commanders was directed to magistrates and the Senate rather than to individual senators. Although little of this epistolary traffic is now extant, our sources often refer to it, and we should neither overlook its existence nor confuse it with the private correspondence that we have.[8] Cicero takes for granted that his correspondents were receiving official letters, and he writes his own with different ends in view.

Equally important, he was only one of those with whom they were communicating privately. They were writing back and forth, not only to their confidants in Rome, but to both allies and opponents abroad, who could change from the one into the other at very short notice.[9] Part of the challenge for Cicero in writing his own letters was to reckon with this concurrent stream of official and private communications, without knowing everything else that his correspondents were hearing.

From this point on, discussion can be organized around the letters themselves. The choice of which to treat has been made with an eye to Cicero's experience of events, which presented itself as a series of abrupt turns separated by stretches of anxiety and confusion. For sampling purposes, the letters that best repay attention are the letters written at turning points, when Cicero's need to mobilize resources was acute.[10] Most of the letters discussed here fall along a timeline that runs from December 44 to July 43 and that in turn defines a storyline of which Mark Antony was the central figure.

December 44–Late April 43: The Stand against Antony at Mutina

Cicero did not commit to an active public stance for many months after the ides of March.[11] Even as late as September, when he began composing the *Second Philippic*, he acted only to slap back after a gross insult from Antony. The speech was not actually delivered, and as of early November the text of it had not been published.[12] Nor did Cicero proceed from words to action. So far from attempting to organize resistance to Antony, he stayed away from Rome for the better part of October and November.

But when Antony headed north in late November to claim command of Cisalpine Gaul, Cicero did finally discern an opportunity for action. In leaving the capital, Antony had to relax his stranglehold over the Senate (Dolabella, his political partner and fellow consul, had also departed from Rome by then). Moreover, an unanticipated counterforce had materialized just a short while earlier, when Octavian began recruiting a private army from among Caesar's veterans and even enticed some of Antony's legions to desert to him. Octavian positioned his troops within easy reach of Rome, offering protection against the threat of force from Antony. It was at this moment that his correspondence with Cicero intensified, and, if it had survived, it would undoubtedly have been the place to begin a study of the wartime letters. Cicero's remarks in many texts that survive leave no doubt that Octavian was the linchpin of his strategy for dealing with Antony.

As it is, however, we must begin with another element in the situation of which Cicero was able to take advantage. A couple of weeks after the assassination, Decimus Brutus, a protégé of Caesar's who nevertheless joined the plot against him, took over the administration of Cisalpine Gaul, as Caesar had arranged before his death.[13] He thus became the only conspirator to gain command of an army during the year 44. That made him a target of attention both from his accomplices, who looked to him for protection, and from Antony, who forced through legislation requiring Decimus to turn over the province to him as soon as Antony laid down his consulate in Rome. Decimus's provisional response was to hold aloof from either side and to busy himself in campaigning at the far end of his province.[14]

After Antony marched north at the end of the year, however, Cicero appealed to Decimus to take a stand. In a letter of about December 9th, he argued that since Decimus had been willing to kill Caesar, he had no reason to balk at defying Antony. For his part, Cicero promised support: "I will do what is up to me, and offer you all my services, efforts, thoughts, and concerns <in everything> pertaining to your praise and glory. Both because of the Republic, which is dearer to me than my life, and because I support you personally and wish for your prestige to be magnified, please understand that at no point will I fail to back your splendid aims, greatness, and glory" (faciam illud quod meum est, ut tibi omnia mea officia, studia, curas, cogitationes <in res omnis> pollicear, quae ad tuam laudem et gloriam pertinebunt. quamobrem velim tibi ita persuadeas, me cum rei publicae causa, quae mihi vita mea est carior, tum quod tibi ipsi faveam tuamque dignitatem amplificari velim, tuis optimis consiliis, amplitudini, gloriae nullo loco defuturum, *Fam.* 11.5.3 = 353 SB).

But Decimus evidently did balk at the prospect of defying a consul without authorization from the Senate. Cicero, who believed at the time that nothing could be accomplished through the Senate until new consuls took office on the first of January,[15] therefore followed up with another letter saying that under current circumstances, Decimus would have to act on his own:

> Marcus Cicero bids greeting to Decimus Brutus, Commander and Consul Elect:
>
> When Lupus [Decimus's liaison in Rome] invited me, Libo, and your cousin Servius to a meeting at my house, I think you learned what my position was from Marcus Seius, who was involved in our conversation. Subsequent details you will be able to learn from Graeceius, though Graeceius follows closely on the heels of Seius.
>
> But the key thing, which I want you to assimilate and remember carefully, is this: in conserving the freedom and welfare of the Roman People, you must not wait for authorization from a Senate that is not yet free. That would be to condemn your own feat (since you liberated the state with no official warrant, and conserving it is still greater and more glorious), and to judge that the lad—or boy, rather—Caesar was rash to take up so great a cause on his own initiative. It would be to judge that those rustic but stout-hearted men and fine citizens were insane—I mean first of all the veterans with whom you served, and second the Martian Legion and the Fourth, who judged their consul to be a public enemy and went over to defend the welfare of the Republic. The wish of the Senate should be counted as authorization, when authorization is impeded by fear.
>
> Finally, you do not have a free hand, since you have already taken up the cause twice, first on the ides of March and most recently when you raised a new army and resources. Hence your overall position and attitude should be not that you will do nothing unless ordered, but that you will accomplish what will be praised by all with the utmost admiration.

M. Cicero s. d. D. Bruto Imp. Cos. Desig.

Cum adhibuisset domi meae Lupus me et Libonem et Servium, consobrinum tuum, quae mea fuerit sententia cognosse te ex M. Seio arbitror, qui nostro sermoni interfuit; reliqua, quamquam statim Seium Graeceius est subsecutus, tamen ex Graeceio poteris cognoscere.

caput autem est hoc, quod te diligentissime percipere et meminisse volam, ut ne in libertate et salute populi Romani conservanda auctoritatem senatus exspectes nondum liberi, ne et tuum factum condemnes—nullo enim publico consilio rem publicam liberavisti, quo etiam est res illa maior et clarior—et adulescentem, vel puerum potius, Caesarem iudices temere fecisse, qui tantam causam publicam privato consilio susceperit, denique homines rusticos sed fortissimos viros civesque optimos dementis fuisse iudices, primum milites veteranos, commilitones tuos, deinde legionem

Martiam, legionem quartam, quae suum consulem hostem iudicaverunt
seque ad salutem rei publicae defendendam contulerunt. voluntas senatus
pro auctoritate haberi debet cum auctoritas impeditur metu.

postremo suscepta tibi causa iam bis est ut non sit integrum, primum
Idibus Martiis, deinde proxime exercitu novo et copiis comparatis.
quamobrem ad omnia ita paratus, ita animatus debes esse, non ut nihil
facias nisi iussus, sed ut ea geras quae ab omnibus summa cum
admiratione laudentur.

Fam. 11.7 = 354 SB[16]

Together, this pair of letters to Decimus illustrates a twofold rhetorical strategy that recurs throughout Cicero's correspondence with army leaders during these months. He constructs an ad hominem appeal for action in terms of personal history and moral principle, and he holds out a prospect of recompense in the form of increased prestige or *dignitas*.

It would be naive to think that Decimus or anyone else was roused to action solely by such appeals from Cicero. In this case, it was Decimus who had written first: he recognized that he had to do something, and he was already exploring options.[17] Moreover, he had reasons of his own for doing what Cicero wanted him to do. Within days of the assassination, he had expressed fear that he would soon be outlawed for his part in the crime (*Fam.* 11.1.2 = 325 SB). If he now allowed Antony to take over his province, he would not only lose the protection of an army whose loyalty he had assiduously cultivated, but he would also have to resume life in Rome as a civilian until he entered office again as consul in January 42. If that prospect made him uneasy, preventing Antony from ousting him was the pragmatic course to follow.

But if Cicero's letters do not identify every consideration that would have weighed with Decimus, the issues they do raise ought at least to be ones that mattered to him. Letters generally presume some consensus between the writer and the addressee. Unless Cicero misjudged the psychology of his peers, Decimus must have been susceptible to an appeal in terms of character and prestige. Both elements invite scrutiny.

In framing an appeal to Decimus's character, Cicero was at a certain disadvantage because the two men were not well acquainted. Although Decimus had served in Caesar's Gallic wars during the same period as Cicero's brother, there is no evidence that he had contact with either brother then or subsequently. The absence of personal intimacy in the correspondence with Decimus gives it a tone different from that of Cicero's other exchanges during these months, not only with the Liberators Marcus Brutus and Cassius, but even with Decimus's fellow Caesarians Cornificius and Plancus.

Lacking an intimate knowledge of his addressee, Cicero chooses the tack that Decimus has defined himself once and for all by slaying Caesar—"the greatest feat in the memory of humankind" (re quae a te gesta est post hominum memoriam maxima, *Fam.* 11.5.1 = 353 SB). He lauds Decimus's role in the assassination in almost every one of the early letters to him.[18] In the letter quoted above, it serves partly to ground an argument about moral consistency: Decimus has an obligation to complete the mission of liberation that he began. But it also allows Cicero to sidle around the objection that Decimus would be acting treasonably if he defied a consul. Legal niceties do not apply, Cicero insinuates, because Antony has placed himself outside the law as Caesar did by becoming a tyrant. He too should be regarded as a public enemy (*hostis*) rather than a head of government. Finally, Cicero suggests that Decimus risks seeing his credit tarnished if he lets lesser men wrest the initiative from him. Octavian is a mere boy, and his recruits are yokels, and yet they have taken Decimus's precedent of forceful action to heart while Decimus now lingers on the sidelines. The assassination of Caesar is the lens through which almost everything that Cicero says is focused.

The second element of Cicero's exhortation is his promise to promote Decimus's *dignitas.* That *dignitas* could be a spur to action had been memorably demonstrated six years earlier, when Caesar urged his troops across the Rubicon to "vindicate his honor and prestige against his enemies" (hortatur...ut eius existimationem dignitatemque ab inimicis defendant, Caes. *BC* 1.7.7).[19] But it was hardly a motive peculiar to Caesar. Cicero and his peers talk often about the claims of *dignitas,* usually in the abstract, as in the passage quoted above from *Fam.* 11.5 = 353 SB. That is, Cicero pledges to augment Decimus's *dignitas* without saying specifically what he intends to do for him. Concrete services are always entailed, however. Earlier in the year, it had been Decimus who broached with Cicero the issue of "safeguarding my prestige," and what he wanted then was for Cicero to sponsor a Senate decree honoring his exploits against Alpine tribesmen (*Fam.* 11.4 = 342 SB—a request that incidentally shows that Cicero had good grounds for assuming a concern with *dignitas* on Decimus's part).

What Cicero would do to enhance Decimus's prestige if he resisted Antony was not made clear until Decimus finally made his move. On the morning of December 20th, he had an edict posted in Rome vowing that he "would keep his province under the control of the Senate and the Roman People" (pollicetur...se provinciam Galliam retenturum in senatus populique Romani potestate, *Phil.* 3.8). As it happened, a meeting of the Senate had been scheduled for later that very day, on which Cicero showed up for the first time in more than three months.[20] He addressed his fellow senators in a speech later published as the *Third Philippic,* then accepted (or solicited) a tribune's invitation to address a few words to the People, which became the *Fourth Philippic.* Then he reported to Decimus what he had done (*Fam.* 11.6a = 356 SB).

The two speeches make Cicero's down payment on his promise to Decimus, who is publicly exalted in both Senate Hall and Forum for defying Antony. To his own words of praise, Cicero managed to attach a Senate endorsement by proposing and carrying a decree of thanks to Decimus. He also carried a decree that countermanded Antony's legislation and instructed Decimus to hold his province until the Senate appointed a successor, thus quelling Decimus's anxiety about the legitimacy of his resistance.[21] A second salvo of praise followed shortly after, when the Senate met on January 1st under the presidency of the new consuls Pansa and Hirtius. Although the only new military development was that Decimus now found himself trapped with his army inside Mutina, he was again acclaimed in Cicero's *Fifth* and *Sixth Philippics* and honored by another Senate decree.[22] And again Cicero wrote assuring him that "in no matter do I, or shall I ever, fail to look out for your prestige" (*me neque deesse ulla in re neque umquam defuturum dignitati tuae, Fam.* 11.8.2 = 360 SB). One more installment on the promise was delivered after news came at the end of April that the armies of Octavian, Hirtius, and Pansa had defeated Antony in battle and lifted the siege of Mutina. Although the beleaguered Decimus had played little if any part in the fighting, he was honored among the victors in the official thanksgiving celebration, and was even voted a triumph.[23]

There was one honor, however, that Cicero failed to procure for Decimus on that occasion. The Senate declined to go along when he proposed an entry in the official calendar celebrating the auspicious coincidence that news of victory had reached Rome on Decimus's birthday.[24] The fizzling of this proposal is instructive on two counts. On the one hand, it points to a problem with the incentives Cicero could offer in exchange for military support. In a letter to Cornificius, another army leader whose *dignitas* he was promising to advance (*Fam.* 12.24.1 = 361 SB), he draws a distinction between "praising" (*laudare*) and "honoring" (*ornare*).[25] Praise he could dispense easily enough and did, out of the well of his eloquence. But the more desirable commodity was honor bestowed by the Senate in the name of the nation. Events of this period are regularly punctuated by the vote of thanksgivings, statues, state funerals, or other tributes to one or another of the Senate's heroes. But a policy of honors was inherently unstable, because each award raised the standard for the honor to be voted on the next occasion. The thanksgiving that Cicero proposed after an initial victory at Mutina was longer than any decreed before, and comments he made about his calendar proposal acknowledged that it had no precedent in historical times.[26] Honors, the chief resource in his power to mediate, were undergoing inflation in a process that paralleled the steady rise in bribes and bonuses being paid to soldiers. But increments of honor were less fungible than extra cash.

It is all the more remarkable, then (and this is the second point), that Decimus felt so deeply aggrieved when Cicero's proposal fell through. On learning the news, he wrote back:

> I am sure the country owes no more to me than I to you. Take it as given that I am capable of more gratitude toward you than those troublemakers are toward me—or if that sounds spoken on the fly, take it that I prefer your judgment to that of the whole crowd on the

other side. You judge of us with a true and unerring sense, which their extraordinary spite and malice keeps them from doing. Well, let them prevent me from being honored, so long as they do not prevent me from managing the business of state effectively.

> *non mihi rem publicam plus debere arbitror quam me tibi. gratiorem me esse in te posse quam isti perversi sint in me exploratum habe; si tamen haec temporis videantur dici causa, malle me tuum iudicium quam ex altera parte omnium istorum. tu enim a certo sensu et vero iudicas de nobis; quod isti ne faciant summa malevolentia et livore impediuntur. interpellent me quo minus honoratus sim, dum ne interpellent quo minus res publica a me commode administrari possit.*
>
> *Fam.* 11.10.1 = 385 SB[27]

Though Decimus was not unique in craving tokens of public esteem, he was more needy at this point than most of his peers. On top of the insecurity that beset any Roman politician away from the center, he suffered the antipathy that many of his countrymen felt toward Caesar's murderers. He was even more hated than Cassius and Marcus Brutus because he had violated a more intimate bond of trust with Caesar.[28] And after he came under siege from Antony, he cannot have been entirely happy that the prospect of rescue depended on two loyal Caesarian officers and the adopted son of the man he had killed. Cicero had perceived the need for reassurance that lay beneath Decimus's concern with *dignitas* and addressed it as the siege was being drawn tight: "I thought I should write first that the Senate and the Roman People worry about you, not only from consideration of their own good but also of your prestige. There is in fact a wonderful affection for your name and a singular love of you on the part of all citizens" (haec ... scribenda existimavi, primum senatum populumque Romanum de te laborare non solum salutis suae causa sed etiam dignitatis tuae. admirabilis enim est quaedam tui nominis caritas amorque in te singularis omnium civium, *Fam.* 11.8.1 = 360 SB).

Late April–Mid-May 43: The Pursuit of Antony

In the initial phase of the struggle, Decimus was required to perform only a holding action, throwing himself in Antony's way until stronger forces could be deployed by Octavian and the consuls.[29] Although the details of Cicero's discussions with the latter three have perished with the loss of the respective letter collections, the plan succeeded. When the new campaigning season opened in the spring of 43, Octavian and the consuls fought two battles in which Antony was trounced. Then the situation shifted abruptly. Antony managed to extricate the remnants of his army and retreat northward, and the two consuls died of wounds they received in battle.

Cicero now expected Decimus to take a more commanding role than heretofore. Decimus was assigned command literally, in that, at Cicero's initiative, he was put in charge of the forces that had been led by the consuls, and he was instructed to pursue Antony.[30] But neither Cicero nor Decimus nor anybody else in that last age of the Republic possessed anything like the authority of a commander in chief of the armed forces. Army leaders had no military superiors, and they were only as observant of Senate authority as they could be compelled to be. On this occasion, Decimus found that he had to operate without any support from Octavian, who kept command of his own soldiers as well as of some who were to have been transferred to Decimus. And Decimus determined for himself the terms on which he would pursue Antony. Over the next three weeks, he trailed him at a distance of at least a day's march almost to the western border of his province. Then when Antony crossed the mountains into southern Gaul, Decimus turned back in the opposite direction.

Cicero's letters to Decimus rarely touch on specifics about military operations (which is true of all his correspondence with army leaders in this period), and so his perception of the strategy at issue is not always clear. Although he initially envisioned that Decimus and Octavian would cooperate in pursuing Antony (*MBrut.* 10[1.3a] = 8 SB), for example, it is not clear how he thought responsibilities should be divided between them, nor how he thought Decimus should adjust when Octavian did nothing at all. It is not clear how he thought Decimus could overtake and stop Antony on the narrow route along which Antony was retreating into Gaul, or what authority he thought Decimus had to lead an army out of his own province and into Lepidus's.[31] But he did have in view one paramount objective, which was that Antony should be destroyed before he had an opportunity to regroup. "The man who crushes Antony puts the finish to the war" (is bellum confecerit qui Antonium oppresserit, *Fam.* 11.12.2 = 394 SB), he told Decimus, and "my wish would be, and I hope, that Antony has been decisively brought down and smashed" (velim equidem, id quod spero, ut plane abiectus et fractus sit Antonius, *Fam.* 11.18.3 = 397 SB).

Hence Cicero looked on with dismay as Antony managed first to link up with new forces raised for him in Italy by his lieutenant, then to pass unimpeded into Gaul, and finally to put himself in position to unite his forces with Lepidus's army. The temperature of Cicero's letters to Decimus cooled. Having earlier declared that Decimus was cherished by all, Cicero now observes that "you do have detractors, as you say" (ut scribis, habes obtrectatores, *Fam.* 11.14.2 = 413 SB). "Some even complain that you people did not give chase, and they think that [Antony] could have been crushed if speed had been employed" (nonnulli etiam queruntur quod persecuti non sitis; opprimi potuisse, si celeritas adhibita esset, existimant, *Fam.* 11.12.2 = 394 SB).[32] Evocations of Decimus's heroic blow against Caesar tail off. Cicero makes one last reference to it, apropos of current mutterings against Decimus, but now the topic cloaks a reproach: "It is so like people—especially our people—to abuse their liberty in the case of the very person through whom they have gained it. All the same, you must take care that some element of criticism is not justified" (omnino est hoc populi maximeque nostri, in eo potissimum abuti libertate per quem eam consecutus sit. sed tamen providendum est ne quae iusta querela esse possit, *Fam.* 11.12.2 = 394 SB). He ceases to speak about promoting Decimus's *dignitas*, tendering only this expression of goodwill in the sign-off of a letter: "The next move is up to you: I cannot do more than I have done. Still, I do want and hope to see you greater and more glorious than anybody" (tuae partes sunt: ego plus quam feci facere non possum. te tamen, id quod spero, omnium maximum et clarissimum videre cupio, *Fam.* 11.14.3 = 413 SB).

The letters written after Antony's escape from Mutina do not take Decimus to task head-on. Criticism is almost always muffled in Cicero's correspondence, and in this case nothing was to be gained by provoking an open breach. Cicero was still counting on Decimus to use his influence on behalf of Cicero's protégés back in Rome (*Fam.* 11.16 = 434 SB and 11.22 = 427 SB). Decimus for his part had reason to ignore any negative undertones in Cicero's letters because he counted on Cicero to move legislation awarding lands and pay to his soldiers.[33]

But between the lines, Cicero's letters are laden with pique and condemnation. When the Senate received a message from Decimus that Cicero judged overcautious, he responded with a letter adverting to Decimus's complete lack of pluck after his rescue from Mutina and invited Decimus to contrast that with the valiant performance of civilian "leaders" whose identity Decimus would readily divine (and who are here, unusually, termed *duces* to point out the comparison between soldiers and civilians): "Your injunctions seemed timorous and out of keeping with the victory of you and the Roman People [at Mutina]. The Senate, my dear Brutus, is brave and has brave leaders. And so it resented being judged timorous and pusillanimous by you, whom it judged the bravest of all men ever. For since all had the greatest hope in your valor when you were hemmed in and Antony was riding high, who could have had any fear once he was beaten and you were freed?" (timidiora mandata videbantur quam erat dignum tua populique Romani victoria. senatus autem, mi Brute, fortis est et habet fortis duces. itaque moleste ferebat se a te, quem omnium quicumque fuissent fortissimum iudicaret, timidum atque ignavum iudicari. etenim cum te incluso spem maximam omnes habuissent in tua virtute florente Antonio, quis erat qui quicquam timeret profligato illo, te liberato? *Fam.* 11.18.1–2 = 397 SB).[34] A couple of weeks later, Cicero found occasion to sound the themes of courage and fear once again (they are the ground bass of his correspondence with Decimus): "As for your telling me to beware of letting fear lead me into a situation of still greater fear, your counsel is sage and most friendly. But please be assured that, though it is obvious that you take first place in that category of valor which consists of never being ruffled or afraid, I come very close to this valor of yours. And so I do not fear anything and will watch out for everything. But see that you are not to blame, my dear Brutus, if I *should* have anything to fear" (quod mihi praecipis ut caveam ne timendo magis timere cogar, et sapienter et amicissime praecipis. sed velim tibi persuadeas, cum te constet excellere hoc genere virtutis ut numquam extimescas, numquam perturbere, me huic tuae virtuti proxime accedere. quam ob rem nec metuo quicquam et cavebo omnia. sed vide ne tua iam, mi Brute, culpa futura sit si ego quicquam timeam, *Fam.* 11.21.4 = 411 SB). Decimus, he suggests, has redefined *virtus* to mean anything but confronting the enemy.

There are other signs of Cicero's displeasure as well. His letters to Decimus become shorter, as he notes expressly, in case Decimus should fail to observe that change for himself. The letters are also increasingly vacuous, reviewing topics raised by Decimus but volunteering little from Cicero's side.[35] Most telling is that by the end of their exchange, Cicero is no longer calling on Decimus to do anything. He had little use for him, once Antony made good his escape into Gaul.[36]

Mid- to Late May 43: The Conjunction of Antony with Lepidus

When Cicero told Decimus that "the man who crushes Antony puts the finish to the war," he had added, "I would rather you guess my point here than that I spell it out more plainly" (hoc quam vim habeat te existimare malo quam me apertius scribere, *Fam.* 11.12.2 = 394 SB). What he meant was that if Decimus failed to finish off Antony, he would lose credit not only for that but for all that he *had* accomplished.[37] Someone else would step in to earn the win. The someone else whom Cicero had in mind was Lucius Munatius Plancus, to whom he made the same remark a couple of days before.[38] But to understand how Plancus became relevant to the situation, it is necessary to backtrack to an earlier point in their correspondence.

Cicero's exchange with Plancus is the second major component of books 10 to 12 of the *Letters to Friends*, filling most of book 10 as that with Decimus fills most of book 11. Like Decimus, Plancus had fought for Caesar in both the Gallic and the civil wars, thereby earning a major command (northern Gaul, with three legions) and designation as consul for the year 42.[39] His relationship with Cicero, however, was very different from Decimus's. Some fifteen to twenty years younger than Cicero, Plancus had entered Cicero's orbit the moment he was born, thanks to Cicero's friendship with his father. Later, Cicero is said to have been his mentor in oratory, in which Plancus made a successful career before joining Caesar.[40]

Rarely if ever did adherence to Caesar cause anyone to forfeit a relationship with Cicero, and that was not the case with Plancus, whose new tie with Caesar opened a channel of influence that Cicero was happy to tap for favors.[41] But after Caesar's death, as Cicero looked ahead to the end of Antony's regime, he set about trying to reclaim Plancus from his aberrant past. The following letter was written at some point in the late autumn of 44, before Octavian's insurgency and Antony's offensive against Decimus made it inevitable that questions about Rome's political future would be settled by arms:[42]

Cicero to Plancus, greetings.

It was a pleasure to see Furnius, for his own sake and all the more because in listening to him, I imagined I was listening to you. He told me about your valor on the battlefield, your justice in governing the province, your general sagacity, and also about the charm of your everyday company, which I know well. He mentioned also your extraordinary generosity to him. All of these things made me glad, and the last one, grateful besides.

I have had a relationship with your family, Plancus, that was established shortly before you were born. For you yourself I have had a love since your early boyhood, and after you were grown, a friendship that was as enthusiastic on my side as it was valued on yours. For these reasons I am incredibly supportive of your prestige, which I see as something in which I share. With valor as your guide and fortune at your side, you have achieved all distinctions, and you achieved them as a young man, to the envy of many persons whom you have confounded by your talent and industry. Now, if you heed me—I who love you dearly, and who maintain that no one could rank higher with you in length of acquaintance—you will base the quest for prestige in future years on an optimal ordering of political life.

I am sure you know (since there is nothing that could escape you) that there was a time when people considered you too much the servant of the times. I would have thought so, too, if I believed that you approved of things which you had to put up with. But since I saw how you felt, I considered that you took a practical view of what was possible.

Now the situation is different. Everywhere you have a choice, and it is free. You are consul designate, in the prime of life, endowed with surpassing eloquence, at a time when the nation is woefully bereft of such men. By the immortal gods, take to heart that care and calculation which will bring you the greatest prestige and glory. The one path to glory, especially in this period when the nation has been troubled for so many years, is the path of sound politics.

I thought I should write you this, more from motives of affection than because I thought you needed my instructions and counsel. I know you have drunk from the same wellspring as I, and so I will make an end. For the present, I thought that no more than this was necessary, to show you my love rather than to show off my wisdom.

In the meantime, I will zealously and carefully attend to anything I think will redound to your prestige.

Cicero Planco sal.

Cum ipsum Furnium per se vidi libentissime tum hoc libentius quod illum audiens te videbar audire. nam et in re militari virtutem et in administranda provincia iustitiam et in omni genere prudentiam mihi tuam exposuit et praeterea mihi non ignotam in consuetudine et familiaritate suavitatem tuam; adiunxit praeterea summam erga se liberalitatem. quae omnia mihi iucunda, hoc extremum etiam gratum fuit.

ego, Plance, necessitudinem constitutam habui cum domo vestra ante aliquanto quam tu natus es, amorem autem erga te ab ineunte pueritia tua, confirmata iam aetate familiaritatem cum studio meo tum iudicio tuo constitutam. his de causis mirabiliter faveo dignitati tuae, quam me tecum statuo habere communem. omnia summa consecutus es virtute duce, comite fortuna, eaque es adeptus adulescens multis invidentibus, quos ingenio industriaque fregisti. nunc, me amantissimum tui, nemini concedentem, qui tibi vetustate necessitudinis potior possit esse, si audies, omnem tibi reliquae vitae dignitatem ex optimo rei publicae statu adquires.

scis profecto—nihil enim te fugere potuit—fuisse quoddam tempus cum homines existimarent te nimis servire temporibus, quod ego quoque existimarem, te si ea quae patiebare probare etiam arbitrarer. sed cum intellegerem quid sentires, te arbitrabar videre quid posses.

nunc alia ratio est. omnium rerum tuum iudicium est idque liberum. consul es designatus, optima aetate, summa eloquentia, maxima orbitate rei publicae virorum talium. incumbe, per deos immortale in eam curam et cogitationem quae tibi summam dignitatem et gloriam adferat; unus autem est, hoc praesertim tempore, per tot annos re publica divexata, rei publicae bene gerendae cursus ad gloriam.

haec amore magis impulsus scribenda ad te putavi quam quo te arbitrarer monitis et praeceptis egere. sciebam enim ex iisdem te haec haurire fontibus ex quibus ipse hauseram. quare modum faciam. nunc tantum significandum putavi ut potius amorem tibi ostenderem meum quam ostentarem prudentiam.

interea quae ad dignitatem tuam pertinere arbitrabor studiose diligenterque curabo.

Fam. 10.3 = 355 SB

The twin components of Cicero's exhortation to Decimus reappear in this letter to Plancus: the appeal to act in keeping with a certain moral character is combined with a promise of public support. And as in the letter to Decimus, the moral appeal is organized with the help of a personalized leitmotif. Cicero's reminders of his long and intimate acquaintance with Plancus are even more insistent than his evocations of Decimus's role in the events of the ides of March.[43] The closeness of their tie serves partly to excuse statements that are blunter than Cicero would risk with others, as he indicates at *Fam.* 10.6.3 = 370 SB. It also lets him draw attention to common experiences that imply common values: the influence of liberal studies, a rapid rise in politics through energy and talent, and the achievement of distinction in oratory. Finally, it enables Cicero to distinguish those elements of Plancus's past behavior that do not represent his true self from those that do.

Possession of a common background bears directly on what Cicero wants from Plancus now. In this early letter, Plancus is not yet being urged to act in his capacity as an army leader.[44] Rather, Cicero has in view the role he will play after his command, when he returns to Rome as consul-designate and then consul.[45] He wants Plancus to renounce the politics of the Caesarian era and to conform again to the spirit of Republican government. The letter is an exercise in political reeducation. As Cicero puts it in the case of another unreformed Caesarian, he is attempting to "make a good man" out of Plancus.[46]

Cicero reiterated the message in sharper form a few months later, when Mutina lay under siege. To his great annoyance, Plancus sent a message to the Senate advocating peace with Antony, which elicited this response:

> Believe me, Plancus, all those rungs of prestige which you have climbed hitherto—very lofty ones, to be sure—will count as honors in name only, not as badges of prestige, unless you associate yourself with the freedom of the Roman People and the authority of the Senate. I beg you, separate yourself at last from those to whom you were attached by ties of opportunity, not your considered judgment. In a time of political upheaval, many have been called consuls, but none has been deemed a consular unless he manifested a consular spirit toward the Republic. And that is the way you should behave, in first detaching yourself from the company of disloyal citizens most unlike yourself, then offering yourself to the Senate and all good men as guide, chief, and leader.

> *Crede igitur mihi, Plance, omnis quos adhuc gradus dignitatis consecutus sis (es autem adeptus amplissimos) eos honorum vocabula habituros, non dignitatis insignia, nisi te cum libertate populi Romani et cum senatus auctoritate coniunxeris. seiunge te, quaeso, aliquando ab iis, cum quibus te non tuum iudicium, sed temporum vincla coniunxerunt. complures in perturbatione rei publicae consules dicti, quorum nemo consularis habitus nisi qui animo exstitit in rem publicam consulari. talem igitur te esse oportet qui primum te ab impiorum civium tui dissimillimorum societate seiungas, deinde te senatui bonisque omnibus auctorem, principem, ducem praebeas.*

> *Fam.* 10.6.2–3 = 370 SB

Cicero does not go quite so far as to say what the Senate supposedly did write to Octavian's legions at one point: that rather than pin their hopes on individuals, they should look to the Senate, "which alone holds everlasting power" (App. *BC* 3.86.354). The letters just quoted do not dwell on practical considerations. Cicero does not argue, for example, that Plancus should take such-and-such a course of action because it will remedy a problem or work to his personal advantage. And fond as he is of political prophecy, he does not here try to motivate Plancus by proposing a program or vision for the future. He does not even do what he does at such length in the *Philippics*, and make a case for action by rehearsing the evils of Antony and his regime. Instead, he focuses his letters on the moral and civic identity of the recipient. Cicero appeals to Plancus, as to Decimus, solely in terms of each man's sense of his worth and position in Roman society.

The asperity of Cicero's response to Plancus's pacifism not only expressed his hostility toward all notions of compromise with Antony but also reflected deepening anxiety about Plancus. By the date of that letter (March 20, 43), Cicero had become less concerned with the part Plancus was going to play as consul in several months than with the military role that he and his legions would play in the next few weeks. In February (if not before), the Senate had summoned Plancus from northern Gaul and Lepidus from southern Gaul to help fight Antony in Italy.[47] Against that background, Plancus's pacific remarks about Antony would have been disquieting enough.[48] But from other directions, too, came indications that his allegiance to the Republican cause might be up in the air. Antony was boasting publicly that Plancus was in league with him. Later, Decimus warned Cicero that he needed to shore up Plancus and reported that he had seized papers showing contact between him and Antony.[49]

But three weeks after the offending letter, Plancus addressed a deliciously insouciant follow-up to the Senate. He declared that in his earlier dispatch he was merely temporizing until he thought it safe to fly his true colors as a patriot, and he announced that he was now ready to do the Senate's bidding (*Fam.* 10.8 = 371 SB). Nevertheless, he did not reach Italy in time for the showdown at Mutina. In fact, he did not move from his distant province until five days after the fighting was over, and by mid-May, when Cicero was casting about for a man who would "put the finish to the war," Plancus was still no more than a couple of days' march nearer to Italy.[50]

By then, however, Antony had entered Gaul, where the war once again changed its aspect. From about May 15th and for the next two weeks, Antony sat encamped within a day's march of Lepidus and his four legions near Forum Iulii on the coast. He could be finished off only if Lepidus could be dissuaded from joining him. Since Decimus was far away in the middle of northern Italy by that time, the only possible dissuader was Plancus, who lay about 140 miles north of the two armies.[51]

Cicero's letters to Plancus become more frequent in this period. Five of them, or a third of the total, were written in the month of May, and their tone is more inveigling than before. Up to then, Cicero had done little to redeem the pledge made in *Fam.* 10.3 = 355 SB that he would attend zealously to Plancus's *dignitas*. He had mentioned him at the end of the *Third Philippic* in December, in his motion to extend the terms of current governors (sec. 38), and he complimented him briefly in the *Thirteenth Philippic* in March (sec. 16 and 44). He responded enthusiastically to Plancus's palinode in April, for which he urged the Senate to pass an official commendation.[52] But when Plancus became the last piece left to play in the match against Antony, Cicero's blandishments swelled into an almost steady stream. If Plancus could snuff out the embers of war, Cicero wrote, "you will bestow a superhuman blessing on the nation and gain eternal glory for yourself" (rem publicam divino beneficio adfeceris et ipse aeternam gloriam consequere, *Fam.* 10.14.2 = 384 SB). "As soon as an opportunity of increasing your prestige presented itself, I did not stint in honoring you, whether with recompense for valor or laudatory words" (ut primum potestas data est augendae dignitatis tuae, nihil praetermisi in te ornando quod positum esset aut in praemio virtutis aut in honore verborum, *Fam.* 10.13.1 = 389 SB). "Strive to wrap up the end of the war: the ultimate in goodwill and glory lies in that....I am little more devoted to my country than to your glory, for which I hope the immortal gods have granted you the greatest opportunity" (incumbe ut belli extrema perficias. in hoc erit summa et gratia et gloria....non multo plus patriae faveo quam tuae gloriae, cuius maximam facultatem tibi di immortales, ut spero, dederunt, *Fam.* 10.19.2 = 393 SB). "In all of time past, I have seen nothing more glorious, more gratifying, more perfectly timed than your letter, Plancus" (nihil post hominum memoriam gloriosius, nihil gratius, ne tempore quidem ipso opportunius accidere vidi quam tuas, Plance, litteras, *Fam.* 10.16.1 = 404 SB).

It is worth noticing how often these effusions were triggered by incoming assurances from Plancus. Cicero had called for a vote of commendation when Plancus wrote that he stood at the service of the Senate. He urged "recompense for valor" when Plancus reported that he had led his forces out of his province (*Fam.* 10.9.3 = 379 SB). He reaffirmed his devotion to Plancus's glory when Plancus wrote that he was a little farther south, and "would prove second to none in spirit, goodwill, and steadfastness" toward the Senate (nec animo nec benevolentiae nec patientiae cuiusquam pro vobis cedam, *Fam.* 10.11.3 = 382 SB). And so on.

As for what Plancus accomplished during these weeks, the simplest way to present it is in the form of a chronicle. He led his army into Lepidus's province on April 26th. On hearing the outcome of the battle of Mutina some days later, he halted where he was north of the Isara, about fifty miles deeper into the province. On May 9th, he built a bridge over the Isara and led his army across, but he halted on the other side. On May 18th he resumed his march south, saying that he expected to reach Lepidus's army within eight days. On May 29th he was within forty miles of Lepidus's army when Antony joined Lepidus and then moved against Plancus. Plancus retreated back to the Isara, which he crossed six days later, on June 4th.[53] If we prescind for a moment from consideration of Plancus's intentions, two striking facts about his behavior are that it took him more than three times as long to march 140 miles south from the Isara as it did to march back, and that for all his marching, he never came within a spear's throw of either Lepidus or Antony. The tributes that Cicero paid to him were responses to plans and promises of action, not to a single deed adversely affecting Antony.

Of Plancus's intentions, more than one interpretation is possible. For purposes of understanding Cicero's exchange with him, however, it is less useful to probe his motives than to see how he presented them to Cicero. Plancus is given to incessant self-explanation (a trait he shares with his old mentor), and what is fascinating in letters of this period is how his explanations keep shifting. He halted after the news about Mutina in order to confront Antony in case Antony were to head toward northern Gaul, and meanwhile he engaged in discussions about cooperation with Lepidus (*Fam.* 10.11.2–3 = 382 SB). He crossed the Isara when Lepidus invited him to make common cause against Antony in the south, but he quickly began to suspect treachery. "I saw that if I should be wiped out, failing the nation as well as myself, I would get no honor or even pity once I was dead. And so I am about to turn back and not let such great resources fall into the hands of rogues.... I will defend the province... and try to keep all options open" (vidi mihi... si ita oppressus essem remque publicam mecum prodidissem, mortuo non modo honorem sed misericordiam quoque defuturum. itaque rediturus sum nec tanta munera perditis hominibus dari posse sinam.... provinciam tuear... omniaque integra servem dabo operam, *Fam.* 10.21.5–6 = 391 SB). But after another appeal from Lepidus, he decided to take the chance. "If Lepidus is true and suffers harm, I saw that it would all be blamed on my intransigence or fear if I failed to aid... a fellow patriot or if I dodged a contest in this crucial war" (si quid Lepidus bene sentiens detrimenti cepisset, hoc omne adsignatum iri aut pertinaciae meae aut timori videbam, si aut hominem... coniunctum cum re publica non sublevassem aut ipse a certamine belli tam necessarii me removissem, *Fam.* 10.18.2 = 395 SB). When Antony and Lepidus combined against him, he scuttled away, "experiencing this pleasure, at all events, that the more they meant to catch me, the greater their grief at being foiled" (in quo hanc capio voluptatem quod certe, quo magis me petiverunt, tanto maiorem iis frustratio dolorem attulit, *Fam.* 10.23.5 = 414 SB). At various points, Plancus's aim is to intercept Antony, to forestall his junction with Lepidus, to protect the province, and to keep himself and his army intact for future operations.[54]

Cicero cannot have been oblivious of the gap between Plancus's professions and his performance. He had no trouble seeing the lameness of Decimus's actions after Mutina, and given the questions about Plancus's loyalty, there was all the more reason to look askance at him. A month before Plancus's circuit of southern Gaul, Cicero wrote: "You have gained great praise from the mere rumor that has circulated about your good intentions, and…the Senate would have expressed gratitude for your effort and preparation by bestowing great honors on you. But in my judgment anyhow, the time for that…was not ripe at present. It is my settled view that an honor is bestowed and granted to illustrious men for great accomplishments rather than for the prospect of a benefit to come" (ipsa fama quae de tua voluntate percrebuit magnam es laudem consecutus. itaque…declaratum esset ab senatu cum tuis magnis honoribus quam gratus esset conatus et apparatus tuus. cuius rei…tempus…ne maturum quidem etiam nunc meo iudicio fuit. is enim denique honos mihi videtur solet qui non propter spem futuri benefici sed propter magna merita claris viris defertur et datur, Fam. 10.10.1 = 375 SB).

The misgivings that pervade this statement (in which the intangibles of fama, voluntas, conatus et apparatus, and spes futuri benefici crowd out merita) lurk in other letters as well. Cicero remarks on the fineness of Plancus's words and sentiments with a frequency that has no parallel in his other exchanges during this period.[55] To Plancus more often than to anyone else, he addresses the expressive command incumbe ("bear down," "put your back into it"), which in turn hints that as a Caesarian, Plancus had proved levis ("lightweight" or "fickle") toward the Republic.[56] The watchword respublica itself is invoked more often in Cicero's letters to Plancus than in parallel exchanges: thirty-six times, or almost thrice per letter on average, as compared with eleven times, or less than once per letter, to Decimus, for example; patria is also common. The unspoken contrast in this case is to partes or factional loyalty, which Cicero was insisting had become an anachronism now that the whole nation was united in opposition to Antony.[57] On occasion, Cicero's misgivings even break the surface, as when he refers to the "hollow cheer" (inanis laetitia, Fam. 10.20.2 = 407 SB) of a letter in which Plancus's assurances had been belied by subsequent events.

If Cicero nevertheless seems less critical of Plancus than of Decimus overall, there are perhaps two reasons. One is that, as noted earlier, he had come to the end of his resources. By the time Plancus was called upon to play his part, Hirtius and Pansa were dead, Octavian had effectively dropped out of the Republican coalition, Decimus had failed, Lepidus was tacitly cooperating with Antony, and Pollio was waiting out the contest in Spain. There were no alternatives to Plancus in the west, and Plancus was at least willing to go through the motions of coming to the rescue—which in itself seems surprising. Since he was on amicable terms with all concerned, unlike Decimus, he had nothing to lose by shirking initiative and standing pat (as Pollio did). Perhaps Cicero does not get as much credit as he deserves for the sway he exercised over Plancus.

A second reason for Cicero's forbearance may be that Plancus had a way of wrapping himself in Ciceronian camouflage when writing letters. At *Fam.* 10.3.2 = 355 SB, for example, Cicero had recalled that his tie to Plancus even predated Plancus's birth, thanks to his tie with Plancus' father (*paterna neces-situdo, Fam.* 13.29.1 = 282 SB). Plancus picked up the idea and riffed, "Be assured that, insofar as our respective ages allow, you are the only person for whom the respect I show has been exalted to the worship of a father" (quod mea tuaque patitur aetas, persuade tibi te unum esse in quo ego colendo patriam mihi constituerim sanctitatem, *Fam.* 10.4.1–2 = 358 SB). When Cicero noted that Plancus's meteoric career was clouded by his reputation as a time-server (*Fam.* 10.3.3 = 355 SB), Plancus echoed back: "All of my successes, whether they have been granted by the kindness of fortune or earned by my exertions—though out of affection you exaggerate them—are so great even from the most hostile perspective that they seem to lack nothing but good repute. Therefore accept this one assurance: all that I can manage through strength and organize through foresight and promote through influence will be dedicated to the nation" (quaecumque in me bona sunt aut fortunae benefi-cio tributa aut meo labore parta, etsi a te propter amorem carius sunt aestimata, tamen vel inimicissimi iudicio tanta sunt ut praeter bonam famam nihil desid-erare videantur. qua re hoc unum tibi persuade, quantum viribus eniti, consilio providere, auctoritate monere potuero, hoc omne rei publicae semper futurum, *Fam.* 10.4.2–3 = 358 SB). After Cicero observed that honor is bestowed for great accomplishments (magna merita, *Fam.* 10.3.3 = 355 SB), Plancus wrote, "I hope you observe that, day after day, increments are being made to my accomplish-ments" (in dies vero meritorum meorum fieri accessiones pervidere te spero, *Fam.* 10.9.11 = 379 SB), but quickly added, "however, I desire nothing for myself—I am the very person who fights against that" (concupisco autem nihil mihi—contra quod ipse pugno). Plancus even tops Cicero's evocations of the *respublica,* using the word thirty-five times for an average of slightly more than three times per letter. In their letters, Cicero and Plancus tend to play off each other's words, to the disadvantage of Cicero, who found it easy to believe that people who talked his talk were talking to the same purpose. None of his corre-spondents could talk the talk better than his protégé. And so it was a fitting irony that, as the author of the latest datable text (*Fam.* 10.24 = 428 SB, dated July 28), Plancus the mockingbird turned out to have the last word in our extant corpus of Cicero's works.

June–July 43: The Aftermath

When Antony and Lepidus united their armies on May 29th, Antony became a much more daunting opponent, and offensive activity against him came to a standstill. Cicero did not altogether abandon hope, however. As late as the end of July, he still imagined that Octavian might prove faithful to the cause (*MBrut.* 26[1.18].3 = 24 SB), and he remained in correspondence with other army leaders throughout June and July. But the war obviously needed rethinking, and Cicero's letters reflect a changed assessment of what was possible.

Shortly after Plancus returned north in June, Decimus led his own army west across the Alps and bivouacked with Plancus on the Isara. There they issued a joint dispatch bidding the Senate to have high hopes and declaring themselves "ready for everything on your behalf."[58] But privately Plancus informed Cicero that even their combined forces were not strong enough to engage Antony (*Fam.* 10.24.3–4 = 428 SB). The war against him would have to pause until the Senate could send reinforcements—if not legions from Octavian's army, then legions summoned from Spain or the east.[59]

Cicero evidently agreed. After learning that Antony and Lepidus had combined, he wrote no more about crushing Antony or wrapping up the war, and he refrained from urging Decimus and Plancus to challenge the enemy. The Senate, meanwhile, had summoned legions from Africa to Italy even before the news of Antony's union with Lepidus, and, after that, it recalled Marcus Brutus and Cassius as well.[60] At this point, the war with Antony became the concern that drove Cicero's communications with army leaders in the east as well as in the west.

For different reasons, there is little to be said about Cicero's correspondence with Cassius and Marcus Brutus prior to this time, in the months in which they began organizing a Republican front overseas.[61] But as in the case of Plancus, Cicero had the advantage of being able to write on the basis of close acquaintance with each man. With Cassius he claimed a relationship going back to Cassius' boyhood.[62] The tie with Brutus was later, mediated by Atticus shortly before the outbreak of the civil war, but it had developed into a much-publicized literary relationship in the 40s.[63] Cicero's position vis-à-vis Brutus and Cassius after Caesar's death, however, lends his correspondence with them a very different aspect than his correspondence with Decimus or Plancus. In the first place, Brutus and Cassius were the unquestioned leaders of the resistance to the Caesarian regime. They had less need than Decimus and far less than Plancus of being exhorted to action by Cicero. Moreover, circumstances limited what Cicero could say. He hoped and believed that when they left Italy in the autumn of 44, they would raise a counterforce against Antony.[64] But since any such initiative would be treasonous as long as Antony was consul, it could not be the subject of frank discussion in letters. Cicero recognized that it did not fall within his area of expertise in any case: "I only wish I had some counsel to give you both! But I do not find even for myself what should be done. For what can be accomplished against force without force?" (utinam haberem quid vobis darem consili! sed ne mihi quidem ipsi reperio quid faciendum sit. quid enim est quod contra vim sine vi fieri possit? *Fam.* 12.3.2 = 345 SB). Yet what surely inhibited Cicero's managerial propensities more than anything else was consciousness of his own passivity for most of the year. When Cassius wrote urging him to put his eloquence and authority to work in the Senate, he had answered that neither he nor any other opponent of Antony could safely set foot there, let alone speak out (*Fam.* 12.2.2–3 = 344 SB). In any comparison with Cassius and Brutus, Cicero could not but come off as the laggard.

Even after Cicero finally began to assert himself in the Senate in December, he did not presume to meddle with Brutus and Cassius but was content to second their agenda. He encouraged them to act audaciously and unilaterally, he applauded their successes before the Senate and the People, and he did his best to have their usurpations of authority regularized after the fact. In only one instance did he try to dictate policy, and that was a manifestation of his personal obsession with Antony. When Brutus captured and imprisoned Antony's brother Gaius in Macedonia, Cicero called in vain for Gaius to be summarily executed.[65] Otherwise, up to the moment of Antony's resurgence in Gaul, he gave full assent to Brutus's and Cassius's strategy of consolidating control in the east. During the siege of Mutina, for example, he envisioned that Republican loyalists might seek refuge with Brutus and Cassius in case Antony won, but he never called for reinforcements to be sent over to Italy.[66] In the brief euphoria that followed Antony's defeat at Mutina, he even thought that Brutus should move further east to deal with Dolabella.[67]

After Antony's conjunction with Lepidus at the end of May, however, Cicero abruptly shifted ground. The first words of a letter to Brutus read, "We still have no letters from you, or even a rumor announcing that you have learned about the Senate's mandate and are bringing your army to Italy—which the nation earnestly desires you to do, and to do quickly" (nullas adhuc a te litteras habebamus, ne famam quidem quae declararet te cognita senatus auctoritate in Italiam adducere exercitus, quod ut faceres idque maturares magno opere desiderabat res publica, *MBrut.* 18[1.10].1 = 17 SB). Almost every one of the ten letters that Cicero wrote to Brutus and Cassius thereafter repeats the entreaty "come to Italy," down to his last letter that is extant (*MBrut.* 26[1.18].1 = 24 SB). The majority are to Brutus, who was nearer, and they make their case more by describing the extremity of the situation than by appealing to Brutus's character. Yet even the restrained protreptic of these letters is carefully targeted to the recipient. Cicero repeats an argument he had used with Decimus, telling Marcus Brutus that the glory won by slaying Caesar now requires him to act again to free the nation.[68] But as the acknowledged leader of the Liberators, Brutus towers over the rest; therefore all citizens will rally around him as soon as he sets foot in Italy.[69] Not only that, but Rome in the present crisis has as much need of his wisdom (a nod to Brutus's philosophical learning) and his *auctoritas* as of his army.[70] It is perhaps a sign of mounting desperation on Cicero's part that his appeals are no longer combined with promises of recompense in the form of heightened *dignitas*.

But this element of Cicero's exchange with the Liberators appears to have encountered only silence from the other side. At any rate, there is no extant letter in which Brutus or Cassius responded to Cicero's call for rescue, and they never crossed back into Italy.

An Overview of the Wartime Correspondence

Letter writing was only one method of action that Cicero mentioned in the *Fourteenth Philippic* when reviewing his conduct of the war against Antony. This chapter has discussed only some of the wartime letters and a few of their themes. By no means does it offer a comprehensive account of Cicero's political leadership during this period, but only an exploration of the relationship bet-ween his leadership and his letter writing.

For the most part, the letters of 44–43 deal with matters of public policy, and Cicero wrote them in his persona as a prominent public figure. That is to say, it was not irrelevant that the letter writer happened to be a powerful opinion maker, an experienced parliamentarian, and a politician with ties throughout Roman society. Cicero could not have had the sort of correspondence we have been examining if he were a layman or a backbench senator. At times, his role as a politician was of key importance to his correspondents, who often wanted him to push through the Senate measures that would benefit them or their soldiers.[71]

Nevertheless, the letters are private in two important senses. In the first place, as noted earlier, Cicero's letters to Cassius, Plancus, and the two Brutuses, as well as theirs to him, are not exchanges between persons writing in an offi-cial capacity.[72] They parallel but do not duplicate official communications bet-ween the Senate and officers of the state, as may be seen in the rare cases in which official and unofficial letters survive side by side.[73] The wartime correspondence of Cicero illustrates the workings of *auctoritas* in a Roman sense, but not of political authority in the modern sense.

It was, indeed, the relative weakness of anything resembling a chain of command in Republican Rome that allowed private correspondence to engross a role in the conduct of policy. The fact that Cicero was regularly receiving letters from almost every major player in the events of 44 and 43 greatly enhanced his plausibility as a leader.[74] He sometimes took theatrical advantage of this traffic when he rose in the Senate to announce, "I hold in my hand a letter from..."[75] His network of correspondents gave him the wherewithal to generate a constant buzz—*fama*—about the progress of a war that was mostly invisible in the capital. As he declared early on, "in any political situation, Senators, the greatest shifts of circumstance are brought about through the least causes, in particular in war and especially civil war, which is governed to a large extent by rumor and opinion" (minimis momentis, patres conscripti, maximae inclinationes temporum fiunt, cum in omni casu rei publicae tum in bello et maxime civili quod opinione plerumque et fama gubernatur, *Phil.* 5.26). Occasionally the letters he received carried news about significant developments on the military front. But at all times they helped him to foster an impression in Rome that forces loyal to the Republic were in motion and that things were being done. They were thus on a level with other symbols that Cicero was manipulating during these months: the honors voted to leaders willing to challenge Antony, the state funerals celebrated for fallen heroes, and the military cloaks which senators and other patriots were asked to wear in public until the emergency had passed. Although they could not determine the outcome of the war, for a while they did allow Cicero to shape public opinion about it.

At the same time, Cicero's epistolary partners had a personal interest in keeping up their side of the exchange. Contact with the center helped reduce the anxiety felt by any politician away from Rome, and all the more so in wartime, when the situation was so volatile. The tie with Cicero also provided a back channel to the Senate through which honors and matériel could be sought. But the most important function of the exchange on this side was that, in the absence of more formal authority, the encouragement of Cicero could be taken to confer a color of legitimacy—*auctoritas* again, if not legality—on Antony's challengers. The issue of legitimacy comes to the surface more than once. Cicero declared that it was with "the approbation of my authority" (approbatione auctoritatis meae, *Phil.* 5.23) that Octavian had raised a private army against the consul. His correspondents echo the same language. Plancus wrote, "I have delivered on everything I undertook at your behest" (omnia me rei p. praestitisse quae...tua exhortatione excepi, *Fam.* 10.7.1 = 372 SB), and Cassius asserted, "I took up arms on your authority and instance" (arma cepi te hortante et auctore, *Fam.* 12.12.2 = 387 SB).

In saying that most of the wartime correspondence that we have was private in the sense of being unofficial, I have been making a point about the status of the letter writers. The second point bears more on the content of the letters: they were written for private consumption rather than for public consumption. That is more often true than not for letters generally, of course. What makes the point relevant to the present argument is that it affected the terms in which Cicero tried to motivate his addressees. His letters appeal to them as individuals rather than as members of a broad public. The difference can be noticed immediately if the *Philippics* are read alongside the letters. Whereas the *Philippics* are addressed to a collective audience (either the Senate or the People), the letters focus much more tightly on the particular persons to whom they are sent. Parties and issues that are relevant to the situation but might undercut the message can be more easily cropped out than in a public utterance. So, for example, after Cicero delivered the *Third* and *Fourth Philippic* on December 20th, he reported to Decimus Brutus as follows:

At the time when the tribunes of the People called a Senate meeting for December 20th and planned a debate about protection of the consuls designate, it had been my policy to attend no meeting before the first of January. But given that your edict was posted on that very day, I thought it would be criminal for a Senate meeting to take place in which nothing was said about your superhuman service to the nation—as would have happened, had I not been there—or even for me not to be on hand in case something complimentary about you were to be said.... How I held forth in the Senate in your regard, and what I said at a very well attended public assembly, I would rather you learn through your correspondence with others. But I do want you to rest assured that I will always take up and defend with the utmost zeal all that pertains to the enlargement of your prestige, great as that already is.

Cum tribuni p. edixissent senatus adesset a.d. XIII Kal. Ian. haberentque in animo de praesidio consulum designatorum referre, quamquam statueram in senatum ante Kal. Ian. non venire, tamen, cum eo die ipso edictum tuum propositum esset, nefas esse duxi aut ita haberi senatum ut de tuis divinis in rem publicam meritis sileretur, quod factum esset nisi ego venissem, aut etiam, si quid de te honorifice diceretur, me non adesse....quae de te in senatu egerim, quae in contione maxima dixerim, aliorum te litteris malo cognoscere; illud tibi persuadeas velim, me omnia quae ad tuam dignitatem augendam pertinebunt, quae est per se amplissima, summo semper studio suscepturum et defensurum.

Fam. 11.6a.2 = 356 SB

Decimus would surely have come away from this letter with the impression that he had been the leading theme of the *Third* and *Fourth Philippic*. But in fact those speeches lavish as much if not more attention on Octavian and his army than on Decimus.[76] On the same day, Cicero presented the same events in yet another light to another correspondent. To a governor in North Africa, he wrote that he had just secured a decree extending all provincial commands indefinitely, and he added, "this I did both for the sake of the nation and especially for the sake of maintaining your prestige" (hoc ego cum rei publicae causa censui tum mehercule in primis retinendae dignitatis tuae, *Fam.* 12.22a.1 = 357 SB).

The difference between letters and speeches does not depend solely on calculated elisions, however. The whole rhetoric of persuasion is different. The evocations of past precedent (*exempla*) that are commonplace in speeches are rare in letters, because they are not personal enough to engage a specific addressee.[77] More surprising, perhaps, is that the vilification of Mark Antony, which takes up a great deal of space in the *Philippics*, likewise plays only a minor part in Cicero's letters. But the reason is the same. It is not that the letters reflect an assessment of Antony different from that of the speeches, but that Cicero's rhetorical objective was different. In letters, the primary task was not to reprobate Antony, about whom Cicero and his correspondents were in rough agreement to start with, but to engage the addressee in a way that would spur him to action. To do that, Cicero needed to appeal to the wants and preoccupations by which each man was susceptible of being influenced.

Yet given that any occasion of action typically brings a range of ego concerns into play, it is remarkable how few of them Cicero chooses to address. For the most part, he does not argue in terms of the military expertise, political insight, practical experience, or private ambitions of his correspondents, and he is guarded in his responses to their requests for reinforcements and money. What he does dwell on are the kinds of things that we have seen: personal connections attesting shared commitments in public life, moral character as demonstrated in past performance, the opinion of citizens, and the craving for prestige.

In a downcast moment after the union between Antony and Lepidus, the failure of Decimus and Plancus, and the dereliction of Octavian, Cicero wrote to Marcus Brutus, "We are being played for fools by the petulance of the soldiery and the arrogance of the commanders. Everyone claims as much leeway in politics as he possesses force. Reason, restraint, law, custom, duty—none of them counts, and not the judgment and evaluation of fellow citizens, nor chagrin before posterity" (illudimur enim, Brute, tum militum deliciis, tum imperatorum insolentia. tantum quisque se in re publica posse postulat quantum habet virium. non ratio, non modus, non lex, non mos, non officium valet, non iudicium, non existimatio civium, non posteritatis verecundia, M Brut. 18[1.10].3 = 17 SB). It was hardly true that the various warlords' motives could be fully interpreted in terms of an antithesis between naked force and the values that Cicero catalogs. But the catalogue is a fair guide to the themes of his letter-writing agenda.

To modern readers, the correspondence from the years 44 and 43 can seem disappointing. It is large and diffuse, and although Cicero had a more significant role to play than when the civil war broke out half a decade earlier, the letters he wrote are not nearly as dramatic as the letters of 49, which form the perfect counterpoint to book 1 of Caesar's *Civil War*. For historians, too, the correspondence of 44–43 has had limited value. Parallel sources do much more to establish the storyline for this period; the letters are spare on facts in proportion to their length and rarely contribute more than sidelights. And although they do cast light on the perspective of the participants, the perspective they illuminate is that of history's losers rather than of the winners, in whom we are always more interested.

What remains uniquely valuable about this correspondence is that it illuminates the mentality of an important set of Roman leaders at a particular time more fully and directly than any other Roman source we have. It provides an excellent dossier for the study of elite motivation in a crisis that put values to the test. Ramsey MacMullen observed some years ago that modern historians of Rome are strongly biased toward sources that furnish information about real-world phenomena. They find it difficult or uncongenial to take account of evidence that he termed "irrational"—"whatever data lie inside the mind, apart from reasoning itself: therefore passion, emotion, prejudice, mood, personality, ideals"—and he contended that "in trying to explain...not *what* happened but *why*, historians must somehow penetrate to the inside."[78] That is the opportunity that a reading of Cicero's wartime correspondence presents.

Afterword

The Collection in Hindsight

Although a letter writer manqué hardly qualifies to be the ideal reader, much less writer, of a book about letter writing, I was the reader I had in mind from the outset of this project. I wanted to sort out things that it would have helped me to understand at the time when I first read Cicero's letters. The preceding chapters gather the results. Their focus has ranged from brute particulars regarding aleatory postal arrangements and the absence of signatures, for example, through social and political pressures that encouraged Cicero and his peers to stay in touch, to implications of some of the topics that recur in their letters. But the aim was always to try to answer one question: What makes these letters the way they are?

Thinking about that question gradually brought home to me the uniqueness of the letters, though such an epiphany might not seem to necessitate a lot of thought. Personal letters from the Roman world are uncommon enough that almost any instance is apt to be unique in some respect, and to have a run of them is always extraordinary. Even if we count the *Moral Epistles* of Seneca along with the letters of Pliny, Fronto, Symmachus, and Sidonius Apollinaris, fewer than half a dozen such collections apart from Cicero's are extant. The next correspondence that genuinely resembles Cicero's—voluminous, articulate but uncosmetized, by turns reflective and impassioned, written from a vantage near the center of events, and deeply involved in them—does not come to light for another six and a half centuries, in the archive of Pope Gregory I. And Gregory's letters were preserved not as a personal correspondence, but as the correspondence of a bishop of Rome.

If for no other reason, then, the Ciceronian corpus would be exceptional by virtue of being a rare example of its kind to have survived from classical antiquity. But to judge by the few collections that can be set beside it, it would still look unique if we had many more examples for comparison than we do. The letter writers and recipients represented in the corpus include almost every one of the leading figures of Cicero's day. For the most part, they are either senators who often have complementary roles as magistrates, governors, and army leaders besides, or other wealthy and well-connected persons in their confidence. They correspond mainly about concerns of public life— about problems of protecting their status, advancing their careers, and managing their relationships with peers, or about political events that bear on those problems. (It may be no accident that in the three component collections of the present corpus, the first letter of each decisively establishes this note.) Also worth noticing is that, during a period of unusually rapid change, they write in the midst of events rather than retrospectively. Time after time, suspense about something in prospect builds through a sequence of letters, only for the topic to vanish when the issue is resolved off stage, as it were, and yields place to some new uncertainty. But the spiral was downward. Cicero feared that the experience of his generation was not just a phase but the finale of a political regime, as was in fact the case. His intimations of the demise of the commonwealth are voiced from early to late in his letters.[1] The pessimism about politics surely contributed in turn to other anxieties evident in them, since little in his life was unconnected with politics.

These features of the correspondence are inseparable from the particular context in which it occurred. The first century B.C. was the most troubled period in the history of the Roman state since literacy enabled the Romans to write about their experience. To find another crisis as profound, we would have to look ahead to the 200s or the 400s. And never again in Roman history could a set of letter writers have been assembled who were at once as diverse and as involved in events as the people of the Ciceronian corpus. That is the important respect in which the corpus is unique: it reflects a unique historical moment. Nor is it simply a matter of chance that these letters happen to overlap with those events. The kind of letters that Cicero and his peers wrote formed part of a strategy for coping with the kind of situation that they faced. Broadly speaking, the correspondence we have would not have existed without the crisis.

Admittedly, there are a few letters in the corpus of which this hardly seems true, such as the note in which Cicero's brother congratulates him on manumitting Tiro (*Fam.* 16.16 = 44 SB), or the short message in which Cicero informs Marius that he will call on him in a couple of days (*Fam.* 7.4 = 199 SB). It is possible, moreover, to envision a selection from Cicero's letter files that would have been much less closely bound up with politics than the selection we have. If our corpus encompassed a series of books containing Cicero's exchanges with foreign intellectuals, with hometown notables and magnates in other towns of Italy and Sicily, with bankers, business associates, and brokers—for that matter, if it encompassed *all* his letters to his family and his staff and to such cronies as Trebatius and Paetus, it is likely that we would come away with a different impression of it. To realize that is to realize that our impressions have been manipulated. If the present corpus can be fairly characterized as a political correspondence from a period of crisis, that quality is the result of somebody's design, and the design can only have been an editor's.

Here again we may be dealing with a feature that makes the Ciceronian corpus unique, at least in Latin literature. The letters of Pliny (except those of the last book) were selected and published by him in his lifetime. The letters of Symmachus were published by his son shortly after his death, but on the basis of evidence internal to the letters it is commonly believed that Symmachus himself readied some two-thirds of the material for publication before he died. The letters of Sidonius were selected, revised, and published in stages by Sidonius himself. We have no information about how Fronto's letters came to be published or when or by whom. But in no other case can it be shown that the selection process formed as important a stage in determining the character of a collection as in the Ciceronian corpus, or that it was carried out by someone other than the letter writer.

To publish any set of letters that were earlier sent privately to individuals creates an anomalous sort of text, in that the parts of it were not composed to be read together. The anomaly is heightened if the author of the letters does not have occasion to read and adjust them at the stage when they are combined (as Cicero probably did not), and when letters by other writers (about thirty others in the present instance) are juxtaposed with them. In reading through the published correspondence, we have an experience of the letters that Cicero himself never enjoyed.

But what sort of inferences can we draw from this textual hybrid? What can we learn from it that we would not learn if we read the letters as they were written, at random moments and in isolation from one another? On the one hand, it would be a mistake to suppose that the published corpus opens an unobstructed view onto Cicero's relationships and activities. Since the letters were in practice written to or from persons not resident in Rome, the activity of people in Rome tends to fall outside their immediate focus. The editor has made the letter collection still less representative of Cicero's relationships and interests by deselecting certain categories of correspondent and subject matter. One element that the collection editor has introduced, on the other hand, which was not present in individual letters, is a semblance of plot. A succession of letters written at close intervals can reveal an unfolding action just as time-lapse photography does. Letter clusters are such a ubiquitous phenomenon in the Ciceronian corpus that one cannot help but suspect that they have been editorially enhanced. Not only do the letters regularly fall into discrete temporal sequences, but often the sequences are emplotted in actions revolving around particular recipients (as in the letters to Lentulus, to Appius, and to Decimus Brutus, for example). The self-image that Cicero inscribes in letters also makes a different impression in the collection than when letters are read separately. In writing a letter, he projects a version of himself meant to cajole, intimidate, or otherwise sway the addressee and sometimes one or more others whom he expects to read it. The effects can vary markedly from one correspondent to another, and even from letter to letter. Readers of the published corpus stand too far away from the situations in which the letters were written to catch every nuance of every performance, but as they read letter after letter, they have occasion to recognize more clearly than original readers could that some degree of role-playing always accompanies the writing of his letters. Though it would be naive to think that the corpus ever reveals to us the real Cicero, it does reveal his favorite repertoire.

Of the two operations by which the letter corpus was created, the manufacture of the letters—Cicero's contribution—has occupied my attention through most of this book. Now at the end, I am sorry that I have not made more headway in understanding what the editor wrought through selection and arrangement. Like the oracle of Delphi, the editor chose neither to explain nor conceal but to offer signs, and the signs are difficult to interpret. Why reserve Caelius's letters to a separate book rather than intersperse them with Cicero's letters, as in other series, for example? Why arrange clearly dated letters out of order? Why leave out Cicero's letters to Pollio, but include Pollio's to him? Why drop the entire correspondence with Atticus and Quintus in the years 53 and 52? What was the attraction that merited inclusion of a vacuous two-line note from Cicero to Basilus?

I finish with many questions that did not occur to me at the beginning. But with these chapters out of the way, I feel I am ready for a fresh reading of the correspondence. If they should help to orient other readers of Cicero's letters, that would be gratifying, too.

Appendix 1: Quantifying the Letter Corpus

NUMBER OF BOOKS IN THE PUBLISHED COLLECTION

As divided by the manuscripts, the extant letter corpus comprises thirty-six books, or a little more than that: one book and evidently part of a second consisting of letters to Marcus Brutus, three books of letters to Quintus, sixteen of letters to Atticus, and sixteen of letters to various persons which acquired the collective designation *Epistulae ad Familiares* in the sixteenth century. But citations in earlier sources suggest that these sixteen books did not originally circulate as a set, but were separately identified by the lead correspondent in each book (for example, "liber epistularum M. Ciceronis ad L. Plancum," Gell. *NA* 1.22.19, "liber M. Tullii epistularum ad Servium Sulpicium," Gell. *NA* 12.13.21). See Peter (1901, 54–57) and Büchner (1939, 1195).

There is also evidence for several books of letters that were published but have perished. They are attested by about one hundred citations in mostly late classical sources, especially Nonius Marcellus. (The citations are conveniently gathered in Watt [1958, 152–75].) Since the sources sometimes specify the number of the book from which a quote is taken, it is possible to estimate the minimum number of books that are missing. Thus there appear to have been a total of at least thirty-eight: two books each containing letters to Axius, Cornelius Nepos, Licinius Calvus, and Marcus junior; at least three each to Caesar, Octavian, and Pansa; four to Pompey; nine to Hirtius; and eight to Marcus Brutus (in addition to the book that is extant), for a total greater than the 36 books that have survived. For details, see Büchner (1939, 1199–1206) and Weyssenhoff (1966 and 1970). However, I do not subscribe to Weyssenhoff's hypothesis that letters attested only as fragments never had an existence as circulating published texts. She believes that either Tiro, or a grammarian who had access to Cicero's unpublished letter files in the century after his death, borrowed from them in writings of his own, and that all later testimonia derive from these excerpts.

NUMBER OF CORRESPONDENTS IN THE PUBLISHED COLLECTION

In addition to Cicero himself, the number of named individuals who send or receive letters in the extant corpus is ninety-seven, conveniently listed at Déniaux (1993, 96–108). (I count only those who receive or send separately in their own right: thus Cicero's brother and his son are counted because there are letters to or by them alone, but not his daughter or his nephew, who write or receive only as part of a group.) Déniaux also identifies the social status of each (with one slip by which M. Terentius Varro has been classified as an *eques*). But the published collection as a whole once included correspondence with eleven others in addition (Axius, Caerellia, Cornelius Nepos, Gorgias, Herodes, Hostilius, Licinius Calvus, Octavian, Pansa, Pelops, and Titinius), for a total of 108 persons.

The majority of Cicero's correspondents are represented only by letters they receive from him. But twenty-nine are represented by letters that they write (the letter writers and their letters are listed in the following section), and within this group four are represented only by letters to Cicero, not by letters from him (Asinius Pollio, Cassius Parmensis, the young Lentulus Spinther, and Sulpicius Galba). The number rises from twenty-nine to thirty-two if both authors of joint letters (Oppius writing along with Balbus, Trebatius writing along with Matius) and one anonymous letter writer (embedded in *Att.* 9.6.3 = 172 SB) are included.

NUMBER OF LETTERS EXTANT

Although the letters contained in the extant correspondence can obviously be added up to obtain some finite number, no consensus exists about what the number is. Peter (1901, 29) reckoned with a total of 864 letters; Riepl (1913, 266 n. 3) with a total of 877. A figure of 914 can be obtained by totaling the number series in each of Shackleton Bailey's commented editions (426 *Att.* + 435 *Fam.* + 27 *QFr.* + 26 *MBrut.*). Tyrrell and Purser presented a total of 931 letters in their edition, with most but not all enclosures separately numbered in the tally. Constans in the first volume of the Budé edition (p. 9) again cited the figure of 931, though the Budé edition actually culminates in 966 items, with enclosures and even some isolated quotations from letters included in the count.

Uncertainty is not likely to be overcome for two reasons. It is beyond question that letter headings have disappeared from the manuscripts at certain points, with the result that two or more originally separate letters appear as one. Yet for the sake of consistency, modern editors generally adhere to the conventional numeration by subdividing a conflated text as "letter 18" and "letter 18a," or as "letter 18a" and "letter 18b," for example, rather than renumbering the whole series. Moreover, while conflation is unmistakable in some texts, in others it is disputed; in still others it may be waiting to be detected. The number of conflated texts therefore remains an unknown quantity. A second problem with counting letters concerns enclosures and embedded letters. In standard editions of the Atticus corpus, editors usually number letters which were sent as enclosures to Atticus as subdivisions of the base text. For example, *Att.* 8.11A, 8.11B, 8.11C, and 8.11D are all enclosures accompanying the base text *Att.* 8.11. Confusingly, however, two enclosures that appear among the *Letters to Friends* are numbered separately (*Fam.* 6.9 accompanying 6.8 and *Fam.* 12.15 accompanying 12.14). More egregiously still, editors have divided *Att.* 9.13 into "*Att.* 9.13" and "*Att.* 9.13a" (lowercase "a") on the basis of a conflation, and have then identified an attachment to the latter as "*Att.* 9.13A" (capital "A"). Such conflations and enclosures at least get designated as distinct items. But there are several enclosures that Cicero copied into the body of his letter text rather than attaching them separately (e.g., *Att.* 8.6.2). Except in Tyrrell and Purser's and the Budé edition, these letters do not normally enter into the numeration at all.

To count the letters is therefore no easy business. Still, there may be readers of this book who want numbers all the same, if only to know by what standard I can claim that certain things are typical of the collection, whereas other things are not. And so I offer one more tally of the letters. I have taken them as they are divided and presented in Shackleton Bailey's Teubner edition of the entire corpus (1987–88). My numbers come out toward the high side of previous estimates because all attachments and embedded letters are included as separate items in the count.

The corpus of *Letters to Atticus* comprises 461 letters: 437 written by Cicero, sixteen written to Cicero, and eight enclosures written neither by nor to Cicero. The corpus of *Letters to Friends* comprises 434 letters in modern editions (not counting the fragment 11.13b = 381 SB). But one letter by Caelius (8.16 = *Att.* 10.9) and another by Cicero (9.14 = *Att.* 14.17A) must be subtracted because they duplicate letters that appear in the Atticus collection. The remaining 432 letters consist of 355 by Cicero, sixty-five to Cicero, and twelve that are neither by nor to Cicero. The corpus of *Letters to Quintus* comprises twenty-seven letters, all by Cicero. The corpus of *Letters to Marcus Brutus* comprises twenty-six letters: seventeen by Cicero, eight to Cicero, and one neither by nor to Cicero.

All in all, 946 letters are extant, 836 of which are written by Cicero. Of the rest, eighty-nine are written to Cicero, as follows:

M. Aemilius Lepidus: *Fam.* 10.34 = 396 SB; 10.34a = 400 SB

M. Antonius: *Att.* 10.8A = 199A SB, 10.10.2 = 201 SB; 14.13A = 367A SB

C. Asinius Pollio: *Fam.* 10.31 = 368 SB, 10.32 = 415 SB, 10.33 = 409 SB

A. Caecina: *Fam.* 6.7 = 237 SB

M. Caelius Rufus: *Fam.* 8.1–17 = 77–79, 81–84, 87–88, 91–92, 94, 97–98, 149, 153, and 156 SB

Q. Caecilius Metellus Celer: *Fam.* 5.1 = 1 SB

Q. Caecilius Metellus Nepos: *Fam.* 5.3 = 11 SB

C. Cassius Longinus: *Fam.* 12.11 = 366 SB, 12.12 = 387 SB, 15.19 = 216 SB

Cassius Parmensis: *Fam.* 12.13 = 419 SB

M. Claudius Marcellus: *Fam.* 4.11 = 232 SB

L. Cornelius Balbus: *Att.* 8.15A = 165 A, 9.7B = 174B SB, 9.13A = 181A SB; Balbus plus C. Oppius: *Att.* 9.7A = 174A SB

P. Cornelius Dolabella: *Fam.* 9.9 = 157 SB

P. Cornelius Lentulus: *Fam.* 12.14 = 405 SB

M'. Curius: *Fam.* 7.29 = 264 SB

A. Hirtius: *Att.* 15.6.2–3 = 386 SB

C. Iulius Caesar: *Att.* 9.6A = 172A SB, 9.16.2–3 = 185 SB, 10.8B = 199B SB

D. Iunius Brutus: *Fam.* 11.4 = 342 SB, 11.9 = 380 SB; 11.10 = 385 SB, 11.11 = 386 SB, 11.13 = 388 SB, 11.19 = 399 SB; 11.20 = 401 SB; 11.23 = 402 SB, and 11.26 = 410 SB

M. Iunius Brutus: *MBrut.* 3(2.3) = 2 SB, 11 (1.4) = 10 SB, 12 (1.4a) = 11 SB, 14
  (1.6) = 12 SB, 15 (1.7) = 19 SB, 19 (1.11) = 16 SB, 21 (1.13) = 20 SB, 24 (1.16) = 25 SB
L. Lucceius: *Fam.* 5.14 = 251 SB
C. Matius: *Fam.* 11.28 = 349 SB; Matius plus Trebatius: *Att.* 9.15a = 184 SB
L. Munatius Plancus: *Fam.* 10.4 = 358 SB, 10.7 = 372 SB, 10.9 = 379 SB, 10.11 =
  382 SB, 10.15 = 390 SB, 10.17 = 398 SB, 10.18 = 395 SB, 10.21 = 391 SB,
  10.21a = 392 SB, 10.23 = 414 SB, 10.24 = 428 SB
Cn. Pompeius: *Att.* 8.11A = 161A SB, 8.11C = 161C SB
Pompeius Bithynicus: *Fam.* 6.16 = 323 SB
M. Porcius Cato: *Fam.* 15.5 = 111 SB
Ser. Sulpicius Galba: *Fam.* 10.30 = 378 SB
Ser. Sulpicius Rufus: *Fam.* 4.5 = 248 SB, 4.12 = 253 SB
C. Trebonius: *Fam.* 12.16 = 328 SB
Q. Tullius Cicero: *Fam.* 16.16 = 44 SB
P. Vatinius: *Fam.* 5.9 = 255 SB, 5.10a.1–2 = 259 SB, 5.10a.3 = 256 SB, 5.10b = 258 SB
anonymous (Lepta?): *Att.* 9.6.3 = 172 SB.

Twenty-one are written neither to nor by Cicero; the majority will have originated as enclosures:

M. Aemilius Lepidus to the Senate: *Fam.* 10.35 = 408 SB
P. Cornelius Lentulus to the Senate: *Fam.* 12.15 = 406 SB
C. Iulius Caesar to C. Oppius and Cornelius Balbus: *Att.* 9.7C = 174 C SB,
  9.13A.1 = 181A SB
C. Iulius Caesar to Q. Pedius: *Att.* 9.14.1 = 182 SB
D. Junius Brutus to M. Iunius Brutus and C. Cassius Longinus: *Fam.* 11.1 = 325 SB
M. Iunius Brutus and C. Cassius Longinus to M. Antonius: *Fam.* 11.2 = 329 SB,
  11.3 = 336 SB
M. Iunius Brutus to Q. Caecilius Atticus: *MBrut.* 25(1.17) = 26 SB.
L. Munatius Plancus to the Senate: *Fam.* 10.8 = 371 SB
L. Munatius Plancus and D. Iunius Brutus to the Senate: *Fam.* 11.13a = 418 SB
Cn. Pompeius Magnus to the consuls: *Att.* 8.6.2 = 154 SB, 8.12A = 162A SB
Cn. Pompeius Magnus to L. Domitius: 8.12B = 162B SB, 8.12C = 162C SB,
  8.12D = 162D SB
Quintus Tullius Cicero to Tiro: *Fam.* 16.8 = 147 SB, 16.26 = 351 SB, 16.27 = 352 SB
Marcus Tullius Cicero the younger to Tiro: *Fam.* 16.21 = 337 SB, 16.25 = 338 SB

DATE OF PUBLICATION

There is no anecdotal information about the circumstances under which Cicero's letters were published, including when they were published. The best that can be achieved is a triangulation from indirect evidence, as follows. No part of the collection appears to have been in general circulation as of early July 44, when Cicero entertained the possibility of revising and publishing some seventy of his letters (*Att.* 16.5.5 = 410 SB). The letters to Atticus were not yet in circulation more than a decade later, at Atticus's death in 32, when Nepos described a large but still private trove of them (*vita Att.* 16.3). They seem to have become current by the end of the century or early in the next, however, because Quintilian (at *Inst.* 6.3.108) cites a quip from a letter of Cicero to

Atticus (*Att.* 8.7.2 = 155 SB) which he drew from a treatise on humor by Domitius Marsus, a contemporary of Maecenas and Ovid. Some part of the *Letters to Friends* must have been current by the end of Tiberius's reign in the 30s A.D., since at *Suas.* 1.5 Seneca the Elder is able to quote explicitly if somewhat inexactly from a letter of Cassius to Cicero corresponding to our *Fam.* 15.19.4 = 216 SB. Then, by the 60s A.D., letters of the younger Seneca cite (again explicitly) the letters to Atticus: *Epist.* 97.4 quotes *Att.* 1.16.5 = 16 SB, and sections 1 and 2 of *Epist.* 118 quote *Att.* 1.12.1 and 4 = 12 SB. The simplest conclusion from these clues would be that the *Letters to Atticus* had come into general circulation not later than the end of Augustus's reign in 14 A.D., and some of the *Letters to Friends* by the end of Tiberius's reign in 37 A.D.

Nevertheless, a preponderance of scholarly opinion has held that at least the *Letters to Atticus*, if not also the *Letters to Friends*, did not circulate publicly until about the 60s A.D., when they are attested by the younger Seneca. On this view, earlier citations are explained as the result of privileged access to the letters while they remained in private hands. The most powerful argument for dating publication to the 60s has been that Asconius, a conscientious researcher, shows no awareness of the letters in commentaries he was writing on Cicero's speeches in the 50s, though the letters contain information that would have been relevant to his enterprise.

To these considerations, I would add only that if the *Letters to Atticus* and the *Letters to Friends* show signs of being compiled on roughly similar editorial principles, it would make sense to put their respective publication dates relatively close together rather than far apart.

How and when the epistolary corpus was published have been endlessly debated questions. Apart from introductions to editions of the letters, the principal discussions have been Boissier (1863), Gurlitt (1879; 1901, 532–58), Peter (1901, 38–96), Meyer (1919, 588–606), Büchner (1939, 1211–23), Carcopino (1947, 1: 9–65 and 2: 217–458), Taylor (1964), Setaioli (1976)—a handy survey of the controversy—and Cugusi (1983, 168–73).

Appendix 2: Contemporary Works Mentioned in the Letters

The following list is limited to works by contemporaries of Cicero which circulated in written form, which are cited in the letter corpus, and which were evidently known to the letter writer. (An asterisk indicates a reference in a letter not by Cicero.)

L. Aelius Tubero: a history (*QFr.* 1.1.10 = 1 SB)

Alexander of Ephesus: a geographical poem (*Att.* 2.20.6 = 40 SB, 2.22.7 = 42 SB)

C. Amafinius: philosophical works (*Fam.* 15.19.2 = 216 SB*)

T. Ampius Balbus: historical or biographical work (*Fam.* 6.12.5 = 226 SB)

L. Antonius: a *contio* (*Att.* 14.20.2 = 374 SB)

M. Antonius: a *contio* (*Att.* 7.8.5 = 131 SB)

Archias: a poem for the Luculli (*Att.* 1.16.15 = 16 SB)

Athenodorus: philosophical work (*Fam.* 3.7.5 = 71 SB)

A. Caecina: *Querelae* (*Fam.* 6.6.8 = 234 SB), an anti-Caesarian work (*Fam.* 6.7.1 = 237 SB*, 6.5.3 = 239 SB), another *liber* (*Fam.* 6.5.1 = 239 SB, 6.7.1 = 237 SB*)

M. Calpurnius Bibulus: *contiones* (*Att.* 2.20.4 = 40 SB)

L. Calpurnius Piso Caesoninus: a speech (*QFr.* 3.1.11 = 21 SB)

Catius: *De rerum natura* (*Fam.* 15.16.1 = 215 SB, 15.19.1–2 = 216 SB*)

Ap. Claudius Pulcher: books on augury (*Fam.* 3.4.1 = 67 SB, 3.9.3 = 72 SB, 3.11.4 = 74 SB), speeches (*Fam.* 3.11.4 = 74 SB)

L. Cornelius Balbus, cos. 40: a *praetexta* (*Fam.* 10.32.3 = 415 SB*)

P. Cornelius Dolabella: a *contio* (*Att.* 14.17A.7 = 371A SB, 14.20.2 and 4 = 374 SB)

Cotta: a *liber* (*Att.* 13.44.2 = 336 SB)

Demetrius Magnes: περὶ ὁμονοίας (*Att.* 8.11.7 = 161 SB, 8.12.6 = 162 SB, 9.9.2 = 176 SB)

M. Fabius Gallus: *Cato* (*Fam.* 7.24.2 = 260 SB)

A. Hirtius: *Anti-Cato* (*Att.* 12.40.1 = 281 SB, 12.41.4 = 283 SB, 12.44.1 = 285 SB, 12.48.1 = 289 SB, 12.45.2 = 290 SB)

C. Julius Caesar: *Apophthegmata* (*Fam.* 9.16.4 = 190 SB), *Anti-Cato* (*Att.*
12.40.1 = 281 SB, 12.41.4 = 283 SB, 13.50.1 = 348 SB, 13.51.1 = 349 SB)

M. Junius Brutus: *Cato* (*Att.* 12.21.1 = 260 SB, 13.46.2 = 338 SB), epitome of
Fannius (*Att.* 12.5b = 316 SB), epitome of Caelius Antipater (*Att.* 13.8 = 313 SB),
a *contio* (*Att.* 15.1a.2 = 378 SB, 15.2.2 = 379 SB, 15.3.2 = 380 SB, 15.4.3 = 381 SB)

C. Licinius Calvus: poem on Tigellius (*Fam.* 7.24.1 = 260 SB)

L. Lucceius: a history of the Sullan period (*Fam.* 5.12.2 = 22 SB)

T. Lucretius Carus: poems (*QFr.* 2.10[9].2 = 14 SB)

Q. Mucius Scaevola: *De iure civili* (*Fam.* 7.22 = 331 SB)

νεώτεροι poets: (*Att.* 7.2.1 = 125 SB)

Nicon: περὶ πολυφαγίας (*Fam.* 7.20.3 = 333 SB)

P. Nigidius Figulus: writings (*Fam.* 4.13.7 = 225 SB)

Octavian: *contiones* (*Att.* 14.20.5 = 374 SB, 14.21.4 = 375 SB, 15.2.3 = 379 SB,
16.15.3 = 426 SB)

Ollius: *Laudatio Porciae* (*Att.* 13.48. 2 = 345 SB)

Phaedrus: περὶ θεῶν (*Att.* 13.39.2 = 342 SB)

Q. Pilius Celer: speech against M. Servilius (*Att.* 6.3.10 = 117 SB)

T. Pomponius Atticus: Greek narrative of Cicero's consulate (*Att.* 2.1.1 = 21 SB),
liber annalis (*Att.* 12.23.2 = 262 SB), epigrams (*Att.* 1.16.15 = 16 SB)

Posidonius: philosophical works (*Att.* 16.11.4 = 420 SB)

Procilius: a geographical work? (*Att.* 2.2.2 = 22 SB)

Cn. Sallustius: *Empedoclea* (*QFr.* 2.10[9].2 = 14 SB)

L. Scribonius Libo: *Annales* (*Att.* 13.30.2 = 303 SB, 13.32.3 = 305 SB, 13.44.3 = 336
SB)

Servilius Casca: a *liber* (*Att.* 13.44.3 = 336 SB)

M. Terentius Varro: *De Lingua Latina* (*Att.* 12.52.3 = 294 SB, 13.12.3 = 320 SB, *Fam.*
9.8.1 = 254 SB), *Laudatio Porciae* (*Att.* 13.48.2 = 345 SB), possible reference to
the Menippean satires (*Fam.* 11.10.5 = 385 SB*), a dialogue (*Att.* 15.13.3 = 416 SB,
16.11.3 = 420 SB, 16.12 = 421 SB), *Imagines* (*Att.* 16.11.3 = 420 SB)

C. Trebonius: political satire (*Fam.* 12.16.3 = 328 SB*, 15.21.1 = 207 SB)

Tyrannio: a work on prosody (*Att.* 12.6.2 = 306 SB)

M. Tullius Cicero: *De Oratore* (*Att.* 4.13.2 = 87 SB, 4.16.2–3 = 89 SB, 4.17.5 = 91
SB, 13.19.4 = 326 SB, *Fam.* 1.9.23 = 20 SB, 7.32.2 = 113 SB, *QFr.* 3.5[5–7].1 = 25
SB), *De Republica* (*Att.* 4.14.1 = 88 SB, 4.16.2 = 89 SB, 5.12.2 = 105 SB,
6.1.8 = 115 SB, 6.2.3 and 9 = 116 SB, 6.3.3 = 117 SB, 6.6.2 = 121 SB, 7.2.4 = 125
SB, 7.3.2 = 126 SB, 8.11.1 = 161 SB, 13.19.4 = 326 SB, *Fam.* 8.1.4 = 77 SB*, *QFr.*
2.13[12].1 = 17 SB, 3.1.11 = 21 SB, 3.5[5–7].1–2 = 25 SB), *Orator* (*Att.* 12.6a.1 = 243
SB, 14.20.3 = 374 SB, *Fam.* 6.7.4 = 237 SB*, 6.18.4 = 218 SB, 12.17.2 = 204 SB,
15.20.1 = 208 SB), *Academica* (*Att.* 12.44.4 = 285 SB, 13.5.1 = 312 SB,
13.12.3 = 320 SB, 13.13–14.1 = 321 SB, 13.14–15.1 = 322 SB, 13.16.1 = 323 SB,
13.18 = 325 SB, 13.19.3 = 326 SB, 13.21.3 = 351 SB, 13.21a .1 = 327 SB, 13.22.1 and
3 = 329 SB, 13.23.2 = 331 SB, 13.24.1 = 332 SB, 13.25.3 = 333 SB, 13.32.3 = 305 SB,
13.35–36.2 = 334 SB, 13.44.2 = 336 SB, 16.6.4 = 414 SB, *Fam.* 9.8 = 254 SB),
Topica (*Fam.* 7.19 = 334 SB), *De Finibus* (*Att.* 12.12.2 = 259 SB, 13.12.3 = 320 SB,
13.19.4 = 326 SB, 13.21a.1–2 = 327 SB, 13.22.3 = 329 SB, 13.23.2 = 331 SB), *De
Officiis* (*Att.* 15.13a.2 = 417 SB, 16.11.4 = 420 SB, 16.14.3 = 425 SB), *Tusculans*

(*Att.* 15.2.4 = 379 SB, 15.4.2–3 = 381 SB), *De Senectute* (*Att.* 14.21.3 = 375 SB,
16.3.1 = 413 SB, 16.11.3 = 420 SB), *De Gloria* (*Att.* 15.27.2 = 406 SB,
16.2.6 = 412 SB, 16.6.4 = 414 SB), philosophical works (*Att.* 12.52.3 = 294 SB,
13.20.4 = 328 SB, *Att.* 13.38.1 = 341 SB, 15.14.4 = 402 SB), *Contra contionem Q.*
Metelli (*Att.* 1.13.5 = 13 SB), *De lege agraria orationes I, II, III, and IV* (*Att.*
2.1.3 = 21 SB), *De Othone* (*Att.* 2.1.3 = 21 SB), *Pro Rabirio* (*Att.* 2.1.3 = 21 SB), *De*
proscriptorum liberis (*Att.* 2.1.3 = 21 SB), *Cum provinciam deposuit* (*Att.* 2.1.3 = 21
SB), *In Catilinam orationes I, II, III, and IV* (*Att.* 2.1.3 = 21 SB), *In Clodium et*
Curionem (*Att.* 3.12.2 = 57 SB), *In Pisonem* (*QFr.* 3.1.11 = 21 SB), *Pro Scauro*
(*QFr.* 3.1.11 = 21 SB), *Pro Plancio* (*QFr.* 3.1.11 = 21 SB), *Pro Ligario* (*Att.*
13.12.2 = 320 SB, 13.19.2 = 326 SB, 13.20.2 = 328 SB, 13.44.3 = 336 SB), *Pro*
Deiotaro (*Fam.* 9.12 = 263 SB), *Second Philippic* (*Att.* 15.13.1 = 416 SB,
15.13a.3 = 417 SB, 16.11.1–3 = 420 SB), *Fifth Philippic* (*MBrut.* 3[2.3].4 = 2 SB*),
Tenth Philippic (*MBrut.* 3[2.3].4 = 2 SB*), *Eleventh Philippic* (*MBrut.* 4.[2.4].2 = 4
SB), speeches (*Att.* 1.13.5 = 13 SB, 4.5.1–2 = 80 SB, 4.15.9 = 90 SB, *Fam.* 1.9.23
= 20 SB, 7.1.3 = 24 SB), *De consiliis suis* (*Att.* 2.6.2 = 26 SB, 14.14.5 = 368 SB,
14.17.6 = 371 SB), a Greek narrative of his consulship (*Att.* 1.19.10 = 19 SB,
1.20.6 = 20 SB, 2.1.1 = 21 SB), a letter to Calvus on oratory (*Fam.* 15.21.4 = 207
SB), *Cato* (*Att.* 12.4.2 = 240 SB, 12.5.2 = 242 SB, 12.40.1 = 281 SB, 13.27.1 = 298
SB, 13.46.2 = 338 SB, *Fam.* 16.22.1 = 185 SB), an auto-consolation for the death
of Tullia (*Att.* 12.14.3 = 251 SB, 12.18.1 = 254 SB, 12.20.2 = 258 SB, 12.21.5 = 260
SB, 12.24.2 = 263 SB, 12.28.2 = 267 SB), *Laudatio Porciae* (*Att.* 13.37.3 = 346 SB,
13.48.2 = 345 SB), a possibly never completed geographical work (*Att.*
2.4.3 = 24 SB, 2.6.1 = 26 SB, 2.7.11 = 27 SB), a possibly never completed
dialogue (*Att.* 15.4.3 = 381 SB, 15.27.2 = 406 SB, 16.2.6 = 412 SB, 15.13.3 = 416
SB), *Prognostica* (*Att.* 2.1.11 = 21 SB, 15.16a = 392 SB), *Marius* (*Att.*
12.49.2 = 292 SB), a Latin poem on his consulship (*Att.* 1.19.10 = 19 SB,
2.3.4 = 23 SB), a poem *De temporibus suis* (*Att.* 4.8a.3 = 82 SB, *Fam.* 1.9.23 = 20
SB, *QFr.* 2.8[7].1 = 13 SB, 2.14[13].2 = 18 SB, 2.16[15].5 = 20 SB, 3.1.24 = 21 SB),
an epic poem for Caesar (*QFr.* 2.16[15].4 = 20 SB, 3.1.11 = 21 SB, 3.6[8].3 = 26
SB, 3.7[9].6 = 27 SB), writings (*Att.* 1.16.18 = 16 SB, 4.5.1 = 80 SB, 4.11.2 = 86
SB, 7.1.4 = 124 SB, 12.38a.1 = 279 SB, 12.40.2 = 281 SB, 13.26.2 = 286 SB, 13.47
= 339 SB, 16.5.2 and 5 = 410 SB, 16.11.3 = 420 SB, *Fam.* 12.17.2 = 204 SB,
MBrut. 25[1.17].5 = 26 SB*).
Q. Tullius Cicero: *Erigona* (*QFr.* 3.1.13 = 21 SB, 3.5[5–7].7 = 25 SB, 3.7[9].6 = 27
SB), *Electra* (*QFr.* 3.5[5–7].7 = 25 SB), two other tragedies (*QFr.* 3.5[5–7].7 = 25
SB), a satirical epigram (*QFr.* 1.3.8 = 3 SB), a historical work (*Att.* 2.16.4 = 36
SB, *QFr.* 1.1.44 = 1 SB).

Notes

1. The phenomenon of linguistic switching in Latin writers has been recently analyzed by Adams (2003), who discusses Cicero's practice in his letters on pages 308–47, commenting, "Since this type of code-switching was a game, and since it took place in private between intimates, it is often light-hearted" (p. 345). Compare Hutchinson (1998, 13–16).

2. Compare Kerbrat-Orecchioni (1998, 27) apropos of both letters and conversation: "Dans toute interaction, les phases d'ouverture et de clôture sont des moments particulièrement délicats pour les interactants, d'où d'ailleurs leur caractère fortement 'ritualisé.'"

3. For statistics about the letter corpus, see appendix 1.

4. Demmel (1962, 325 n. 2) noted the rarity of comment regarding family: "allein dem Briefwechsel mit Atticus der Austausch von Familienangelegenheiten vorbehalten war; wenigstens findet sich sonst nichts dergleichen."

5. Cic. *Phil.* 11.5. Appian has a more circumstantial and grisly account at *BC* 3.26.100–101.

6. The social background of Cicero's correspondents is conveniently set out in the table in Déniaux (1993, 96–108).

7. The exchange of letters between persons who are both in Rome is treated as unusual at Plut. *Caes.* 17.8 and Nep. *Att.* 20.2. At most a handful of letters in the Ciceronian corpus are intra-urban, including possibly *Fam.* 6.15 = 322 SB, 7.22 = 331 SB, and 11.1 = 325 SB. Déniaux (1993, 114) notes the correlation between absence from Rome and risk: "le départ d'un magistrat pour sa province lui impose un éloignement dommageable au soin de sa *dignitas.*"

8. The Romans were familiar with carrier pigeons (Steier 1932, 2493–94), but then as now, pigeons could not haul much, they traveled in only one direction, and they are scarcely relevant to the topic of letter writing. After a long survey of alternative

forms of communication, Riepl (1913, 124) sensibly concluded, "Die Universalform der Nachrichtenbeförderung im Altertum war und blieb der Brief."

9. For transit time from Rome to Tusculum, see *Att.* 12.53 = 295 SB; for Rome to Puteoli, see *Att.* 14.13.1 = 367 SB, 14.17.1 = 371 SB, 14.18.1 = 373 SB, 14.20.1 = 374 SB; from Britain to Rome, *QFr.* 3.1.13, 17, and 25 = 21 SB; from Syria, *Att.* 14.9.3 = 363 SB. Fuller details are compiled by Bardt (1866) and Riepl (1913, 137–47). For a discussion of time in the letters, see Hutchinson (1998, 139–71).

10. A fourth option, not always distinct from the other three, applied in the case of letters of recommendation, which were often carried by the recommendee.

11. For the expectation of speed, see *Att.* 9.4.3 = 173 SB, 11.23.2 = 232 SB, and 16.14.2 = 425 SB. For the expectation of a return letter, see *Fam.* 9.9.3 = 157 SB and *Att.* 12.39.1 = 280 SB.

12. *Att.* 13.21.2 = 351 SB, 13.27.2 = 298 SB. Smadja (1976) catalogs and discusses (at pp. 91–93) Cicero's *tabellarii*.

13. Arrangements for regular couriers may be glimpsed at *Att.* 12. 42.1 = 282 SB, 15.8.1 = 385 SB, 16.13.3 = 423 SB, 16.15.3 = 426 SB, *QFr.* 2.11(10).5 = 15 SB, 2.12(11).4 = 16 SB, *Fam.* 14.18.2 = 144 SB, 16.5.2 = 124 SB. But Cicero indicates at *Att.* 8.14.1 = 164 SB and 16.2.6 = 412 SB that such arrangements were exceptional.

14. *Fam.* 11.8.1 = 360 SB, 3.3.1 = 66 SB, and 12.22a.4 = 357 SB.

15. For a survey of the hazards with evidence, see Riepl (1913, 279–85) and Nicholson (1994).

16. For example, *Att.* 6.1.9 = 115 SB, 13.29.3 = 300 SB, *Fam.* 4.4.1 = 203 SB (with SB's note), 7.18.2 = 37 SB, 9.16.1 = 190 SB, 10.5.1 = 359 SB, 10.33.3 = 409 SB, 11.11.1 = 386 SB, 12.12.1 = 387 SB, 12.30.7 = 417 SB. Much more common than the sending of duplicate letters, however, was the repetition in successive letters of the same material, as at *Att.* 7.1 = 124 SB with 6.9 = 123 SB, *Fam.* 3.3.1 = 66 SB with 3.2.1 = 65 SB, and 14.14 = 145 SB with 14.18 = 144 SB.

17. The opening of this letter, in which Cicero thanks Atticus for a long letter after a series of short, uninformative messages, is also relevant to the issue of confidentiality: he implies that Atticus finally sent a long letter because he had a trusted *hospes* who would carry it. For other instances in which distrust of the messenger gives Cicero pause, see *Att.* 1.13.4 = 13 SB, 1.18.2 = 18 SB, 2.19.5 = 39 SB, 4.15.3 = 90 SB, 10.11.1 = 202 SB, 15.4.4 = 381 SB, *QFr.* 3.1.21 = 21 SB, 3.6(8).2 = 26 SB.

18. Some other excuses: *Att.* 1.13.1 = 13 SB, 1.16.16 = 16 SB, 4.17.1 = 91 SB, *Fam.* 1.7.1 = 18 SB.

19. For annoyance over someone's failure to make use of a courier, see *Fam.* 7.14.1 = 38 SB, *Att.* 12.39.1 = 280 SB.

20. A letter writer could also encounter the opposite problem. If delivery of the letter depended on another man's agent, and if the agent waited to accumulate a batch of mail before beginning his run, the letter could be stale before it left Rome (Cic. *QFr.* 3.1.8 = 21 SB).

21. *Att.* 7.9.1 = 132 SB, 7.15.1 = 139 SB, 7.20.2 = 144 SB, 8.12.1 = 162 SB, 8.14.1 = 164, 9.16.1 = 185 SB, 12.12.2 = 259 SB, 12.27.2 = 266 SB, 12.39.2 = 280 SB, 12.42.1 = 282 SB, 14.4.2 = 358 SB, 15.28 = 405 SB, 16.13.3 = 423 SB, 16.15.3 = 426 SB. The only other correspondents with whom Cicero tries to establish a daily exchange are Quintus

and Terentia, likewise at a time when the parties are relatively nearby, *QFr.* 2.10(9).2 = 14 SB, 2.11(10).5 = 15 SB), *Fam.* 14.18.2 = 144 SB.

22. However, it is possible that that the two short series of letters to Marius and to Curius in book 7 of the *Letters to Friends* represent the vestiges of a more prolonged correspondence with persons living permanently away from Rome.

23. Another reason pertains only to members of the senatorial class and has its basis in Roman political organization. Senators were required to be in Rome when they were not conducting the public business abroad. Apart from some military commands, foreign service did not usually keep them abroad for longer than a year or two. Therefore situations did not often arise in which two senators could carry on an exchange lasting for several years. The salient exception would be Cicero's correspondence with Caesar, which is unfortunately not extant. But the set of moral epistles from Seneca to Lucilius, which *is* extant, does not fit this category for several reasons. They were written in the period after Seneca had retired from the Senate, and his epistolary partner was not a fellow senator but an *eques*, serving as an imperial procurator in Sicily (imperial posts did often keep incumbents abroad for several years). But more important, there is good reason to suspect that this series of philosophical reflections represents an idealized correspondence rather than an actual one.

24. Whether Cicero's correspondence files included copies of letters that he wrote as well as the letters he received is a matter of perennial controversy. In fact, we know almost nothing about the procedures by which members of the Roman elite disposed of their private correspondence. The only direct evidence consists of Nepos's reference to a large archive of Cicero's letters to Atticus that he had seen (*vita Att.* 16.3), plus a small handful of references by Cicero to letters by himself or others that he has saved. The extent to which this information can be validly eked out with the help of papyrological evidence for letter archives in Egypt is uncertain. Peter (1901, 32–35) summarized the information available when he wrote; for more recent accounts, see Cugusi (1983, 139–41; 1989, 415–17). But despite the dearth of hard evidence, I take it as an article of faith that Cicero did retain copies of his letters, for two main reasons. First, I think that a publication project that was to generate more than seventy books of letters (see appendix 1) would have been far less practicable if the originals had to be retrieved from each of Cicero's hundred-odd addressees than if copies of them could be found in Cicero's own archives. And second, Tiro's diligence in composing a biography of his former master in at least four books (Asc. *in Milon.* 48.26 Clark), in recording his jokes (Quint. *Inst.* 6.3.5), and in preserving preliminary sketches of his speeches (Quint. *Inst.* 10.7.30–31) disposes me to believe that he would have been equally obsessive about saving letters.

25. From Cicero's exchange with Caesar there are examples of both sorts. Cicero's letters to Caesar are passed on to Atticus at *Att.* 8.2.2 = 152 SB and 13.51.1 = 349 SB; Caesar's letters to Cicero are passed on at *Att.* 7.23.3 = 147 SB, 9.6.6 = 172 SB, 10.3a.2 = 194 SB, and 13.22.5 = 329 SB.

26. Andrew Dyck adds *per litteras*, "Not only that, but if the letter were lost, the oral message might still arrive; and if the bearer and recipient were not known to each other, the oral message could provide a guarantee of authenticity."

27. Hence the main exceptions to Cicero's habit of not reporting political news are found in his correspondence with Quintus, with Atticus, and with Lentulus

Spinther, who as consul had organized Cicero's recall from exile. Vis-à-vis each of these recipients and especially Quintus, Cicero occupied the trusted position of being one of the *sui*.

28. Caelius complied with Cicero's request for news not only by sending the letters that survive in book 8 of the *Letters to Friends* but by attaching to them supplements (none extant) that he paid to have compiled from various public sources, as he describes at *Fam.* 8.1.1 = 77 SB and 8.11.4 = 91 SB; see also *Fam.* 2.8.1 = 80 SB. Caesar likewise made detailed arrangements for intelligence gathering when he was away from Rome (Cic. *QFr.* 3.1.10 = 21 SB and *Fam.* 9.16.4 = 190 SB).

29. Some examples culled from the letters: *Att.* 10.16.5 = 208 SB, 14.20.2 = 374 (with Shackleton Bailey's note), 15.15.2 = 393 SB, 15.27.1 = 406 SB.

30. *Att.* 1.11.1 = 7 SB; a similar situation is described in *Att.* 1.17 = 17 SB. Other clear statements that letters are a poor substitute for live contact are found at *Fam.* 3.5.4 = 68 SB, 12.30.1 = 417 SB, and 15.14.2–3 = 106 SB.

31. Other letter readings at *Att.* 11.9.2 = 220 SB, 13.45.1 = 337 SB, *Fam.* 9.1.1 = 175 SB, 10.12.2 = 377 SB. Robert Kaster points out to me that reading aloud is implied in the scene described at *Fam.* 7.5.2 = 26 SB, where a letter from Caesar is delivered to Cicero during a meeting between him and Balbus. Cicero provides a graphic instance of the letter as presentification when he describes how he "complexus...sum cogitatione te absentem, epistulam vero osculatus" at *Fam.* 3.11.2 = 74 SB. The kissing of a letter received is parodied in a text quoted at Stowers (1986, 65–66), which suggests that it became a commonplace motif.

32. On the persistence of generic elements in ancient letters, see especially Koskenniemi (1956), Thraede (1970), and Cugusi (1983). Cugusi (1998) surveys motifs and phraseology that Cicero shares with writers of letters on papyri.

33. As Dziatzko (1899, 838–39) and Koskenniemi (1956, 155) point out.

34. Apart from *Fam.* 2.4.1 = 48 SB (which follows), the relevant passages are *Fam.* 4.13.1 = 225 SB, 6.10.4 = 222 SB, 15.14.3–4 = 106 SB, *Att.* 5.5.1 = 98 SB, 7.5.4–5 = 128 SB, 9.4.1 = 173 SB, and *QFr.* 1.1.37 = 1 SB. The background of these statements is discussed by Peter (1901, 21–24), Koskenniemi (1954), and Hutchinson (1998, 6–7), and several are presented in translation along with other proto-theoretical pronouncements on the letter in Malherbe (1988).

35. Examples only: "utemur bono litterarum et eadem fere absentes quae si coram essemus consequeremur" (Cic. *Fam.* 15.14.3 = 106 SB), "non...quicquam libentius facio quam scribo ad te: videor enim cum praesente loqui et iocari" (Cic. *Fam.* 15.19.1 = 216 SB), "ego, etsi nihil habeo quod ad te scribam, scribo tamen quia tecum loqui videor" (Cic. *Att.* 12.53 = 295 SB), "colloqui videbamur in Tusculano cum essem; tanta erat crebritas litterarum" (Cic. *Att.* 13.18 = 325 SB).

36. A reader for Oxford University Press points out a case in which a letter resumes a live conversation. Cicero wrote *Fam.* 7.22 = 331 SB after a dinner party debate with Trebatius about a point of law, when he returned home to his library and tracked down juristic authorities that supported his position.

37. The ideal is articulated in a remark of Valerius Cato quoted at Quint. *Inst.* 6.3.104, "urbanus homo erit...qui in sermonibus circulis conviviis, item in contionibus, omni denique loco ridicule commodeque dicet"; for a discussion of Roman *urbanitas* in the age of Cicero, see Ramage (1973, 52–76). Quintilian locates

the natural ground of wit "in conviviis et sermonibus" (6.3.14, cf. 6.3.28), and discusses the difficulty of transplanting it. Needless to say, the association of joking with conversation is not peculiar to Roman society: "Everyday conversation is the natural showplace—or better, playground—of joking: joking everywhere informs the overall progress and the step-by-step construction of conversation" (Norrick 1993, 139).

38. Cicero dwells more often on joking than on any other function of letters: *Att.* 5.5.1 = 98 SB, 6.5.4 = 119 SB, 7.5.5 = 128 SB, *Fam.* 2.4.1 = 48 SB, 4.13.1 = 225 SB (with Shackleton Bailey's note), 7.11.3 = 34 SB, 15.18.1 = 213 SB, and 15.19.1 = 216 SB.

39. Cic. *Att.* 7.1.8 = 124 SB. Four of these letters are preserved in the published corpus: *Fam.* 3.9.4 = 72 SB (cf. 3.13.1 = 76 SB), 15 = 110 SB, 15.10 = 108 SB, and 15.13 = 109 SB.

40. [Cic.] *Fam.* 8.11 = 91 SB. Cicero himself can be glimpsed in such canvassing efforts on other occasions, at *Fam.* 1.2.1 = 13 SB, 5.6.1 = 4 SB, 12.24.1 = 361 SB; and he describes Clodius engaged in one at *Att.* 1.14.5 = 14 SB. At *Fam.* 3.5.4 = 68 SB Cicero declines to communicate a *mandatum* by letter until there is no chance of communicating in person, and at *Fam.* 15.14.3 = 106 SB he observes that congratulations, too, are better expressed live than by letter.

41. Predominantly joking letters from Cicero are *Fam.* 1.10 = 21 SB, 7.6 = 27 SB, 7.10 = 33 SB, 7.11 = 34 SB, 7.12 = 35 SB, 7.13 = 36 SB, 7.14 = 38 SB, 7.16 = 32 SB, 7.18 = 37 SB, 7.27 = 148 SB (unpleasantly joking), 7.32 = 113 SB, 9.10 = 217 SB, 9.19 = 194 SB, 9.20 = 193 SB, 9.21 = 188 SB, 9.24 = 362 SB, 9.25 = 114 SB, 9. 26 = 197 SB, and 15.19 = 216 SB. Two-thirds of these nineteen letters are directed to just two of Cicero's correspondents, Trebatius and Paetus, who, not coincidentally, are his social inferiors. Cicero's practice (in the published correspondence, at least) thus affords a corollary to the maxim later articulated by Iulius Victor (*Ars Rhetorica* 27) "epistula, si superiori scribas, ne iocularis sit." For recent discussions of humor in Cicero, with references to earlier bibliography, see Hutchinson (1998, 172–99) and Corbeill (1996, 3–13). Norrick (1993), written from the perspective of modern discourse analysis, provides a helpful complement.

42. Cic. *Att.* 5.2.1 = 95 SB, *Fam.* 3.9.2 = 72 SB, 8.17.1 = 156 SB, 13.7.1 = 320 SB.

43. Single examples only: *Fam.* 10.1.4 = 340 SB, 13.8.1 = 321 SB, 13.25 = 291 SB, 13.28.2 = 294 and SB 13.51 = 61 SB. Déniaux (1993), who comments on some of these effects in pages 28–53, observes that a letter of recommendation not only projects a relationship with the recommendee, but "renforce aussi les liens qui unissent Cicéron et son correspondant" (28). In that respect, it contrasts with a modern recommendation, which typically "présente une personne à une autre en lui demandant une faveur, mais ne présuppose pas une amitié entre l'auteur et le destinataire de la lettre" (29). Robert Kaster adds *per e-litteras*, "In fact, one could probably go even farther and say that the modern recommendation will typically attempt to disguise or downplay any pre-existing relationship in the interest of creating an impression of 'objectivity' (this is certainly true of formal recommendations in our line of work). In that respect, the different dynamics between the ancient and the modern forms seem exactly parallel to the different dynamics of ancient and modern advocacy, where the norm in antiquity was to stress the personal relationship between the advocate and the client, whereas the norm today is to establish a 'professional' distance, again in the interest of objectivity."

44. *Fam.* 1.7.11 = 18 SB (the son of Lentulus Spinther, who with *Fam.* 12.14 = 405 SB becomes a correspondent of Cicero in his own right), 4.3.4 = 202 SB and 4.4.5 = 203 SB (the son of Servius Sulpicius Rufus), 5.8.4 = 25 SB (the sons of Crassus), 5.17.4–5 = 23 SB (the son of Publius Sittius), 6.5.1 = 239 SB and 6.6.13 = 234 SB (the son of Caecina), 6.18.4–5 = 218 SB (the son of Lepta), 12.14.8 = 405 SB (Cicero's son, mentioned in a letter from the younger Lentulus), 13.27.4 = 293 SB, and *MBrut.* 3(2.3).6 = 2 SB (Cicero's son again, mentioned in a letter from Brutus). *MBrut.* 4(2.4).6 = 4 SB also implies that Brutus had written to Cicero about his son. Compare *Fam.* 13.68 = 211 SB, regarding a father rather than a son.

45. Apart from the passages cited, other instances of the metaphor in the letters are, for *vinculum*, *Fam.* 5.15.2 = 252 SB, 15.11.2 = 118 SB, *Att.* 3.24.1 = 69 SB, 6.2.1 = 116 SB, and, for *devincire*, *Fam.* 1.7.3 = 18 SB, 1.9.21 = 20 SB, 3.13.2 = 76 SB, 6.11.1 = 224 SB, 13.3.1 = 315 SB, 13.7.5 = 320 SB, 13.11.3 = 278 SB, 13.27.2 = 293 SB, 13.29.1 = 282 SB, *Att.* 1.13.2 = 13 SB, 16.16B.2 = 407B SB, and *QFr.* 1.2.4 = 2 SB.

46. Not only is this metaphor missing, but at two points at which Cicero resorts to related images (*adligare* in sec. 42 and *habenae amicitiae* in sec. 45), he applies them to models of friendship that he rejects.

47. That conception is ubiquitous in the *De Amicitia*: see secs. 15, 20, 23, 27, 48, 61, 80–81, 92, and 100. Cicero explains that he is speaking of the ideal and not the actual in sects. 22 and 100.

48. A complication frankly acknowledged at *Amic.* 64: "verae amicitiae difficillime reperiuntur in iis qui in honoribus reque publica versantur: ubi enim istum invenias qui honorem amici anteponat suo?"

49. Compare *Fam.* 3.9.4 = 72 SB, 5.11.2 = 257 SB, and Sall. *Cat.* 35.6 (Catiline's letter to Catulus).

50. *Fam.* 9.16.1–6 = 190 SB. Paetus, Cicero's informant in this case, reported on talk that he had heard to Cicero's disadvantage on another occasion according to *Fam.* 9.24 = 362 SB.

51. For another intervention by Cicero, see Cic. *Fam.* 13.24 = 290 SB.

52. For an essay in understanding the role of gossip in Roman political society, see Laurence (1994). Bergmann (1993) has a thoughtful and intelligent discussion of gossip by a sociologist. Among other points that seem pertinent to the understanding of gossip in Rome, he relates it to the craving for information (cf. p. 147, drawing on the work of Robert Paine: "It is the urgent interest of every gossiper to receive information about what is going on around him. Therefore he is anxious to maintain the flow of information that provides him with messages and news") and to the dynamics of friendship groups.

53. Cicero first uses *confirmare* in sec. 2, and there, as if to make sure that the figurative coloring remains in force, he modifies it with the adverb *vehementius*: "tu multis de causis vellem me convenire potuisses, primum ut...postremo ut amicitia nostra...confirmaretur vehementius."

54. Jakobson (1987, 68).

55. "The illocutionary force of the letter is bound up with its autoreferential capacity, which is the capacity it has to refer to itself and to its own communicative function independently of any propositional content it may express...the letter...can communicate no other content than its own communicativeness," Violi (1985, 160).

Or more simply put, "the real subject matter of letter-writing is the writing of the letters" (Chartier 1997, 19). The essays of both Violi and Chartier offer valuable insights into Cicero's correspondence, though neither is concerned with it.

CHAPTER 2

1. I share Mary Beard's conviction (2002) that the ancient editions of Cicero's correspondence afford clear evidence of conscious arrangement and design. She suggests that the principles of arrangement in ancient poetry books provide a model for the way that themes, personality, and personal relationships are highlighted in the various letter collections. I will focus on more formalistic patterns of organization that complement those which she discerns.

2. The last complete letter written by Cicero is *MBrut.* 26(1.18) = 24 SB, which Cicero dated "July 27th." The very latest one, however, is thought to be a letter to Octavian from which Nonius Marcellus quotes a fragment (3: 702.23–24 Lindsay = frag. 23B, p. 160 Watt)—though if this was Cicero's final communication, it is odd to find it lodged in book 1 or book 2 of the letters *ad Caesarem iuniorem* (so the Nonius manuscripts) rather than in book 3. The last datable letter from one of Cicero's correspondents is *Fam.* 10.24 = 428 SB, written by Plancus and dated "July 28th."

3. One work that Cicero seems to have intended for posthumous publication was the outspoken *De consiliis suis,* which is occasionally mentioned in the letters to Atticus. Dio says that it was not published until after his death (39.10.3), though Büchner (1939, 1267–69) argues that it may have been published during the last year of Cicero's life.

4. *Att.* 16.5.5 = 410 SB. Since the context in which Cicero makes this statement will be relevant to the following argument, I quote the entire section: "Nepotis epistulam exspecto. cupidus ille meorum, qui ea quibus maxime γαυριῶ legenda non putet? et ais 'μετ' ἀμύμονα'. tu vero ἀμύμων, ille quidem ἄμβροτος. mearum epistularum nulla est συναγωγή; sed habet Tiro instar septuaginta, et quidem sunt a te quaedam sumendae. eas ego oportet perspiciam, corrigam; tum denique edentur." Peter (1901, 36 n. 1) noted a similar use of the word *synagoge* at *Att.* 9.13.3 = 180 SB to mean a selection of texts: it there refers to a compilation of quotations from Atticus's letters that Cicero incorporated into a letter of his own, *Att.* 9.10 = 177 SB.

5. The numeration in printed editions of the *Letters to Friends* gives seventy-nine letters for book 13, but conflations have been detected which raise the current count to eighty-one. In its pristine form, the book contained a still higher number of letters, since it included duplicates of three letters of recommendation that in modern editions are printed only where they first appear, at *Fam.* 2.14, 12.21, and 12.29 (see Nardo 1961–64, 205.). That Tiro's seventy letters were the core of book 13 was argued by Gurlitt (1879, 14–16; 1901, 534–35). He convinced Peter (1901, 36), Büchner (1939, 1217 and 1222), Shackleton Bailey (1965–70, 1: 65), and others. For some dissenters, see Tyrrell and Purser (1904, 1: 68–69), Nardo (1961–64), Hutchinson (1998, 5 n. 4), and both Constans and Beaujeu in the Budé edition (1969–96, 1: 10 and 9: 214 n. 1).

6. Cicero's attitude toward the publication of letters is thus of a piece with his practice regarding orations, which he published in revised form, not as he delivered

them. There is, however, this important difference: in the case of a speech, by contrast with a letter, a fully written script did not exist before publication.

7. Cicero often comments that politics was using up all his energies in these months (*Fam.* 9.24.4 = 362 SB, 10.1.1 = 340 SB, 10.19.2 = 393 SB, 10.28 = 364 SB, 12.24.2 = 361 SB, 12.25a.6 = 383 SB, 12.30.1–2 = 417 SB, *MBrut.* 9(1.3).2 = 7 SB) and apart from publishing his *Philippics* against Antony, there are no other literary projects on which he is known to have been working in 43.

8. The "main focus of debate" according to Beard (2002, 118 n. 47).

9. The letters to Atticus are contrasted with *libri* of Cicero "qui in vulgus sunt editi" at Nep. *Att.* 16.3. This passage comes from the first edition of the life, which was evidently written in the early to mid-30s, though Nepos allowed it to stand in a second edition written after Atticus's death in 32. Nepos speaks as though access to the letters is possible in future but not a certainty: "Should anyone read them, he would feel no great need for a detailed history of those times" (quae qui *legat*, non multum *desideret* historiam contextam eorum temporum, Nep. *Att.* 16.3).

Nepos's statement about the letters has been taken to imply that he saw them at Atticus's house, an inference which is not unreasonable given that they were addressed to Atticus, that the statement comes up in a biography of Atticus, and that Nepos boasts of hospitality enjoyed at Atticus's house (Nep. *Att.* 13.7). Nevertheless it is an inference, not a circumstance that Nepos makes explicit. If Cicero kept copies of his letters to Atticus, Nepos may have read those rather than Atticus's originals. In support of that inference, one could point to Nepos's eagerness to see Cicero's letters in mid-44 and to the fact that at some point Nepos produced a (lost) two-book biography of Cicero as well as the short sketch of Atticus.

10. The relevant numbers in Shackleton Bailey's edition of the *Ad Familiares* are 209, 260, 261, 210, and 148. Older editions cite the recipient's name as "M. Fadius Gallus"; Shackleton Bailey (1962, 196) was responsible for pointing out that all manuscripts give the nomen as "Fabius" and for restoring it to the text.

11. Exactly how the confusion arose is not clear. The recipient of *Fam.* 7.27 = 148 SB is identified in the heading as "Gallus," which most naturally suggests that Cicero's former quaestor, identified as "T. Fadius" in the heading of *Fam.* 5.18 = 51 SB, bore the full name "T. Fadius Gallus." He would thus have had the same cognomen and almost the same nomen as Cicero's other friend. But Shackleton Bailey has questioned whether the quaestor in fact bore the name "Gallus," which is attested only by the heading of the letter in question. If he did not, the error presumably developed in two stages. The name "Fadius" will first have been confused with "Fabius," and then after the five letters were combined, "Fadius" will have been ousted from its place in the heading of *Fam* 7.27 = 148 SB by the cognomen belonging to Fabius. "In any case, the publisher of the collection presumably confused...T. Fadius with M. Fabius Gallus and for that reason placed vii. 27 where we find it," Shackleton Bailey (1962, 196).

12. See Shackleton Bailey's commentary on *Fam.* 11.17 = 435 SB. Another editorial misidentification may have occurred in *Fam.* 13.64 = 138 SB, where Shackleton Bailey argues that a letter to Q. Minucius Thermus, the governor of Asia, has strayed into a contemporary set of letters to the governor of Bithynia, P. Silius, and suggests that "the mistake may have arisen when the letters were first edited."

13. For the principal scholarly discussions of publication of the letters, see appendix 1.

14. Boissier (1863, 28) noted another important reason for suspecting Tiro's involvement with the letters: it was Tiro who published the sketches (*commentarii*) left for those speeches that Cicero had chosen not to write up and publish himself (Quint. *Inst.* 10.7.30–31).

15. Carcopino developed a two-part case about the letters. The bulk of it consisted of a dossier of testimony, gathered especially from the letters to Atticus, which either cast a sorry light on Cicero's own performance as a human being, father, husband, friend, and statesman, or which reflected badly on the behavior of Pompey, Brutus, Antony, and the Roman leadership class generally. The one person not tarred by these backstage revelations was the newly emergent Octavian. On that foundation Carcopino built his theory of publication. As the only person with an interest in having such a damaging correspondence made public and the only person with the power to prevent or effect publication at the time, Octavian saw an opportunity to achieve a propaganda coup during the years leading up to his final confrontation with Antony. With the more-than-willing compliance of the conscienceless Epicurean Atticus and of Cicero's feckless son Marcus, who together had inherited the letter files, and with Tiro's assistance, he therefore instigated a crash program of selective publication in the years 33 and 32.

Prolix, florid, bullying, and intemperate, *Les secrets de la correspondance de Cicéron* ranks as perhaps the most irritating book in the modern Cicero bibliography. But obnoxious as it was, Carcopino's influence has been difficult to shake off because on points of detail, he sometimes had a case. For some reactions, see Piganiol (1949) and Balsdon (1950 and 1952), which review, respectively, the French and the English editions, and Taylor (1951).

16. This was one of the principal points at issue between Gurlitt (1879 and 1901) and Peter (1901), the latter holding that the published corpus reflects an editorial design and therefore a degree of editorial discrimination, while Gurlitt maintained that it was a more or less mechanical transcription of everything recovered from various letter files. Gurlitt's view prevailed in subsequent scholarship, perhaps because he had the tactical advantage of uttering the last word in the dispute. But neither argument had much of an empirical footing in letters that could be shown to be missing.

17. In his commentaries, Shackleton Bailey generally notes cross-references in the correspondence, both to letters that are extant and to letters that are not. But he is not always consistent on this point, and he nowhere lists the missing letters he does note. The same is true of the Budé editors. Weyssenhoff (1966, 13) noted how desirable it would be to have such a register but specified that she was not undertaking to provide it herself. The lost letters with which she is concerned are from collections of Cicero's letters known in antiquity but not transmitted to us. Cugusi (1979) has collected most of the evidence for missing letters written by Cicero's epistolary partners, but not for missing letters by Cicero himself.

18. I have excluded from the table an earlier letter of recommendation to Plancus (*Fam.* 13.29) that does not form part of the series in book 10, as well as two official despatches from Plancus to the Senate that do.

19. On the subject of archives of personal correspondence, see note 24 in chapter 1.

20. *Fam.* 16.16 = 44 SB; two other letters by Quintus, both to Tiro, are preserved in the same book (*Fam.* 16.26 = 351 SB and 16.27 = 352 SB).

21. *QFr.* 2.10[9]. 2 = 14 SB and 2.11[10].5 = 15 SB. One letter specifically promised was a report on the events of February 14 (*QFr.* 2.12[11].4 = 16 SB).

22. *Att.* 3.26 = 71 SB and 4.1.4 = 73 SB.

23. "Velim tibi curae sit…ut aliquid istinc bestiarum habeamus; Sittianamque syngrapham tibi commendo. libertum Philonem istoc misi et Diogenem Graecum, quibus mandata et litteras ad te dedi," *Fam.* 8.8.10 = 84 SB; probably the same letter to which Cicero refers at *Att.* 6.1.21 = 115 SB.

24. "Minucium $\overline{\text{XII}}$ sola curasse scripsi ad te antea," *Att.* 11.15.2 = 226 SB; "scripsi enim ad te de hortis," *Att.* 13.34 = 350 SB; "ego ad te alia epistula scripsi de HS $\overline{\text{CX}}$ quae Statio curarentur," *Att.* 15.15.1 = 393 SB. The missing letter mentioned at *Att.* 5.20.10 = 113 SB also concerned a matter of personal finances, though not Cicero's own finances.

25. The missing letter was evidently a follow-up to the extant *Fam.* 10.12 = 377 SB, which reported an earlier phase of Cicero's intervention on behalf of Plancus.

26. *Fam.* 11.11.1 = 386 SB. It happens that in this case Cicero summarizes what the letter must have said in a contemporary letter to Marcus Brutus (*MBrut.* 23[1.15].8–9 = 23 SB).

27. *Fam.* 12.22A.4 = 357 SB, 12.25.3 = 373 SB, and 12.29.2 = 433 SB.

28. *Att.* 6.1.10 = 115 SB, 6.4.2 = 118 SB (evidently a reference to the same letter as the preceding), 6.6.1 = 121 SB, *Fam.* 2.15.2 = 96 SB, 3.10.5 = 73 SB, and 8.6.2 = 88 SB (the last three passages all refer to one letter).

29. The Curius series (*Fam.* 7.28–31) does not include a letter mentioned at *Fam.* 16.4.2 = 123 SB (cf. *Att.* 8.5.2 = 157 SB), in which Cicero asked Curius to look after the ailing Tiro at Patrae. The letters to Quintus do not include Cicero's announcement (see *Fam.* 16.16.1 = 44 SB) that he had manumitted Tiro.

30. *Fam.* 3.6.2 = 69 SB, 4.1.2 = 150 SB, *Att.* 10.5.1 = 196 SB (cf. 10.6.1 = 197 SB), 16.6.1 = 414 SB. I know two examples of a published letter that consists solely of such an arrangement, *Fam.* 7.4 = 199 SB in the Marius series and 9.4 = 180 SB in the Varro series.

31. Not wanting to encourage speculation about editorial revision, Shackleton Bailey considered the possibility (in his comments on these two letters, ad loc.) that the deletions discussed in this and the preceding paragraph took place earlier, when Cicero had the letter to Appius copied for his file in the first case, and when Atticus received and filed the letter about Quintus in the second. Possibly. But insofar as both these changes may have been undertaken with an eye to future readers, the hypothesis does not negate editorial activity but merely relocates it.

32. For example, *Att.* 8.12C.4 = 162C SB, 9.6.3 = 172 SB, 10.4.7 = 195 SB, 12.11 = 249 SB, 16.15.4 = 426 SB, *Fam.* 12.12.5 = 387 SB, 12.15.7 = 406 SB, 16.15.4 = 426 SB.

33. See also the discussion of this passage by Nicholson (1994, 46).

34. Latin letter writers sometimes use words like *coniungere* (*Fam.* 7.30.3 = 265 SB), *infra scribere* (*Fam.* 6.8.3 = 235 SB), or *subicere* (Pliny *Epist.* 10.58.4) when referring to an enclosure, but the usual formula is simply *mittere exemplum, mittere epistulam* (e.g., *Att.* 8.11.6 = 161 SB, 15.5.1 = 383 SB). For further information about enclosures in

Latin letters, see Cugusi (1983, 142–44). Letters addressed to a third party are sometimes sent merely to be forwarded by the recipient rather than as enclosures to be read, but context usually distinguishes between one kind and another.

35. *Att.* 8.6.2 = 154 SB, 8.11A = 161A SB, 8.11B = 161B SB, 8.11C = 161C SB, 8.11D = 161D SB, 8.12A = 162A SB, 8.12B = 162B SB, 8.12C = 162C SB, 8.12D = 162D SB, 8.15A = 165A SB, 9.6.3 = 172 SB, 9.6A = 172A SB, 9.7A = 174A SB, 9.7B = 174B SB, 9.7C = 174C SB, 9.11A = 178A SB, 9.13A = 181A (which in its turn contains an embedded enclosure), 9.14.1 = 182 SB, 9.15a = 184 SB, 9.16.2–3 = 185 SB, 10.8A = 199A SB, 10.8B = 199B SB, 10.9A = 200A SB, 10.10.2 = 201 SB, 11.12.2 = 223 SB, 14.13A = 367A SB, 14.13B = 367B SB, 14.17A = 371A SB, 15.6.2–3 = 386 SB, 15.14.2–3 = 402 SB, 16.16A = 407A SB, 16.16B = 407B SB, 16.16C = 407C SB, 16.16D = 407D SB, 16.16E = 407E SB, 16.16F = 407F SB, *Fam.* 6.8 = 235 SB, and 12.15 = 406. At first glance, *Fam.* 10.8 = 371 SB appears to be a letter enclosed with 10.7 = 372 SB, and so the ancient editor doubtless meant it to appear. But the details related at *Fam.* 10.12.2 = 377 SB reveal that the two letters did not accompany each other. *Fam.* 8.8.5–8 = 84 SB is an enclosed document, but not a letter.

Note that I have counted embedded letters, which are not usually counted as separate items in modern editions. Note also that those enclosures that do get counted in modern editions are counted differently in the Atticus corpus and in the *Letters to Friends*. In the first collection, an enclosure is not given a separate number but carries the number of the letter to which it is attached, from which it is distinguished alphabetically (letter 11A or 11B as opposed to letter 11, for example). In the *Letters to Friends*, the two enclosures are counted independently of their base letters.

36. Evidence for letters—and letters only—which were sent as attachments but not published as attachments is as follows: *Att.* 3.8.4 = 53 SB, 5.11.6 = 104 SB (extant as *Fam.* 13.1 = 63 SB), 5.18.1 = 111 SB (extant as *Fam.* 15.1 = 104 SB), 7.23.3 = 147 SB, 8.2.2 = 152 SB, 8.2.4 = 152 SB, 9.12.1 = 179 SB (two letters, cf. 9.13.1 = 180 SB), 10.3a.2 = 194 SB, 12.18.2 = 254 SB, 12.21.1 = 260 SB, 12.34.3 = 273 SB, 12.37.1 = 276 SB (two letters), 12.38.2 = 278 SB (cf. 12.39.1 = 280 SB), 13.29.3 = 300 SB, 13.3.2 = 308 SB, 13.22.5 = 329 SB, 13.38.1 = 341 SB, 13.51.1 = 349 SB, 13.47a.2 = 352 SB, 14.17.4 = 371 SB (two letters, one of which is extant as *Fam.* 12.1 = 327 SB), 15.5.1 = 383 SB, 15.26.2 = 404 SB, 15.29.1 = 408 SB, 16.11.8 = 420 SB, 16.12.1 = 421 SB, 16.15.3 = 426 SB, *Fam.* 2.17.7 = 117 SB, 5.9.1 = 255 SB, 7.30.3 = 265 SB (extant as *Fam.* 13.50 = 266 SB), 10.31.6 = 368 SB, 10.32.5 = 415 SB, 10.33.2 = 409 SB, 11.19.1 = 399 SB, 13.19.1 = 285 SB, 13.26.3 = 292 SB, *QFr.* 2.11(10).5 = 15 SB (with Shackleton Bailey's note), *MBrut.* 14(1.6).3 = 12 SB.

37. Only one letter in the Pliny corpus (*Epist.* 10.58) carries attachments, and the few attachments published in Fronto's corpus are limited to letters written by Fronto himself.

38. Among various documents mentioned as attachments in the letters we find *senatusconsulta* (*Att.* 4.2.5 = 74 SB, *Fam.* 3.2.2 = 65 SB), edicts (*Att.* 5.3.2 = 96 SB, 16.7.7 = 415 SB), legal texts (*Att.* 3.20.3 = 65 SB, *Fam.* 7.22 = 331 SB), speeches (*Att.* 15.13.1 = 416 SB, *Fam.* 9.12 = 263 SB), and other literary compositions (*Att.* 1.19.10 = 19, *Fam.* 7.19 = 334 SB).

39. Three of the enclosures were in fact published twice: a letter of Caelius appears both as an enclosure (*Att.* 10.9A = 200A SB) and in a Caelius series (*Fam.*

8.16 = 153 SB); a letter of Dolabella appears at *Att.* 14.17A = 371A SB and *Fam.* 9.14 = 326 SB; and one of the enclosures accompanying *Att.* 8.11.6 = 161 SB was also published in a (nonextant) Pompey series (Nonius 2:455.39–40 Lindsay).

40. The treatment of enclosures regarding Pompey's situation at Brundisium suggests that some care was taken in deciding which ones to publish. Two are extant, an embedded letter at *Att.* 9.6.3 = 172 SB that gives a partly true and partly false report and a more accurate bulletin from Matius and Trebatius at *Att.* 9.15a = 184 SB. However, Cicero also received and passed on to Atticus two other reports (mentioned at *Att.* 9.12.1 = 179 SB and 9.13.1 = 180 SB). But Cicero soon learned that the news they contained was erroneous, and these texts the editor did not include.

41. The letters are *Fam.* 10.35 = 408 SB, 11.1 = 325 SB, 11.2 = 329 SB, 11.3 = 336 SB, and 11.13A = 418 SB; *MBrut.* 25(1.17) = 26 SB may be a parallel case if it is authentic. The Tiro book of the *Letters to Friends* also features several letters neither to nor by Cicero (*Fam.* 16.8 = 147 SB, 16.21 = 337 SB, 16.25 = 338 SB, 16.26 = 351, 16.27 = 352 SB), but these may have originated as part of a primary correspondence addressed to Tiro rather than as enclosures in letters to Cicero.

42. At least they suggest that cover letters from Cicero's epistolary partners were apt to be deselected. But it should be noted that the Atticus corpus features three short messages from Cicero himself that function purely as cover letters: *Att.* 9.15a = 184 SB, 9.16 = 185 SB, and 16.16 = 407 SB.

43. Good studies of Cicero's letters of recommendation have been published by several scholars in recent years, notably by Élisabeth Déniaux and Hannah Cotton (bibliography in Déniaux 1993, 17–24). In this section, however, my focus is exclusively on the recommendations as an editorial problem.

44. Strictly speaking, manuscripts of book 13 present a block of eighty-three recommendations, since it includes three recommendations that also appear elsewhere (see n. 5). Editors delete the three duplications, and I have not included them in my count.

45. Recommendations located outside book 13 are *Fam.* 1.3 = 56 SB, 2.6 = 50 SB, 2.14 = 89 SB, 3.1.3 = 64 SB, 5.5 = 5 SB, 6.9 = 236 SB, 7.5 = 26 SB, 7.21 = 332 SB, 9.13 = 311 SB, 9.25.2–3 = 114 SB, 10.1.4 = 340 SB, 11.16 = 434 SB, 11.17 = 435 SB, 11.22 = 427 SB, 12.6 = 376 SB, 12.21 = 429 SB, 12.24.3 = 430 SB, 12.26 = 431 SB, 12.27 = 432 SB, 12.29 = 433 SB, *MBrut.* 6(1.1) = 13 SB, 15(1.7) = 19 SB, 16(1.8) = 15 SB, 23(1.15).1–2 = 23 SB, *QFr.* 1.2.10–11 = 2 SB, 2.13(12).3 = 17 SB, *Att.* 11.12.2 = 223 SB, 15.14.2–3 = 402 SB, 16.16A-F = 407A–F SB. My tally differs slightly from that of Déniaux (1993, 22–24), who does not count *Fam.* 10.1.4 = 340 SB or *MBrut.* 23(1.15).1–2 = 23 SB. The epistolary corpus also preserves five recommendations written *to* Cicero: *Fam.* 11.19.2 = 399 SB, *MBrut.* 14(1.6).2 and 4 = 12 SB, 15(1.7) = 19 SB, 19(1.11) = 16 SB, and 21(1.13) = 20 SB.

46. In fact the corpus contains several testimonia to recommendations which were not published, for example, *Fam.* 2.17.7 = 117 SB, 5.10a.1 = 259 SB, 13.19.1 = 285 SB, 13.40 = 59 SB, 13.49 = 313 SB, 13.64.1 = 138 SB, 13.75.1 = 60 SB, and *Att.* 16.2.5 = 412 SB (the letter to Oppius).

47. In the five cases in which the recommendations come from Cicero's correspondents (see note 45 of this chapter), either they are combined with other epistolary items or the persons recommended are involved in the political events which are the focus of the exchange.

NOTES TO PAGES 46–48   193

48. The extant letter (an embedded text) is *Att.* 11.12.2 = 223 SB. For a trace of a letter on Quintus's behalf that did not survive, see *Att.* 2.6.2 = 26 SB.

49. The evidence is handily set out in the prosopographical table at Déniaux (1993, 96–108), where the first column lists Cicero's correspondents and the status of each, and the last column notes which correspondents receive letters of recommendation. (A slip has intruded into her entry for M. Terentius Varro, who is not an *eques Romanus* but a senator.) The status of three of the addressees (Cluvius, Cupiennius, and Rutilius) is uncertain, but all played a part in land apportionments of the 40s, and they may have been senators. Of the four remaining, Papirius Paetus and the officials of *Fam.* 13.76 = 62 SB are asked to act in their capacity as leading men of their respective towns and Trebatius in his capacity as a prominent and well-connected jurist. Caesius's situation is not known.

50. Cicero's *commendati* can be surveyed most easily in the table at Déniaux (1993, 145–60).

51. Déniaux (1993, 1–2).

52. See Cotton (1985) and Déniaux (1993, 44–46) on the *vulgaris commendatio*.

53. In practice, of course, a letter of recommendation may bear witness to more than two relationships, since there will often be someone behind the recommendee urging Cicero to act. Atticus emerges as an instigator at *Fam.* 13.1.5 = 63 SB, 13.17.1 = 283 SB, and 13.23.1 = 289 SB.

54. *Fam.* 3.1.3 = 64 SB, 9.25.2–3 = 114 SB, 10.1.4 = 340 SB, 12.6 = 376 SB, 12.24.3 = 361 SB, *QFr.* 1.2.10–11 = 2 SB, 2.13(12).3 = 17 SB.

55. I am assuming here that when Cicero kept a copy of a recommendation, he had it filed with correspondence relating either to the recipient of the letter or to the commendee or both and not with other letters of recommendation. Although I (and doubtless many other academics) do in fact keep a file consisting only of such letters, there is no reason to think that Cicero did. I keep letters of recommendations together because I learned that any recommendation might later need to be recycled, because I rarely have other correspondence with either the addressee or the commendee under which to file them, and because recommendations represent some of my most artistic writing. None of these considerations would have had any significant application to Cicero.

56. It would be rash to assume that recommendations were all that the editor found when he looked through these files: compare *Fam.* 13.41.2 = 54 SB for Culleolus and *Att.* 7.1.8 = 124 SB for Silius. But why an editor would have chosen to omit the rest of Cicero's correspondence with such persons one can only speculate. Perhaps it did not lend itself to the sort of episodic and thematic schemes of organization that the editor favored elsewhere. Or perhaps the correspondence was of the "phatic" type (see chapter 1, p. 29), important for maintaining a relationship but uninteresting to a later reader. Or perhaps there were just not that many letters to these men. Most of Cicero's exchanges with all his peers would have been live exchanges in Rome.

57. For the duplicates, see note 5 of this chapter. It is fair to ask, of course, why under a concerted plan of publication there should be even three duplicates. To this question I can make no better answer than to recall that the books which now constitute the *Letters to Friends* were not originally a corpus but were published separately and probably at intervals. Lapses can be more easily forgiven (and, perhaps

more to the point, overlooked) in a project that lasted months or years than in a publication of everything at once.

58. The only case in which recommendations to the same person from different periods are clustered together in book 13 is the set of four letters to Valerius Orca (*Fam.* 13.4–6a = 57, 58, 318, and 319 SB). One of the noticeable patterns of this book is that although half the addressees receive multiple recommendations, all the recommendations usually date to the same phase of their careers.

59. Conceivably the editor calculated that, whereas he had no other recommendations to put with the one to Furfanus, book 13 contained plenty of other recommendations to Acilius. But in fact the recommendation for Curius is not merged with the other letters to Acilius in book 13 (*Fam.* 13.30–39 = 301–310 SB). One reason for its separation may be that it is from a period different from that of the other recommendations to Acilius. But it is also possible (as Shackleton Bailey hints in his commentary on the recommendation of Curius) that two different governors with the name Acilius are involved.

A further complication about *Fam.* 13.50 is that Acilius never received it. From *Fam.* 7.31 = 267 SB, it is clear that Cicero gave Curius the original recommendation, not a copy, and that Curius then decided not to use it. In this case there can be no doubt that the editor took the letter to Acilius from a letter file concerning Curius rather than Acilius.

60. In section 2, Cicero intimates that political letters may be too risky for him to write to Isauricus in future, and the two men had divergent political sympathies in any case.

61. *Att.* 16.16 = 407 SB. Although this letter stands last in the manuscripts, it is not chronologically the latest and stands twenty letters from the end of Shackleton Bailey's commented edition.

62. It almost certainly follows that the editor suppressed short cover messages in which Cicero sent the other five letters of recommendation to Atticus, preferring instead to attach the entire set to the first cover letter. For another case in which the editor has created a false attachment, see note 35 of this chapter on *Fam.* 10.8 = 371 SB.

63. The most systematic analysis of the way in which the various letter series were constructed is given by Peter (1901, 38–96), who is especially good at pointing out thematic links between letters to different persons in the *Letters to Friends*. His assumptions about editorial competence differ significantly from mine, however. He tends to credit all manifestations of intelligible design to an early editor and all manifestations of sloppiness and disorder to a later one, who enlarged the letter corpora and put them into the form in which they have come down to us. My working assumption, on the other hand, is that a single editor was sometimes more successful and sometimes less successful at dealing with the mass of intractable material confronting him.

64. See *QFr.* 1.4.5 = 4 SB, *Att.* 3.22.2 = 67 SB, 6.1.1 = 115 SB, 9.11.1 = 178 SB.

65. Missing letters from Cicero are implied at *Fam.* 1.7.2 = 18 SB and 1.10 = 21 SB.

66. The dedication is referred to in *Fam.* 3.4 = 67 SB, 3.9.3 = 72 SB, and 3.11.4 = 74 SB.

67. *Fam.* 3.8.6 = 70 SB, 3.10.8 = 73 SB, 3.13.1 = 76 SB.

68. Beard (2002, 125) has recently observed that the book divisions of the Atticus manuscripts "construct an episodic narrative out of the letters."

69. See Shackleton Bailey's notes on missing letters at 7.11 = 134 SB (4: 298 of his Cambridge edition), 7.16.1 = 140 SB (4: 312), 7.26 = 150 SB (4: 322), 8.6.1 = 154 SB (4: 333), 9.10.6 = 177 SB (4: 379), 9.11.2 = 178 SB (4: 381), 10.2 = 192 SB (4: 400), and 10.5.1 = 196 SB (4: 405). Note also that in a period when Cicero implies that he was writing almost daily, there are gaps of four days or more between 10.3A = 194 SB and 10.4 = 195 SB, 10.5 = 196 SB and 10.6 = 197 SB, 10.7 = 198 SB and 10.8 = 199 SB, and 10.15 = 207 SB and 10.16 = 208 SB.

70. There is a gap of a month and a half between 11.10 = 221 SB and 11.11 = 222 SB. Shackleton Bailey notes indications of missing letters at 11.14.1 = 225 SB (5: 284 of his edition), 11.15.2 = 226 SB (5: 285) and 11.20.2 = 235 SB (5: 295).

71. Introduction of an extraneous letter into the series is only the plainest sign of the editor's desire to frame it as a story. But two complementary decisions about placement were involved, both entailing departures from the dominant principle of grouping letters by addressee. The governor who reported Marcellus's death was Servius Sulpicius Rufus, subject of a letter series of his own earlier in book 4 (letters 1–6 = 150–51, 202–203, and 248–49 SB). Although the letter about Marcellus's death was contemporary with some others in the Servius series, the editor chose to group it with the Marcellus letters instead. The second decision concerns a letter to Marcellus that has been detached from the rest. The published correspondence includes a letter (*Fam.* 15.9 = 101 SB) written five years earlier than the ones collected in book 4. But that letter the editor chose to present in a sequence organized by chronology rather than by recipient.

72. Whatever the editor had in mind in pairing the letters of Trebonius with those of Cassius, the juxtaposition cannot have been fortuitous. The Trebonius and the Cassius correspondence are the two most conspicuous cases in which the editor has split up letters which could have been amalgamated into one series. Other letters to or from Trebonius were published at *Fam.* 10.28 = 364 SB and 12.16 = 328 SB. Other letters to or from Cassius Longinus are at *Fam.* 12.1–13 = 327, 344–45, 363, 365–67, 376, 387, 416, 421, and 425 SB.

73. The exception is *Fam.* 5.6 = 4 SB to Sestius, then Gaius Antonius's quaestor in Macedonia. But the letter to Sestius immediately follows and partly complements the letter to Antonius.

74. The exception is *Fam.* 7.5 = 26 SB to Caesar, a letter of recommendation on behalf of Trebatius, which the editor used to introduce the seventeen letters to Trebatius that follow. Technically, *Fam.* 7.27 = 148 SB is also an exception, since this letter is to Cicero's former quaestor Fadius. But as noted earlier, the editor has confused Fadius with Fabius Gallus, and mistakenly attached the Fadius letter to the Gallus series.

75. By adding, say, *Fam.* 2.17–19 = 115–17 SB and 7.32 = 113 SB (to say nothing of letters to Curio and Caelius in book 2).

76. Beard (2002, 127–28) suggests that the nonchronological ordering of dated letters in the Atticus series may in some cases reflect the order in which letters were received rather than written, or that the editor has rearranged letters for the sake of literary or dramatic effect. I can offer no better explanation for these anomalies, which I find baffling.

77. Apart from Peter (1901) and Beard (2002), Shackleton Bailey (1977, 1: 23) has commented on this feature of the *Letters to Friends*: "All the Books show varying degrees of internal cohesion, some of them more than has generally been recognized."

78. The letters and letter writers are listed in appendix 1. Yet another category is formed by twenty-one letters in the collection that were written neither by nor to Cicero. About a third of these occur as enclosures in the *Letters to Atticus*, but the others are presented as independent items in the *Letters to Marcus Brutus* and the *Letters to Friends* (they, too, are listed in appendix 1).

79. By an isolated letter pair, I mean the combination of a letter by Cicero with a letter by a correspondent who appears nowhere else in the corpus as sender or recipient. There are only four such pairs altogether: *Fam.* 11.27–28 = 348–49 SB (Cicero/Matius), 5.1–2 = 1–2 SB (Metellus Celer/Cicero), 5.3–4 = 10–11 SB (Metellus Nepos/Cicero), and 6.16–17 = 323–24 SB (Pompeius Bithynicus/Cicero). It should be noted that the latter two are artificial pairs, in that the one letter is not actually a response to the other.

80. Servius Sulpicius Galba: *Fam.* 10.30 = 378 SB, Cassius (Parmensis?): *Fam.* 12.13 = 419 SB, Publius Lentulus (son of the consul of 57): *Fam.* 12.14 = 405 SB, and the most extreme case, Asinius Pollio: *Fam.* 10.31 = 368 SB, 10.32 = 415 SB, and 10.33 = 409 SB.

81. However, they must certainly have shared this focus with the lost books to Octavian, Hirtius, and Pansa.

82. Déniaux (1993, 96–108).

83. See Weyssenhoff (1966, 6; 1970, 6) and Büchner (1939, 1199–1206).

84. There is a partial list in Déniaux (1993, 203–204), table 6. Cicero's Sicilian *hospites* and clients are the implicit background of *Fam.* 13.30–39 = 301–10 SB, however.

85. The only letters of Cicero to Greeks which are known to have been published were to teachers of his son (Plut. *Cic.* 24.7), and they may have been published in the context of that correspondence.

86. The absence of the Balbus correspondence from the Ciceronian corpus stands in contrast with a decision taken about Caesar's correspondence. Caesar's literary executors, who included Balbus, seem to have published *only* his letters to Balbus and Oppius (Suet. *Iul.* 56.6, Gell. *NA* 17.9.1–5)—a decision which perhaps parallels the appearance of a book of letters to Tiro in the published corpus of Cicero's correspondence.

87. Pliny *Epist.* 9.11. Perhaps the undistinguished Curius who receives letters in book 7 of the *Letters to Friends* gained a place in the published correspondence thanks to his personal connection with Tiro.

88. See Shackleton Bailey (1995, 142–54) on doubtfully authentic headings. However, if Cicero's letters were published not from the originals that went out to the addressees but from copies made for Cicero's files, the careless transcriber may have been the secretary who first copied them rather than the editor who later published them.

CHAPTER 3

1. Demetrius, whose discussion of letter writing is perhaps the earliest extant source on the subject, leads off by criticizing the view that a letter is comparable to a dialogue exchange (secs. 223–24). Differences between letters and conversation have

often been noted in modern analyses of the letter, see especially Duchene (1995), Kerbrat-Orecchioni (1998), and Müller (1985).

2. The physical aspect of ancient letters is well described by Dziatzko (1899, 836–38), Büchner (1939, 1207–11), and Cugusi (1983, 43–72). For good modern photos of papyrus letters rolled and sealed, see Capasso (1995, plates 29–32) and Gallazzi (1997, 53–54); for ancient letter tablets, see the plates in Lalou (1992). Ermert (1979, 107–18) outlines the range of materially based sign possibilities in modern letters. But in the following paragraphs, I take note only of formats and effects that can be verified in the correspondence of Cicero and his friends. That wax tablets were often associated with love notes, for example, is true but not verifiable from Cicero's corpus. Notice, however, that Martial's verse labels for what we might characterize as different varieties of notebook stationery at *Epigr.* 14.3–10 generally treat the material base as a signifier of content.

3. *Att.* 12.7.1 = 244 SB, *Fam.* 4.12.2 = 253 SB, 6.18.1 = 218 SB, 9.26.1 = 197 SB, 12.20 = 339 SB, *QFr.* 2.10(9).1 = 14 SB, *MBrut.* 4(2.4).1 = 4 SB. The verb *exarare* (meaning literally "to cut a furrow") is regularly though not exclusively used for inscribing a tablet, and often conveys similar associations. For a broader discussion of the semiotics of letters written on tablets, see Meyer (2001).

4. Like tablets, papyrus was manufactured in different formats for different purposes, including stationery: Pliny *HNat.* 13.79–80, Mart. *Epigr.* 14.11.

5. That letters were rolled rather than folded is implied by Sen. *Epist.* 45.13 and Cass. Dio 46.36.4 and shown by surviving examples; see also Peter (1901, 34 n. 3).

6. When the word *volumen*, which normally designates a book roll, is applied to letters, it indicates a monster letter: *Att.* 10.4.1 = 195 SB, *Fam.* 3.7.2 = 71 SB, 12.30.1 = 417 SB; compare *Schol. Bob.* on Cic. *Planc.* 85, p. 167 Stangl. Cicero's "ponderosa epistula" (*Att.* 2.11.1 = 32 SB) conveys the same idea. At *Att.* 6.9.1 = 123 SB, Cicero registers dismay at the manifest *smallness* of a long-awaited letter.

7. Pliny *Epist.* 8.15.2 worries about the availability of papyrus when he is writing from the Italian countryside.

8. At *Att.* 5.4.4 = 97 SB, Cicero arranges a supply of stationery for Atticus as the latter is about to leave Rome for Epirus. People sometimes made such arrangements even in the heartland of papyrus: Capasso (1995, 26 n. 28), Cugusi (1989, 402 n. 104; and 1992–2002, 1:150, lines 18–19).

9. "An hoc significas, nihil fieri, frigere te, ne chartam quidem tibi suppeditare?" *Fam.* 7.18.2 = 37 SB.

10. Cicero acknowledges at *Att.* 16.15.1 = 426 SB that *not* writing to Atticus in his own hand could be construed as a sign of laziness (*pigritia*).

11. See especially *Att.* 2.23.1 = 43 SB and *QFr.* 2.2.1 = 6 SB. The same is likely to have been true for at least some of the letters to his wife Terentia, e.g., *Fam.* 14.1.5 = 8 SB and 14.2.1 = 7 SB. Autograph letters partly overlap with those letters in the corpus not written in rhythmic prose. "To all correspondents except Atticus, his wife Terentia, and his freedman Tiro, Cicero normally writes rhythmic letters. The final part of letters may sometimes be unrhythmic, and occasionally the start; when Cicero is writing to close friends or to his brother Quintus, there can be other brief unrhythmic passages," Hutchinson (1998, 10). For a rapid introduction to the subject of rhythmic prose, see Powell (1996).

12. For example, the pressure of work is cited at *QFr.* 2.2.1 = 6 SB, 3.3.1 = 23 SB; eye trouble at *Att.* 7.13a.3 = 137 SB, 10.14.1 = 206 SB; inconvenience at *Att.* 5.17.1 = 110 SB, 14.21.4 = 375 SB.

13. The terms here are Cicero's own. For *signum*, see *QFr.* 3.3.1 = 23 SB, *Att.* 4.16.1 = 89 SB; for *indicare*, *Att.* 7.2.3 = 125 SB; for *colligere*, *Att.* 2.23.1 = 43 SB; for *iudicare*, *QFr.* 2.16(15).1 = 20 SB.

14. *Fam.* 16.15.2 = 42 SB, *Att.* 5.4.4 = 97 SB, *QFr.* 2.15(14).1 = 19 SB.

15. *Fam.* 2.13.3 = 93 SB, *Att.* 8.1.1 = 151 SB, *Fam* 10.21.1 and 3 = 391 SB.

16. Confidentiality is unmistakably the concern when Cicero switches to his own handwriting in domestic letters: *Att.* 11.24.2 = 234 SB, 12.32.1 = 271 SB, 13.9.1 = 317 SB, 13.28.4 = 299 SB, 15.20.4 = 397 SB. But there he is trying to restrict information about family business, gossip about which was most to be feared from other members of the household. To take over the writing of a letter from a secretary under those circumstances was an effective way to foreclose a leak. To cut out the secretary when writing about political matters, on the other hand, seems a less practical means of ensuring confidentiality.

17. The clearest example is *QFr.* 3.1.17–19 = 21 SB, but *Fam.* 8.6.5 = 88 SB (in conjunction with *Fam.* 2.13.3 = 93 SB) can also be interpreted as a simple postscript rather than as a confidential note. Last-minute addenda are numerous in letters of the Ciceronian corpus (much more numerous than in modern letters), and for the most part obvious as well, since they follow epistolary closing formulas or identify themselves as written after the letter had already been finished or after fresh news has supervened. Formally, they resemble the postscript in a modern letter, though the Romans lacked a formula corresponding to our "PS:" with which to introduce them. Functionally, however, they seem rather different. In modern letters the postscript often is or purports to be an afterthought to what precedes, occurring independently of any external stimulus. Postscripts in the Ciceronian corpus respond more to the rhythms and products of epistolary traffic They rarely represent further thoughts on something in the body of the letter, and still more rarely are *calculated* afterthoughts. On postscripts in Latin letters generally, see Cugusi (1983, 71–72).

18. 1 Cor. 16.21, Gal. 6.11, Col. 4.18, 2 Thess. 3.17, Philem. 19.

19. According to Julius Victor (Halm 1863, 448.27–28), however, the closing formula itself (if not the whole letter) would be written in the sender's hand in correspondence between close friends. Cicero, too, may have followed this practice, though neither he nor his correspondents happened to remark on it if he did.

20. For example, *Att.* 3.15.8 = 60 SB, 3.21 = 66 SB, 11.2.4 = 212 SB, 11.3.3 = 213 SB, 12.17 = 255 SB; *Att.* 11.2.4 = 212 SB makes certain that what is meant is not merely writing on behalf of Cicero, but writing in the guise of Cicero. It may be worth noting that—in the extant correspondence, at any rate—Cicero never has his wife write for him at such times, though he does ask her to let him know to whom he should write. We have no evidence to show whether Tiro ever ghostwrote Cicero's letters. But Cicero thought that his brother's staff did sometimes ghostwrite his (*QFr.* 1.2.9 = 2 SB).

21. Cic. *QFr.* 1.2.8–9 = 2 SB, App. *B.C.* 5.144.599, Pliny *HNat.* 37.10, Cass. Dio 51.3.6.

22. The letter in question is discussed at *Att.* 11.16.1–4 = 227 SB, 11.17a.3 = 229 SB, *Fam.* 14.8 = 164 SB. Not but what Cicero's suspicion may have been correct.

23. Compare Cic. *Att.* 5.18.1 = 111 SB, *Fam.* 11.19.1 = 399 SB, 12.12.1 = 387 SB, and Cass. Dio 51.3.6.

24. One letter certainly sent incognito, though its content hardly seems sensitive, was *Fam.* 14.6 = 158 SB, which Cicero wrote to his wife and daughter from Pompey's camp during the civil war. The letter heading "_____ bids greeting to his own" (suis s. d.) suppresses the names of both sender and addressee. But letter headings are the subject of the next section. Another means of masking authorship and content was to write in code. But although Cicero at one point contemplated using code names (*Att.* 2.19.5 = 39 SB, 2.20.3 and 5 = 40 SB) and although Caesar (Caes. *BG* 5.48.4, Suet. *Iul.* 56.6, Gell. *NA* 17.9.1), Brutus (Isid. *Orig.* 1.25.1), and Augustus (Suet. *Aug.* 88, Isid. *Orig.* 1.25.1) are said to have written letters in code, no such letters are extant in the Ciceronian corpus. To publish letters written in code form would, of course, be something of an anomaly. The nearest Cicero comes to writing in code is to switch from Latin to Greek in sections of a letter in which a sensitive topic is raised (*Att.* 6.4.3 = 118 SB, 6.5.1–2 = 119 SB, *Fam.* 7.18.1 = 37 SB).

25. At *Att.* 2.20.5 = 40 SB, Cicero lists three means of suppressing his identity as a letter writer: not using his seal, not writing in his own hand, and substituting a pseudonym for his real name in the letter heading, all of which he proposes to employ. The same elements came into play in the correspondence of the Catilinarian conspirators, out of which Cicero created so much theater in the *Third Catilinarian*. Because Cicero had prepped the Allobrogian ambassadors about how to entrap the conspirators, he was able to capture letters that each man had written in his own hand and sealed, and Cicero turned these into key props for his performance at an emergency session of the Senate. He summoned each conspirator in turn to acknowledge his seal, snipped the sealing string and had him verify his handwriting, then read the letter aloud. That the conspirators set their own hand and seal to letters addressed to the Allobrogian people should not be put down to simple stupidity. The ambassadors presumably left little wiggle room about the kind of commitment they had to have from their allies in Rome. In any case, it emerges between the lines of Cicero's narrative (at sec. 10) that the letters left all specifics about the conspiracy to an oral message accompanying the written one. But a kind of inconsequence does seem evident in the most incriminating of the captured documents, which was Lentulus's celebrated message to Catiline beginning "Who I am, you will know from him whom I have sent to you" (sec. 12). By not naming himself (or the addressee or the bearer) in the letter, Lentulus employed the third of the concealment strategies mentioned above. Yet this letter, like the others, apparently carried the sender's handwriting and seal. Butler (2002, 85–102) has a fine account of Cicero's handling of the captured letters.

26. For an overview of these elements, with bibliography, see Cugusi (1983, 47–67) and Corbinelli (2008, 36–56 and 89–125). An interesting comparandum for Cicero's practice is afforded by Ovid's more self-conscious manipulation of these quintessentially generic features in the *Heroides* and other poetic letters. Kirfel (1969, 11–36) provides a good survey of the way epistolary conventions are exploited in poetic letters. For Ovid as for Cicero, the opening is the point at which the letter writer is most likely to vary or underscore a formula.

27. For letter headings, see, in addition to Cugusi (1983, 47–56), Shackleton Bailey (1995, 1–10, 142–54, a very handy conspectus of letter headings in the

Ciceronian corpus), together with Déniaux (1993, 75–83) and Adams (1978). But
Adams is more concerned with naming practices in general than with the specific
format of letter headings.

There are two complications that must be acknowledged in any account of letter
headings in the Ciceronian correspondence. The first is that slightly more than a
quarter of the letters appear without headings in the manuscripts. Whereas letters that
lack other epistolary elements are generally printed in modern texts as they have been
transmitted, editors assume—rightly, in my opinion—that every letter must originally
have carried a heading, and they therefore supply missing headings, with suitable
typographical signals. At a minimum, this situation makes it difficult if not impossible
to advance statistical claims about the letter headings. Furthermore, although some
headings doubtless disappeared as a result of copying mistakes, the very large number
of omissions cannot be simply the result of random accident. In certain books of the
corpus (*Att.* 12, 13, 15, 16, *Fam.* 1), all or almost all letters lack headings. It is also
noteworthy that omissions do not occur where they would obscure the author or
recipient of a letter, but only in letter series. The systematic character of many
omissions suggests deliberate action taken at the editorial or copying stage. And that
in turn relates to a second caveat that must be borne in mind. Critics have found
reason to suspect that some letter headings which are transmitted in the
manuscripts—again, usually in letter series—originated not with the author but with
the editor (see, most recently, Shackleton Bailey 1995). There remain, of course,
several hundred letter headings with a presumption of authenticity, but opinions will
differ about the strength of that presumption.

28. That the letter heading is expressed in the third person is shown by the
formula *salutem dicit* in Plautine parodies of the letter form at *Bacch.* 734, *Curc.* 431,
and *Persa* 501, and by the fact that the possessive adjective sometimes attached to the
name in the dative is *suus* rather than *meus.*

29. Strictly speaking, the letter heading may not have been needed for
identification purposes at all. If Cicero's letters conformed to the pattern of extant
documentary texts, sender and addressee may already have been identified on the
outside of the letter, just as on a modern envelope (on the external address, see Cugusi
1983, 64–67). And of course, the recipient of any letter hardly needed to be informed
of his or her identity once the letter was opened.

30. The one extant letter from Quintus to Cicero (*Fam.* 16.16 = 44 SB) follows the
same pattern.

31. Servius Sulpicius Rufus, on whose name see Shackleton Bailey's note on
Fam. 4.2.1 = 151 SB; Appius Claudius Pulcher, on whom see Shackleton Bailey (1995,
146); and Appius's nephew Appius.

32. So to the proconsul (and unofficial triumvir) M. Licinius Crassus *Fam.* 5.8 =
25 SB, the praetors C. Titius Rufus and C. Curtius Peducaeanus at *Fam.* 13.58–59 =
140–41 SB, the quaestor C. Sextilius Rufus at *Fam.* 13.48 = 142 SB, and Q. Valerius
Orca, governor and later land commissioner, at *Fam.* 13.6 = 57 SB and 13.4 = 318 SB;
all but the first of these are favor-seeking letters. The unique heading at *Att.* 3.20 = 65
SB, "Cicero s. d. Q. Caecilio Q. f. Pomponiano Attico," is partly a joke, as the extreme
imbalance in name styles for sender and addressee indicates. The first line of the letter
congratulates Atticus on his adoption by his uncle Caecilius, which carried with it both

an inheritance and a change of name from "Pomponius" to "Caecilius Pomponianus." It is less obvious why the formal style is used with M. Fabius Gallus at *Fam.* 7.23 = 209 SB and 7. 24–25 = 260–61 SB.

33. Julius Victor says as much: "praefationes...litterarum computandae sunt pro discrimine amicitiae aut dignitatis, habita ratione consuetudinis," Halm (1863, p. 448.23–25).

34. "Gentilicium + cognomen in either order is unknown," according to Shackleton Bailey (1995, 143). But on this point, epistolary fashion changed after the time of Cicero.

35. *Att.* 15.14.2 = 402 SB, *Fam.* 9.14 = 326 SB (to his ex-son-in-law, Dolabella), all but two of the letters to Terentia (or Terentia and Tullia) in *Fam.* 14, and half the letters from Cicero to Tiro in *Fam.* 16.

36. *Att.* 15.6.2 = 386 SB, *Fam.* 5.9 = 255 SB, 5.10a = 259 SB, 7.29 = 264 SB, 11.1 = 325 SB, 12.12 = 387 SB, 12.14 = 405 SB. Adams (1978, 164) observes that in the body of his letters, too, "Vatinius...uses the familiar form of address (with *mi*)...but Cicero does not reciprocate."

37. Shackleton Bailey (1995, 142) thinks that the headings of Caelius's letters as given in the manuscripts must be spurious because "Caelius cannot reasonably be believed to have omitted titles." Yet the formality of Cicero's headings, which is paralleled in no other extended letter series, remains almost equally problematic.

38. Demmel (1962, 14–18) interprets the anomalous heading as part of a joking response to a joking letter from Paetus. But given the anxiety that Paetus expressed about Cicero's safety on other occasions (*Fam.* 9.16 and 24 = 190 and 362 SB), I think it is at least as likely that he took seriously the possibility that his friend might have to do battle with the Parthians.

39. Cicero's anxiety about having to reinsert himself into Roman politics becomes explicit in a roughly contemporary letter in which he asks Atticus to brief him so that he can "model himself" appropriately before he reaches the capital (*Att.* 6.3.4 = 117 SB).

40. For a pseudo-title used in a letter heading with an even sharper edge, see *Att.* 10.11.5 = 202 SB, with Shackleton Bailey's note.

41. *Fam.* 12.17–18 = 204–5 SB, 13.68 = 211 SB, 68–72 = 211, 297–300 SB, 15.8 = 100 SB. Senators do not address one another as "collega" simply by virtue of being senators, since membership in that body was not a magistracy as it is with us.

42. *Fam.* 7.32.1 = 113 SB, 16.18 = 219 SB, *Att.* 10.11.5 = 202 SB, *MBrut.* 5(2.5).3 = 5 SB, *Verr.* 2.3.154, *Leg. Agr.* 2.53, *Dom.* 22, and *Phil.* 13.22.

43. For the greeting formula, see Cugusi (1983, 48–56) and Lanham (1975).

44. *Fam.* 6.12 = 226 SB, 9.10 = 217 SB, 13.68 = 211 SB, 13.69–71 = 297–99 SB, 14.7 = 155 SB, 14.9 = 161 SB, 14.14 = 145 SB, 14.18 = 144 SB, 16.1 = 120 SB, 16.4–6 = 123–25 SB, 16.9 = 127 SB, 16.11 = 143 SB. Other correspondents represented in the collection (at *Fam.* 4.12 = 253 SB, 10.33 = 409 SB, 12.14 = 405 SB, 16.26–27 = 351–52 SB) also have occasional recourse to the more expansive formula, which is attested since Plautus *Curc.* 431–32.

45. The following list comprises instances of the basic formula with its variations: *Att.* 8.11C = 161C SB, 9.7B = 174B SB, *Fam.* 5.1 = 1 SB, 5.2 = 2 SB, 5.7 = 3 SB, 5.9 = 255 SB, 5.10a = 259 SB, 5.14 = 251 SB, 7.29 = 264 SB, 9.9 = 157 SB, 10.33 = 409 SB, 10.34

= 396 SB, 10.35 = 408 SB, 11.3 = 336 SB, 12.11 = 366 SB, 12.12 = 387 SB, 12.13 = 419
SB, 12.15 = 406 SB, 12.16 = 328 SB, 13.6 = 57 SB, 14.5 = 119 SB, 14.8 = 164 SB, 14.11 =
166 SB, 14.14 = 145 SB, 14.15 = 167 SB, 14.16 = 163 SB, 14.17 = 162 SB, 14.21 = 165 SB,
14.22 = 172 SB, 14.23 = 171 SB, 14.24 = 170 SB, 15.1 = 104 SB, 15.2 = 105 SB, 15.19 = 216
SB.

46. Sen. *Epist.* 15.1, Pliny *Epist.* 1.11.1, Plautus *Persa* 502–503.

47. Adams (1978, 164 n. 20). However, Adams draws a forced distinction when
he classifies letters 1–4 to Terentia, which never use the formula, as intimate, and
6–24, which often do employ it, as distant. This categorization ignores letter 5 (= 119
SB), which begins with the formula "si tu et Tullia, lux nostra, valetis, ego et
suavissimus Cicero valemus," but contains the vocative "mea suavissima et
optatissima Terentia" in the body of the text. It also gives a misleading impression of
letter 14 (= 119 SB), which begins "si vos valetis, nos valemus," but later addresses
Terentia and Tullia as "meae carissimae animae."

48. Except perhaps for the word *consulto*, the interpretation of Babl (1893, 24)
seems close to the mark: "Quod...illud prooemium adhibuit, ei brevi ante divortium
consulto, ut suspicor, solemniter scripsit, ut quam amoris dulcedinem animo non
haberet, eam verbis formulisque simularet."

49. For the closing formula, see Cugusi (1983, 56–64).

50. In which case it would be tempting to see it in relation to Cicero's repetition
of the standard opening in letters to Terentia of exactly the same period.

51. Hutchinson (1998, 10).

52. For the dateline, see, in addition to Cugusi (1983, 57), Gurlitt (1903). Since
the last line of a letter was as exposed to mutilation as the heading, generalizations
about the dating of letters involve a similar uncertainty. In most cases, we simply
cannot know whether a date was omitted by the letter writer, the editor, or a copyist.
But there is one case in which the omission is clearly secondary. *Att.* 8.11C = 161C SB,
a short letter from Pompey to Cicero that Cicero forwarded to Atticus, carries no date
as it stands. Yet Pompey's original must have recorded the date and place of despatch,
since Cicero is able to cite that information at *Att.* 8.11D.4 = 161D SB.

53. The aversion to dates in letters of recommendation may be seen in another
way in the *MBrut*. The extant series contains eight letters from Brutus, four of which
are dated. Of the four not dated, one is a letter fragment whose conclusion is missing
(*MBrut*. 11[1.4] = 10 SB), one is a letter under suspicion of being spurious (*MBrut*.
24[1.16] = 25 SB), and two are letters of recommendation (*MBrut*. 15[1.7] = 19 SB and
19[1.11] = 16 SB).

54. For the usefulness of a dateline in fixing the sender's whereabouts, see Gurlitt
(1903, 26). William Stull points out to me that a dateline also clarifies the order in
which a succession of letters were written (since letters do not always reach the
addressee in the order in which they were sent). A note of the place of dispatch would
have been unnecessary in most cases in which letters were carried back and forth by
private couriers, since shuttle couriers would know the route that the master was
traveling.

55. In the series preserved in *Fam.* books 10–12 and in *MBrut*.

56. The letters from Brundisium—the same series that Cicero so obsessively
closed with the *vale* formula—are in *Att.* 11. A similar argument could be made about

the letters that Cicero wrote from exile in 58–57, when he dated all but one of fourteen letters he sent to Atticus during the months in which he languished at Thessalonica (*Att.* 3.8–21 = 53–66 SB).

57. Cic. *Att.* 12.53 = 295 SB. Variations on "nihil habeo quod ad te scribam" are most frequent in the correspondence with Atticus (for example, *Att.* 4.4 = 76 SB, 5.5 = 98 SB, 13.8 = 313 SB), but not uncommon elsewhere (for example, *Fam.* 2.4 = 48 SB, 9.3 = 176 SB, 11.25 = 420 SB, 14.2 = 7 SB). Pari passu, Cicero sometimes exhorts his correspondents to write even though *they* have nothing to say (*Att.* 1.12.4 = 12 SB, 12.12.2 = 259 SB, 12.42.1 = 282 SB, 12.44.4 = 285 SB).

58. A good account of epistolary tenses is provided by Mellet (1988, 189–206), who emphasizes that they are not limited to the imperfect, but involve a range of tenses; see also Rauzy (2000). Although not unknown in Greek letters, the phenomenon is best represented in Latin, if for no other reason than that we have a larger corpus of Latin letters. In English and other modern languages, the same tense shift can be heard in messages left on telephone answering machines, which Dingwall (1992, 96) has observed "'behave' more like letters than telephone calls."

59. The imposition on Atticus is implicit not only in the verb *exspectabamus*, but also in the presence of the courier who delivers Cicero's note, since Atticus will be expected to give the courier a message to take back.

60. The study of linguistic politeness was launched by Brown and Levinson (1987), a version of which first appeared in 1978, and politeness, together with the related concept of "face," soon became the subject of such intensive scholarly discussion that it has necessitated periodic bibliographic reviews. A recent retrospective may be found in a special issue of the *Journal of Pragmatics* 35 (2003: 1451–1710). Politeness theory has been applied to Cicero's correspondence by Hall (1996, 1998, and 2009), and by Roesch (2004).

61. Cugusi (1992, 23). Cugusi's meager list, compiled entirely from documentary letters, has the incidental value of emphasizing by contrast the more elaborate politeness language of the Ciceronian corpus.

62. Compare *Fam.* 4.1–2 = 150–151 SB and 4.3–4 = 202–203 SB with *Mur.* 15–53.

63. For Servilius Isauricus, contrast *M Brut.* 2(2.2).3 = 3 SB and *Fam.* 10.12.4 = 377 SB with *Fam.* 13.66–72 = 211, 238, 296–300 SB. For Antony, contrast *Att.* 14.13B = 367B SB with the *Philippics*.

64. *Att.* 9.6A = 172A SB, 9.11A = 178A SB, 9.16.2–3 = 185 SB, 9.18 = 187 SB.

65. Cicero's correspondence is not the only material to call in question the sufficiency of Brown and Levinson's model. The reduction of politeness to the management of face-threatening acts has been criticized as unsuited to modern societies as well. Yu (2003, 1685) contrasts it with the situation in Chinese society, where politeness is "positively reciprocal, with both parties engaged in mutually shared orientation to negotiate, elevate, and attend to each other's face." See also the critiques by Kerbrat-Orecchioni (2000, 23–24) and by Hall (2009, 7–8), who modifies Brown and Levinson's approach to achieve a better fit with the norms of Roman society.

66. I subscribe to the argument made by Préchac (1913), although it entails that the name *Talnam* at *Att.* 16.6.1 = 414 SB must be emended.

67. *Desiderabatur* and *verebantur* in sec.1, and perhaps *fuit* and *sensi* as well.

68. For an account of the cadences that Cicero favors in formal prose, see Hutchinson (1995; for the letters specifically, 1998, 9–12). Not all the letters to Trebatius are rhythmic, but the one under discussion here is.

69. The variety of lotus that Cicero saw at Trebatius's house was evidently a shade tree rather than a shrub or plant, however. See Pliny *HNat.* 16.123–24.

70. The vicissitudes through which Trebatius rose to a position of influence and honor under the Augustan regime are described by Sonnet (1937).

71. Cicero characterizes his outlook during this period as "despair" at *Att.* 15.20.1 = 397 SB and *Fam.* 12.25.3 = 373 SB.

72. Cicero associates these themes directly with himself in another letter written at a low ebb in his fortunes, *Att.* 2.6 = 26 SB (quoted in chap. 1), where he extols the livability of Antium over Rome and relishes the affection with which he is regarded there.

73. The politeness campaign did not end with this letter. A week later, Cicero presented Trebatius with a Latin adaptation of Aristotle's *Topics* which he had written while he was sailing down the coast (*Fam.* 7.19 = 334 SB). He repeats the account in the introduction to the *Topica* (1–5). Apart from Atticus and Cicero's son, Trebatius is the only non-senator to have had one of Cicero's works formally directed to him.

74. One of Cicero's stranger performances in the art of managing the addressee is *QFr.* 3.1 = 21 SB, a rambling, ten-page letter to his brother written at intervals during a period of two and a half weeks in September of 54. The message content ranges over a variety of political and private projects concerning the two brothers, and it progressively expands in response to incoming letters from Quintus. But in a recent commentary that elaborates on the eccentricities of the text, Henderson (2007) shows how an aura of fraternal amity that Cicero initially projects as a haven in a hostile world breaks down under the force of his own megalomania.

75. The only reason Cicero divulges even this much about the conversation with Pompey is that Caelius had explicitly asked about it, *Fam.* 8.1.3 = 77 SB. Cicero is hardly more forthcoming about the visit with Pompey when he writes to Atticus: *Att.* 5.7 = 100 SB.

76. *Fam.* 2.8–15 = 80, 85–86, 89–90, 93, and 95–96 SB; 3.3–13 = 66–76 SB; and *Att.* 5.1–6.7 = 94–121 SB.

77. *Fam.* 7.6–18 = 27–39 SB and *QFr.* 2.13(12)–3.7(9) = 17–27 SB.

78. *Fam.* 7.7.1 = 28 SB and 7.17.1 = 31 SB.

79. "Quod scire vis qua quisque in te fide sit et voluntate, difficile dictu est de singulis," *Fam.* 1.7.2 = 18 SB.

80. "De qua ratione tota iam videtur mihi exponendi tempus dari, ut tibi rescribam ad ea, quae quaeris," *Fam.* 1.9.3 = 20 SB.

CHAPTER 4

1. For representative views, see Eagleton (1983, 1–16) and Guillory (1993, 63–71).

2. The capaciousness of the term is reflected in the divergence between the content of this chapter and chapter 1 of Hutchinson (1998), despite identical chapter titles.

3. Deissmann articulated his views of the letter in *Biblelstudien* (1895, 187–252) and again, more summarily, thirteen years later in *Licht vom Osten*, which I have seen in its fourth edition (1923, 116–19, 193–98). Deissmann is regularly invoked among classicists, as by Peter (1901, 11), Luck (1961), Kirfel (1969, 11–12), and Scarpat (1989, 495–99), and in modified form his distinction has been recently defended by Klauck (2006, 70–71). It is not free of ideological tilt, however. As his book titles indicate, Deissmann's chief concern was with New Testament studies, and his understanding of letters was ultimately related to what he wanted to find in the letters—definitely not "epistles," in his view—of St. Paul.

4. An empirical survey may be found in Gavoille (1998).

5. The distinction is ubiquitous in studies of the epistolary genre, but for recent consideration of its bearing on Cicero's letters, see Hutchinson (1998), where it is of central concern in chapter 1. Hutchinson (2007) returns to the problem, concluding (p. 35) that "the nature of the division between literary and non-literary seems ever less straightforward."

6. At *Phil.* 2.7 and *Fam.* 15.21.4 = 207 SB.

7. *Fam.* 15.21.4 = 207 SB. For further testimonia to this exchange, see Cugusi (1979, I: 390–91).

8. For private letter collections prior to Cicero, see Sykutris (1931, 197), Trapp (2003, 12–13), and Hutchinson (1998, 4 n. 4).

9. For example, *Att.* 9.13.4 = 180 SB, *Off.* 1.22 and 2.96.

10. He cites one to Cato's son at *Off.* 1.37. But it is doubtful whether more than that one ever came into circulation. See Astin (1978, 183–84).

11. Enclosures are discussed in chapter 2; for some requests that letters be destroyed upon receipt, see *Att.* 8.2.4 = 152 SB, 10.12.3 = 203 SB, *Fam.* 5.20.9 = 128 SB, 7.18.4 = 37 SB.

12. Examples only: a sensitive topic broken off, *Att.* 13.9.1 = 317 SB, *Fam.* 4.8.2 = 229 SB; obfuscated, *Att.* 13.21a.4 = 327 SB; names avoided, *Att.* 7.12.2 = 135 SB, *Fam.* 2.9.1 = 85 SB; Latin to Greek, *Att.* 6.9.2 = 123 SB, 15.12.2 = 390 SB, with Shackleton Bailey's note; preemption of the copyist, *Att.* 4.17.1 = 91 SB, 12.32.1 = 271 SB.

13. Caesar, *Att.* 8.2.2 = 152 SB, 9.11A = 178A SB, 11.12.2 = 223 SB; Pompey, *Att.* 3.8.4 = 53 SB, 8.11B and 8.11D = 161B and 161D SB; Varro, *Att.* 13.25.3 = 333 SB; Brutus, Cassius, and Dolabella (the last extant as an enclosure), *Att.* 14.17.4 = 371 SB; Brutus, *Att.* 12.18.2 = 254 SB, 12.37.1 = 276 SB; Dolabella, *Att.* 15.14.2–3 = 402 SB; Antony, *Att.* 14.13B = 367B SB; Plancus, *Att.* 16.16.1 = 407 SB; Octavian, *MBrut.* 24(1.16).1 = 25 SB.

14. *Att.* 8.9.1 = 188 SB, 12.51.2 = 293 SB, 13.27.1 = 298 SB.

15. Examples: *Att.* 5.11.6 = 104 SB, 16.16.1 = 407 SB, *Fam.* 2.17.7 = 117 SB, 7.30.3 = 265 SB.

16. So, correctly, Schneider (1998, 553).

17. Eco (1976, 48–150; 1979, 19–21), Violi (1985, 158–59). Alternatively, one might have recourse to the ancient distinction between "exoteric" and "esoteric" writings.

18. Marchesi (2008, 221). The pairings she discusses are *QFr.* 1.1 = 1 SB with Pliny *Epist.* 7.33, *Fam.* 5.12 = 22 SB with Pliny *Epist.* 5.8 and 7.33, and *Fam.* 7.1 = 24 SB with Pliny *Epist.* 9.6.

19. The following letters, all appreciably shorter than the three described, might be added to the list: *Fam.* 9.1 = 175 SB (to Varro, announcing Cicero's return to literary

pursuits after the perturbations of the civil war), 9.4 = 180 SB (an invitation to Varro to pay a visit, cast as a conceit on the Stoic analysis of decision making), 9.21 = 188 SB (to Papirius Paetus, on the history of the Papirian *gens*), 9.22 = 189 SB (to Paetus, a philosophically oriented riff on the linguistics of obscenity), 15.16 = 215 SB (to the Epicurean Cassius, a teasing application of Epicurean doctrine on mental images), 15.19 = 216 SB (again to Cassius and again teasing, about contemporary politics in light of Epicurus's teaching on pleasure and pain), 16.17 = 186 SB (to Tiro, bantering about the meaning of *fideliter*).

20. In fact, and despite the conjectures of Shackleton Bailey and others, we do not know that Cicero put *any* of these letters into circulation, and he seems to imply in one case that the letter was not in circulation. When he urged Atticus to have a look at the letter he wrote to Lucceius (*Att.* 4.6.4 = 83 SB), he told him to get it from Lucceius. (Presumably he could have made a copy available himself, but he wanted Atticus to intervene with Lucceius in furtherance of Cicero's desire for a monograph on the Catilinarian affair.)

21. This was the point of Hutchinson's discussion (2007) of papyrus letters.

22. For a few examples out of many in which *scribere accurate* is applied to letters, see *Att.* 6.1.21 = 115 SB, 6.9.3 = 123 SB, 13.24.2 = 332 SB, *Fam.* 2.19.2 = 116 SB, 13.8.1 = 321 SB, *MBrut.* 23(1.15).1 = 23 SB. In the dedicatory letter to his collection, Pliny says that he selected for publication "epistulas…quas paulo curatius scripsissem," *Epist.* 1.1.1.

23. Pointed out by Griffin (1995, 333 n. 36).

24. See *Fam.* 13.7.1 = 320 SB, 13.8.1 = 321 SB, and *Att.* 6.6 = 121 SB (described as carefully written at *Att.* 6.9.3 = 123 SB). Three other prime examples would be *Fam.* 9.8 = 254 SB, the letter presenting the *Academica* to Varro, apropos of which Cicero vows at *Att.* 13.25.3 = 333 SB that he will never take such pains over a letter again, *Fam.* 13.15 = 317 SB to Caesar, which Cicero vaunts as *non vulgaris*, and the *valde bella* letter to Lucceius (*Fam.* 5.12 = 22 SB).

25. Others are *Fam.* 2.19.2 = 116 SB, 13.7.1 = 320 SB, 13.8.1 = 321 SB, 13.75.1 = 60 SB.

26. The total includes the ninety-seven correspondents represented among the extant letters, plus eleven additional correspondents attested in books no longer extant; see appendix 1. It does not include everyone who can be identified as having exchanged letters with Cicero, however. So far as I know, that list has never been compiled.

Correspondents appearing in Schanz-Hosius are as follows (numbers in parentheses refer to the relevant page of the Erster Teil, or to volume and page of the Zweiter Teil): T. Ampius Balbus (351), M. Antonius (388), C. Asinius Pollio (2:24), Q. Caecilius Metellus Celer (389), Q. Caecilius Metellus Nepos (389), A. Caecina (602), M. Caelius Rufus (399), C. Cassius Parmensis (315), Ap. Claudius Pulcher (599), C. Claudius Marcellus, pr. 80 (599), L. Cornelius Balbus (350), P. Cornelius Lentulus Spinther, cos. 57 (389), Q. Cornificius (308), M. Fabius Gallus (334, but registered there as "Fadius"), C. Furnius (2:329), A. Hirtius (344), C. Iulius Caesar (332), M. Iunius Brutus (394), M. Licinius Crassus (480), L. Lucceius (327), C. Matius (605), C. Memmius (310), P. Nigidius Figulus (552), C. Oppius (351), T. Pomponius Atticus (329), M. Porcius Cato (490), C. Scribonius Curio (398), P. Sestius (430), Ser. Sulpicius Rufus (593), M. Terentius Varro (555), M. Tullius Tiro (547), C. Trebatius Testa (596), C. Trebonius (544), Q. Tullius Cicero (550), L. Valerius (263),

P. Volumnius Eutrapelus (315). Among lost correspondents, add Cornelius Nepos (351) and C. Licinius Calvus (392). Octavian's literary career had not begun by the time of Cicero's death, though Cicero refers to *contiones* of which he had seen transcriptions.

Greek literary friends (for that matter, Greeks absolutely) are completely absent from the recipients and writers of the extant letters, and almost completely absent from known correspondents of the lost corpora. Their minimal representation in Cicero's letter corpus parallels the situation in Latin poetry: they rarely appear among the friends mentioned by Latin poets from Catullus on.

27. For Cicero's *emendatio*, see Helm (1956, 149 g), under the year 94 B.C. Cicero refers to Lucretius's poems at *QFr.* 2.10[9].3 = 14 SB.

28. *Fam.* 7.11.2 = 34 SB, 12.18.2 = 205 SB, Sen. *Contr.* 7.3.9, Macr. *Sat.* 2.3.10.

29. For example, Laelius with Pacuvius and Terence (*Amic.* 24 and 89), Servius Galba with Ennius (*Luc.* 51), Lutatius Catulus with Furius (*Brut.* 132), Decimus Brutus with Accius (*Arch.* 27).

30. For a recent discussion of Cicero's relations with contemporary Latin poets, see Spahlinger (2000), who provides ample references to earlier bibliography on the subject. Cicero also speaks in vague terms of having listened to recitations by poets at *QFr.* 2.9(8).1 = 12 SB, and some experience of readings may be implied at *Att.* 14.20.3 = 374 SB.

31. *Fam.* 15.21.2 = 207 SB, 12.16.3 = 328 SB.

32. *Fam.* 13.1–3 = 63 and 314–15 SB; 12.13 = 419 SB.

33. For the circumstances under which *contiones* were transcribed and circulated in this period, see White (2009, 279–80).

34. One from the poem on his consulate (at *Att.* 2.3.4 = 23 SB) and one from the *De Republica* (at *Att.* 8.11.1 = 161 SB).

35. Stahlenbrecher (1957, 16) counts 177 quotations from Greek and Latin poetry in the letters; his list on pages 260–63 includes quotations in prose as well as verse.

36. See Shackleton Bailey's note here for *tamen* in this and the preceding passage.

37. Given the lost exchange with Calvus on oratory (*Fam.* 15.21.4 = 207 SB), however, it would be imprudent to deny the possibility altogether.

38. Pliny the Elder: *Epist.* 3.5; Silius: *Epist.* 3.7; Martial: *Epist.* 3.21; recitations: *Epist.* 4.27, 5.17, 6.17, 6.21, 7.17, 8.12, 8.21.

39. Sherwin-White (1966, 44–45).

40. Horsfall (1993), whose claim has been criticized by Spahlinger (2000, 250–53).

41. A correspondence closer to Cicero than Pliny's might be instanced to illustrate the same point. According to Cornelius Nepos, the triumvir Octavian carried on an almost daily correspondence with Atticus: "numquam ad suorum quemquam litteras misit, quin Attico mitteret quid ageret, inprimis quid legeret quibusque in locis et quam diu esset moraturus ... nullus dies temere intercessit quo non ad eum scriberet, cum modo aliquid de antiquitate ab eo requireret, modo aliquam quaestionem poeticam ei proponeret" (*vita Att.* 20.2). As Augustus, he later carried on a literary correspondence with Vergil and Horace; see Cugusi (1979, 349–51, nos. 60–66), or Malcovati (1948, 21–24, nos. 35–40).

42. On this motif in Cicero's letters of recommendation, see Déniaux (1993, 177–79).

43. See Goldberg (2005, 87–97), speaking of the expression of "class solidarity" on p. 96, and Damon (2008), who speaks of "literature as a form of

social glue" at p. 175. In Cicero's own parlance, literature is a bond or *vinculum*
(*Fam.* 3.10.9 = 73 SB, 13.29.1 = 282 SB).

44. Apart from Atticus and Quintus, for whom the evidence is too abundant to be
summarized here, there are thirty-two correspondents with whom Cicero adverts to
something literary. They are as follows (all citations are to the *Letters to Friends*, unless
otherwise indicated):

T. Ampius Balbus (writings, *studia* 6.12.5 = 226 SB)
A. Caecina (writings, 6.6.8 = 334 SB; *studia*, 6.6.1 = 334 SB, 6.9.1 = 236 SB,
     13.66.1 = 238 SB)
M. Caelius Rufus (allusions, 2.9 = 85 SB)
C. Cassius Longinus (writings, 12.2.1 = 344 SB; allusions, 15.16 = 215 SB, 15.19 =
     216 SB; *studia*, 7.33.2 = 192 SB)
C. Claudius Marcellus, cos. 50 (*studia*, 15.11.2 = 118 SB)
M. Claudius Marcellus (*studia*, 15.9.1 = 101 SB)
Ap. Claudius Pulcher (writings, 3.4.1 = 67 SB, 3.9.3 = 72 SB, 3.11.4 = 74 SB;
     quotation, 3.7.6 = 71 SB; *studia*, 3.10.9 = 73 SB, 3.13.2 = 76 SB)
P. Cornelius Dolabella (writings, 9.12.2 = 263 SB; allusion, 9.10.1 = 217 SB, 9.14.2
     = 326 SB)
P. Cornelius Lentulus Spinther (cos. 57) (writings, 1.9.23 = 20 SB; allusions,
     1.9.12 and 18 = 20 SB; *studia*, 1.7.11 = 18 SB)
Q. Cornificius (writings, 12.17.2 = 204 SB, 12.20 = 339 SB; quotation, 12.25.5 = 373 SB)
M'. Curius (writings, 7.28.2 = 200 SB; quotations, 7.28.2 = 200 SB, 7.30.1 = 265 SB)
M. Fabius Gallus (writings, 7.24.2 = 260 SB; quotations, 7.24.1 = 260 SB, 7.26.1
     = 210 SB)
C. Iulius Caesar (quotations, 13.15 = 317 SB; writings, 13.16.4 = 316 SB)
M. Iunius Brutus (writings, *MBrut.* 4[2.4].2 = 4 SB; quotations, *MBrut.*
     8[1.2a].2 = 6 SB, *MBrut.* 18[1.10].2 = 17 SB, *MBrut.* 23[1.15].3 = 23 SB; *studia*,
     13.10.2 = 277 SB, 13.12.2 = 279 SB)
L. Lucceius (writings, 5.12 = 22 SB; quotation, 5.12.7 = 22 SB)
M. Marius (writings, 7.1.2–3 = 24 SB)
C. Matius (writings, 11.27.5 = 348 SB; *studia*, 11.27.6 = 348 SB)
L. Mescinius Rufus (*studia*, 5.19.2 = 152 SB, 5.21.2–3 = 182 SB)
L. Munatius Plancus (allusion, 10.13.2 = 389 SB; *studia*, 10.3.4 = 355 SB, 13.29.1
     and 5 = 282 SB)
P. Nigidius Figulus (writings, 4.13.7 = 225 SB; *studia*, 4.13.4 = 225 SB)
Q. Paconius Lepta (writings, 6.18.4 = 218 SB; quotation, 6.18.5 = 218 SB)
L. Papirius Paetus (writings, 9.16.4 = 190 SB, 9.20.3 = 193 SB, 9.25.1 = 114 SB,
     9.26.3 = 197 SB; allusion and quotation: 9.15.2 = 196 SB, 9.16.4–6 = 190 SB,
     9.20.1 = 193 SB, 9.21.1 = 188 SB, 9.22 = 189 SB; 9.26.2 = 197 SB)
M. Porcius Cato (writings, 15.4.12 and 16 = 110 SB; quotation, 15.6.1 = 112 SB)
Ser. Sulpicius Rufus (writings, 4.4.1 = 203 SB; *studia*, 4.1.1 = 150 SB, 4.3.3 = 202
     SB, 4.4.4 = 203 SB, 13.28.2 = 294 SB, 13.28a.2 = 295 SB)
M. Terentius Varro (writings, 9.2.5 = 177 SB, 9.4 = 180 SB, 9.8 = 254 SB;
     quotation, 9.7 = 178 SB; *studia*, 9.1.2 = 175 SB, 9.2.5 = 177 SB, 9.3.2 = 176 SB,
     9.6.4–5 = 181 SB)

Titius (writings, 5.16.3 = 187 SB)

C. Trebatius Testa (writings, 7.19 = 334 SB, 7.20.3 = 333 SB; quotations and
   allusions, 7.6 = 27 SB, 7.10.4 = 33 SB, 7.13.2 = 36 SB, 7.16.1 = 32 SB,
   7.20.1 = 333 SB)

Trebianus (studia, 6.10.4 = 222 SB)

C. Trebonius (writings, 15.20.1 = 208 SB, 15.21 = 207 SB)

M. Tullius Tiro (writings, 16.10.2 = 43 SB, 16.17.1 = 186 SB, 16.18.3 = 219 SB,
   16.20 = 220 SB, 16.22.1 = 185 SB; quotation, 16.8.2 = 147 SB; studia,
   16.14.2 = 41 SB)

L. Valerius (allusion, 1.10 = 21 SB)

P. Volumnius Eutrapelus (writings, 7.32.2 = 113 SB; quotation, 7.33.1 =
   192 SB)

45. See Stahlenbrecher (1957, 17–18).

46. Appius Pulcher, Caesar, Paconius Lepta, Tiro, and Varro (for whom, see the
list in n. 44 of this chapter).

47. Att. 1.19.10 = 19 SB, 2.1.11 = 21 SB, 13.5.1 = 312 SB, 15.13.1 = 416 SB,
16.2.6 = 412 SB, 16.3.1 = 413 SB, 16.11.3 = 420 SB (all books sent by Cicero to
Atticus), Fam. 6.18.4 = 218 SB (to Lepta), 7.19 = 334 SB (to Trebatius), 9.8 = 254
SB (to Varro), 9.12.2 = 263 SB (to Dolabella), 12.17.2 = 204 SB (to Cornificius).
Cicero is also the recipient of other authors' work: Att. 2.1.1–2 = 21 SB (from
Atticus), 12.40.1 = 281 SB (from Hirtius), Fam. 3.9.3 = 72 SB (from Appius), 7.24.2
= 260 SB (from Fabius Gallus), 12.16.3 = 328 SB and 15.21 = 207 SB (from
Trebonius).

48. The line first occurs in Hector's speech to Andromache at Il. 6.442, but since
Cicero sometimes quotes it in conjunction with Il. 22.100, he probably has in mind
Hector's soliloquy as he is deciding whether to confront or flee from Achilles at Il.
22.99–130 (where the line recurs as 22.105). Cicero quotes the line in whole or in part
six times: Att. 2.5.1 = 25 SB, 7.1.4 = 124 SB, 7.12.3 = 135 SB, 8.16.2 = 166 SB, 13.13.2 =
321 SB, 13.24.1 = 332 SB.

For quotations from the Odyssey in the letters, see the careful study by De Caro
(2006), who concludes that citations from the Odyssey and the Iliad alike serve
"innestare significati epici nella vita quotidiana o nelle vicende politiche.... Il testo
Greco viene così re-interpretato et ri-semantizzato in base al contesto, come
significante per nuovi significati" (149).

49. More understated but still surprising is a passage in which Cicero figures
himself as an Iliadic hero in one of the speeches. At Pro Sulla 50, he declares that he
will not allow the prosecutor to torment his client after having brought him down in a
previous trial: "tu ornatus exuviis huius venis ad eum lacerandum quem interemisti,
ego iacentem et spoliatum defendo et protego." Winterbottom (2004, 222 n. 34; 224 n.
41) has noted other instances of Iliadic characterization in the speeches, though not of
Cicero himself.

50. This passage from the letters is discussed by Goldberg (2005, 87–88).

51. Fam. 9.18.3 = 191 SB and 9.20.2 = 193 SB, both to Papirius Paetus. In a letter
to Caelius Rufus, Cicero casts himself in yet another role from comedy (Fam. 2.9.2 =
85 SB).

52. For example, by Curius according to *Fam.* 7.28.2 = 200, by Atticus according to *Att.* 8.2.2 = 152, and by the imposter Marius according to *Att.* 12.49.2 = 292. Compare also the criticisms of Cicero at *Att.* 16.7.3 = 415 SB and *MBrut.* 25(1.17).5 = 26 SB.

53. The meaning of the last sentence is disputed. See Zetzel (1995, 4 n. 11) for an argument that it refers, not to a change of *dramatis personae*, but to the addition of those prefaces addressed to Quintus that the dialogue now features.

54. Cicero's comments about revising his *Academica* are spread across a series of letters (see appendix 2, under "M. Tullius Cicero"), but they evince the same preoccupation with practical rather than literary objectives.

55. Although the letter in question (*Fam.* 9.6 = 181 SB) is the latest of Cicero's letters to Varro in 46, it does not actually stand last in the Varro series of book 9, for two reasons. First, the editor chose to conclude that series with a letter that Cicero wrote a year later to accompany his presentation of the *Academica* to Varro (*Fam.* 9.8 = 254 SB). And second, the letters of 46 themselves do not stand in chronological order, perhaps because none of them contained an explicit date.

56. Cicero had tried out the same line in the peroration of a letter to Cato a few years earlier (*Fam.* 15.4.16 = 110 SB).

57. See *Att.* 2.25.1 = 45 SB and 13.25.3 = 333 SB.

CHAPTER 5

1. Springer (1927) was led to compile his dossier concerning letters that Cicero received partly because of his surprise that the consultative aspect of the correspondence had not drawn more discussion: "adhuc parvum animadversum videtur, quantum Cicero cum in domesticis tum in publicis rebus amicorum consiliis quantumque suo arbitrio atque iudicio deberet" (p. 1). Yet the subject of advice in the letters has attracted little discussion since. Although the collection by Spencer and Theodorakopoulos on advice in Greece and Rome (2006) includes an essay on Pliny's exchange with Trajan, it offers nothing on Cicero's letters. Habinek (1990), discussed later in this chapter, is the only paper I know that deals with the subject directly.

2. Examples only: *Att.* 12.47.2 = 288 SB, 13.18 = 325 SB, 13.19.5 = 326 SB, 15.22 = 399 SB, *Fam.* 9.8.2 = 254 SB, 9.14.8 = 326 SB, 16.17.1 = 186 SB.

3. Crook (1955, 4). One of the blackest marks in Livy's portrait of King Tarquinius Superbus is that he refused to consult with the Senate and that he decided all matters by himself (1.49.7).

4. A record of proceedings in the Senate (on occasion even a public record) was kept in some form, but has left no traces for the period of the Roman Republic. And although there are many references to the panels which assisted Roman magistrates and governors, we have no summaries of the discussion which took place in them. Anecdotes are rare, and more or less obviously slanted in some way. But we catch glimpses of Verres's *consilium* in Cicero's *Verrine Orations* and of an imperial official's panel of assessors at Aug. *Conf.* 6.10.16. Pliny describes a meeting of the emperor with his advisers at *Epist.* 6.31, and Juvenal parodies one in *Sat.* 4. Cicero's letters offer some of the most circumstantial accounts of Romans taking counsel with one another, including a debate in the Senate at *Att.* 1.16.9–10 = 16 SB

and private conferences between Caesar and Cicero at *Att.* 9.18 = 187 SB, Cicero, Cassius, and Brutus at *Att.* 15.11 = 389 SB, and Cicero and his nephew at *Att.* 13.42 = 354 SB.

5. For Cicero's classification of letter types, see chapter 1, note 34.

6. The dilemmas of advice giving that arise in a contemporary American context make a useful point of comparison; see Goldsmith and Fitch (1997, 461–70).

7. Not that advice giving is unproblematic in other societies. A discussion of the phenomenon from the standpoint of modern communication theory leads off with the question, "Why do people persist in offering a type of support with such dicey prospects for success?" Goldsmith (2004, 52).

8. The letter to Quintus contains other passages to similar effect in secs. 8, 18, and 45.

9. Compare "non quo ea te fugere existimem" at *Fam.* 4.5.1 = 248 SB (Servius to Cicero).

10. Cicero similarly deprecates the quality of his advice and emphasizes his goodwill in letters to Marcellus (*Fam.* 4.7.1 = 230 SB) and Caecina (*Fam.* 6.6.2 = 234 SB).

11. Cicero resorts to the "si videbitur" formula also at *Att.* 12.51.3 = 293 SB, where Atticus has advised him to do one thing, and Cicero proposes that he do something else.

12. Redressive phrasing continues in what follows, where Cicero wants to say that if Servius is determined to come, he should come quickly. I underscore the mitigating touches: "sin autem est quod communicare velis, ego te exspectabo. tu, quod tuo commodo fiat, quam primum velim venias, sicut intellexi et Servio [i.e., Servius junior] et Postumiae placere."

13. Other examples are found at *Att.* 1.20.2 = 20 SB, 9.7.3 = 174 SB, 14.19.1 = 372 SB, and *Fam.* 3.3.1 = 66 SB.

14. *Fam.* 8.5.2 = 83 SB, *QFr.* 1.1.45 = 1 SB.

15. For examples, see *Fam.* 6.19 = 262 SB, 7.17 = 31 SB, and 6.20 = 247 SB.

16. Compare *Amic.* 91, "monere et moneri proprium est verae amicitiae"; *Off.* 1.58, "consilia sermones cohortationes consolationes, interdum etiam obiurgationes in amicitiis vigent maxime"; 1.91, "etiam in secundissimis rebus maxime est utendum consilio amicorum"; Lucilius 611 Marx, "porro 'amici est bene praecipere, bene tueri' praedicant."

17. See Goldsmith and Fitch (1997, 462).

18. This may be seen at a glance from Déniaux (1993, 96–108, table 2, third column: "relation à Cicéron"), quoting the language of friendship which Cicero uses in relation to each person.

19. *Att.* 10.8A = 199A SB, 14.13A = 367A SB, 14.13B = 367B SB.

20. For example, *Att.* 13.40.2 = 343 SB "quid mi auctor es? advolone an maneo?," 15.11.1 = 389 SB "auctor non sum ut te urbi committas," *Fam.* 6.8.2 = 235 SB "a me consilium petis quid sim tibi auctor."

21. "τῶν μελλόντων ἐπὶ πλεῖστον τοῦ γενησομένου ἄριστος εἰκαστής." Cicero quotes the whole passage on Themistocles' foresight in Greek, as if he knew it by heart, at *Att.* 10.8.7 = 199 SB, and he alludes to it at *De Orat.* 2.299, 3.59, and *Brut.* 28.

22. Interestingly, Cornelius Nepos picked up on this feature of the correspondence. Speaking of a collection of letters from Cicero to Atticus that he had seen, he writes, "sic enim de studiis principum, vitiis ducum, mutationibus rei publicae perscripta sunt ut nihil in his non appareat et facile existimari possit prudentiam quodam modo esse divinationem," *vita Att.* 16.4. Mitchell (1991, 18–19) has a good treatment of foresight in his chapter on Cicero's "political ideas."

23. The prediction of an impending augurate for Oppius at *Fam.* 2.16.7 = 154 SB was false, and the prediction of one for Vatinius at *Att.* 2.9.2 = 29 SB was about ten years premature. Cicero's prediction, in May of 49, that a Caesarian regime would not last six months (*Att.* 10.8.7 = 199 SB) was inaccurate. But his most flagrant misjudgment has to be his guarantee of Octavian's loyalty to the Republic at *Phil.* 5.50–51. Vaticinations in hindsight include those on the consequences of Pompey's alliance with Caesar at *Fam.* 6.6.4 = 234 SB (with Shackleton Bailey's note), on Curio's embrace of Caesar at 2.13.3 = 93 SB, and on Octavian's putsch in south Italy at *Att.* 16.8.2 = 418 SB. For a rare confession of failure at prophecy, see *Fam.* 15.15.2 = 174 SB.

24. See, for example, Cic. *Off.* 1.15. Cicero comments on the derivation of *prudentia* from *providere* at *Leg.* 1.60; for the similarity between them, see *Off.* 2.33.

25. Kaster (2005, 76).

26. The exchange between Caesar and Cicero is discussed from a different perspective in White (2003, 81–86). Let it be noted here that Caesar's overture to Cicero set an example that Octavian would later follow; see *Att.* 16.9 = 419 SB.

27. In fact, the perspectives available to us on this exchange are even more diverse. Apart from Caesar's letter, Cicero's reaction to Caesar's letter, and Cicero's reply to Caesar, we also have Cicero's report of Matius's interpretation of Caesar's letter (*Att.* 9.11.2 = 178 SB), Cicero's exegesis of his own letter to Caesar (*Att.* 8.9.1 = 188 SB), a follow-up letter from Caesar (*Att.* 9.16.2–3 = 185 SB), and Cicero's report of a face-to-face meeting in which Caesar renewed his request in blunter terms (*Att.* 9.18.3 = 187 SB).

28. Shacketon Bailey (at *Att.* 15.1.2 = 377 SB) cites *Att.* 14.13.5B = 367B to Antony as another declaration in the same vein.

29. Plut. *Cic.* 20, *An seni* 27 [797 D]. What is known about Lucceius is that he prosecuted Catiline under the *lex Cornelia de sicariis* in the previous year (sources in Alexander 1990, 108–109, no. 217). It is within the compass of the word *auctor* that Cicero could mean, not that Lucceius counseled him in 63, but that he set him an example in 64. For Cicero's known advisers during the Catilinarian affair, see Dyck (2008, 176), apropos of *Cat.* 3.7.

30. The letters Cicero wrote to Appius comprise one of the most completely preserved series within the *Letters to Friends*: between the initial letter and the last, only one item appears to be missing (the letter mentioned at *Fam.* 3.6.2 = 69 SB). Moreover, almost every one of Cicero's letters takes up and carefully replies to something Appius had written. The lack of any earlier reference to Appius's advice about the *supplicatio* strongly suggests that it could have been conveyed only in person rather than by letter. There was only one moment at which Appius and Cicero could have conferred in person, and that was when their paths briefly converged near Iconium in early September of 51 (as described in *Fam.* 3.7.4 = 71 SB). Yet it is not clear that they actually met on that occasion.

31. For three more cases in which Cicero imputes to someone a decisive but otherwise undocumented influence on his own conduct in the past, see *Fam.* 1.8.2 = 19 SB (Lentulus), 11.29.1 = 335 SB (Oppius), and 13.29.7 = 282 SB (Ateius Capito). Roman literary historians will recognize here something akin to the *carmen iussum* trope by which a poet credits someone else with instigating his work.

32. Quintus: *Att.* 3.15.6 = 60 SB, 3.17.1 and 3 = 62 SB, 3.18.2 = 63 SB, 3.22.1–2 = 67 SB, 3.26 = 71 SB, *Fam.* 5.4.1 = 10 SB, *QFr.* 1.4.5 = 4 SB; Piso: *Att.* 3.22.1 = 67 SB, *Fam.* 14.2.2 = 7 SB, *QFr.* 1.4.2 = 4 SB; Pompey: *Att.* 3.8.4 = 53 SB; Lentulus: *Att.* 3.22.2 = 67 SB; Metellus Nepos: *Fam.* 5.4 = 10 SB; Sestius: *Att.* 3.19.2 = 64 SB, 3.20.3 = 65 SB, 3.23.4 = 68 SB, *QFr.* 1.4.2 = 4 SB; Fadius: *Att.* 3.23.4 = 68 SB; other tribunes: *Att.* 3.24.1 = 69 SB; Axius: *Att.* 3.15.3 = 60 SB; others: *Att.* 3.17 = 62 SB, 3.19.2 = 64 SB, *Fam.* 14.1.1 = 8 SB, 14.2.2 = 7 SB, *QFr.* 1.3.5 = 3 SB. This list is limited to those with whom it can be proved that Cicero corresponded. But the actual number is surely much larger. Nicholson (1992, 47–88) lists and describes the roles of about fifty people altogether who were working on Cicero's behalf at this time.

33. *Att.* 5.4.1 = 97 SB, 5.14.3 = 107 SB, 5.17.4 = 110 SB, 5.21.14 = 114 SB, 6.1.10 = 115 SB, 6.4.2 = 118 SB, 6.6.1 = 121 SB.

34. *Fam.* 8.6.2 = 88 SB. *Att.* 5.17.4 = 110 SB suggests that Cicero may have asked Sestius to do the same.

35. Tiberius Nero, *Att.* 6.6.1 = 121 SB; compare *Fam.* 13.64 = 138 SB, written after a visit by Nero to Cilicia.

36. *Att.* 6.6.1 = 121 SB, *Fam.* 3.12.2 = 75 SB. Treggiari (2007, 83–94) gives a good account of the negotiations preceding Tullia's marriage to Dolabella.

37. *Att.* 15.25 = 403 SB, 16.5.3 = 410 SB, 16.2.4 = 412 SB, 16.7.1 = 415 SB. Oppius was one of those whose *consilium* he says counted heavily with him: *Fam.* 11.29.1 = 335 SB. *Att.* 8.9a.1 = 160 SB affords a glimpse into a parallel round of consultations back in the year 49.

38. Cic. *Phil.* 2.89, *Att.* 14.10.1 = 364 SB, 14.14.2 = 368 SB, 15.11.2 = 389 SB.

39. *Att.* 3.9.2 = 54 SB, 3.10.2 = 55 SB, 3.13.1 = 59 SB.

40. Shackleton Bailey (1965, 1: 20–21), discusses Atticus's role at this point; his introduction to the first volume of *Cicero's Letters to Atticus* provides the fullest general treatment of Atticus's advisory relationship to Cicero.

41. He does, however, retroactively *defend* a decision he had taken about whom to represent at *Fam.* 1.9.19 = 20 SB.

42. *Att.* 1.12.3 = 12 SB, 1.13.3 = 13 SB, 1.14.1–2 and 5 = 14 SB, 1.16 = 16 SB (sec. 1 of which makes clear that Cicero did not consult Atticus, though he claims that he would have liked to), and 1.18.2–3 = 18 SB.

43. In one case, when his friend Paetus presumed to offer him advice on military action, Cicero scoffingly brushed it aside. See chapter 3, p. 70.

44. The evidence of the letters thus bears out a general observation by Habinek (1990, 171) about advice giving in Roman society: "social status and a sense of *virtus* depend on the constant and comparative evaluation by external assessors." A more specific claim put forward in that paper is open to question, however. Habinek argues that Cicero was innovating in the *De Amicitia* when he called on upper-class friends to be candid in rebuking one another, especially where interests of state were involved. Up until then, he argues, the pattern that had prevailed was that candid

criticism was confined to relationships between unequal friends, such as Scipio and Polybius, or Servilius and the good companion described by Ennius. Cicero's message in the *De Amicitia*, however, was that aristocratic peers must also engage in honest criticism and advice, because that will improve the ability of the aristocracy to self-correct and so to maintain supremacy. It is difficult to say anything certain about social behavior before the age of Cicero because evidence is extremely scarce. But one problem with Habinek's argument as it applies to Cicero's milieu turns on the distinction between "equal" and "unequal" friendships. Though it is easy to distinguish social superiors and social inferiors if one looks to the extremes of the social spectrum, it is less easy to draw such distinctions within Cicero's circle. That Cicero and the aristocrat Appius Pulcher can be counted as social equals, as they are for purposes of Habinek's argument, or that Cicero and Caelius Rufus or Cicero and Atticus can be counted as unequals, is at least not self-evident. But the larger difficulty is that in the epistolary corpus overall, most of which predates the *De Amicitia*, rebuke and criticism seem to be freely practiced without regard for the relative status of the parties.

45. *Fam.* 7.21 = 332 SB to Trebatius, for example, records a consultation on a point of law, for which there must have been many occasions among members of the upper class. But they are scarcely represented in the letters.

46. In 44, for example: "laudas me quod nihil ante de profectione constituam quam ista quo evasura sint videro," *Att.* 14.19.6 = 372 SB; "quod me mones ut pedetemptim, adsentior," 16.14.2 = 425 SB. Atticus practiced a related advisory stance which he described as "holding back" on judgment (ἐποχή, *Att.* 6.6.3 = 121 SB, 6.9.3 = 123 SB, 15.21.2 = 398 SB). Andrew Dyck points out to me that the term was a watchword of Academic philosophy, which suggests in turn that it was meant to commend Atticus's temporizing as a principled rather than a merely expedient course of action.

47. The governor was Gabinius, whose *maiestas* trial is documented in Alexander (1990, 145, no. 296).

48. Cicero was equally noncommittal in dispensing advice on less portentous matters at *Fam.* 1.9.25 = 20 SB (to Lentulus again), 15.14.4 = 106 SB (to Cassius), and *Att.* 16.13.4 = 423 SB (to Atticus).

49. The professionalization of advice giving makes it difficult to find modern studies of the phenomenon that can shed light on the Roman situation. Most social studies research that I have seen focuses on advice given by accredited figures such as health care professionals or academic advisers (no doubt because such environments make survey situations relatively easy to control, and significant statistics easier to obtain). Advice exchanged less formally between nonexperts, which would be the best parallel for the Roman situation, seems to have been little studied. Goldsmith (2004, 52–79), however, has studied informal advice giving.

CHAPTER 6

1. For evidence regarding books no longer extant, see appendix 1.

2. The following discussion assumes that readers recall or can learn the timeline of the sixteen months with which this chapter is concerned, notwithstanding its

intricacy (a well-annotated Goldilocks survey, with neither too much nor too little detail, is Holmes 1928, 1: 1–71). Only those points that bear most closely on the present argument will be accorded footnotes here.

3. Good snapshots of the Senate after Caesar's death are provided by Syme (1939, 162–75), Mitchell (1991, 308–10), and Gotter (1996, 155–72).

4. *Phil.* 5.32, compare 13.38–39, 42, 46–47, *MBrut.* 4(2.4).5 = 4 SB.

5. *Gubernacula rei publicae, MBrut.* 1(2.1).2 = 1 SB; *principatus, Phil.* 14.17–18; *princeps, Fam.* 12.24.2 = 361 SB, *Phil.* 4.16, and 14.20; *dux, MBrut.* 8(1.2a).3 = 6 SB; *auctor, Phil.* 4.16.

6. Brutus observed that in the struggle against Antony, the Senate and the Roman People wanted Cicero's *auctoritas* "to be the very greatest that any one man can have in a free republic," *MBrut.* 12(1.4a).2 = 11 SB, while Antony described Cicero as the *dux* and *lanista* orchestrating the clash of forces at Mutina, *Phil.* 13.30 and 40.

7. In Latin, the distinction is between *litterae publicae* or *publice scriptae*, written to the Senate by a commander in the field or vice versa (e.g., *Fam.* 10.7.1 = 372 SB, 10.12.2 = 377 SB, 15.1.1 = 104 SB, 15.3.2 = 103 SB, *Att.* 5.20.7 and 9 = 113 SB, 6.1.9 = 115 SB) and *litterae privatae*, which is how Cicero labels his correspondence with Marcus Brutus at *Fam.* 11.25.2 = 420 SB. He draws the distinction between public and private correspondence very clearly at *Fam.* 15.9.3 = 101 SB. Appian similarly distinguishes between official directives and the private communications that Decimus Brutus was receiving from individual senators at *BC* 3.27.103. To ascribe a "halb-amtlicher Charakter" (Gotter 1996, 145) to either side of Cicero's wartime correspondence obscures the terms on which the parties engaged each other.

8. The few official letters that are extant from this period evidently survived as enclosures in letters to Cicero: letters to the Senate from Lentulus (*Fam.* 12.15 = 406 SB), Lepidus (*Fam.* 10.35 = 408 SB), Plancus (*Fam.* 10.8 = 371 SB), and Decimus Brutus and Plancus (*Fam.* 11.13a = 418 SB). But there are allusions to many more: from Gaius Antonius (*MBrut.* 5[2.5].1 and 3 = 5 SB), Decimus Brutus (*Fam.* 11.4.2 = 342 SB, 11.19.1 = 399 SB, 11.26.1 = 410 SB, App. *BC* 3.81.333), Marcus Brutus (Cass. Dio 47.22.1, *Phil.* 10.1, 13, 24–26, *MBrut.* 5[2.5].1–3 = 5 SB, Cassius (Cass. Dio 47.28.5, Cic. *Fam.* 12.12.1 = 387 SB, *MBrut.* 3[2.3].3 = 2 SB), Cornificius (*Fam.* 12.25.1 = 373 SB), Dolabella (*MBrut.* 5[2.5].3 = 5 SB), Hirtius (Cic. *Phil.* 8.6, 14.22), Lepidus (Cass. Dio 46.51.1, Cic. *Fam.* 10.6.1 = 370 SB, 10.16.1 = 404 SB, *MBrut.* 20[1.12].1 = 21 SB), Octavian (Cic. *Phil.* 14.22, App. *BC* 3.73.301), Pansa (Cic. *Phil.* 14.22, App. *BC* 3.73.301), Plancus (*Fam.* 10.16.1 = 404 SB), and Pollio (*Fam.* 10.31.6 = 368 SB, evidently the same as 10.33.3 = 409 SB). Official letters from the Senate are mentioned at App. *BC* 3.86.354, Cass. Dio 46.50.3- 5, 46.51.4–5, Cic. *Fam.* 10.31.4 = 368 SB. Cicero assumes that senatorial decrees will have been communicated to his correspondents at *Fam.* 10.13.1 = 389 SB, 10.16.1 = 404 SB, 10.22 = 423 SB, 12.28.2 = 374 SB, 12.29.2 = 433 SB, 12.30.7 = 417 SB, *MBrut.* 18(1.10).1 = 17 SB.

9. For example, Decimus Brutus was also in communication with Octavian (*Fam.* 11.10.4 = 385 SB, Cass. Dio 45.15.1) and with Plancus (*Fam.* 10.20.2 = 407 SB, 11.11.1 = 386 SB, 11.14.3 = 413 SB); Marcus Brutus in communication with Trebonius and Tillius Cimber (App. *BC* 3.6.18), with Cassius (Plut. *Brutus* 28.3), and with Octavian (Cass. Dio 47.22.2); Cassius in communication with Octavian (Cass. Dio. 47.28.5) as well as with Trebonius, Tillius Cimber, and Marcus Brutus (above);

Plancus in communication with Lepidus (*Fam.* 10.11.3 = 382, 10.15 = 390 SB, 10.21.1 = 391 SB, 10.18.2 = 395 SB, 10.17.1 = 398 SB), with Octavian (*Fam.* 10.24.4 = 428 SB), and with Antony (*Phil.* 13.44, *Fam.* 11.11.1 = 386 SB), in addition to Decimus Brutus (above); Pollio in communication with Antony (*Fam.* 10.32.4 = 415 SB), with Lepidus (*Fam.* 10.32.4 = 415 SB, 10.33.2 = 409 SB), and with Octavian (*Fam.* 10.33.3 = 409 SB, App. *BC* 3.81.330).

10. For readers who desire a complete and in-depth treatment of the wartime letters, the best available resources are Shackleton Bailey's commented editions: vol. 2 of the *Ad Familiares* (1977), vol. 6 of *Cicero's Letters to Atticus* (1967), and *Cicero: Epistulae ad Quintum Fratrem et M. Brutum* (1980).

11. As Cicero wrote later to Trebonius, "ad illum animum meum reverti pristinum" (*Fam.* 10.28.1 = 364 SB) only after Antony's departure from Rome in late November.

12. Cicero was still revising on about November 5th, when he makes his last mention of the speech to Atticus, a week before the *Letters to Atticus* come to an end (*Att.* 16.11 = 419 SB), and at that time he was still anxious to keep it out of general circulation.

13. Evidence for Decimus's career is assembled by Münzer (1931).

14. Cicero, who after the assassination expressed doubt about Decimus's fortitude (*Att.* 15.4.1 = 381 SB), later told Marcus Brutus that Decimus never stirred until Octavian came out in arms against Antony (*MBrut.* 23[1.15].7 = 23 SB). Decimus's campaigns in the Alps, which won him the title of "Imperator" that both men inscribe in letter headings, are attested in *Fam.* 11.4 = 342 SB.

15. *Att.* 16.9 = 419 SB, 16.11.6 = 420 SB, 16.15.3 = 426 SB, *Fam.* 11.6a.2 = 356 SB.

16. The place of this letter in the sequence of events from December 44 to January 43 is well explained by Sternkopf (1901).

17. According to *Fam.* 11.5.1 = 353 SB, that letter was preceded by one from Decimus, and *Fam.* 11.7 = 354 SB followed a meeting arranged by Decimus's emissary Lupus. *Fam.* 11.5.1 = 353 SB shows that Decimus was consulting at the same time with the incoming consul Pansa, and according to Cass. Dio 45.15.1, he was being encouraged by Octavian as well.

18. Most extravagantly in *Fam.* 11.5 = 353 SB and 11.7 = 354 SB, but also in 11.6a = 356 SB and 11.8.1 = 360 SB. It occurs for the last time in *Fam.* 11.12 = 394 SB. Decimus himself never harks back to his role in the assassination, apart from the oblique phrase "cum ad rem publicam liberandam accessi" at *Fam.* 11.10.5 = 385 SB—if indeed those words refer to the plot against Caesar rather than to the decision to resist Antony.

19. The meaning and motivational force of *dignitas* in this phase of the civil wars is well explored by Raaflaub (1974).

20. It is a tantalizing question how the Senate came to meet on December 20th, after Cicero had been saying for weeks that it would not act before January 1st. Who authorized the meeting (the new tribunes ostensibly, but surely not acting alone), whether it was deliberately coordinated with the arrival of Decimus's edict, and what part if any Cicero played in orchestrating events are questions answerable only in the realm of speculation.

21. Cicero's praise of Decimus takes up *Phil.* 3.8–12 and 4.8–9. The decrees are moved at *Phil.* 3.37–38, and *Phil.* 5.28 proves that they carried.

22. *Phil.* 5.24, 26, 28, 35–57, 6.6–9.

23. Whether Decimus accomplished anything at the second Battle of Mutina depends upon the interpretation of *eruptio* at Cic. *MBrut.* 11(1.4).1 = 10 SB and *Fam.* 11.14.1 = 413 SB. For an argument that it refers to a successful sortie by Decimus, see Shackleton Bailey's commentary on the former passage. But the word can also used more loosely; see Shackleton Bailey on Cic. *Fam.* 12.18.1 = 205 SB. The thanksgiving in honor of Decimus is mentioned at Cic. *Fam.* 11.18.3 = 397 SB, Cass. Dio 46.40.1, and App. *BC* 3.74.302. The triumph is attested by Cass. Dio 46.40.2, Vell. Pat. 2.62.4, and Livy *per.* 119.

24. Cic. *MBrut.* 23(1.15).8 = 23 SB, *Fam.* 11.14.3 = 413 SB.

25. An equivalent distinction between *honos verborum* and *praemium virtutis* is made at *Fam.* 10.13.1 = 389 SB, cf. *MBrut.* 23(1.15).7 = 23 SB.

26. *Phil.* 14.11 (a passage which incidentally comments on the problem of inflation) and 37, App. *BC* 3.74.302.

27. The text is as emended by Shackleton Bailey, but Decimus's sense of grievance is not in doubt.

28. App. *BC* 2.143.597, Cass. Dio 44.14.3–4, Cic. *Phil.* 10.15.

29. At *Phil.* 6.9, Cicero characterizes Decimus's move as a sort of self-sacrifice: "quid egit aliud nisi ut paene corpore suo Gallia prohiberet Antonium?" Plancus later opined that Decimus erred in letting himself be rushed into confronting Antony before he was ready (Cic. *Fam.* 10.8.4 = 371 SB).

30. Cass. Dio 46.40.1, App. *BC* 3.74.302, Livy *per.* 120. That this mandate happens not to be documented in the correspondence between Cicero and Decimus is one more indication that their exchange is private rather than official.

31. Although Cicero seems to have expected Decimus to carry the pursuit of Antony into Gaul if need be, it is not clear that Decimus ever held that view of his responsibility. Decimus writes as though his aim was to crush Antony in Italy if he could, but only to prevent him from later returning to Italy if he succeeded in crossing into Gaul (*Fam.* 11.9.2 = 380 SB, 11.20.4 = 401 SB, 11.23.2 = 402 SB). That was also the understanding of Plancus, who was in regular communication with Decimus during these weeks (*Fam.* 10.15.4 = 390 SB). (Cassius Dio 46.50.1, on what authority it is not known, contends that Decimus did not attack Antony because he wanted to ensure that Octavian faced a viable rival.) That Decimus eventually did cross into Gaul and join Plancus in June was not a move already envisioned in April.

32. As often, the criticism that Cicero here ascribes to "some people" corresponded precisely to his own sentiments, as is clear from his words to Marcus Brutus at *MBrut.* 18(1.10).2 = 17 SB.

33. *Fam.* 11.10.5 = 385 SB, 11.14.2 = 413 SB, 11.20.1 and 3 = 401 SB. Decimus also sought Cicero's help on behalf of civilian clients; see *Fam.* 11.19.2 = 399 SB.

34. Andrew Dyck points out to me that Cicero's stylization of himself as a *dux* is another evocation of his role in the struggle against Catiline twenty years earlier (*Cat.* 2.28). Apropos of tense usage in this letter, Shackleton Bailey comments that "the imperfects are epistolary throughout," which may be correct. But I am not sure that the constant shift in this passage between past and present does not hint that the former high opinion of Decimus no longer holds.

35. *Fam.* 11.24 = 412 SB, 11.25 = 420 SB, 11.15 = 422 SB.

36. In June, however, when Decimus took his army across the Alps to join Plancus in northern Gaul, he regained credit with Cicero to the extent of being treated as part of a new united front.

37. Just to be on the safe side, Cicero did spell out this part of his point for Decimus earlier in the letter, in sec. 1.

38. *Fam.* 10.13.2 = 389 SB, reiterated at 10.19.2 = 393 SB and 10.20.3 = 407 SB. Still earlier, Cicero had told Plancus, "spes omnis est in te" (*Fam.* 10.14.1 = 384 SB), and when Decimus was still under siege, Cicero was anticipating the possibility that Plancus might assume "huius belli principatum" (*Phil.* 13.44).

39. The evidence for Plancus's career is assembled by Hanslik (1933) and in *PIR*² M 728. Plancus is also the subject of a (sympathetic) recent monograph by Watkins (1997).

40. With one exception, however, the only source attesting Cicero's early relationship with Plancus is the correspondence they exchanged in the 40s. The exception is a note in Jerome's adaptation of Eusebius's chronicle, under the year 25 B.C., "Munatius Plancus Ciceronis discipulus orator habetur insignis," p. 164 h Helm.

41. *Fam.* 13.29 = 282 SB, *Att.* 12.52.1 = 294 SB. It is uncertain whether the Plancus whose help Cicero solicits in *Att.* 16.16A = 407A SB is Munatius or Plotius.

42. The absence of any allusion to military action on the part of Octavian, Antony, or Decimus led Ruete (1883, 33), followed by Walser (1957, 57), to date this letter to late September or early October, which I find more plausible than Shackleton Bailey's dating of it to mid-December, when a confrontation was already under way. The December date is based on Plancus's comment (at *Fam.* 10.4.1 = 358 SB) that Cicero wrote *Fam.* 10.3 = 355 SB after returning from a trip, in combination with another passage (*Fam.* 11.5.1 = 353 SB) in which Cicero mentions coming to Rome on December 9th. But Plancus may be referring to an earlier occasion than is Cicero.

43. In addition to the present letter, *Fam.* 10.1.3 = 340 SB, 10.2.1 = 341 SB, 10.5.1 = 359 SB, 10.6.2 = 370 SB, 10.10.2 = 375 SB, 10.12.5 = 377 SB, 13.29.1 and 5 = 282 SB. Plancus also advertises the closeness of their tie at *Fam.* 10.4.2 = 358 SB and 10.11.1 = 382 SB.

44. The first hint that Plancus's army might be relevant occurs later, in *Fam.* 10.5.3 = 359 SB, written probably in December: "magna spes in te et in tuo exercitu, magna exspectatio." The reference to Plancus's military prowess in *Fam.* 10.3.1 = 355 SB has to do with campaigns that he (like Decimus) was conducting in this period against natives, not with the prospect of a civil war.

45. The focus of *Fam.* 10.3 = 355 SB thus remains the same as in the first letter to Plancus in the series, *Fam.* 10.1 = 340 SB, in which Cicero emphasizes the "exspectatio consulatus tui."

46. *Att.* 15.5.1 = 383 SB, apropos of Hirtius; for the language, compare *Att.* 14.21.4 = 375 SB and 15.6.1 = 386 SB. Other attempts at political reeducation during this period include Cicero's letters to Dolabella (*Att.* 14.17A = 371A SB) and Matius (*Fam.* 11.27 = 348 SB).

47. Cass. Dio 46.29.6, 46.50.2, [Cic.] *Fam.* 10.33.1 = 409 SB (by Pollio); Cicero implies at *Phil.* 13.16 and 44 that Plancus is on the way. Again, the Senate's summons to Plancus formed part of an official correspondence, and so it is not documented in the personal exchange between him and Cicero.

48. All the more disquieting if Plancus's remarks formed the substance of his reply to the summons from the Senate, as seems chronologically likely. Lepidus wrote in a similar vein to the Senate at roughly the same time (Cic. *Fam.* 10.6.1 = 370 SB, *Phil.* 13).

49. Cicero refers to Antony's boast at *Phil.* 13.43. Decimus raised warnings in *Fam.* 11.9.2 = 380 SB and 11.11.1 = 386 SB, and still later, Pollio reminded Cicero of the friendship between Antony and Plancus (*Fam.* 10.33.2 = 409 SB). Appian at *BC* 3.72.297 also has Antony voice confidence that Plancus will join him (compare also *BC* 3.46.190).

50. Plancus says that he crossed the Rhone on April 26th (*Fam.* 10.9.3 = 379 SB), and as of May 18th he was no farther south than the Isara (*Fam.* 10.18.4 = 395 SB).

51. The distance figure is taken from Shackleton Bailey's commentary on *Fam.* 10.18 = 395 SB. That Cicero did not consider Lepidus himself a likely ally against Antony is indicated by the absence of a sustained exchange of letters between him and Lepidus; book 10 of the *Letters to Friends* contains only one to him from Cicero (*Fam.* 10.27 = 369 SB) and two to Cicero from him (*Fam.* 10.34 and 34a = 396 and 400 SB). In Cicero's eyes, Lepidus had probably disqualified himself as a good-faith partner when the force he sent to Mutina at the Senate's bidding fought on Antony's side (Cass. Dio 46.38.6–7, [Cic.] *Fam.* 10.30.1 = 378 SB).

52. *Fam.* 10.12 = 377 SB and *M Brut.* 2(2.2).3 = 3 SB. Cicero describes a three-day argument over the resolution honoring Plancus, which was blocked by a tribunician veto. Historians and commentators surmise that Cicero overcame the veto, but he stops short of saying that. He does not mention a *senatusconsultum* (as he does later at *Fam.* 10.13 = 389 SB), and Plancus in *Fam.* 10.11.1 = 382 SB appears to be thanking him for the effort rather than the result.

53. The dates are as given according to the manuscripts in Plancus's own letters at *Fam.* 10.9.3 = 379 SB, 10.11.2 = 382 SB, 10.15.3 = 390 SB, 10.18.4 = 395 SB, and 10.23.2–3 = 414 SB, except that Shackleton Bailey follows Sternkopf (1910, 256–57) in emending May 12th at *Fam.* 10.15.3 = 390 SB to May 9th or thereabouts.

54. Sternkopf (1910) 297–98 commented aptly, "Was Plancus betrifft, so liegt seine Tatenscheu, sein Mangel an Initiative… seine schwankende Unentschlossenheit, seine zaudernde Ängstlichkeit am Tage. Seine Briefe verdecken dies nicht…. Aber er hat, wie manche seinesgleichen, die Gewohnheit und die Fähigkeit, für die Notwendigkeit dessen, was er getan oder vielmehr unterlassen hat, nachmals in seinen Relationen die trefflichsten Gründe anzuführen."

55. "verborum sententiarumque gravitas" *Fam.* 10.12.1 = 377 SB and 10.19.1 = 393 SB, "gravissimis verbis ac sententiis" 10.16.1 = 404 SB.

56. "in rem publicam omni cogitatione curaque incumberes," *Fam.* 10.2.2 = 340 SB, "incumbe, per deos immortalis in eam curam et cogitationem quae tibi summam dignitatem et gloriam adferat," 10.3.3 = 355 SB, "hortor… ut tota mente omnique animi impetus in rem publicam incumbas," 10.5.2 = 359 SB, "incumbe toto pectore ad laudem, subveni patriae," 10.10.2 = 375 SB, "in illam… curam incumbe," 10.14.2 = 384 SB, "incumbe ut belli extremi perficias," 10.19.2 = 393 SB. Elsewhere in letters of this period only once in a letter to Cornificius, *Fam.* 12.24.1 = 361 SB. For *levitas* as an attribute of the disloyal, compare "scelus… summamque levitatem et inconstantiam" *Fam.* 12.8.1 = 416 SB, "scelere et levitate" *Fam.* 12.10.1 = 425 SB, "levitatem et

inconstantiam animumque semper inimicum rei publicae" *MBrut.* 2(2.2).1 = 3 SB, "levissimus homo" *MBrut.* 23(1.15).9 = 23 SB, all in reference to Lepidus.

57. *Phil.* 13.39, *MBrut.* 4(2.4).5 = 4 SB, *Fam.* 12.5.3 = 365 SB. Cicero was responding to Antony's claim that the war against him was no more than a recrudescence of the old conflict between Pompeians and Caesarians (*Phil.* 5.32, 13.26).

58. "Ad omnia pro vobis…paratos," *Fam.* 11.13a.5 = 418 SB. Though this dispatch boasts of the speed with which Decimus crossed the Alps, he does not appear to have been any more rapid in his movements than Plancus. He was already expected in Gaul as of May 18th (*Fam.* 10.18.2 = 395 SB), yet he did not actually arrive before about June 9th (*Fam.* 10.23.3 = 414 SB).

59. The call for reinforcements, first raised by Plancus in mid-May (*Fam.* 10.21.6 = 391 SB), was then often repeated by both Plancus and Decimus (*Fam.* 11.26.1 = 410 SB, 11.14.2 = 413 SB, 10.23.6 = 414 SB, 11.13a.5 = 418 SB, 10.24.4 = 428 SB).

60. Cic. *Fam.* 11.14.3 = 413 SB, App. *BC* 3.85.351, Cass. Dio 46.51.5.

61. After Cassius sailed from Italy in August of 44, he was simply out of touch for most of the time. He was leery of providing information in any case because his efforts to raise money and troops were illegal, and he was operating in the Levant, from which letters could take longer than two months to reach Rome. From his departure through May of 43, the collection comprises only two letters from him, with the consequence that Cicero's letters to Cassius often declare that he does not know where Cassius is or what he is doing. Marcus Brutus, on the other hand, who was operating just across the Adriatic, was able to maintain more regular contact with Cicero. The problem in this case is that most of his exchange with Cicero has perished; no letters of the *MBrut.* are extant before April of 43.

62. See *Fam.* 15.14.6 = 106 SB and 15.18.22 = 213 SB.

63. The formation of the tie with Brutus is attested by letters Cicero wrote during his Cilician proconsulate in books 5 and 6 of the Atticus correspondence. Cicero later made Brutus the honorand of the dialogue named for him, the *Orator*, the Stoic *Paradoxes*, the *Tusculan Disputations*, the *De Finibus*, and the *De Natura Deorum*.

64. Cicero's hopes are expressed in *Fam.* 12.2.3 = 344 SB and 12.3.2 = 345 SB to Cassius—again, no letters of the *MBrut.* are extant before April of 43.

65. *MBrut.* 5(2.5).5 = 5 SB, 7(1.2).2 = 14 SB, 8(1.2a).2 = 6 SB, 9(1.3).3 = 7 SB, and 10(1.3a) = 8 SB. Cicero's persistence has at least the excuse that Brutus had invited him to say what he thought should be done with Gaius, *MBrut.* 3(2.3).2 = 2 SB. Months later, Brutus did have Gaius killed in retaliation for the killing of Cicero (Plut. *Brut.* 28.1, cf. Cass. Dio 47.24.4).

66. *Fam.* 12.6.2 = 376 SB, 12.8.1 = 416 SB, *MBrut.* 13(1.5).2 = 9 SB.

67. *MBrut.* 13(1.5).1 = 9 SB, 7(1.2) = 14 SB.

68. *MBrut.* 18(1.10).4 = 17 SB, 20(1.12).2 = 21 SB, 22(1.14).2 = 22 SB, 26(1.18).2 = 24 SB.

69. *MBrut.* 18(1.10).4 = 17 SB, 22(1.14).2 = 22 SB, 23(1.15).12 = 23 SB.

70. *MBrut.* 20(1.12).2 = 21 SB, 22(1.14).2 = 22 SB, 23(1.15).12 = 23 SB; Cicero puts the same argument to Cassius, *Fam.* 12.10.2–3 = 425 SB.

71. Decimus: *Fam.* 11.4 = 342 SB, 11.10.4–5 = 385 SB, 11.14.2 = 413 SB, 11.20.3 = 401 SB, 11.21.5 = 411 SB, 11.24.2 = 412 SB, 11.26 = 410 SB; Plancus: *Fam.* 10.2 = 341

SB, 10.7.2 = 372 SB, 10.9.2 = 379 SB, 10.10.1 = 375 SB, 10.12.3 = 377 SB, 10.13.1 = 389 SB, 10.16.1 = 404 SB, 10.21.6 = 391 SB, 10. 21a = 392 SB, 10.22.1 = 423 SB, 10.23.6 = 414 SB, 10.24.2 = 428 SB; Cassius: *Fam.* 12.7.1 = 367 SB, 12.10.2 = 425 SB, 12.12 = 387 SB; Brutus: *MBrut.* 3(2.3).5 = 2 SB, 4(2.4).4 = 4 SB, 13(1.5).1 = 9 SB, 14(1.6).4 = 12 SB, 21(1.13) = 20 SB, 23(1.15).13 = 23 SB; Cornificius: *Fam.* 12.30.4 and 6 = 417 SB.

72. A Roman model of which would be the correspondence between Pliny the governor of Bithynia and the Emperor Trajan in book 10 of Pliny's *Letters*.

73. The best example of such a pair is *Fam.* 12.14–15 = 405–406 SB. But those two letters, by Lentulus junior, are from the eastern theater of operations rather than from the west.

74. It was a further advantage that Cicero's correspondence with Cassius, Plancus, Cornificius, and both Brutuses was already well under way before he decided to claim a leading role in the struggle with Antony.

75. *Phil.* 12.9, 13.22, *Fam.* 10.12.2 = 377 SB, *MBrut.* 2(2.2).3 = 3 SB.

76. Hence, to judge by indications in the letters, Cicero did not send copies of his speeches to Decimus or to any of his other wartime correspondents except Marcus Brutus, a fellow connoisseur of oratory.

77. See Oppermann (2000), who provides a table of *exempla* in the letters on pages 317–24. It shows that Cicero cites four *exempla* in letters to Marcus Brutus (three of them in one letter), one in a letter to Plancus, and none with other wartime correspondents except for Atticus.

78. MacMullen (1990, 21–22). MacMullen (2003) returns to this theme, but the range of motivation discussed here is more narrowly conceived as "feelings," and the argument is more expressly cast as a protest against historiography in the mode of Ronald Syme.

AFTERWORD

1. For example, "rei publicae statum…elapsum scito esse de manibus," *Att.* 1.16.6 = 16 SB, in July of 61; "de re publica quid ego tibi subtiliter? tota periit," *Att.* 2.21.1 = 41 SB, in mid-59; "circumspice omnia membra rei publicae…nullum reperies profecto quod non fractum debilitatumve sit," *Fam.* 5.13.3 = 201 SB, in mid-46; "fuit meum quidem iam pridem rem publicam lugere," *Att.* 12.28.2 = 267 SB, in March of 45.

Bibliography

Adams, James N. 1978. Conventions of Naming in Cicero. *Classical Quarterly* 28: 145–66.

———. 2003. *Bilingualism and the Latin Language.* Cambridge: Cambridge University Press.

Alexander, Michael C. 1990. *Trials in the Late Roman Republic, 149 BC to 50 BC.* Phoenix Supplementary Vol. 26. Toronto: University of Toronto Press.

Astin, Alan E. 1978. *Cato the Censor.* Oxford: Oxford University Press.

Babl, Johann. 1893. De epistularum Latinarum formulis. Bamberg: Königliches Alte Gymnasium Programm.

Bailey, David Roy Shackleton. 1962. Two Tribunes, 59 B.C. *Classical Review* 12: 195–97.

———. 1965–70. *Cicero's Letters to Atticus.* Cambridge Classical Texts and Commentaries 3–9. Cambridge: Cambridge University Press.

———. 1977. *Cicero: Epistulae ad Familiares.* Cambridge Classical Texts and Commentaries 16–17. Cambridge: Cambridge University Press.

———. 1980. *Cicero: Epistulae ad Quintum Fratrem et M. Brutum.* Cambridge Classical Texts and Commentaries 22. Cambridge: Cambridge University Press.

———. 1987. *M. Tullius Cicero: Epistulae ad Atticum.* Stuttgart: B. G. Teubner.

———. 1988a. *M. Tullius Cicero: Epistulae ad Familiares.* Stuttgart: B. G. Teubner.

———. 1988b. *M. Tullius Cicero: Epistulae ad Quintum Fratrem, Epistulae ad M. Brutum.* Stuttgart: B. G. Teubner.

———. 1995. *Onomasticon to Cicero's Letters.* Stuttgart: B. G. Teubner.

Balsdon, John P. V. D. 1950. Review of *Les secrets de la correspondance de Cicéron,* by J. Carcopino. *Journal of Roman Studies* 40: 134–35.

———. 1952. Review of *Cicero: The Secrets of His Correspondence,* by J. Carcopino. *Classical Review* 2: 178–81.

Bardt, Karl. 1866. Quaestiones Tullianae. Diss., Frederick William University. Berlin: G. Schale.

————. 1897. Zur Provenienz von Ciceros Briefen ad Familiares. *Hermes* 32: 264–72.

Beard, Mary. 2002. Ciceronian Correspondences: Making a Book Out of Letters. In *Classics in Progress: Essays on Ancient Greece and Rome*, ed. Timothy P. Wiseman, pp. 104–44. Oxford: Oxford University Press.

Bergmann, Jörg R. 1993. *Discreet Indiscretions: The Social Organization of Gossip.* Translated by John Bednarz. New York: Aldine de Gruyter.

Boissier, Gaston. 1863. *Recherches sur la manière dont furent recueillies et publiées les lettres de Cicéron.* Paris: Librairie d'Auguste Durand.

Brown, Penelope, and Stephen C. Levinson. 1987. *Politeness: Some Universals in Language Usage.* Cambridge: Cambridge University Press.

Büchner, Karl. 1939. M. Tullius Cicero (Tullius 29). In *Paulys Realencyclopädie* 7A: 827–1274.

Butler, Shane. 2002. *The Hand of Cicero.* London: Routledge.

Caffi, Claudia. 1986. Writing Letters. In *Pragmatics and Linguistics: Festschrift for Jacob L. Mey on his 60th Birthday 30th October 1986*, ed. Jørgen D. Johansen and Harly Sonne, pp. 49–57. Odense: Odense University Press.

Capasso, Mario. 1995. *Volumen: Aspetti della tipologia del rotolo librario antico.* Cultura 3. Naples: Procaccini.

Carcopino, Jérôme. 1947. *Les secrets de la correspondance de Cicéron.* Paris: L'Artisan du livre = 1951. *Cicero: The Secrets of His Correspondence.* Translated by Emily O. Lorimer. London: Routledge and Kegan Paul.

Chartier, Roger. 1997. Introduction: An Ordinary Kind of Writing: Model Letters and Letter-Writing in Ancien Régime France. In *Correspondence: Models of Letter-Writing from the Middle Ages to the Nineteenth Century*, ed. Roger Chartier et al., trans. Christopher Woodall, pp. 1–23. Princeton, N.J.: Princeton University Press.

Constans, Léopold A., Jean Bayet, and Jean Beaujeu. 1969–96. *Cicéron: Correspondance.* Paris: Société d'Édition Les Belles Lettres.

Corbeill, Anthony. 1996. *Controlling Laughter: Political Humor in the Late Republic.* Princeton, N.J.: Princeton University Press.

Corbinelli, Silvia. 2008. Amicorum colloquia absentium: *La scrittura epistolare a Rome tra comunicazione quotidiana e genere letterario.* Naples: M. D'Auria.

Cotton, Hannah M. 1985. Mirificum genus commendationis: Cicero and the Latin Letter of Recommendation. *American Journal of Philology* 106: 328–34.

————. 1986. The Role of Cicero's Letters of Recommendation: Iustitia versus Gratia? *Hermes* 114: 443–60.

Crook, John. 1955. *Consilium Principis: Imperial Councils and Counsellors from Augustus to Diocletian.* Cambridge: Cambridge University Press.

Cugusi, Paolo. 1979. *Epistolographi Latini Minores.* Vol. 2: *Aetatem Ciceronianam et Augusteam Amplectens.* Turin: G. B. Paravia.

————. 1983. *Evoluzione e forme dell' epistolografia latina nella tarda Repubblica e nei primi due secoli dell' Impero.* Rome: Herder.

————. 1989. L'epistolografia: modelli e etiologie di comunicazione. In *Lo Spazio Letterario di Roma Antica*, ed. Guglielmo Cavallo, Paolo Fedeli, and Andrea Giardini, Vol. 2, pp. 379–419. Rome: Salerno.

————. 1992–2002. *Corpus Epistularum Latinarum Papyris, Tabulis, Ostracis Servatarum.* Florence: Edizioni Gonnelli.

———. 1998. L'epistola Ciceroniana: strumento di comunicazione quotidiana e modello letterario. *Ciceroniana* 10: 163–89.

Damon, Cynthia. 2008. Enabling Books. *New England Classical Journal* 35: 175–84.

De Caro, Antonio. 2006. 'Ut Ulixes' (*fam.* 1.10): La ricezione dell' 'Odissea' nelle lettere di Cicerone. *Paideia* 61: 125–52.

Deissmann, Gustav Adolf. 1895. *Bibelstudien: Beiträge zumeist aus den Papyri und Inschriften zur Geschichte der Sprache, des Schrifttums, und der Religion des hellenistichen Judentums und des Urchristentums*. Marburg: N. G. Elwert.

———. 1923. *Licht vom Osten: Das Neue Testament und die neuentdeckten Texte der hellenistisch-römischen Welt*, 4th ed. Tübingen: J. C. B. Mohr.

Demmel, Meinolf. 1962. *Cicero und Paetus (ad fam. IX 15–26)*. Diss., Cologne University.

Déniaux, Élisabeth. 1993. *Clientèles et pouvoir à l'époque de Cicéron*. Rome: École Française de Rome.

Dingwall, Silvia. 1992. Leaving Telephone Answering Machine Messages: Who's Afraid of Speaking to Machines? *Text* 12: 81–101.

Duchene, Roger. 1995. Lettre et conversation. In *Art de la lettre, art de la conversation à l'époque classique en France*, ed. Bernard Bray and Christoph Strosetzki, pp. 93–102. Paris: Klincksieck.

Dyck, Andrew R. 2008. *Cicero: Catilinarians*. Cambridge: Cambridge University Press.

Dziatzko, Karl. 1899. Brief. In *Paulys Realencyclopädie* 3: 836–43.

Eagleton, Terry. 1983. *Literary Theory: An Introduction*. Minneapolis: University of Minneapolis Press.

Eco, Umberto. 1976. *A Theory of Semiotics*. Bloomington: Indiana University Press.

———. 1979. *The Role of the Reader: Explorations in the Semiotics of Text*. Bloomington: Indiana University Press.

Ermert, Karl. 1979. *Briefsorten: Untersuchungen zu Theorie und Empirie der Textklassifikation*. Tübingen: Max Niemeyer Verlag.

Gallazzi, Claudio. 1997. Cinque campagne di scavo a Tebtyni. *Rivista Ca' de Sass* 138: 50–57

Gavoille, Laurent. 1998. 'Epistula' et 'litterae': Étude de synonomie. *Epistulae Antiquae* 1: 13–36.

Goldberg, Sander M. 2005. *Constructing Literature in the Roman Republic: Poetry and Its Reception*. Cambridge: Cambridge University Press.

Goldsmith, Daena J. 2004. *Communicating Social Support*. Cambridge: Cambridge University Press.

Goldsmith, Daena J., and Kristine Fitch. 1997. The Normative Context of Advice as Social Support. *Human Communications Research* 23: 454–76.

Gotter, Ulrich. 1996. *Der Diktator Ist Tot: Politik in Rom zwischen den Iden des März und der Begründung des Zweiten Triumvirats*. Historia Einzelschriften 110.

Griffin, Miriam. 1995. Philosophical Badinage in Cicero's Letters to his Friends. In *Cicero the Philosopher: Twelve Papers*, ed. Jonathan Powell, pp. 325–46. New York: Oxford University Press.

———. 1997. From Aristotle to Atticus: Cicero and Matius on Friendship. In *Philosophia Togata II: Plato and Aristotle at Rome*, ed. Jonathan Barnes and Miriam Griffin, pp. 86–109. New York: Oxford University Press.

Guillory, John. 1993. *Cultural Capital: The Problem of Literary Canon Formation*.
    Chicago: University of Chicago Press.
Gurlitt, Ludwig. 1879. *De M. Tulli Ciceronis epistulis earumque pristina collectione*.
    Diss., Georg-August University. Göttingen: H. Gerlach.
———. 1901. Die Entstehung der Ciceronischen Briefsammlungen. *Neue Jahrbücher*
    für das classische Altertum 7: 532–58.
———. 1903. Über das Fehlen der Briefdaten in den Ciceronischen
    Korrespondenzen. In *Festschrift zu Otto Hirschfelds sechzigstem Geburtstage*,
    pp. 16–29. Berlin: Weidmann.
Habinek, Thomas N. 1990. Towards a History of Friendly Advice: The Politics of
    Candor in Cicero's *De Amicitia*. *Apeiron* 23: 165–85.
Hall, Jon. 1996. Cicero *Fam.* 5.8 and *Fam.* 15.5 in the Light of Modern Politeness
    Theory. *Antichthon* 30: 19–33.
———. 1998. Cicero to Lucceius (*Fam.* 5.12) in Its Social Context: *Valde Bella?*
    Classical Philology 93: 308–21.
———. 2005. Politeness and Formality in Cicero's Letter to Matius (*Fam.* 11.27).
    Museum Helveticum 62: 193–213.
———. 2009. *Politeness and Politics in Cicero's Letters*. Oxford: Oxford University
    Press.
Halm, Karl. 1863. *Rhetores Latini Minores*. Leipzig: B. G. Teubner.
Hanslik, Rudolf. 1933. Munatius 30. In *Paulys Realencyclopädie* 16: 545–51.
Hartung, Wolfdietrich. 1983. Briefstrategien und Briefstrukturen, Oder: Warum
    Schreibt Man Briefe? In *Sprache und Pragmatik: Lunder Symposium 1982*, ed. Inger
    Rosengren, Lunder germanistisch Forschungen 52, pp. 215–28. Stockholm:
    Almqvist and Wiksell.
Helm, Rudolf. 1956. *Eusebius Werke*, Vol. 7: *Die Chronik des Hieronymus*. Berlin:
    Akademie Verlag.
Henderson, John. 2007. '…when who should walk into the room but…' : Epistoliterarity
    in Cicero *Ad Qfr*. 3.1. In *Ancient Letters: Classical and Late Antique Epistolography*, ed.
    Ruth Morello and A. D. Morrison, pp. 37–85. Oxford: Oxford University Press.
Holmes, Thomas Rice. 1928. *The Architect of the Roman Empire*. Oxford: Clarendon
    Press.
Horsfall, Nicholas. 1993. Cicero and Poetry: The Place of Prejudice in Literary History.
    In *Papers of the Leeds International Latin Seminar, Seventh Volume*. ARCA 32,
    pp. 1–7. Leeds: Francis Cairns.
Hutchinson, Gregory O. 1995. Rhythm, Style, and Meaning in Cicero's Prose. *Classical*
    Quarterly 45: 485–99.
———. 1998. *Cicero's Correspondence: A Literary Study*. Oxford: Oxford University
    Press.
———. 2007. Down among the Documents: Criticism and Papyrus Letters. In
    Ancient Letters: Classical and Late Antique Epistolography, ed. Ruth Morello and
    A. D. Morrison, pp. 17–36. Oxford: Oxford University Press.
Ioannatou, Marina. 2006. *Affaires d'argent dans la correspondance de Cicéron:*
    L'aristocratie face à ses dettes. Paris: De Boccard.
Jakobson, Roman. 1987. Linguistics and Poetics. In *Language in Literature*, ed. Krystyna
    Pomorska and Stephen Rudy, pp. 62–94. Cambridge, Mass.: Belknap.

Kaster, Robert A. 2005. *Emotion, Restraint, and Community in Ancient Rome*. Oxford: Oxford University Press.

Kerbrat-Orecchioni, Catherine. 1998. L'interaction épistolaire. In *La lettre entre réel et fiction*, ed. Jürgen Siess, pp. 15–36. Paris: Sedes.

————. 2000. Est-il bon, est-il méchant: Quelle représentation de l'homme-en-société dans les théories contemporaines de la politesse linguistique? In *Politesse et idéologie: Rencontres de pragmatique et de rhétorique conversationelles*, ed. Michel Wauthion and Anne Catherine Simon, pp. 21–35. Louvain-la-Neuve: Peeters.

Kirfel, Ernst-Alfred. 1969. *Untersuchungen zur Briefform der Heroides Ovids*. Noctes Romanae 11. Bern: Paul Haupt.

Klauck, Hans-Josef. 2006. *Ancient Letters and the New Testament: A Guide to Context and Exegesis*. Translated by Daniel P. Bailey. Waco, Tex.: Baylor University Press.

Koskenniemi, Heikki. 1954. Cicero über die Briefarten (genera epistularum). *Arctos* 1: 97–102.

————. 1956. *Studien zur Idee und Phraseologie des griechischen Briefes bis auf 400 n. Chr*. Annales Academiae Scientiarum Fennicae 102, 2.

Lalou, Élisabeth. 1992. *Les tablettes à écrire de l'antiquité à l'époque moderne*. Actes du colloque international du CNRS 10–11 octobre 1990. Bibliologia 12. Turnhout: Brepols.

Langeheine, Volker. 1983. Textpragmatische Analyse schriftlicher Kommunikation am Beispiel des Briefes. In *Schriftsprachlichkeit*, ed. Siegfried Grosse, pp. 190–211. Dusseldorf: Schwann.

Lanham, Carol D. 1975. *Salutatio Formulas in Latin Letters to 1200: Syntax, Style, and Theory*. Münchner Beiträge zur Mediävistik und Renaissance-Forschung 22. Munich: Arbeo Gesellschaft.

Laurence, Ray. 1994. Rumour and Communication in Roman Politics. *Greece and Rome* 41: 62–74.

Leach, Eleanor W. 1999. Ciceronian 'Bi-Marcus': Correspondence with M. Terentius Varro and L. Papirius Paetus in 46 B.C.E. *Transactions of the American Philological Association* 129: 139–79.

————. 2006. An gravius aliquid scribam: Roman *seniores* Write to *iuvenes*. *Transactions of the American Philological Association* 136: 247–67.

Leonhardt, Jürgen. 1995. Theorie und Praxis der *deliberatio* bei Cicero: Der Briefwechsel mit Atticus aus dem Jahre 49. *Acta Classica Universitatis Scientiarum Debreceniensis* 31: 153–71.

Lintott, Andrew. 2008. *Cicero as Evidence: A Historian's Companion*. New York: Oxford University Press.

Luck, Georg. 1961. Brief und Epistel in der Antike. *Altertum* 7: 77–84.

MacMullen, Ramsay. 1990. Roman Elite Motivation: Three Questions. In *Changes in the Roman Empire: Essays in the Ordinary*, pp. 13–24. Princeton, N.J.: Princeton University Press.

————. 2003. *Feelings in History, Ancient and Modern*. Claremont, Calif.: Regina Books.

Malcovati, Enrica. 1948. *Imperatoris Caesaris Augusti operum fragmenta*. 3rd ed. Turin: G. B. Paravia.

Malherbe, Abraham J. 1988. *Ancient Epistolary Theorists*. Society of Biblical Literature: Sources for Biblical Study 19. Atlanta: Scholars Press.

Marchesi, Ilaria. 2008. *The Art of Pliny's Letters: A Poetics of Allusion in the Private Correspondence.* Cambridge: Cambridge University Press.

McDonnell, Myles. 1996. Writing, Copying, and Autograph Manuscripts in Ancient Rome. *Classical Quarterly* 46: 469–91.

Mellet, Sylvie. 1988. *L'imparfait de l'indicatif en latin classique: temps, aspect, modalité.* Paris: Société pour Information grammaticale.

Meyer, Eduard. 1919. Ciceros Briefwechsel. In *Caesars Monarchie und das Principat des Pompejus: Inner Geschichte Roms von 66 bis 44 v. Chr.*, 2nd ed., pp. 588–606. Stuttgart: Cotta.

Meyer, Elizabeth A. 2001. Wooden Wit: *Tabellae* in Latin Poetry. In *Essays in Honor of Gordon Williams: Twenty-Five Years at Yale*, ed. Elizabeth I. Tylawsky and Charles G. Weiss, pp. 201–12. New Haven, Conn.: Henry R. Schwab.

Mitchell, Thomas N. 1991. *Cicero: The Senior Statesman.* New Haven, Conn.: Yale University Press.

Münzer, Friedrich. 1931. Iunius 55a. In *Paulys Realencyclopädie* Supplbd. 5: 369–85.

Nardo, Dante. 1961–64. I 'duplicati' dell' epistolario ciceroniano. *Ciceroniana* 3–6: 199–232.

Nicholson, John. 1992. *Cicero's Return from Exile: The Orations* Post Reditum. Lang Classical Studies 4. New York: P. Lang.

———. 1994. The Delivery and Confidentiality of Cicero's Letters. *Classical Journal* 90: 33–63.

Nikitinski, Oleg. 2001. Die (mündliche) Rolle von Briefboten bei Cicero. In *ScriptOralia Romana: Die römische Literatur zwischen Mündlichkeit und Schriftlichkeit*, ed. Lore Benz, pp. 229–47. Tübingen: Narr.

Norrick, Neal R. 1993. *Conversational Joking: Humor in Everyday Talk.* Bloomington: Indiana University Press.

Oppermann, Irene. 2000. *Zur Funktion historischer Beispiele in Ciceros Briefen.* Beiträge zur Altertumskunde 138. Munich: K. G. Saur.

Peter, Hermann. 1901. *Der Brief in der römischen Litteratur: Litterargeschichtliche Untersuchungen und Zusammenfassungen.* Leipzig: B. G. Teubner = *Abhandlungen der philologisch-historischen Classe der königlichen Sächsischen Gesellschaft der Wissenschaften* 20.

Piganiol, André. 1949. Un ennemi de Cicéron: A propos d'un livre récent. *Revue Historique* 201: 224–34.

Powell, Jonathan G. F. 1996. Prose-rhythm, Latin. In *The Oxford Classical Dictionary*, 3rd ed., pp. 1261–62. Oxford: Oxford University Press.

Préchac, François. 1913. Notes on Trebatius the Velian. *Classical Quarterly* 7: 273–81.

Raaflaub, Kurt. 1974. *Dignitatis Contentio: Studien zur Motivation und politischen Taktik im Bürgerkrieg zwischen Caesar und Pompeius.* Vestigia 20. Munich: Beck.

Ramage, Edwin S. 1973. *Urbanitas: Ancient Sophistication and Refinement.* Norman: University of Oklahoma Press.

Rauh, Nicholas K. 1986. Cicero's Business Friendships: Economics and Politics in the Late Roman Republic. *Aevum* 60: 3–30.

Rauzy, Estelle. 2002. Les déplacements de point de vue dans la correspondance de Cicéron. In *Epistulae Antiquae II: Actes du IIe colloque "Le genre épistolaire antique et ses prolongements européens" (Université François-Rabelais, Tours*

18–19 septembre 1998), ed. Léon Nadjo and Élisabeth Gavoille, pp. 113–25. Leuven: Peeters.

Riepl, Wolfgang. 1913. *Das Nachrichtenwesen des Altertums mit Besonderer Rücksicht auf die Römer.* Leipzig: B. G. Teubner.

Roesch, Sophie. 2004. La politesse dans la correspondance de Cicéron. In *Epistulae Antiquae III: Actes du IIIe colloque "Le genre épistolaire antique et ses prolongements européens" (Université François-Rabelais, Tours 25–27 septembre 2002)*, ed. Léon Nadjo and Élisabeth Gavoille, pp. 139–52. Leuven: Peeters.

Ruete, Edmund. 1883. Die Korrespondenz Ciceros in den Jahren 44 und 43. Diss., Strassburg University.

Scarpat, Giuseppe. 1989. L'epistolografia. In *Introduzione allo studio della cultura classica*, Vol. 1: *Letteratura*, pp. 473–512. Milan: Marzorati.

Schanz, Martin and Carl Hosius. 1927. *Geschichte der römischen Literatur bis zum Gesetzgebungswerk des Kaiser Justinian*, Erster Teil, 4th ed. Munich: C. H. Beck.

———. 1935. *Geschichte der römischen Literatur bis zum Gesetzgebungswerk des Kaiser Justinian*, Zweiter Teil, 4th ed. Munich: C. H. Beck.

Schneider, Wolfgang C. 1998. *Vom Handeln der Römer: Kommunikation und Interaktion des politischen Führungsschicht vor Ausbruch des Bürgerkriegs im Briefwechsel mit Cicero.* Spudasmata 66. Hildesheim: Olms.

Setaioli, Aldo. 1976. On the Date of Publication of Cicero's Letters to Atticus. *Symbolae Osloenses* 51: 105–20.

Sherwin-White, Adrian N. 1966. *The Letters of Pliny: A Historical and Social Commentary.* Oxford: Oxford University Press.

Showalter, English. 1986. Authorial Self-Consciousness in the Familiar Letter: The Case of Madame de Graffigny. *Yale French Studies* 71: 113–130.

Smadja, E. 1976. Esclaves et affranchis dans la corrrespondance de Cicéron: Les relations esclavagistes. In *Texte, politique, idéologie: Cicéron. Pour une analyse du système esclavagiste: Le fonctionnement du texte cicéronien*, pp. 73–108. Annales de l'Université de Besançon 187.

Sonnet, Paul. 1937. Trebatius 7. In *Paulys Realencyclopädie* 6A: 2251–61.

Spahlinger, Lothar. 2000. Cicero als Literaturförderer: Ein Beitrag zur System des Literaturpatronats in der ausgehenden Republik. *Philologus* 144: 239–66.

Spencer, Diana and Elena Theodorakopoulos. 2006. *Advice and Its Rhetoric in Greece and Rome.* Nottingham Classical Literature Studies, Midlands Classical Studies vol. 9. Bari: Levante.

Springer, Karl. 1927. *Supplementum Tullianum: Συναγωγὴ epistularum quae ad Ciceronianas annorum 68–49 spectant.* Charlottenberg: Gebrüder Hoffmann.

Stahlenbrecher, Werner. 1957. Die Dichterzitate in Ciceros Korrespondenz. Diss., Hamburg University.

Sternkopf, Wilhelm. 1901. Ciceros Briefwechsel mit D. Brutus und die Senatssitzung vom 20. Dez. 44. *Philologus* 60: 282–306.

———. 1910. Plancus, Lepidus und Laterensis im Mai 43. *Hermes* 45: 250–300.

Stowers, Stanley K. 1986. *Letter Writing in Greco-Roman Antiquity.* Philadelphia: Westminster Press.

Sykutris, Johannes. 1931. Epistolographie. In *Paulys Realencyclopädie* Supplbd. 5: 185–220.

Steier, A. 1932. Taube. In *Paulys Realencyclopädie* 4A: 2479–2500.

Syme, Ronald. 1939. *The Roman Revolution*. Oxford: Clarendon Press.

Taylor, Lily Ross. 1951. Review of *Cicero: The Secrets of His Correspondence*, by Jérôme Carcopino, *American Historical Review* 57: 414–16.

———. 1964. Cornelius Nepos and the Publication of Cicero's Letters to Atticus. In *Hommages à Jean Bayet*, ed. Marcel Renard and Robert Schilling. Collection Latomus 70, pp. 678–81. Brussels: Latomus.

Thraede, Klaus. 1970. *Grundzüge griechisch-römischer Brieftopik*. Zetemata 48. Munich: Beck.

Trapp, Michael. 2003. *Greek and Latin Letters: An Anthology with Translation*. Cambridge: Cambridge University Press.

Treggiari, Susan. 2007. *Terentia, Tullia, and Publilia: The Women of Cicero's Family*. London: Routledge.

Tyrrell, Robert Y. and Louis C. Purser. 1904–13. *The Correspondence of M. Tullius Cicero*. 2nd ed. Dublin: Hodges, Figgis.

Violi, Patrizia. 1985. Letters. In *Discourse and Literature*, ed. Teun A. van Dijk, pp. 149–67. Amsterdam: J. Benjamins

Walser, Gerold. 1957. *Der Briefwechsel des L. Munatius Planeus mit Cicero*. Basel: Helbing und Lichtenhahn.

Watkins, Thomas H. 1997. *L. Munatius Plancus: Serving and Surviving in the Roman Revolution*. Illinois Classical Studies Supplement 7. Atlanta: Scholars Press.

Watt, William S. 1958. *M. Tulli Ciceronis Epistulae*. Vol. 3: *Epistulae ad Quintum Fratrem, Epistulae ad M. Brutum, Fragmenta epistularum*. Oxford: Oxford University Press.

Weyssenhoff, Christina. 1966. *De Ciceronis epistulis deperditis*. Wroclaw: Zaklad Naradowy im. Ossolinskich.

———. 1970. *Ciceronis Epistularum Fragmenta*. Wroclaw: Zaklad Naradowy im. Ossolinskich.

White, Peter. 2003. Tactics in Caesar's Correspondence with Cicero. In *Caesar against Liberty? Perspectives on His Autocracy*. Papers of the Langford Latin Seminar 11, ed. Francis Cairns and Elaine Fantham, pp. 68–95. Cambridge: Francis Cairns.

———. 2009. Bookshops in the Literary Culture of Rome. In *Ancient Literacies*, ed. William A. Johnson and Holt Parker, pp. 268–87. New York: Oxford University Press.

Winterbottom, Michael. 2004. Perorations. In *Cicero the Advocate*, ed. Jonathan Powell and Jeremy Paterson, pp. 215–30. Oxford: Oxford University Press.

Yu, Ming-chung. 2003. On the Universality of Face: Evidence from Chinese Compliment Response. *Journal of Pragmatics* 35: 1679–1710.

Zetzel, James E. G. 1995. *Cicero, De Re Publica: Selections*. Cambridge: Cambridge University Press.

Index of Persons

The following register is limited to contemporaries of Cicero who are named in the text; a few very minor characters have been omitted.

Index of Passages

CPSIA information can be obtained at www.ICGtesting.com
Printed in the USA
BVOW020000010212

281667BV00003BA/1/P